FRAUD EXAMINATION FOR MANAGERS AND AUDITORS

1997 edition

Jack C. Robertson, PhD, CPA, CFE
C.T. Zlatkovich Centennial Professor of Accounting
The University of Texas at Austin

published by
VIESCA BOOKS
Austin, Texas

printed by Atex Austin, Inc.

Portions of Chapters 1-5 are adapted from the *Fraud Examiners Manual*, by Joseph T. Wells, Nancy S. Bradford, Gilbert Geis, W. Michael Kramer, James D. Ratley, and Jack C. Robertson, © 1993-1995 by the Association of Certified Fraud Examiners, Inc., used with permission.

Portions of Chapters 6-12 and 14 are adapted from Auditing, 8th Edition, by Jack C. Robertson, © by the Richard D. Irwin Company, a McGraw-Hill company, 1976, 1979, 1982, 1988, 1990, 1993, 1996, used with permission.

Fraud Examination for Managers and Auditors
1996 edition published by Association of Certified Fraud Examiners, Inc.
1997 edition published by Viesca Books

Printed by: Atex Austin, Inc., Austin, Texas

Viesca Books
5804 Westslope Drive
Austin, TX 78731-3633

Printed in the United States of America   **ISBN 0-9656785-0-4**

THE PAST IS PROLOGUE

"The object of an audit may be said to be threefold:
1. THE DETECTION OF FRAUD
2. THE DETECTION OF TECHNICAL ERRORS
3. THE DETECTION OF ERRORS OF PRINCIPLE.

"On account of its intrinsic importance, the detection of fraud is clearly entitled to be considered an 'object' in itself, although it will be obvious that it can only be concealed by the commission of a technical error, or of an error of principle. It will be appropriate, therefore, to combine the search after fraud with search for technical and fundamental errors; but it can never be too strongly insisted that the auditor *may* find fraud concealed under *any* item that he is called upon to verify. His search for fraud should therefore be unwearying and constant.

"Having thoroughly made himself master of the [accounting] system, the Auditor should look for its weakest points. 'Where is fraud most likely to creep in?' he should ask himself; and, if he can find a loop-hole, let him be doubly vigilant there. But never let him for a moment suppose that, because he sees no opportunity for fraud, none can exist."

Source: Dicksee, Lawrence R., edited by Robert H. Montgomery. *Auditing: A Practical Manual for Auditors*. Authorized American Edition (1905).

PREFACE

This book is an ideal resource for beginners in the fields of fraud examination and fraud-aware auditing. Its purposes are: (1) to introduce the important elements of fraud examination as a foundation for dealing with fraud, and (2) to explain independent audits of financial statements in terms of a fraud-detection perspective. The fraud examination section (Chapters 1-5) is condensed from the *Fraud Examiner's Manual* (Association of Certified Fraud Examiners, 2nd edition, 1994). The auditing section (Chapters 6-12) is drawn from *Auditing* (Richard D. Irwin, Inc., 8th edition, 1996). The closing section--Skills and Responsibilities--contains original chapters on fraud-detection audit procedures and auditors' official responsibilities.

The goal in this book is to give practical guidance and enhance managers' and auditors' abilities to recognize, prevent, and detect financial frauds in organizations. The primary interest is spreading the word about fraud examination and enabling more people to be able to fight fraud effectively. As authors, we welcome the opportunity to bring these materials to a wide audience.

FRAUD EXAMINATION

Fraud is the crime of choice in modern economies. It pays better than street crime. The physical dangers are minor. The risk of detection is not great. Punishments are usually not very serious in terms of fines and jail time. It can be carried out in a wide variety of organizations--churches, schools, governments, businesses, hospital, trade associations--any place that has money or property. A variety of locales and property targets are described in this book to acquaint managers and auditors with numerous fraud possibilities.

Frauds can be grouped in two major classifications--employee frauds and management frauds. Employee fraud--also known as internal fraud and occupational crime--refers to the actions of people taking money or property from their employers. Embezzlement, theft, and kickbacks are typical schemes designed to take advantage of an employer's trust. Management fraud--also known as fraudulent financial reporting and organizational crime--refers to the actions of managers to inflate reported earnings or assets for the purpose of deceiving parties outside the organization. Falsified financial statements are used to obtain loans, sell stock, obtain trade credit, and secure bonuses and other managerial compensation.

Fraud control is important for managers of all kinds of organizations. The crucial questions about fraud are: How is it detected? How is it investigated and resolved? What actions will help prevent it? These questions are answered with the activities known as *fraud examination*.

Fraud examination is a broad field that begins in the sociology of white-collar crime, incorporates elements of civil and criminal law, acknowledges the discovery potential of audit procedures, and draws intensively on a variety of investigation techniques. It consists of four principal steps: (1) **Audit procedures**--knowledge of accounting systems and document examination intricacies designed to find signs and signals of fraud cover-up, (2) **Observation**--ability to perceive evidence in a suspect's movements and activities, and to notice the importance of documents and physical evidence, (3) **Exploratory interviewing**--skills of extracting damaging testimony from collaborators, accomplices, and co-workers, and (4) **Admission-seeking interviewing**--skills of confronting the suspect for the purpose of obtaining a confession.

The first five chapters of this book provide the conceptual and technical background for fraud examination work. They deal with law and criminology directed toward an understanding of the white-collar criminal's motivation and risk. Particular characteristic schemes of both employee fraud and management fraud are detailed so managers and auditors can be aware of various manifestations of fraud. Investigation techniques are explained in a useful, how-to manner, so managers and auditors can put the lessons into practice.

CHAPTER 1 covers the law related to fraud. It defines various types of fraud, ranging from misrepresentation to embezzlement. Numerous fraud-related statutes are identified and described to provide a breadth of knowledge about the law of fraud. Features of the important corporate sentencing guidelines are explained.

CHAPTER 2 covers criminology related to fraud. Criminology is the social-psychological explanation of people and organizations in fraud activities. The chapter explains fraudulent behavior in terms of *organizational crime* (frauds by organizations) and *occupational crime* (frauds by persons against organizations).

CHAPTER 3 contains detail descriptions of employee fraud schemes. It covers cash schemes (e.g., skimming, kiting), accounts receivable schemes (e.g., lapping, write-offs), inventory schemes (e.g., embezzlement, false charges), purchasing schemes (e.g., fictitious invoices, duplicate payments), fixed asset schemes, payroll schemes, and expense account schemes. Auditors and examiners must know about the various schemes if they expect to detect and investigate them. The chapter also contains guidance on internal fraud prevention, and an appendix contains a sample fraud policy statement.

CHAPTER 4 contains detail descriptions of management fraud--the ways and means of producing misleading financial statements. Various schemes are described in terms of improper revenue recognition (e.g., misclassification, early booking, fictitious sales, manipulated percentage-of-completion accounting), inadequate disclosure of related-party transactions, improper asset valuation (e.g., inventory and accounts receivable overstatement), improper deferral of costs and expenses (e.g., omission of liabilities), and inadequate disclosure. Auditors and examiners must know about the various schemes if they expect to detect and investigate them.

CHAPTER 5 explains many aspects of fraud investigations. It concentrates on document examination and interviewing, with particular emphasis on the "tricks of the trade" for conducting interviews. Interviews are very important, and this chapter provides many practical guides. It also covers the rights of employees during investigations--matters of lawful search, defamation, false imprisonment, and lawful surveillance. The chapter closes with guidelines for fraud examination reports.

AUDITING FOR FRAUD DETECTION

The public accounting profession stands accused of not looking hard enough for fraud in the independent audits of financial statements. Independent auditors acknowledge responsibilities for detecting material fraud that produces misleading financial statements, but they have said little about any responsibility to try to detect employee fraud. No manuals exist to specify fraud detection procedures, excepting those in the private hands of forensic accounting consulting firms and the forensic services divisions of CPA firms. The general audit staffs have very little technical guidance. In general, independent auditors do not put a high priority on detection of employee fraud and management fraud.

CPA firms have faced hundreds of lawsuits involving their association with allegedly misleading financial statements. Damages aggregating billions of dollars have been sought by aggrieved plaintiffs. At the same time, accounting firms' clients have lost millions if not billions of dollars to internal frauds. A large proportion of U.S. corporations have experienced serious frauds by trusted insiders. If fraud-aware independent auditors had detected signs of even a small portion of these fraud, clients could have saved large sums.

The chapters in this section build upon the foundation of fraud examination (Chapters 1-5) and concentrate on ways and means independent auditors can pay attention to fraud potential by performing fraud-detecting procedures. The chapters introduce fraud-aware independent auditing, cover technical details of internal control, and explain procedural applications for various accounts in the context of business operations.

CHAPTER 6 is the introduction to fraud awareness auditing. It contains an overview of a fraud "model" (i.e., motive, opportunity, and lack of integrity) and some thoughts on fraud prevention through enlightened management. Fraud detection is presented in terms of documents, sources of information, and "extended procedures." Five case stories tell tales about fraud situations and related audit detection potential.

CHAPTER 7 is an introduction to auditors' concepts of internal control--a crucial feature in business operations. Internal control holds a special relevance for fraud awareness auditing. Frauds occur most often when people have an *opportunity* made easy by lack of control checks and supervision. The chapter describes various segregations of duties and error-checking techniques often mentioned in connection with fraud investigations.

CHAPTERS 8-12 carry a consistent organization. They contain detail descriptions of transactions, data sources, control, and audit procedures in the major business activities. The chapters cover cash collections and receivables (Chapter 8), cash disbursements and payables (Chapter 9), payroll (Chapter 10), cost accounting (Chapter 11), and investments, liabilities, and equities (Chapter 12). The general principles of transaction processing and control are specified for particular business areas. The coverage is most appropriate for auditors who need to slant their audit knowledge toward fraud detection. The case stories in each chapter are particularly informative about fraud situations and audit detection potential. These chapters are not about "fraud auditing," which is conducted after allegations of fraud are known, much like a full-blown fraud examination. Instead, the emphasis is on the potential for fraud detection in the ordinary course of an independent audit. In many respects, this fraud awareness auditing can be applied in internal and governmental audit assignments.

SKILLS AND RESPONSIBILITIES

Auditors need to expand the frontier of audit procedures. Few readily-available sources contain descriptions of fraud-detecting procedures auditors might perform. Many of these are well-known implements in fraud examiners' toolkits. Independent auditors, internal auditors, and government auditors have produced statements of expectations and responsibilities--the "rule book" of auditor behavior, but these fall short of practical technical guidance. Chapters in this section deal with both these areas.

CHAPTER 13 contains specifications and explanations of fraud detection audit procedures. The procedures are organized like an audit program with sections on cash receipts-sales-accounts receivable, cash disbursements-purchasing-accounts payable, inventory, payroll, employee expense accounts, property-plant-equipment, and income taxes. They are expressed in practical, how-to-do-it terms, ready for transfer to audit field work.

CHAPTER 14 explains the fraud-related standards in the professional literature of independent auditors (American Institute of Certified Public Accountants), internal auditors (The Institute of Internal Auditors, Inc.), government auditors (U.S. General Accounting Office Generally Accepted Government Auditing Standards), and fraud examiners (Association of Certified Fraud Examiners). For each organization, the standards are expressed in terms of specific requirements. These standards represent the official current state of fraud detection auditing.

What has the past shown? What is the present situation? What does the future hold? These questions are provocative. This book is not the last word on fraud examination and auditing. Developments will proceed, and changes will occur. However, for the time being, the present states of fraud examination and auditing knowledge are important entries in the fight against white-collar crime in organizations all over the world.

I deeply appreciate all the contributors to the fields of fraud examination and auditing. They are too numerous to mention here by name without risk of omitting important people. However, in particular, I thank the Association of Fraud Examiners for permission to use material from the *Fraud Examiner's Manual*, and I thank the Richard D. Irwin company for permission to condense and reprint certain chapters from *Auditing*. Without their cooperation, this book would not have been possible. Nevertheless, I remain responsible for errors of commission and omission and for the zeal in the desire to emphasize all aspects of efforts to improve fraud examination and auditing.

Jack C. Robertson
Austin, Texas
April 1997

FRAUD EXAMINATION FOR MANAGERS AND AUDITORS

Table of Contents

FRAUD EXAMINATION

AUDITING FOR FRAUD DETECTION

SKILLS AND RESPONSIBILITIES

CHAPTER 1
LAW RELATED TO FRAUD

Legal issues related to fraud are often complex and their interpretation may require the assistance of an experienced attorney. Certified Fraud Examiners and auditors should consult with counsel if legal questions arise during a fraud examination or audit.

The two sources of substantive law in the United States are *statutes* passed by Congress and state legislatures (including regulations enacted by administrative and regulatory agencies) and the *common law*. The common law consists of usages and customs of society interpreted by the judicial system, and it is often called "judge-made law." Criminal law prosecutions are always based on statutes, but civil actions can be based both on statute and common law.

Criminal fraud statutes often contain provisions that do not have any obvious connection to basic principles of right and wrong. For example, a violation of the federal Mail Fraud statute can be charged only if the wrongdoers placed or received a letter in the U.S. mail, regardless of how serious the underlying fraud may be. Similarly, defendants are liable under the Racketeering Influenced and Corrupt Organizations (RICO) statute only if they engage "in a pattern of racketeering activity" through "an enterprise" that is engaged in interstate commerce. Violations of the federal Money Laundering statute occur only if the defendants have engaged in "specified unlawful activity" and have thereafter conducted a "prohibited financial transaction." Certified Fraud Examiners preparing criminal cases must be familiar with the specific technical elements of the applicable statutes, and must carefully review the evidence to make certain that all essential elements of proof are met. Auditors should be aware of the many types of frauds that are prohibited by statute and common law.

The common law is based not on statutes passed by the legislatures but upon "precedent" established by previously decided cases stretching back hundreds of years in United States and British courts. Decisions in individual cases bind judges in later cases of a similar nature until the precedent is overturned by a higher court or by a statute enacted by a legislature. Although most civil actions are based on the common law, an increasing number of civil statutes are being enacted in the fraud area, including the federal Civil RICO and Civil False Claims statutes.

Civil cases prosecuted under the common law usually contain fewer technical elements. They tend to incorporate traditional principles of fairness and morality. For example, a plaintiff may file a common law claim for fraud by alleging that the defendant misrepresented important facts upon which the plaintiff relied, resulting in loss to the plaintiff.

CRIMINAL AND CIVIL ACTIONS FOR FRAUD

Fraud may be prosecuted in a criminal action, a civil action, or both, in sequence or simultaneously. Certified Fraud Examiners and auditors should be familiar with a number of differences between criminal and civil actions.

INVESTIGATION AND PROSECUTION

Criminal actions for fraud are brought by the government acting through the prosecutor's office. The prosecutor has considerable discretion to decide whether to bring a criminal case, what charges to file, who to charge and who not to charge, and whether to try the case or to negotiate a plea-bargain. Civil actions may be brought by private individuals or by organizations, usually without the involvement or permission of the government or a court.

Criminal cases are investigated by law enforcement agencies, at times with the assistance of a prosecutor's office and a grand jury. A grand jury is an investigative body that is empowered to issue subpoenas for testimony and documents to determine whether a violation of the law has occurred. Law enforcement agencies and the prosecution therefore can subpoena evidence before charges are filed to determine whether an offense has occurred. However, in civil actions for fraud, private parties generally have no opportunity to compel the production of testimony or other evidence until a complaint is filed.

Criminal investigations and prosecutions for fraud are subject to Constitutional limitations, such as those in the Fourth, Fifth and Sixth Amendments, and in procedural rules designed to protect the rights of defendants. In general, these requirements do not apply in civil actions. Violations of constitutional rights in a criminal case can result in the "suppression" or exclusion of any evidence or statement obtained by improper means, or in some instances, in dismissal of the indictment. In civil cases, evidence obtained improperly may still be used and the action may proceed. However, unreasonable searches and other abusive or improper acts may be remedied through civil actions brought by the aggrieved party against the wrongdoer. The burden of proof in a criminal case requires evidence "beyond a reasonable doubt," and a jury must reach a unanimous verdict. In civil cases the burden of proof is lower, usually termed a "preponderance of the evidence." In some jurisdictions, the jury decision in a civil case does not need to be unanimous. Guilty criminals are punished by outcomes such as imprisonment, fines, orders of restitution, probation, and community service. Civil cases, when the plaintiffs are successful, result in an award of monetary damages or in some instances the entry of an order or injunction that compels the losing party to take remedial action to avoid future illegal acts.

Criminal and civil actions for fraud may proceed simultaneously even though such parallel proceedings present a dilemma for defendants. For example, a defendant may lawfully assert the fifth amendment right against self-incrimination to avoid answering questions or producing certain documents in the criminal investigation. However, this right may not be available in the corresponding civil case without suffering sanctions, which may include entry of a judgment. A defendant in a civil action may be compelled to produce documents or to otherwise provide information, which then could be used adversely in the criminal case.

Generally, courts have not been sympathetic to the defendants' dilemma, and have allowed civil discovery to proceed even though criminal charges are pending. In some instances, the court or the parties may agree to seal the civil record. In rare cases the court may order that the civil case be stayed pending resolution of the criminal case. Normally, however, the court will allow the cases to proceed simultaneously despite any substantial prejudice to the defendant. In parallel civil and criminal cases in which the government is a party, the criminal process (including the use of grand jury subpoenas) may not be used to obtain evidence solely for a civil case.

Criminal and civil actions for fraud may be brought in federal or state court. Federal courts have jurisdiction over federal criminal and civil statutes and certain common law claims that usually involve parties who are residents of different states and controversies where $50,000 or more is at issue. State courts have jurisdiction over state statutes and most common law civil claims.

THE CIVIL JUSTICE SYSTEM

Fraud examiners, auditors, accountants, security personnel, private investigators, and attorneys often are involved in actions to investigate and recover losses due to fraud. Many of these cases will be processed in the civil justice system.

Civil Litigation

Most common-law fraud actions are filed in state courts. Suits involving parties from different states and those involving more than $50,000 in controversy, or actions brought on the basis of federal statutes, such as the civil RICO provisions, may be brought in federal court. Federal court is generally preferred by plaintiffs in larger cases because federal rules of evidence provide easier access to witnesses and documents located in different states. The procedures described below are largely drawn from the federal rules.

Beginning the Civil Action

A civil action begins with the filing of a complaint in the appropriate court, usually in the jurisdiction in which the defendant or the plaintiff resides, or where the claim arose. Court rules provide that the complaint should be a "short and plain statement" showing the court's jurisdiction to hear the case (e.g., in federal court, that there is diversity of citizenship and more than $50,000 in issue), the grounds for relief, and a demand for judgment. Rule 9(b) of the Federal Rules of Civil Procedure requires that the facts entitling the plaintiff to relief be stated with "particularity." Thus, a plaintiff in a negligence case may get into court by merely alleging--without any details or supporting evidence--that the defendant operated his automobile in a negligent manner at a particular place and time. However, a fraud plaintiff must plead the alleged fraud in detail--the actual misrepresentations that were made, to whom, how they were false, and the damages suffered.

The federal Rule 9(b) requirement often creates a problem for fraud plaintiffs. For example, a company may have good grounds to believe that it is the victim of a kickback fraud, but may need access to the discovery system (e.g., subpoenas for documents and witnesses) to prove the illegal payments. In such circumstances, particularly where the specific information needed is within the sole control of the defendant, the court may relax the 9(b) requirement.

The complaint and a summons must be served on the defendant. The summons advises the defendant of a certain time to answer (usually 20 days) or suffer a default. A corporation may be served through any officer, managing agent, or other agent authorized by law to received process. Process may be served on a defendant outside the court's state if the defendant has significant contacts within the state, such as a corporation conducting business in the state.

A defendant may file an answer to the complaint, deny liability, add counterclaims against the plaintiff, or file motions to dismiss the action based on grounds such as failure to state a claim, expiration of the statute of limitations, and improper service. In major litigation these procedural challenges may consume a year or more and result in large legal fees before the case reaches the merits of the issue.

BASIC DEFINITION AND TYPES OF FRAUD

Black's Law Dictionary defines fraud as:

> "all multifarious means which human ingenuity can devise, and which are resorted to by one individual to get an advantage over another by false suggestions or suppression of the truth. It includes all surprise, trick, cunning or dissembling, and any unfair way by which another is cheated."

Thus, fraud includes any intentional or deliberate act to deprive another of property or money by guile, deception or other unfair means.

The principal types of fraud (often called white-collar crime) are:

- Misrepresentation of material facts
- Concealment of material facts
- Bribery
- Conflicts of interest
- Theft of money or property
- Theft of trade secrets or intellectual property
- Breach of fiduciary duty
- Statutory offenses

MISREPRESENTATION OF MATERIAL FACTS

Misrepresentation cases can be prosecuted criminally or civilly under a variety of statutes, such as false statements, false claims, mail and wire fraud. They may be the basis for common law claims. The essence of the offense is deliberately making false statements to induce an intended victim to part with money or property.

The specific elements of proof of misrepresentation vary somewhat according to the jurisdiction, and whether the case is prosecuted as a criminal or civil action. The elements normally include:

- A material false statement
- Knowledge of its falsity
- Reliance on the false statement by the victim
- Damages suffered.

In a civil case, a victim must prove reliance on the false statements and actual loss. These elements of proof may not be necessary in a criminal prosecution. Also, in some statutes, materiality is assumed and need not be proved.

In most instances, only false representations of "presently existing facts" may be prosecuted. Opinions and speculative statements about future events (even if made with the intent to mislead) may not be the basis for a fraud case. For example, a used car salesman who assures a naive customer that the 20 year-old car that was towed to the lot will give "years of driving pleasure" probably cannot be prosecuted for fraud. However, the salesman might be prosecuted for misrepresentation of material facts upon telling the customer that the car has been driven only 15,000 miles when the known mileage is 150,000 miles.

The rule limiting fraud cases to misrepresentations of presently existing facts is often applied to bar fraud claims in contract disputes. A party to a contract who promises to perform certain services by a particular date in the future, but who fails to do so, generally may not be prosecuted for fraud unless the plaintiff can demonstrate that the defendant had the intent not to perform the promised services when the contract was made. Of course, the other party may file an action for breach of contract.

The rule precluding fraud actions based on false "opinions" is subject to a certain exceptions, principally cases involving opinions provided by professional advisers, such as Certified Public Accountants. An accountant may be prosecuted for fraud who:

- Certifies that a financial statement fairly presents the financial condition of the audited company when the accountant knows it does not

- Falsely states that an audit was conducted in accordance with generally accepted auditing standards
- Deliberately distorts the audit results.

Normally, only material false statements may serve as the basis for a fraud case. Materiality usually refers to statements sufficiently important or relevant that they influence a victim's decision. For example, a claim that a company enjoyed a 50 percent growth in profits would probably be material to a prospective investor. On the other hand, a statement that the company was considering moving its headquarters from New York City to Chicago may not be. The materiality of allegedly false statements is often a central issue in securities fraud cases.

In all fraud cases, the prosecution or plaintiff must prove that a false statement was intentional and part of a deliberate scheme to defraud. Under law, frauds cannot be accidental or unintentional. (Whether a "fraud" can result from mere negligent mistake is often a point of contention.) In some instances, particularly those involving civil actions for fraud and securities cases, the intent requirement is met if the prosecution or plaintiff is able to show that the false statements were made recklessly; that is, with gross negligence or complete disregard for truth or falsity.

Although a misrepresentation fraud case may not be based on negligent or accidental misrepresentations, in some instances a civil action may be filed for negligent misrepresentation. This action is appropriate if a defendant suffered a loss as a result of the carelessness or negligence of another party upon which the defendant was entitled to rely. Examples would be negligent false statements to a prospective purchaser regarding the value of a closely held company's stock or the accuracy of its financial statements.

CONCEALMENT OF MATERIAL FACTS

An action for fraud may be based on the concealment of material facts, but only if the defendant had a duty to disclose them in the circumstances. The essential elements of fraud based on failure to disclose material facts are:
- That the defendant had knowledge
- Of a material fact
- That the defendant had a duty to disclose
- And failed to do so
- With the intent to mislead or deceive the other party.

The duty to disclose usually depends on the relationship between the parties. Persons who occupy a special relationship of trust, such as the officers or directors of a corporation, an attorney, accountant, trustee, stockbroker, or other agent may be found to have a duty to fully and completely disclose material facts to the parties who rely upon them. Statutes have expanded the duty to disclose to areas which traditionally had no such duty, such as to the sellers of personal or real property, and purchasers or sellers of securities.

Proof that a concealed fact was material is the most important element in concealment cases. No liability exists if the withheld information would not have affected the other party. In addition to fraudulent concealment, a defendant may also be liable for negligent failure to discover and disclose material facts. For example, an accountant may be liable for failure to discover or report material facts in a financial statement audit. Of course, as with negligent misrepresentation, the penalties are less severe for negligence than for fraudulent misrepresentation.

BRIBERY

Bribery includes (a) official bribery, which refers to the corruption of a public official, and (b) commercial bribery, which refers to the corruption of a private individual to gain a commercial or business advantage. The elements of official bribery vary by jurisdiction, but generally are:
- Giving or receiving
- A thing of value
- To influence
- An official act.

The "thing of value" is not limited to cash or money. Courts have held that such things as lavish gifts and entertainment, payment of travel and lodging expenses, payment of credit card bills, "loans," promises of future employment, and interests in businesses may be bribes if they were given or received with the intent to influence decisions. Some state statutes may distinguish between felonies or misdemeanors according to the amount of illegal payment.

Proof of corrupt influence often involves demonstration that the person receiving the bribe favored the bribe-payer in some improper or unusual way, such as by providing preferential treatment, bending or breaking the rules, taking extraordinary steps to assist the bribe-payer, or allowing the bribe-payer to defraud the agency or company. However, the prosecutor or plaintiff is not required to demonstrate that the bribe-taker acted improperly. A bribe may be paid to induce an official to perform an act that otherwise would be legal, or one may be paid to induce an act the official might have performed without a bribe. Bribery schemes involving these circumstances, however, are difficult to prove and lack appeal for prosecution.

ILLEGAL GRATUITY

An illegal gratuity is a lesser offense of official bribery. The elements of an illegal gratuity are:
- Giving or receiving
- A thing of value
- For or because of
- An official act.

An illegal gratuity charge does not require proof of intent to influence. Statutes prohibit public officials from accepting any payment of money or other thing of value other than lawful compensation. In practice, statutes often are applied when relatively small payments, such as gifts or entertainment, are used to attempt to influence public officials.

COMMERCIAL BRIBERY

Commercial bribery may be prosecuted either as a criminal act or as a civil matter. About half of the states have criminal statutes that prohibit commercial bribery. If a state does not have a commercial bribery statute, such schemes can usually be prosecuted under criminal fraud statutes on the theory that the payment of a commercial bribe defrauds the business owner of the right to an employee's unbiased and loyal services.

No federal statute prohibits commercial bribery. However, such offenses may be prosecuted at the federal level as mail or wire fraud, or as RICO or other violations. The elements of commercial bribery vary by jurisdiction, but typically include:

- Giving or receiving
- A thing of value
- To influence
- A business decision
- Without the knowledge or consent of the principal.

The fifth element is included on the theory that a private business owner is not defrauded if the owner knows of or allows employees to accept gifts, favors or other payments from vendors or other business contacts. Most state commercial bribery statutes are misdemeanors punishable by a jail term of not more than one year. Commercial bribery is a felony in Colorado, Kansas, Texas, Arizona (if the value of the bribe payment is $100 or more) and New Hampshire (if the value of the bribe is $500 or more). The New York commercial bribery law is a typical statute that makes it a misdemeanor to give or receive (or to offer or solicit) "any benefit" without the consent of the employer, with the intent of influencing the employee's business conduct. The Louisiana, Michigan, and New Jersey commercial bribery statutes confer immunity on the party to the scheme who first agrees to testify against the other party in a criminal proceeding.

Businesses injured by commercial bribery schemes may sue for treble damages and attorneys' fees under the Civil RICO statute (Title 18, U.S. Code, § 1964) and the Clayton Act (Title 15, U.S. Code, § 13(c)), and for compensatory and punitive damages for common law fraud, conflict of interest, and breach of fiduciary duty. Civil actions may be brought even if commercial bribery is not a crime in a jurisdiction.

EXTORTION

An extortion case is often the other side of a bribery case. Extortion is defined as the obtaining of property from another with the other party's "consent" having been induced by wrongful use of actual or threatened force or fear. Fear may include the apprehension of possible economic damage or loss. A demand for a bribe or kickback may also constitute an extortion. In most states and in the federal system, extortion is not a defense to bribery. That is, a person who makes a bribe payment upon demand of the recipient is still culpable for bribery. In New York, however, extortion may be a defense in certain circumstances.

CONFLICT OF INTEREST

Statutes in every state and the in federal system (as well as common law decisions in all jurisdictions) prohibit persons from engaging in conduct which involves a conflict of interest. A conflict of interest may be prosecuted civilly or criminally. The criminal statutes vary widely and include prohibitions on public officers accepting employment with government contractors or lobbying government agencies during specified time periods.

Elements of a typical civil claim for conflict of interest include:

- An agent taking an interest in a transaction
- That is actually or potentially adverse to the principal
- Without full and timely disclosure to and approval by the principal.

An agent includes any person who, under the law, owes a duty of loyalty to another, including officers, directors, and employees of a corporation, public officials, trustees, brokers, independent contractors, attorneys, and accountants. Persons who do not occupy positions of trust with another party, such as arms-length commercial parties, do not owe a duty of loyalty to each other and therefore are not subject to conflict of interest restrictions.

The defendant in a civil conflict-of-interest case must repay any losses the conflict caused and must disgorge any profits received as a result of the conflict even if the principal suffered no actual loss. The "disloyal" party may also be required to forfeit all compensation received during the period of disloyalty. The victim of a conflict of interest may also void any contracts entered into on its behalf that were influenced by the conflict.

THEFT OF MONEY AND PROPERTY

Theft is a term often used to describe a wide variety of fraudulent conduct. For example, many state statutes describe misrepresentation fraud as "theft by deception" or "larceny by trick." As used here, the term theft is limited to embezzlement, larceny, and misappropriation of trade secrets and proprietary information.

Embezzlement

Embezzlement is the wrongful appropriation of money or property by a person to whom it has been lawfully entrusted. Embezzlement implicitly involves a breach of trust, although a fiduciary relationship between the parties is not required. The elements of embezzlement vary somewhat by jurisdiction, but generally are:

- The defendant took or converted
- Without the knowledge or consent of the owner
- Money or property of another
- That was properly entrusted to the defendant.

Larceny

Larceny is defined as the wrongful taking of money or property of another with the intent to convert or to deprive the owner of its possession and use. In larceny, unlike embezzlement, the defendant never has lawful possession of the property. The elements of larceny typically include:

- Taking or carrying away
- Money or property of another
- Without the consent of the owner
- With the intent to permanently deprive the owner of its use or possession.

Theft of Trade Secrets

Theft or misappropriation of trade secrets may be prosecuted under a variety of federal and state statutes and the common law. Trade secret includes not only secret formulas and processes, but more mundane proprietary information, such as customer and price lists, sales figures, business plans, or any other confidential information that has a value to the business and would be potentially harmful if disclosed.

The elements of a typical theft of trade secret claim are:

- That a party possessed information of value to the business
- That was treated confidentially
- That the defendant took or used by breach of an agreement, confidential relationship, or other improper means.

A critical feature is that the information being sought to be protected be treated confidentially, although absolute secrecy is not required. It is sufficient if the information was "substantially" undisclosed. Limited disclosure to persons with a need to know or pursuant to confidentiality agreements will not void the secret. Methods of demonstrating that information was intended to be kept confidential include a written policy describing the information as proprietary or secret, strict limitations on distribution of the information, and physical security to prevent unauthorized access and use of the information. The owners of the information should also enforce restrictive agreements and act promptly to remedy any inadvertent disclosures. Failure to do so may be construed as a waiver of confidentiality and make it impossible to prevent future use or disclosures.

The most typical defense is that the information was developed independently. If the aggrieved party demonstrates that the information came to the defendant as the result of or during a confidential relationship, the burden of proof shifts to the defendant to demonstrate independent discovery. The defendant may also defend a misappropriation claim by showing that the information was not in fact a secret, that the third party's use was authorized, or that the trade secret or proprietary information had been abandoned by the owner.

BREACH OF FIDUCIARY DUTY

Persons in a position of trust or fiduciary relationship, such as officers, directors, high-level employees of a corporation or business, agents and brokers, owe certain duties imposed by law to their principals or employers. The principal fiduciary duties are loyalty and care.

Duty of Loyalty
The duty of loyalty requires that employees and agents act solely in the best interest of their employers and principals, free of any self-dealing, conflicts of interest, or other abuse for personal advantage. Thus, corporate directors, officers, and employees are barred from using corporate property or assets for their personal pursuits or taking corporate opportunities for themselves. More traditional fraudulent conduct, such as embezzlements, thefts, acceptance of kickbacks, and conflicts of interest also violate the duty of loyalty, and may be prosecuted as such in addition to or instead of the underlying offense.

A breach of duty of loyalty is easier to prove than fraud. The plaintiff does not need to prove criminal or fraudulent intent or the other elements of fraud. To prevail, the plaintiff must show only that the defendant occupied a position of trust or fiduciary relationship and that the defendant breached that duty for personal benefit.

A breach of fiduciary duty claim is a civil action. The plaintiff may receive a monetary damage award for lost profits and recover profits that the disloyal employee earned--in some instances, even the salary paid to the employee or agent during the period of disloyalty. The plaintiff may recover profits received by the disloyal agent even if the principal did not suffer an actual loss. The plaintiff may also void any contracts entered into on its behalf that were influenced by the employee's or agent's disloyalty.

Duty of Care

Corporate officers, directors, amd high-level employees, as well as other persons in a fiduciary relationship, must conduct business affairs prudently with the skill and attention normally exercised by persons in similar positions. Fiduciaries who act carelessly or recklessly are responsible for any resulting loss to corporate shareholders or other principals. Damages may be recovered in a civil action for negligence, mismanagement, or waste of corporate assets.

However, persons in a fiduciary relationship are not guarantors against all business reverses or errors in judgment. The Business Judgment Rule protects corporate officers and directors from liability for judgments that were made in good faith (e.g., free of self-dealings or conflicts) and that appeared to be prudent based on the then-known circumstances.

Corporate officers breach their duty of loyalty if they accept kickbacks, engage in a conflict of interest, or otherwise are disloyal. Corporate officers who carelessly fail to prevent such conduct, or fail to enforce controls, or to pursue recovery of losses may breach their duty of care. Corporate defendants in such cases may raise the Business Judgment Rule in defense by showing that they had no reasonable grounds to suspect such conduct or that the cost of prevention or recovery was too high compared to the anticipated returns.

FEDERAL CRIMINAL FRAUD STATUTES

The purpose of this section is to give fraud examiners and auditors a basic overview of several federal statutes that cover fraud-related crimes. It is not intended to be an exhaustive explanation of the laws.

The criminal fraud statutes in the U.S. Code require a federal jurisdictional basis, such as an effect on interstate commerce or use of the mail. The U.S.

laws are often used to prosecute the larger and more serious crimes primarily because of the generally superior resources of federal law enforcement agencies and their nationwide jurisdiction.

MAIL FRAUD (TITLE 18, U.S. CODE, §1341)

The mail fraud statute is the workhorse of federal white-collar prosecutions. It has been used against virtually all types of commercial fraud, public corruption, and security law violations. The statute provides: Anyone who uses the U.S. Postal Service to help perpetrate a fraud shall be fined or imprisoned, or both.

The essence of the offense is the use of the mails, lacking which, no matter how large or serious the fraud, there is no federal jurisdiction. The mailing does not itself need to contain the false and fraudulent representations, as long as it is an integral part of the scheme. What is integral or incidental depends on the facts of each case. Generally, a mailing that helps advance the scheme in any significant way will be considered sufficient.

Frauds and swindles are not defined in the mail fraud statute or elsewhere in the U.S. Code. Most of the cases treat any intentional scheme to deceive and deprive another of a tangible property right as being within the statute. Under Title 18, U.S. Code, § 1346, the mail fraud statute may be used to prosecute official corruption, along with the bribery laws, under the theory that the payment or receipt of bribes deprived the public of its right to honest and unbiased services of public servants.

The fraudulent scheme need not be successful and a victim need not suffer a loss for the statute to apply. Also, the mailing need not travel in interstate commerce. Any use of the U.S. postal system provides sufficient grounds for federal jurisdiction.

WIRE FRAUD (TITLE 18, U.S. CODE, §1343)

The pertinent part of this statute provides that: "anyone who uses wire, radio, or television communication in interstate or foreign commerce to help perpetrate a fraud shall be fined or imprisoned, or both."

The wire fraud statute is often used in tandem with mail fraud counts in federal prosecutions. Unlike mail fraud, however, the wire fraud statute requires an interstate or foreign communication for a violation.

INTERSTATE TRANSPORTATION OF STOLEN PROPERTY (TITLE 18, U.S. CODE, § 2314)

The pertinent part of this statute provides that: "anyone who (a) transports in interstate or foreign commerce any goods, wares, merchandise, securities or money, of the value of $5,000 or more, knowing the same to have been stolen, converted or taken by fraud; or (b) travels in interstate commerce in connection with a fraud of $5,000 or more...shall be fined or imprisoned, or both."

§ 2314, popularly known as "ITSP" (Interstate Transportation of Stolen Property), is often used in fraud prosecutions in conjunction with mail or wire fraud counts, or to provide federal jurisdiction in their absence, when proceeds of a value of $5,000 or more obtained by fraud are transported across state lines. The statute is also violated if a defendant induces the victim to travel in interstate commerce as part of the scheme to defraud. Individual transportation of money or other items valued at less than $5,000 as part of the same scheme may be aggregated to meet the value requirement.

RACKETEER INFLUENCED AND CORRUPT ORGANIZATIONS (RICO) (TITLE 18, U.S. CODE, §1961, et. seq.)

RICO is probably the best-known and most controversial federal statute in use today. Originally enacted in 1970 to fight organized crime's infiltration of legitimate business, its powerful criminal and civil provisions have come to be used in a wide range of fraud cases. The statute outlaws the investment of ill-gotten gains in another business enterprise, the acquisition of an interest in an enterprise through certain illegal acts, and the conduct of the affairs of an enterprise through such acts. Criminal penalties include stiff fines and prison terms as well as the forfeiture of all illegal proceeds or interests. Civil remedies include treble damages, attorney fees, dissolution of the offending enterprise, and other penalties.

The pertinent parts of the complex statute are in the next sections.

§ 1962: Prohibited Activities

(a) It is unlawful for anyone to use income derived from a pattern of racketeering activity or through collection of an unlawful debt to acquire any interest in any enterprise which is engaged in interstate or foreign commerce.

(c) It is unlawful for anyone employed by or associated with any enterprise engaged in interstate or foreign commerce, to conduct or participate in the conduct of the enterprise's affairs through a pattern of racketeering activity or collection of unlawful debt.

(d) It is unlawful for any person to conspire to violate any of the provisions of this law.

§ 1963: Criminal Penalties

(a) Whoever violates any provision of § 1962 of this chapter shall be fined or imprisoned, or both, and shall forfeit to the United States any interest the person has acquired or maintained in violation of § 1962.

§ 1964: Civil Remedies

(a) The U.S. district courts shall have jurisdiction to prevent and restrain violations of § 1962 by issuing appropriate orders, including, but not limited to: divestiture, restriction of future activities, dissolution of an enterprise, and reorganization of an enterprise.

(c) Any person injured in his business or property by reason of a violation of § 1962 of this chapter may sue therefor in any appropriate United States district court and shall recover threefold the damages sustained and the cost of the suit, including reasonable attorney's fees.

(d) A final judgment or decree rendered in favor of the United States in any criminal proceeding brought by the United States under this chapter shall stop the defendant from denying the essential allegations of the criminal offense in any subsequent civil proceeding brought by the United States.

§ 1962(c) is probably the most commonly charged offense. The elements of a 1962(c) offense are:

- The defendant was associated with an "enterprise" as defined in the statute, which may be a business, a union, a group of individuals "associated in fact," or even a single individual
- The enterprise was engaged in or affected interstate commerce
- The defendant conducted the affairs of the enterprise through a "pattern of racketeering activity," that is, two or more illegal acts, enumerated in

the statute as predicate violations, such as mail and wire fraud or ITSP violations.

The most controversial aspect of RICO is its civil provisions. Civil actions may be brought by the government or any private party injured in business or property. Critics complain that private party suits have been used to reach "deep pocket" defendants, such as accounting firms, who ought not be characterized as "racketeers," and to coerce unwarranted settlements from blameless defendants fearful of possible treble damage judgments. Supporters contend that a plaintiff cannot recover unless fraud or other criminal acts are proved--making the stigma of being alleged a racketeer and the award of treble damages justified. Several bills to repeal or amend RICO, particularly the civil provisions, have been introduced in Congress in recent years, and some amendment is widely expected.

FEDERAL SECURITIES LAW (THE 1933 AND 1934 ACTS)

Numerous federal statutes prohibit false statements and other fraudulent activity in connection with securities transactions. The most commonly used are § 17(a) of the Securities Act of 1933 (popularly known as the 1933 Act), and Rule 10(b)5, promulgated under the Securities and Exchange Act of 1934 (the 1934 Act). Both contain civil and administrative remedies (e.g., the power to initiate actions to enjoin further violations) enforced by the Securities and Exchange Commission as well as criminal sanctions enforced by the Department of Justice. Whether a particular violation is prosecuted civilly or criminally depends in large measure on the degree of willfulness that can be proved.

§ 17(a) of the 1933 Act makes it unlawful to employ fraudulent devices or misrepresentations in connection with the offer or sale of securities through jurisdictional facilities (e.g., the U.S. mail). Rule 10(b)5 prohibits the same conduct "in connection with the purchase or sale" of any security by "any person." Rule 10(b)5 is used most often because it has the broadest reach--including insider trading. The Rule accompanying § 10(b)5, found in Title 17, Code of Federal Regulations, § 240.10b-5, specifically provides:

> It shall be unlawful for any person, directly or indirectly, by the use of any means or instrumentality of interstate

commerce, or of the mails or of any facility of any national securities exchange,

(a) To employ any device, scheme, or artifice to defraud,

(b) To make any untrue statement of a material fact or to omit to state a material fact necessary in order to make the statements made, in the light of the circumstances under which they were made, not misleading, or

(c) To engage in any act, practice, or course of business which operates or would operate as a fraud or deceit upon any person, in connection with the purchase or sale of any security.

Specific intent to defraud is an essential element of a violation of § 17(a) and Rule 10(b)5. However, intent to defraud is defined more broadly in securities regulations than in other areas of common-law fraud, and includes reckless statements, as well as the knowing circulation of half truths and false opinions or predictions that elsewhere may be considered non-actionable puffing.

To allow action, a false statement must be material. The test for materiality is whether there is a substantial likelihood under all the circumstances that a reasonable investor would have considered the misstated or omitted facts significant in making investment decisions. Materiality is most often expressed in dollar terms or in terms of its effect on financial statements, but it may also relate to serious questions of management's integrity regardless of the dollar amount involved.

THE FOREIGN CORRUPT PRACTICES ACT OF 1977 (TITLE 15, U.S. CODE, § 78m(b)2)

The FCPA prohibits publicly held companies from making corrupt payments to foreign officials or political organizations. The Act also makes it illegal for any U.S. citizen to make such payments. The statute was the result of disclosures from the Watergate investigations of corporate payments to foreigners to obtain business overseas. Of more current interest are the separate books and records provisions of the FCPA (§ 13(b)2--amending the Securities and Exchange Act of 1934) that requires public companies to:

(a) make and keep books, records, and accounts, which, in reasonable detail, accurately and fairly reflect the transactions and dispositions of the assets of the issuer; and

(b) devise and maintain a system of internal accounting controls sufficient to provide reasonable assurance that
   (i)   transactions are executed in accordance with management's general or specific authorization;
   (ii) transactions are recorded as necessary (1) to permit preparation of financial statements in conformity with generally accepted accounting principles or any other criteria applicable to such statements, and (2) to maintain accountability for assets;
   (iii) access to assets is permitted only in accordance with management's general or specific authorization; and
   (iv) the recorded accountability for assets is compared with the existing assets at reasonable intervals and appropriate action is taken with respect to any differences.

SEC Regulations enforcing these provisions specifically require:

- Rule 13(b)(2)-1: No person shall falsify or cause to be falsified, any book, record or account subject to § 13(b)(2)(A) of the Securities Exchange Act.

- Rule 13(b)(2)-2: (a) No director or officer of an issuer shall make or cause to be made a materially false or misleading statement, or (b) omit to state any material fact necessary in order to make [financial reporting] statements not misleading to an accountant in connection with (1) any audit or examination of the financial statements, or (2) the preparation or filing of any document or report required to be filed with the Commission.

The statute and regulations effectively give the SEC supervisory authority over the financial management and reporting functions of publicly-held corporations. The SEC has interpreted its powers under the FCPA broadly, announcing that "it is important that issuers...review their accounting procedures, systems of internal accounting controls and business practices in order that they may take any actions necessary to comply with the requirements of the Act."

Violations of the bribery parts of the statute may be punished by large corporate fines and long prison terms. Individuals may also be penalized with large fines and prison terms. Administrative and civil relief is also available.

CONSPIRACY (TITLE 18, U.S. CODE, §371)

The principal federal conspiracy statute provides: "if two or more persons conspire to commit any offense against the United States or its agencies, and one or more of such persons do any act to effect the object of the conspiracy, each shall be fined or imprisoned, or both."

The essential elements of this extremely important statute are:

- The conspiracy was willfully formed
- The accused willfully became a member of it
- At least one of the conspirators knowingly committed at least one overt act in furtherance of the conspiracy.

The essence of the offense is a combination or agreement of two or more persons to accomplish an unlawful purpose by lawful or unlawful means or a lawful purpose by unlawful means. The purpose of the conspiracy need not be accomplished for a violation to occur. However, at least one of the co-conspirators must have carried out at least one overt act in furtherance of the conspiracy. The overt act need not be criminal in itself and may be as innocuous as making a phone call or writing a letter.

Conspiracy counts are favored by prosecutors because they provide evidentiary and pleading advantages. If a conspiracy is shown, the acts and statements of one co-conspirator may be admitted into evidence against all, and each co-conspirator may be convicted for the underlying substantive offense (e.g., destroying government property) committed by any one of its members. A corporation cannot conspire with one of its own employees to commit an offense because the employee and employer are legally viewed as one. However, a corporation may conspire with other business entities or third parties to violate the statute.

AIDING AND ABETTING (TITLE 18, U.S. CODE, §2)

The aiding and abetting statute provides: "(a) Whoever commits an offense against the United States or aids, abets, counsels, commands, induces, or procures its commission is punishable as a principal, and (b) Whoever willfully causes an act to be done which if directly performed by him or another would be an offense against the United States, is punishable as a principal."

Under this fundamental tenet of criminal law, anyone who induces another to commit an offense, or who actively aids in its commission may also be charged and convicted of the underlying offense and subject to its penalties.

OBSTRUCTION OF JUSTICE (TITLE 18, U.S. CODE, §1503, et. seq.) AND PERJURY (TITLE 18, U.S. CODE, §1621 and 1623)

These statutes punish efforts to impede or obstruct the investigation or trial of other substantive offenses. Prosecutors usually are pleased to discover such violations because they add a more sinister flavor to what may be colorless white-collar charges and help to prove underlying criminal intent. In many instances, these charges draw the stiffest penalties.

Several obstruction statutes in the federal code punish, among other things, the attempted or actual destruction of evidence; tampering with or threatening witnesses, jurors or other court personnel. Perjury is an intentional false statement given under oath on a material point. Under a related federal statute (Title 18, U.S. Code, § 1623), the government may allege and prove perjury if the defendant makes two irreconcilable contradictory statements without proving which is true and which is false. False and fraudulent statements--orally or in writing--made to a government agency on a material matter may also be punished as a felony under a variety of statutes even if not given under oath.

OBSTRUCTION OF FEDERAL AUDIT (TITLE 18, U.S. CODE, §516)

This statute makes it a felony to obstruct a federal auditor in the performance of official audit duties. The statute provides: "(a) Whoever, with intent to deceive or defraud the United States, endeavors to influence, obstruct, or impede a Federal auditor in the performance of official duties relating to a person receiving in excess of $100,000 from the United States in any 1 year period shall be fined under this title or imprisoned, or both, (b) For purposes of this section, the term 'Federal auditor' means any person employed on a full- or part-time or contractual basis to perform an audit or a quality assurance inspection for or on behalf of the United States."

OBSTRUCTING EXAMINATION OF FINANCIAL INSTITUTION (TITLE 18, U.S. CODE, §1517)

This statute, similar to the prohibition of obstructing an audit, makes it a felony to obstruct the examination of a financial institution: "Whoever corruptly obstructs or attempts to obstruct any examination of a financial institution by an agency of the United States with jurisdiction to conduct an examination of such financial institution shall be fined under this title or imprisoned, or both."

TAX EVASION, FALSE RETURNS AND FAILURE TO FILE (TITLE 26, U.S. CODE, §7201, 7203, 7206(1), et. seq.)

Fraud and corruption prosecutions may include tax evasion, false returns, or failure to file charges if--as is often the case--the recipient of illegal payments has not reported them as income or the payer has attempted to conceal and deduct them as a legitimate business expense.

BANKRUPTCY FRAUD (TITLE 18, U.S. CODE, §151, et. seq.)

Two related but somewhat different types of criminal conduct fall under the general heading of bankruptcy fraud. The first is the planned bankruptcy or bust-out scheme where the wrongdoer sells off for cash, usually below cost, inventory obtained on credit (often through false or inflated financial statements) and then absconds with the proceeds. Formal bankruptcy proceedings are often not initiated and the crime may be prosecuted under general fraud statutes, such as mail or wire fraud.

The second type of bankruptcy offense involves misconduct by a person or entity actually involved or contemplating being involved in a formal bankruptcy proceeding.

FEDERAL CORRUPTION STATUTES (TITLE 18, U.S. CODE, §201, et. seq.)

Chapter 11 of Title 18 of the U.S. Code, § 201, et. seq. has 19 separate criminal provisions that define and prohibit a wide variety of conflicts of interest and other corrupt and unethical conduct involving public officials. The statutes of particular interest to fraud examiners are briefed below.

§201. Bribery of Public Officials and Witnesses

The essence of this law is the prohibition of both giving and receiving influence on the part of officials and jurors in connection with their official duties or testimony. However, the law exempts payment or receipt of lawful witness fees and expenses. The details are as follow:

"(a) For the purpose of this section: (1) The term "public official" means Member of Congress, Delegate, or Resident Commissioner or an officer of any department, agency or branch of Government thereof, including the District of Columbia, in any official function, under or by authority of any such department, agency, or branch of Government, or a juror; (2) The term "person who has been selected to be a public official" means any person who has been nominated or appointed to be a public official, or has been officially informed that such person will be soon nominated or appointed; and (3) The term "official act" means any decision or action on any question, matter, cause, suit, proceeding or controversy, which may at any time be pending, or which may by law be brought before any public official, in such official's official capacity, or in such official's place of trust or profit.

"(b) Whoever (1) corruptly gives, offers or promises anything of value to any public official or person who has been selected to be a public official, or offers or promises to give anything of value to any other person or entity, with intent to (A) influence any official act; or (B) influence such public official or person who has been selected to be a public official to commit or aid in committing any fraud on the United States; or (C) induce such public official or such person who has been selected to be a public official to do or omit to do any act in violation of the lawful duty of such official or person; (2) being a public official or person selected to be a public official corruptly demands, seeks, receives, accepts, or agrees to receive or accept anything of value personally or for any other person or entity, in return for being influenced to commit a fraud or to violate an official duty, (3) corruptly gives, offers, or promises anything of value to any person with intent to influence testimony under oath at a trial, hearing, or other proceeding, before any court, any committee of either House or both Houses of Congress, or any agency, commission, or officer, (4) corruptly demands, seeks, receives, accepts or agrees to receive or accept anything of value in return for being influenced in testimony under oath; Shall be fined no more than three times the monetary equivalent of the thing of value or imprisoned, or both, and may be disqualified from holding any office of honor, trust, or profit under the United States."

§212. Offer of Loan or Gratuity to Bank Examiner

"Whoever, being an officer, director or employee of a bank which is a member of the Federal Reserve System or the deposits of which are insured by the Federal Deposit Insurance Corporation [and other federal financial institutions] makes or grants any loan or gratuity, to any examiner or assistant examiner who examines or has authority to examine such bank, corporation, or institution, shall be fined or imprisoned, or both; and may be fined a further sum equal to the money so loaned or gratuity given."

§ 213. Acceptance of Loan or Gratuity by Bank Examiner

"Whoever, being an examiner or assistant examiner of member banks of the Federal Reserve System or banks the deposits of which are insured by the Federal Deposit Insurance Corporation [and other federal financial institutions] accepts a loan or gratuity from any bank, corporation, association or organization examined by him or from any person connected herewith, shall be fined or imprisoned, or both; and may be fined a further sum equal to the money so loaned or gratuity given, and shall be disqualified from holding office as an examiner."

§ 215. Receipt of Commissions or Gifts for Procuring Loans

"Whoever (1) corruptly gives, offers, or promises anything of value with intent to influence or reward an officer, director, employee, agent, or attorney of a financial institution in connection with any business or transaction of such institution; or (2) as an officer, director, employee, agent, or attorney of a financial institution, corruptly solicits or demands, or corruptly accepts or agrees to accept, anything of value intending to be influenced or rewarded in connection with any business or transaction of such institution; Shall be fined or imprisoned, or both."

The essence of this law is the prohibition of both giving and receiving influence in connection with private lending decisions. However, the law exempts payment or receipt of bona fide salary, wages, fees, or other compensation paid, or expenses paid or reimbursed, in the usual course of business.

The illegal gratuity statute deals with the offense of bribery. A bribe is a payment made with the purpose of influencing (changing) official conduct. A gratuity is a payment made to reward or compensate an official for performing duties lawfully required. Bribery is punishable by imprisonment, fine, and disqualification from holding public office. An illegal gratuity carries a lesser prison term, a fine, or both.

§212 and 213 forbid giving a loan or gratuity to a bank examiner. The only reported case construing these statutes held that the prosecution need not prove that the loan or gratuity was given or received with a corrupt or wrongful intent. The strict application of the statute has been justified by the public's need for disinterested bank examiners.

§ 215 bars the corrupt giving or receiving of anything of value to influence the action of an employee or agent of a federally-connected financial institution. The statute is aimed primarily at reducing corrupt influence in loan-making. Unlike § 212 and 213, a specific intent to influence or be influenced through the illegal payment must be proved to obtain a conviction. A payment made after a loan has been approved and disbursed may be in violation of the law if it is part of a prearranged plan or agreement.

EMBEZZLEMENT AND MISAPPLICATION OF BANK FUNDS (TITLE 18, U.S. CODE, §656, et. seq.)

§ 656 and 657 are the principal federal bank embezzlement statutes. The statutes provide:

§ 656. Theft, Embezzlement, or Misapplication by Bank Officer or Employee

"Whoever, being an officer, director, agent or employee of, or connected in any capacity with any federally-connected financial institution ["bank"], embezzles, abstracts, purloins or willfully misapplies any of the funds or credits of such institution, shall be fined or imprisoned, or both."

§ 657. Lending, Credit and Insurance Institutions

"Whoever, being an officer, agent or employee of or connected in any capacity with "lending, credit, and insurance institutions," and whoever, being a receiver of any such institution, or agent or employee of the receiver, embezzles, abstracts, purloins or willfully misapplies any money, funds, credits, securities or other things of value belonging to such institution, shall be fined or imprisoned, or both."

The bank embezzlement law covers a wide variety of lending, credit and insurance institutions, including the Reconstruction Finance Corporation, Federal Deposit Insurance Corporation, National Credit Union Administration, Home Owners' Loan Corporation, Farm Credit Administration, Department of Housing and Urban Development, Federal Crop Insurance Corporation, Farmers' Home Corporation, the Secretary of Agriculture acting through the Farmers' Home Administration, or any land bank, intermediate credit bank, bank for cooperatives or any lending, mortgage, insurance, credit or savings and loan corporation or association authorized or acting under the laws of the United States or any institution the accounts of which are insured by the Federal Savings and Loan Insurance Corporation, or by the Administrator of the National Credit Union Administration or any small business investment company.

FALSE STATEMENTS AND ENTRIES (TITLE 18, U.S. CODE, §1001, et. seq.)

Chapter 47 of Title 18, U.S. Code, contains a number of related provisions that punish false or fraudulent statements, orally or in writing, made to various federal agencies and departments. The principal statute is § 1001 that prohibits such statements generally and overlaps with many of the more specific laws, such as § 1014, that apply to false statements made on certain loan and credit applications.

§ 1001 most often is used to prosecute false statements to law enforcement or regulatory officials, not made under oath, in the course of an official investigation, or on an application for such things as federal employment, credit, and visa applications. The statute (establishing a felony) may also be used in lieu of the misdemeanor provisions of the IRS Code for filing false documents with tax returns.

The false statement statutes of greatest importance to the fraud examiner are these:

§ 1001. Statements or Entries Generally

"Whoever [within the jurisdiction of any department or agency of the United States] knowingly and willfully falsifies, conceals or covers up a material fact, or makes any false, fictitious or fraudulent statements or representations, or makes or uses any false writing or document, shall be fined or imprisoned, or both."

§ 1005. Bank Entries, Reports and Transactions

"Whoever, being an officer, director, agent or employee of any Federal Reserve Bank, member bank, national bank or insured bank, without authority from the directors of such bank, issues or puts in circulation any notes of such bank; or whoever without authority makes, draws, issues, puts forth, or assigns any certificate of deposit, draft, order, bill of exchange, acceptance, note, debenture, bond, or other obligation, or mortgage, judgment or decree; or whoever makes any false entries of such bank with intent to injure or defraud such bank, or any other person or organization; shall be fined or imprisoned, or both."

A statement is false for the purposes of § 1001 if it was known to be untrue when it was made, and is fraudulent if it was known to be untrue and was made with the intent to deceive a government agency. For a violation to occur, the agency need not actually have been deceived nor must the agency have in fact relied upon the false statement. The statement must have been capable, however, of influencing the agency involved.

§ 1005 makes it unlawful, among other things, for any officer, director, agent, or employee of a federally insured or chartered bank to make any false entries on the books of such institution with the intent to injure or defraud the bank or third parties, or to deceive any bank officer, examiners, or government agency. § 1014 prohibits false statements or reports in any credit application or related document submitted to a federally insured bank or credit institution for the purpose of influencing such organization's action in any way. As with § 1001, the false statements must be willful, but it need not have been relied upon or actually deceived the agency for a violation to occur.

BANK FRAUD (TITLE 18, U.S. CODE, §1344, et. seq.)

This law makes it a crime to defraud or to attempt to defraud a federally charted or insured bank. Previously, such offenses were prosecuted under the more generic fraud statutes, such as mail or wire fraud. The bank fraud statute and the related §1345 that provides for civil actions by the government to enjoin fraudulent activity are set out below.

§ 1344. Bank Fraud
"(a) Whoever knowingly executes, or attempts to execute, a scheme or artifice (1) to defraud a federally chartered or insured financial institution; or (2) to obtain any of the assets owned by or under the custody or control of a federally chartered or insured financial institution by means of false or fraudulent pretenses, representations, or promises, shall be fined or imprisoned, or both."

§1345. Injunctions Against Fraud
"Whenever it shall appear that any person is engaged or is about to engage in any act which constitutes or will constitute a violation, the Attorney General may initiate a civil proceeding in a district court of the United States to enjoin such violation. The court shall proceed as soon as practicable to the hearing and determination of such an action, and may, at any time before final determination, enter such a restraining order or prohibition, or take such other action, as is warranted to prevent a continuing and substantial injury to the United States or to any person or class of persons for whose protection this action is brought."

As in the mail and wire fraud statutes, the terms "scheme" and "artifice to defraud" include any misrepresentations or other conduct intended to deceive others in order to obtain something of value. The prosecution must prove only an attempt to execute the scheme and need not show actual loss, or that the victim institution was deceived, or that the defendant personally benefited from the scheme.

FRAUD IN CONNECTION WITH FEDERAL INTEREST COMPUTERS (TITLE 18, U.S. CODE, §1030)

Computer crime is a new and somewhat amorphous term referring both to cases in which a computer is the instrument of a crime and those in which it is the object. As the instrument, for example, a computer may be used to direct calls in a scheme to sell shares in a nonexistent gold mine or may be used to steal funds from a bank account. As the object of a crime, the information contained in a computer may be stolen or destroyed.

Most computer crimes are prosecuted under traditional fraud, theft, and embezzlement statutes. A statute enacted in 1984, Title 18, U.S. Code, § 1030, makes certain computer-related activity a specific federal offense. The statute provides:

§1030. Fraud and Related Activity in Connection with Computers
"(a) Whoever (1) knowingly accesses a computer without authorization and obtains information that is protected for reasons of national defense or foreign relations with the intent or reason to believe that such information so obtained is to be used to the injury of the United States or to the advantage of any foreign nation; (2) intentionally accesses a computer without authorization and thereby obtains information contained in a financial record of a financial institution or of a card issuer as defined in § 1602(n) of Title 15, or contained in a file of a consumer reporting agency on a consumer, as such terms are defined in the Fair Credit Reporting Act (15 U.S.C. 1681 et. seq.); (3) intentionally, without authorization to access any computer of a department or agency of the United States, accesses such a computer that is used by or on behalf of the Government of the United States and such conduct affects the use of the Government's operation of such computer; (4) knowingly and with intent to defraud, accesses a Federal interest computer without authorization and by means of such conduct furthers the intended fraud and obtains anything of value; (5) intentionally accesses a Federal interest computer without authorization and damages or destroys information in any such Federal interest computer, or prevents authorized use of any such computer or information; (6) knowingly and with intent to defraud traffics (as defined in § 1029) in any password or similar information through which a computer may be accessed without authorization; shall be punished as provided in subsection (c) of this section."

The term "federal interest computer" basically means a computer exclusively for the use of a financial institution or the United States Government, or, in the case of a computer not exclusively for such use, used by or for a financial institution or the United States Government and the conduct constituting the offense affects the use of the financial institution's operation or the Government's operation of such computer. This section does not prohibit any lawfully authorized investigative, protective, or intelligence activity of a law enforcement agency of the United States, a State, or a political subdivision of a State, or of an intelligence agency of the United States.

In brief, § 1030 punishes any intentional, unauthorized access to "federal interest" computers for the purpose of:
- Obtaining restricted data regarding national security
- Obtaining confidential financial information
- Using a computer which is intended for use by the United States government
- Committing a fraud, or
- Damaging or destroying information contained in the computer.

THE ELECTRONIC FUNDS TRANSFER ACT (TITLE 15, U.S. CODE, §1693n)

This Act provides, in part, that "whoever (1) knowingly, in a transaction affecting interstate or foreign commerce, uses or attempts or conspires to use any counterfeit, fictitious, altered, forged, lost, stolen, or fraudulently obtained debit instrument (i.e., card, code, or other device, other than a check, draft, or similar paper instrument, by the use of which a person may initiate an electronic fund transfer) to obtain money, goods, services, or anything else of value; or (2) transports such a debit instrument in interstate or foreign commerce; or (3) uses any instrumentality of interstate or foreign commerce transport such a debit instrument; or (4) knowingly receives, conceals, uses or transports money, goods, services, or anything else of value in interstate commerce which was obtained with a counterfeit, fictitious, altered, forged, lost, stolen, or fraudulently obtained debit instrument...; shall be fined or imprisoned, or both."

Federal and state legislatures have moved to make criminal all manner of computer fraud and abuses, such as hardware theft and destruction, misappropriation of software, unauthorized accessing of computers and data communications facilities to steal data or money or to cause mischief. The elements of the crime seem to include unauthorized access (or exceeding one's authority), an intent to defraud, and obtaining anything of value. Software, as a thing of value, seems to be included, as well as cash money.

MAJOR FRAUD AGAINST THE UNITED STATES (TITLE 18, U.S. CODE, §1031)

This statute drastically increases the penalties for fraud upon the United States involving procurement contracts of $1,000,000 or more. The act provides, in its pertinent parts: "Whoever knowingly executes, or attempts to execute, any scheme or artifice with the intent to defraud the United States...in any procurement of property or services as a prime contractor with the United States or as a subcontractor or supplier on a contract in which there is a prime contract with the United States; shall, be fined or imprisoned, or both."

Other provisions of the statute allow for penalties of up to $10,000,000 in fines or twice the amount of the gross loss or gain involved in the offense. The statute contains a special seven-year statute of limitations compared to the normal five-year statute applicable to federal crimes.

The statute also contains a whistle-blower protection clause that provides that any individual who is discharged, demoted, harassed, or otherwise mistreated as a result of the individual's cooperation in the prosecution of offenses under this section may obtain reinstatement, two times the amount of back-pay due, and other damages, including litigation costs and attorney's fees.

Another provision authorizes the Attorney General to pay up to $250,000 in certain circumstances for information regarding possible prosecutions under this section. This and the "whistle-blower" provisions do not apply to persons who participated in the offense.

LAUNDERING OF MONETARY INSTRUMENTS (TITLE 18, U.S. CODE, §1956)

This complex statute forbids money-laundering in connection with a large number of enumerated federal crimes, including but not limited to narcotics trafficking. Pertinent parts of the statute prohibit persons from engaging in certain financial transactions (e.g., transferring money instruments within and outside the United States) when they know the money comes from unlawful activities, and their actions conceal or disguise the nature, location, source, ownership, or control of the proceeds of specified unlawful activity or avoid a transaction reporting requirement under State or Federal law,

The statute provides for fines of up to $500,000 or twice the value of the property involved in the transaction, whichever is greater, or long prison terms, or both. The statute also provides for a civil penalty related to the value of the property, funds, or monetary instruments involved in the transaction.

The statute includes extensive definitions of technical terms. "Specified unlawful activity" includes narcotics-related transactions, transactions related to bankruptcy fraud, bribery, false statements, embezzlement, mail or wire fraud, bank fraud, and environmental violations. Assets acquired as a result of violations of the money-laundering statutes are subject to forfeiture by the government.

ANTI-KICKBACK ACT OF 1986 (TITLE 41, U.S. CODE, §51-58)

The act prohibits giving or receiving anything of value ("kickback") by a subcontractor to a prime contractor in U.S. government contracts. Pertinent parts of the statute prohibit the payment of any fee, commission, or compensation of any kind, or the granting of any gift or gratuity of any kind by or on behalf of a subcontractor to any officer, partner, employee, or agent of a prime contractor holding a negotiated contract entered into by any agency of the United States for the furnishing of supplies, materials, equipment, or services of any kind whatsoever.

Willful violations can be punished by a fine, a prison term, or both. Civil penalties up to twice the amount of the kickback may also be assessed. The United States may also offset the amount of any kickback against the amount owed on the prime contract.

Title 41, U.S. Code, § 57, requires that the prime contractor have in place in its operations reasonable procedures to prevent and detect kickbacks. The prime contractor is also required to cooperate fully with any federal agency investigation and to report any suspected violations promptly.

According to the Congressional notes following the statute, "reasonable procedures to detect and prevent kickbacks" include

- Educational programs for employees and subcontractors
- Policy manuals
- Special procurement and audit procedures

- Ethics policies
- Applicant screening
- Reporting procedures.

CORPORATE SENTENCING GUIDELINES

The Sentencing Reform Act of 1984 provided for the development of guidelines for sentencing individual and organizational offenders. The guidelines for individuals became effective in 1987, and the guidelines for organizations in 1991. The sentencing guidelines seek to make punishments more uniform, and they unquestionably and dramatically increase the severity of punishment. In some cases, the fine may be $290 million or more. However, corporations that have a program to prevent and detect violations of the law may be rewarded with a more lenient sentence. The reward may be worth several million dollars at the time of sentencing.

Under the guidelines, sentencing determinations are made by cross-referencing the base offense level assigned to a particular offense with the "defendant's criminal history category." There are 43 basic offense levels (murder and treason being level 43 offenses) and 6 criminal history categories. Adjustments may be made up or down in each table based on the particular facts and circumstances of the case. For example, the base offense level for crimes involving fraud or deceit is 6, but if the fraud involved a loss of more than $2,000, more than minimal planning, or other aggravating circumstances, the base offense level can be substantially increased. The final applicable offense level is then coordinated with the criminal history category of the defendant (which is computed on a point basis according to the number and type of previous convictions and other factors) to arrive at the final sentencing level. The court may depart from the recommended sentence if unique factors are present but any such departure must be supported by specific reasons.

As an example, a defendant with no prior convictions convicted of fraud involving the loss of $10,000 would be sentenced to a term of 4 to 10 months, absent unusual circumstances. If the fraud resulted in the loss of $1,000,000, involved more than minimal planning, and was perpetrated by a defendant who had a previous conviction punishable by more than a year in prison, the recommended term of imprisonment would be 41 to 51 months. Under the Sentencing Act, the defendant will serve substantially the sentence received (a small reduction is possible for good behavior). The act abolished parole in federal cases.

SENTENCING OF ORGANIZATIONS

Corporations and other organizations may be criminally liable for offenses committed by their agents if committed in the scope of the agent's duty and with the intended purpose of benefiting the organization. A corporation can be held criminally responsible even if its management had no knowledge or participation in the underlying criminal events and even if specific policies or instructions prohibited the activity undertaken by the employees. In fact, a corporation can be criminally responsible for the collective knowledge of several of its employees even if no single employee intended to commit an offense. Thus, the combination of vicarious or imputed corporate criminal liability and the sentencing guidelines creates an extraordinary risk for corporations.

Sentencing guidelines for organizations indicate that:
* The court must, whenever practicable, order the organization to remedy any harm caused by the offense
* If the organization operated primarily for a criminal   purpose, the fine should be set sufficiently high to   divest the organization of all assets
* The fine range for any other organization should be based on the seriousness of the offense and the culpability of the organization. Culpability generally will be determined by the steps taken by the organization prior to the offense to prevent and detect criminal conduct, the extent of involvement in or tolerance of the offense by the organization's personnel, and the organization's response after an offense had been committed.

SETTING THE AMOUNT OF THE FINE

First, the base fine is determined by figuring the greatest of:
* The amount from the offense level fine table
* The pecuniary gain to the organization from the offense
* The pecuniary loss from the offense caused by the organization, to the extent the loss was caused intentionally, knowingly, or recklessly.

The fine amounts on the base offense level fine table range from $5,000 to $72,500,000. Next, the court calculates the appropriate multipliers for the base fine level, depending on the particular circumstances. Factors that are considered include:

- Involvement in or tolerance of criminal activity
- Prior history
- Whether the organization violated a judicial order or injunction during the offense
- The existence of an effective program to prevent and detect violations of law
- Any self-reporting, cooperation, and acceptance of responsibility
- Obstruction of justice by the organization.

The culpability score is then converted to a multiplier that generates the recommended fine range. The court will consider a number of additional factors to determine where in the range the actual fine will be imposed. An organization must be ordered to serve a period of probation, if the court finds that:

- Probation is necessary to secure payment of restitution, to enforce a remedial order, or to ensure completion of community service
- A monetary penalty is ordered and has not been paid at the time of sentencing and probation is necessary to ensure payment
- Probation is necessary to assure that changes are made to reduce the likelihood of crime
- Probation is necessary to accomplish Sentencing Act purposes
- The sentence does not include a fine.

The length of probation may not exceed five years. In addition, the court has discretion to order the defendant organization to publicize its conviction and the nature of the offense. The court may also order the organization to make periodic reports to the court or the probation department and subject itself to unannounced examinations of its books and records. Finally, the court may order the organization to develop and submit for court approval an effective compliance program.

EFFECTIVE PROGRAM TO DETECT AND PREVENT VIOLATIONS OF LAW

The guidelines provide credit in the calculation of a fine if the organization has in place an effective program to detect and prevent violations of law. The Act defines such a program as one that is reasonably designed, implemented, and enforced so that it generally will be effective in preventing and detecting criminal conduct. The organization must use due diligence in seeking to prevent and detect criminal conduct by its employees.

DUE DILIGENCE

The organization must take at least seven minimum steps to meet the requirement of due diligence:
1. Implement policies defining standards and procedures to be followed by the organization's agents and employees.
2. Assign specific high-level personnel ultimate responsibility to ensure compliance
3. Use due care not to delegate significant discretionary authority to persons whom the organization knows or should have known had a propensity to engage in illegal activities.
4. Communicate standards and procedures to all agents and employees and require participation in training programs.
5. Take reasonable steps to achieve compliance (e.g., by the use of monitoring and auditing systems and by having and publicizing a reporting system where employees can refer criminal conduct without fear of retribution--hot line or ombudsman program.)
6. Consistently enforce standards through appropriate discipline ranging from reprimand to dismissal.
7. After detection of an offense, the organization must take all reasonable steps to respond appropriately to the offense and to prevent further similar offenses, including modifying its program and appropriate discipline for the individuals responsible for the offense and for those who failed to detect it.

CONCLUDING REMARKS

The description of sentencing guidelines and companies' obligations to implement and manage systems for deterrence of frauds is a fitting conclusion for this section on the law related to fraud. Numerous aspects of common law and numerous statutes exist to combat fraud. However, no matter how many laws are written, and no matter how many cases are decided to convict and punish fraudsters, prevention and detection still resides largely in the private sector. Government and the judicial system will never be large enough to cope with fraud. The cooperation of millions of businesses and individuals must fill the gap.

CHAPTER 2
CRIMINOLOGY RELATED
TO FRAUD

White-collar and economic crime are not legal terms. In criminology, they refer to a wide variety of offenses. The major common elements of such behaviors are: (1) They grow out of occupational efforts in business, politics, and the professions, and (2) they rarely involve force or threat of force. Perpetrators typically do not seek out their jobs to commit crime. Their lawbreaking typically occurs after they are confronted with temptation or faced with circumstances they believe they cannot satisfactorily resolve in any lawful manner.

Economic crimes can be defined as acts in violation of civil and criminal law designed to bring financial reward for the offender. These are crimes against property, not crimes characterized by force or violence against people. Most criminologists have noted that property crimes are treated with indifference by the average citizen compared to violent crime. Studies suggest that nearly every person has participated in a theft of some sort: petty shoplifting, cheating on income taxes, stealing a book from a college bookstore, or pilfering from a place of employment. Another reason for the public's tolerance is the belief that economic crimes "really don't hurt anyone." Mild punishment for economic crimes is common.

AMATEURS AND PROFESSIONALS

Much economic street crime is caused by occasional criminals. Their decision to steal is largely related to opportunity, and these thefts are neither well planned nor well-executed. In addition, included in this group of amateurs, are the millions of occasional thieves who earn their incomes legitimately, but engage in such activities as shoplifting, pilfering, and tax fraud.

Occasional property crimes occur when people have an opportunity or situational inducement to commit crime. Opportunities are available to all members of all classes, but members of the upper class have more opportunity to engage in lucrative business-related crimes.

Professional thieves make the bulk of their income from law violations. Most are not deterred by the law, and many are very skilled at their craft. Not a great deal is known about the professional thief, except that three types of offenders can be identified. One group is young people who are taught the craft of theft by older professionals; another is gang members who continue their thefts after maturing out of gang activity; and the third category includes youths who are incarcerated for minor offenses and learn the techniques of professional theft while in prison.

"Organized crime" is a special case. It is a conspiratorial activity, involving the coordination of many people in planning and executing illegal activity or in the pursuit of a legitimate activity through unlawful means (for example, using threats to secure a stake in a legitimate corporation). Organized crime involves continuous commitment by primary members, although individuals with specialized skills (such as contract killers) may be brought in when the need arises. Organized crime organizations are usually structured along hierarchical lines--a chieftain supported by close advisors, and then lower echelon members.

Organized crime has economic gain as its primary goal, though achievement of power and status also may be a motivating factor. Organized crime is not limited to providing illicit services. It includes such sophisticated activities as laundering illegal money through legitimate business, land fraud, and computer crimes. Most organized crime income comes from narcotics distribution, loan sharking, and prostitution. However, billions of dollars are gained from white-collar crime, gambling, theft rings, pornography, and other illegal enterprises.

Until fairly recently, federal and state governments did little to combat organized crime. One of the first anti-organized crime measures was the Interstate and Foreign Travel or Transportation in Aid of Racketeering Enterprises Act (the Travel Act). The Travel Act prohibits interstate facilities and interstate commerce with the intent to promote, establish, carry on, or facilitate an unlawful activity. In 1970, Congress passed the Organized Crime Control Act. It provides for special grand juries in localities where major organized crime appears to be active. It also creates a general federal immunity statute whereby a witness can be ordered to jail for 18 months for refusal to testify, after having been granted immunity from prosecution for specified offenses.

People acting alone or in small groups are basically amateurs. The "organized criminals," popularized by the government and the media, are the professionals.

WHITE-COLLAR CRIME

Most fraud is "white-collar crime." Scholars differ widely in their definitions of white-collar crime. The Dictionary of Criminal Justice Data Terminology, published by the Bureau of Justice Statistics, defines white-collar crime as:

"non-violent crime for financial gain committed by means of deception by persons whose occupational status is entrepreneurial, professional or semi-professional and utilizing their special occupational skills and opportunities; also non-violent crime for financial gain utilizing deception and committed by anyone having special technical and professional knowledge of business and government, irrespective of the person's occupation."

This definition may be incomplete in two ways. First, by limiting offenses to the course of persons' occupational work, it overlooks other possible perpetrators and other possible violations. While many people can commit larceny in the course of their daily activities, only a few corporate executives can violate the Sherman Antitrust law. Second, the definition overlooks the role of the "criminal" corporation.

Several distinct differences distinguish street crimes/economic crimes from white collar crime. Opportunity is the first distinguishing characteristic. An unemployed poor youth without funds might turn to armed robbery. However a bank teller, who is also short of cash, might embezzle because a different opportunity presented itself. Most criminals will commit crimes with which they are the most familiar, are the most easily accomplished, and have the fewest dire consequences. An often unheralded bonus of social status is access to opportunities for the less dirty, "more decent" kinds of crime.

PUBLIC PERCEPTION OF WHITE-COLLAR CRIME

According to some criminologists, the apparent increase in fraud is due to the lack of seriousness with which the public regards white-collar crime. However, some studies show that fraud-related offenses are perceived by the public to be as serious if not more serious than more traditional crimes, especially for white-collar violations that have harmful physical consequences.

Illustrating this point is a poll conducted by the National Survey of Crime Severity in 1977. Sixty thousand (60,000) respondents 18 years of age or older were given a list of offenses and each was asked to rate and assign a value to each crime. The survey results showed that both occupational and "common" crime are viewed as serious behavior, although the degree of seriousness varies with the offense. Fraud by a grocer and a ten-dollar embezzlement are perceived to be as serious as an obscene phone call. A bribe accepted by a city politician and a $1,000 armed robbery rate about the same. Table 1 shows the study results.

TABLE 1
National Survey of Crime Severity Ratings: Selected Offenses
(White-collar crimes in bold)

Rating	Offense
1.9	**An employee embezzles $10 from his employer.**
1.9	A store owner knowingly puts "large" eggs into containers marked "extra large."
1.9	A person makes an obscene phone call.
3.1	A person breaks into a home and steals $100.
3.2	**An employer illegally threatens to fire employees if they join a labor union.**
3.6	A person knowingly passes a bad check.
3.7	A labor union official illegally threatens to organize a strike if an employer hires nonunion workers.
5.4	A real estate agent refuses to sell a house to a person because of that person's race.
5.4	A person threatens to harm a victim unless the victim gives him money. The victim gives him $10 and is not harmed.
5.7	A theater owner knowingly shows pornographic movies to a minor.
6.1	**A person cheats on his Federal income tax return and avoids paying $10,000 in taxes.**
6.1	A person runs a prostitution racket.
6.2	A person beats a victim with his fists. The victim requires treatment by a doctor but not hospitalization.
6.2	**An employee embezzles $1,000 from his employer.**

TABLE 1 (Continued)
Rating   Offense
------   --

6.4   An employer refuses to hire a qualified person because of that person's race.

6.5   A person uses heroin.

6.9   A factory knowingly gets rid of its waste in a way pollutes the water supply of a city. As a result, one person becomes ill but does not require medical treatment.

6.9   A person beats a victim with his fists. The victim requires hospitalization.

8.0   A person steals an unlocked car and sells it.

8.2   Knowing that a shipment of cooking oil is bad, a store owner decides to sell it anyway. Only one bottle is sold and the purchaser is treated by a doctor but not hospitalized.

8.6   A person performs an illegal abortion.

9.0   A city official takes a bribe from a company for his help in getting a city building contract for the company.

9.0   A person, armed with a lead pipe, robs a victim of $1,000.

9.2   A person robs a victim of $10 at gun point. No physical harm occurs.

9.4   A public official takes $1,000 of public money for his own use.

9.6   A police officer knowingly makes a false arrest.

9.6   A person breaks into a home and steals $1,000.

10.0   A government official intentionally hinders the investigation of a criminal offense.

10.9   A person steals property worth $10,000 from a locked building.

11.2   A company pays a bribe to a legislator to vote for a law favoring the company.

11.8   A man beats a stranger with his fists. He requires hospitalization.

12.0   A police officer takes a bribe not to interfere with an illegal gambling operation.

12.0   A person gives the floor plans of a bank to a bank robber.

13.3   A person, armed with a lead pipe, robs a victim of $10. The victim is injured and requires hospitalization.

13.5   A doctor cheats on claims he makes to a Federal health insurance plan for patient services. He gains $10,000.

13.9   A legislator takes a bribe from a company to vote for law favoring the company.

TABLE 1 (Continued)

Rating	Offense
14.6	A person, using force, robs a victim of $10. The victim is hurt and requires hospitalization.
15.5	A person breaks into a bank at night and steals $10,000.
15.7	A county judge takes a bribe to give a light sentence in a criminal case.
16.6	A person, using force, robs a victim of $1,000. The victim is hurt and requires treatment by a doctor but not hospitalization.
17.8	Knowing that a shipment of cooking oil is bad, a store owner decides to sell it anyway. Only one bottle is sold and the purchaser dies.
19.5	A person kills a victim by recklessly driving an automobile.
19.7	A factory knowingly gets rid of its waste in a way that pollutes the water supply of a city. As a result, 20 people become ill but none require medical treatment.
19.9	A factory knowingly gets rid of its waste in a way that pollutes the water supply of a city. As a result, one person dies.
20.1	A man forcibly rapes a woman. Her physical injuries require treatment by a doctor but not hospitalization.
33.8	A person runs a narcotics rings.
39.1	A factory knowingly gets rid of its waste in a way that pollutes the water supply of a city. As a result, 20 people die.
43.9	A person plants a bomb in a public building. The bomb explodes and one person is killed.
72.1	A person plants a bomb in a public building. The bomb explodes and 20 people are killed.

Source: The National Survey of Crime Severity by Marvin Wolfgang, Robert Figlio, Paul Tracy, and Simon Singer (1985). Washington, D.C.; U.S. Government Printing Office (Pp. vi-x).

KINDS OF WHITE-COLLAR CRIME

Criminologists have used a variety of white-collar crime classification schemes. One of them comprehends these categories:
- Ad hoc violations committed for personal profit on an episodic basis; for example, welfare fraud and tax cheats

- Abuses of trust committed by persons in organizations against organizations; for example, embezzlement, bribery, and kickbacks
- Collateral business crimes committed by organizations in furtherance of their business interests; for example, false weights and measures, antitrust violations, environmental crimes
- Con games committed for the sole purpose of cheating clients; for example, fraudulent land sales, bogus securities.

However, white-collar crime also can be broken down simply into two categories--organizational crime and occupational crime. Organizational crime is committed by business and government. Occupational crime is largely committed by individuals or small groups of individuals working in connection with their occupations.

ORGANIZATIONAL CRIME

Organizational crime occurs in the context of complex relationships and expectations among boards of directors, executives, and managers on the one hand; and among parent corporations, corporate divisions, and subsidiaries on the other. Most of the time it is "crime by committee."

While corporations cannot be jailed, their activities can be restricted. Most corporate lawbreakers are handled by government regulatory agencies like the Federal Trade Commission, the Environmental Protection Agency, and the Food and Drug Administration. Enforcement measures may include warning letters, consent agreements or decrees not to repeat the violation, orders of regulatory agencies to compel compliance, seizure or recall of goods, administrative or civil monetary penalties, and court injunctions to refrain from further violations.

Corporate crime is certainly not limited to the United States. Clinard and Yeager say it appears to be extensive in Europe, Japan, Australia and other areas. According to Delmas-Marty, French multinationals violate the law in many ways. They utilize both legal and illegal means in tax evasion. They may transfer profits from one subsidiary to another located in a country that has a more lenient tax system or presents a tax haven. According to Cosson, French manufacturing corporations also falsify their bookkeeping to avoid payment of industrial and commercial taxes.

In Japan, the Diet (legislature) has passed a law for the punishment of crimes "relating to environmental pollution that adversely affects the health of persons." Under this law intentional or negligent emission by industries of a substance that causes danger to human life or health is to be punished with imprisonment or fines.

The Swiss banking system has often been accused of offering a hiding place for stolen or looted money, providing a screen for stock manipulations and shady promoters and helping tax evaders conceal both income and assets. Deposits in Swiss banks may be laundered to obscure their illegal origins, and then the money is made legal through new commercial transactions and therefore concealed from tax authorities.

CORPORATE ORGANIZATION AND CRIMINAL BEHAVIOR

Large corporations have contributed to the industrial and commercial development of the United States and most Western countries. These corporations wield much wealth and social and political powers, and they affect the lives of almost every person. The corporations influence prices and therefore inflation, quality of goods, and employment rates. They know how to manipulate public opinion through the use of the mass media, and they can influence foreign relations.

Clinard and Yeager believe the public perceives business as being motivated by self-interest rather than by broader national or social interests, perhaps with good reason. They found that 1,553 white-collar crime cases had been filed against the 562 Fortune 500 businesses whose records were examined for two years--an average of 2.7 violations for each company. About 60 percent of the companies had at least one case against them, and for these companies, the average was 4.4 cases. The oil, pharmaceutical, and motor vehicle industries had the largest number of violation cases. They found that large corporations were far more likely to commit violations than small corporations and that large corporations bear a widely disproportionate share of sanctions for serious and moderate violations.

Irwin Ross analyzed 1,043 companies that at one time or another had appeared on the Fortune list of large industrial companies. Included in his study were five kinds of offenses: bribe-taking or bribe-giving by high-level executives, criminal fraud, illegal campaign contributions, tax evasion, and antitrust violations. One hundred seventeen (117), 11 percent of the corporations, were violators.

The costs of corporate crimes not only include financial losses, but also injuries, deaths and health hazards. Such crimes destroy public confidence in businesses and hurt the image of corporations. Clinard and Yeager say price-fixing offenses victimize the consumer and federal, state, and municipal governments. Income tax crimes deprive the government and those dependent on it of needed revenue.

Clinard and Yeager believe that corporate violations are increasingly difficult to discover, investigate, or develop successfully into cases due to their complexity and intricacy. The characteristic complex nature of corporate crimes is particularly true of antitrust cases, foreign payoffs, illegal political contributors, and computer fraud. Victims of corporate crime are often unaware that they have been victimized (e.g., large numbers of consumers pay a modestly inflated price for a product as a result of antitrust collusion).

Legal responses have been slow and ineffectual for dealing with organizational crime. The law has emphasized the role of the individual actor in criminality but has not examined the role of the organization very much. Criminal activities are often rooted in organizational subculture and attitudes, developed over time, and cannot be traced to individuals or groups within the organization. While individuals still carry out the criminal enterprise, their attitudes and characteristics are of little importance, because an organization can replace employees who are unwilling to participate in a criminal activity.

TYPES OF VIOLATIONS

Clinard and Yeager found six main types of corporate illegal behavior: administrative, environmental, financial, labor, manufacturing, and unfair trade practices.

Administrative violations involve noncompliance with the requirements of an agency or court and information-reporting violations such as refusal to produce information, failure to report information, and failure to file, secure certification, or acquire permits.

Environmental violations include incidents of air and water pollution, including oil and chemical spills, as well as violations of air and water permits that require capital outlays by the corporations for construction of pollution control equipment.

Financial violations include illegal payments or failure to disclose such violations (i.e., domestic commercial bribery), illegal domestic political contributions, payments to foreign officials, illegal gratuities and benefits, and violations of foreign currency laws. Examples of securities-related violations are false and misleading proxy materials, misuse of nonpublic material information, and the issuance of false financial statements and other data.

Transaction violations, involve the following: terms of sale (overcharging customers), exchange agreements (failure to apply increased prices equally to classes of purchasers, illegal changing of lease conditions, illegal termination of supplier-purchaser relationships, imposition of more stringent credit terms, and payment maneuvers (failure to pay full price when due, insufficient funds checks, making preferential payments). Also included are tax violations involving fraudulent returns and deficiency in tax liability, accounting malpractices such as failure to record terms of transactions involving questionable pricing and promotional practices, false entries such as recording fictitious sales, and improper estimates such as misreporting of costs.

Labor violations fall into four major types: discrimination in employment, occupational safety and health hazards, unfair labor practices, and wage and hour violations. The four agencies responsible for bringing actions concerning these violations are the Equal Employment Opportunity Commission, the Occupational Health and Safety Administration, the National Labor Relations Board, and the Wage and Hour Division of the Department of Labor.

Manufacturing violations involve three government agencies. The Consumer Product Safety Commission responds to violations of the Federal Hazardous Substances Act, the Poison Prevention Packaging Act, the Flammable Fabrics Act and the Consumer Product Safety Act. Violations in this arena include electric shock hazards, chemical and environmental hazards, and fire and thermal burn hazards. The main categories of manufacturing violations involving the Food and Drug Administration regulations are misbranding, mispackaging, mislabeling (packaging in incorrect or defective containers, lack of adequate or correct content or ingredient statements, lack of adequate or correct directions for use on labels), contamination or adulteration (such as lack of assurance of sterility; product prepared, held, or stored under unsanitary conditions), lack of effectiveness of product (failure to meet standards, defect in product), inadequate testing procedures and inadequate standards in blood or plasma collection and laboratory processing (improper procedures in choice and use of blood donors, lack of assurance of sterility).

The Federal Trade Commission investigates unfair trade practices involve abuses of competition (monopolization, price discrimination, credit violations, misrepresentation), vertical combinations (tying agreements), and horizontal combinations (price fixing, bid rigging, illegal mergers, illegal interlocking directorships, agreements among competitors to allocate markets, jobs, customers, accounts, sales and patents).

CAUSES OF ORGANIZATIONAL CRIMES

Sociologist Robert K. Merton first theorized that social structures provide motivation for misconduct. Merton focused on competition, the importance of money in society, and the erosion of norms that encourage legitimate money-making behavior. Two key elements of cultural structure are the goals that are deemed worthy for all members of society and the norms that spell out how they may be legitimately achieved. When the goals receive more emphasis than the norms, the norms will lose their power to regulate behavior. This produces a state of "anomie," or normlessness--an important concept in sociology that is said to lead to lawlessness.

Merton also defined competitive economic activity as a "culturally-legitimated success-goal." Regardless of the cultural emphasis on profits, an organization must seek profits, and profits will be a prime indicator of prestige within a society, as well as the key to social mobility within hierarchies of organizations. In short, money talks in the business world.

Not all economists agree with the notion that profit maximization is the primary goal for businesses. Managerial goals often tend in a direction other than profit--as when a company seeks growth, stability, a larger market share, or better perquisites for its own employees. These goals oriented away from money-making may result in companies that are satisfied to settle for minimal profit levels so they can accomplish other important goals as well.

Vaughan noted that organizations engage in intense competition for such resources as personnel, product development, land acquisition, advertising space, and sales territories. The ability to obtain these resources may be limited by scarcity, by the behavior of competing organizations, by consumer behavior, and by the ability of a business to take on new responsibilities. When the lack of strategic resources threatens a loss, unlawful conduct may follow.

Whether a company will cheat does not depend solely on competition for resources. Economic success is relative. One company may be satisfied with a much smaller profit than its older competitor. Another company may be satisfied by continuing improvement with respect to its competitors, while an industry giant may remain happy simply by maintaining market share. A company's goals may change over time, but companies practically never desire to lose ground.

When illegal conduct succeeds in an organization, it tends to reinforce the bad behavior. While society frowns on the wrongdoing, the organization may come to think of the behavior as normal. The success then breeds further wrongdoing among individuals who are swayed into departing from rules they once regarded as legitimate. Without outside social controls (e.g., law enforcement), a corrupt organization can affect the entire societal structure. For example, companies can lobby legislatures to enact laws to legitimize formerly unlawful behavior.

According to Vaughn, the erosion of normative support for legitimate procedures can produce such anti-competitive activities as price-fixing, discriminatory price-cutting, theft of trade secrets, false advertising, and bribery. These examples of misconduct can be viewed sociologically as the victimization of one organization by another to obtain resources that provide upward mobility in the organizational pecking order.

OPPORTUNITIES FOR UNLAWFUL ORGANIZATIONAL BEHAVIOR

Social structures alone do not explain an organization's use of illegal methods to seek scarce resources. Another necessary ingredient in the mix is opportunity. The opportunity to act unlawfully is present in some degree in all complex businesses. The legitimate processes of business--for example, computerized commodity trading conducted in milli-seconds and in huge quantities--may provide the opportunity for wrongdoing and a minimal risk of detection.

Much information on businesses (e.g., products, financial performance, market size) is publicly available, but other organizational characteristics that set the stage for illegal behavior are usually shrouded in secrecy. These secrets include internal processes and structures that are not necessarily related to size or market clout. Vaughan hypothesized that the complexity of internal processes and structures of a business, regardless of a company's size, often sets the stage for organizational misbehavior.

Organizational Structure

Complex companies provide a structure that can foster misbehavior. Companies isolate those settings in departments and in locations around a city, the country, or the world. This isolation means that information about what one part of a company is doing may be unknown in another part. All this reduces the risk that misbehavior will be detected and punished. The larger a company grows, the more specialized its subunits tend to become. An internally diversified company may have few employees who fully understand all the detailed operations.

Specialized departments in a large company compete for resources not only with other companies, but with departments within their own company. The need to outperform not only other businesses, but also other units within their own business, can generate sufficient pressure to lead to misconduct. Vaughan noted that departments often have survival concerns that conflict with the larger interests of an organization. When given a chance to make decisions, lower-level managers will tend to act not in the interest of the whole company, but in the interests of their departments.

Specialization also hides illegal activities, especially where a company's tasks are kept separate and unrelated. Employees' fragmented knowledge protects a company from the effects of personnel turnover and leaks of information. No single person one can offer much more than a piece of the jigsaw puzzle that paints the overall company picture. The same secrecy, however, raises the chances for misconduct.

Vaughan believes that organizational growth naturally leads to a progressive loss of control over departments. Executives cannot hope to keep track of all the units in a huge company and must rely on subordinates to carry out policy. When the distance between top executives and subordinate units grows to a sufficient level "authority leakage" results. Such leakage can make the company too unwieldy for an executive to enforce rules at all levels. The organization can diversify beyond the capability of those at the top to master it.

This leakage allows subsidiaries, company researchers, accountants, or other personnel to engage in misconduct without any assurance that internal controls will check the behavior. In some cases, as with computer crime, detecting misconduct may be beyond the ability of most employees.

The tiered structure of most organizations obscures personal responsibility and tends to spread it throughout the company. Thus, determining where a decision to engage in misconduct originated can be difficult. John E. Conklin put it this way: "The delegation of responsibility and unwritten orders keep those at the top of the corporate structure remote from the consequences of their decisions and orders, much as the heads of organized crime families remain `untouchable' by law."

The Nature of Transactions

Transactions among and within complex organizations can add to the potential for misconduct by offering seemingly legitimate means of pursuing scarce resources unlawfully and by providing an opportunity to hide the unlawful behavior. According to Vaughan, transactions carry four distinguishing characteristics: formalization, complex processing and recording methods, reliance on trust, and general rather than specific monitoring procedures.

As organizations increase in complexity, the likelihood that they will engage in informal transactions diminishes. Exchanges between companies that are formal, complex, and impersonal are likely themselves to be formal, complex, and impersonal. Because large companies engage in large volumes of daily transactions, they adopt formal rules aimed at making the exchanges routine.

An offshoot of this formal behavior is the growth of technological means for recording and carrying out business transactions. Computers and accounting systems use specialized languages that can mask huge masses of information from an ordinary employee. Specialization means the rules and procedures governing the processing and recording of exchanges will vary among companies, as will the equipment and language used.

Thus, companies presuppose a degree of trust when doing business with outsiders. Managers may supervise employees, and somewhat limit embezzlement, fraud and other illegal conduct, but doing so to an extreme will probably restrict business. Vaughan argued that limits on the degree to which an organization can monitor its employees render trust a key to interorganizational exchanges. Efficient companies usually rely not on a "Big Brother approach" to monitoring employees, but on such techniques as spot checks, sampling, and checking of selected business indicators. These general oversight techniques will not always be sufficient for a company to learn of rules violations, but if they are known throughout the company, they may provide some general deterrence.

The large size of corporations, delegation of most responsibilities, and the degree of specialization of jobs allow for a degree of irresponsibility that may allow individuals in the corporation to remain largely unaccountable. According to Conklin, executives at the higher levels of the corporation can absolve themselves of responsibility for crimes in stating that the illegal means used be their employees was done without the executives' knowledge, much the same way heads of organized crime families remain "untouchable" by the law by keeping themselves remote from the illegal activity.

CRIMINOGENIC ORGANIZATIONAL STRUCTURES

Gross asserted that all organizations are inherently criminogenic (prone to committing crime), but not necessarily criminal. Gross made this assertion because of business' reliance on "the bottom line." Without conscious intent, organizations can invite fraud as a means of achieving goals.

Organizations can also be criminogenic because they encourage loyalty. According to Vaughan, the reasons are that:

- The organization tends to recruit and attract similar individuals
- Rewards are given out to those who display characteristics of the "company man"
- Long-term loyalty is encouraged through company retirement and benefits
- Loyalty is encouraged through social interaction such as company parties and social functions
- Frequent transfers and long working hours encourage isolation from other groups
- Specialized job skills may discourage company personnel from seeking employment elsewhere.

These features may cause company personnel sometimes to perceive that committing crime to maintain and further organizational goals might be worthwhile. The use of formal and informal rewards and punishments, plus social activities and pressures to participate, link an employee's needs and goals to the success of the company. When a company achieves its goals, its employees prosper. In short, the interests of an organization and its employees coincide, and this situation may set the stage for unlawful conduct by individuals on the organization's behalf. Of course, not all agents will act unlawfully on a company's behalf, and individual employee behavior will be linked to factors that may not be related to the world of the organization. The fact that corporate and individual goals are often joined in organizations does not invariably create a climate for illegal actions. As with any major decision, complexities often enter the picture. Temptations vary not only among departments, but within them as well. The availability of information and individual risk-reward assessments may generate lawful behavior that resists organizational pressures to violate the law. Put plainly, the likelihood that organizational processes will generate misbehavior is highly variable and cannot be measured with any degree of precision.

CORPORATE EXECUTIVES AND CRIMINAL LIABILITY

Many of the ethical and legal problems of a corporation result from the corporate structure that separates ownership from management. Typical large corporations are administered by a group of salaried managers and a board of directors that exercises little direct power other than hiring or firing the managers. Thus, corporate managers as a group have great autonomy over decisions regarding production, investment, pricing, and marketing.

Executives tend to believe that their jobs are at risk if they cannot show a profit to higher management or the board of directors. Clinard and Yeager hold that if goals for managers are set too high, they then confront hard choices of risking being thought incompetent or taking unethical or even illegal shortcuts.

According to Clinard and Yeager, corporations often try to protect their executives from liability by agreeing to pay fines, court costs, and attorney's fees with corporate funds. Generally, executive compensation and tenure remain untouched. The complexity of the legal proof required in complex corporate crimes allows businessmen to test the limits of the law. Businessmen can hire highly-skilled lawyers who present arguments about lack of previous convictions or unlikelihood of becoming a repeat offender as well as being able to cite numerous precedents where businessmen were charged but not imprisoned for similar violations.

Even if prosecuted and convicted, business executives typically receive relatively mild sentences. They are considered low-risk inmates. Some corporate offenders are given community service as punishment, such as giving speeches about their offenses to businesses and civic groups, working in programs designed to aid the poor, or helping former ordinary criminal offenders secure job pledges from businesses.

MANAGEMENT BEHAVIOR

Brenner and Molander found that superiors are the primary influence in unethical decision making. Stone found that the success of law enforcement "ultimately depends upon its consistency with and reinforcement of the organization's rules for advancement and reward, its customs, conventions, and morals." Stone said if the law is too much at odds with the corporation's "culture," employees will tend more carefully to cover up their tracks before they will change their behavior. In fact, in some corporations, operating illegally may become the norm of ethical tone of the company as set by the president or chief executive officer. In the language of accountants' control theory, the executives' role is to set the "tone at the top."

Silk and Vogel found several rationalizations used by business people to justify questionable conduct:

● Government regulations are unjustified because the additional costs of regulations and bureaucratic procedures cut heavy into profits.

● Regulation is unnecessary because the matters being regulated are unimportant.

● Although some corporate violations involve millions of dollars, the damage is so diffused among a large number of consumers that individually there is little loss.

● Violations are caused by economic necessity; they aim to protect the value of stock, to insure an adequate return for stockholders, and to protect the job security of employees by insuring the financial stability of the corporation.

Braithwaite views white-collar crime as a product of the corporate subculture. In Braithwaite's view, corporations will turn to crime as a result of "blocked opportunities." Because white-collar crime can exist only in secrecy, deviant subcultures develop (conspiracy among executives, for example), lines of communication are not allowed to develop, and people operate within spheres of responsibility.

CONTROLLING ORGANIZATIONAL CRIME

Efforts to control corporate crime follow three approaches: voluntary change in corporate attitudes and structure; strong intervention of the political state to force changes in corporate structure, accompanied by legal measures to deter or punish; and consumer action. Voluntary changes involve the development of stronger business ethics and certain corporate organizational reforms. Government controls may involve federal corporate chartering, deconcentration and divesture, larger and more effective enforcement staffs, stiffer penalties, wider use of publicity as a sanction, and possibly the nationalization of corporations. Consumer group pressures may be exerted through lobbying, selective buying, boycotts, and the establishment of large consumer cooperatives.

Clinard and Yeager suggest that a wide, comprehensive industrial code of ethics, which many businessmen favor, could be of great help when a businessman wished to refuse an unethical request. A universal code could help define more clearly the limits of acceptable or ethical conduct, improve the ethical climate of business, and serve to reduce cutthroat practices where competition is intense.

Clinard and Yeager found that mass media publicity about law violations probably represents the most feared consequence of sanctions imposed on a corporation. Publicity can also inform the public about the operation of regulatory controls and enable people to understand the purposes of the controls. Informal publicity is ordinarily carried as news items from the media while formal publicity is a requirement that a corporation must, as part of an enforcement action, publish an advertisement or some other statement acknowledging a violation and that corrective measures are being taken.

If illegal behavior consistently resulted in decreased patronage or even consumer boycotts, consumer pressure could be an effective tool in the control of illegal corporate behavior. However, Clinard and Yeager found that consumer action appears not to be very effective. Consumers are often unaware when a corporation's products are unsafe or when it has violated antitrust laws or polluted the environment. Without organized behavior, a consumer's withdrawal of individual patronage is generally ineffective.

Many corporations settle charges, without admitting or denying guilt, by entering into a consent to an administrative- or a court-ordered decree banning future violations. Sporkin says consent decrees have enabled the appointment of special officers to investigate and pursue claims against errant managements and others on behalf of the corporation and its shareholders, the placement of persons independent of management and not previously associated with the company on the board of directors, and the appointment of special review or audit committees. A problem with consent orders, however, is that they are frequently not followed up to find out whether the terms imposed are being met.

Criminal fines and civil and administrative penalties against corporations are forms of monetary penalties. Criminal cases average about one year from indictment to conviction; civil actions about two years; and administrative cases about four months. Criminal action against corporations is difficult to initiate because government agencies generally depend on the records of the corporation and its ability or willingness to furnish needed information. Some of the criteria considered when deciding to bring criminal action against a corporation include: the degree of loss to the public, the duration of the violation, the level of complicity by high corporate managers, the frequency of the violation, evidence of intent to violate, evidence of extortion, the degree of notoriety given by the media, precedent in law, a history of serious violations by the corporation, deterrence potential, and the degree of cooperation demonstrated by the corporation.

THE ENFORCEMENT EFFORT: PREVENTING AND REDUCING FRAUD

Enforcement strategies include two main theories--compliance and deterrence. Compliance hopes to achieve conformity to the law without having to detect, process, or penalize violators. Compliance systems provide economic incentives for voluntary compliance with the laws. They use administrative efforts to control violations before they occur. For example, the SEC and the IRS have many administrative mechanisms to encourage voluntary compliance with securities laws and tax laws. Most environmental crimes are also controlled by these means. In a compliance system, an offense is most often characterized as a technical violation rather than as a crime.

On the other hand, a sanctioning strategy is designed to detect law violations, determine who is responsible, and penalize offenders to deter future violations. Deterrence by sanctioning tries to control the immediate behavior of individuals, not the long-term behaviors targeted by compliance systems.

Deterrence theory assumes that humans are rational in their behavior patterns. Humans seek profit and pleasure while they try to avoid pain. Deterrence assumes that an individual's propensity toward lawbreaking is in inverse proportion to the perceived probability of negative consequences.

Increased Enforcement

Formal levels of enforcement in white-collar crime are, by all measures, extremely low. One view holds that increased enforcement can only come with a complete and total revision of the criminal justice system. Currently, people have little fear of detection because they know that the police and courts cannot keep up with the pace of criminal offenses. Some people believe that longer prison sentences for offenders are neither necessary nor even desirable because we do not have the courts and jails to accommodate them. These commentators believe a better plan is to sacrifice the severity of punishment for its certainty. Until potential offenders have the perception that they will be caught and punished, no one can expect a reversal of the crime trend.

Monetary Penalties

Not all experts agree that monetary penalties are appropriate. For example, a $1 million fine levied against a multi-billion dollar organization may have no effect. One novel approach to punishing corporations was proposed by Coffee. He advocated stock dilution or "equity fining." Under this approach, the convicted corporation would issue additional shares of stock to the state equal to the cash value of a fine. The state could collect the equity shares and sell them, trade them, or keep them for their earnings power.

With respect to monetary penalties, some argue that these sanctions are limited to a person's own worth and therefore have limited utility. In 1992, Congress implemented the corporate sentencing guidelines, providing up to $290 million in fines for illegal corporate behavior. It is too early to determine the deterrent impact of penalties of this size.

OCCUPATIONAL CRIME

Occupational crime is committed by individuals or small groups of individuals in connection with their occupations. It includes violations of law by businessmen, politicians, labor union leaders, lawyers, doctors, pharmacists, and employees who embezzle money from their employers or steal merchandise and tools.

Green fine-tuned the white-collar crime concept using the term "occupational crime," which he defined as "any act punishable by law which is committed through opportunity created in the course of an occupation which is legal." Green further delineated occupational crime in four categories:

- Crimes for the benefit of an employing organization (organizational occupational crime)
- Crimes by officials through exercise of their state-based authority (state authority occupational crime)
- Crimes by professionals in their capacity as professionals (professional occupational crime)
- Crimes by individuals as individuals

Some scholars debate whether individuals should be held responsible for crimes committed on behalf of their organizations. Although some direct benefit accrues to the perpetrator, far more benefit accrues to the organization. Regardless of whether the organization is held liable, the fraud is as a direct result of some human action or interaction. In the words of Parisi, "If an organization is like a gun, then there must be someone comparable to a triggerman." Sometimes the line between occupational crime and organizational crime is very thin.

WHY EMPLOYEES COMMIT FRAUD

A number of theories attempt to explain why employees steal. The various techniques of neutralization--denial of injury and the victim--are commonly used: "It was a big bank, they had lots of money; I was only `borrowing' from the company; I don't get paid enough." Benson said that three-fourths of the embezzlers he studied "referred explicitly to extraordinary circumstances and presented the offense as an aberration in their life history." In other words, the offenders saw themselves as completely law abiding, except for the incident in question.

Cressey's model for the embezzler--immediate financial need, perceived opportunity, and rationalization--no doubt describes many fraud offenders. However, even Cressey, who pioneered the study of embezzlement, later said that the unsharable financial problem was not critical in all instances. Stress theories no doubt account for some people who have set financial goals they cannot otherwise achieve. In one interesting study, only a third of 160 employee thefts--most of them long-term employees--were committed by persons who actually needed money.

In contrast to actual need, living beyond one's means is often a principal motivator. Dailey concluded that females claim they steal for the family, while males admit to stealing for business reasons. Females apparently commit less fraud than males for three important reasons. First, they tend to occupy fewer managerial positions as a percentage of the work force, and therefore do not have as much opportunity to commit thefts. Second, they are more closely supervised because of their lower positions, making the possibility less likely. Third, several studies concluded that women are just more honest than men.

Rationalization
Economic offenders are known for providing elaborate excuses for their crimes, and the nature of such explanations may be a major distinguishing mark between them and street offenders. Cressey found that embezzlers typically insisted that they were only borrowing the money and that they intended to repay it once they had covered the bills and other financial demands vexing them. Antitrust violators usually maintain they are seeking to stabilize an out-of-control price situation when they conspire with others to fix prices. Psychologists arrested for phony and unauthorized charges against government medical benefit programs are likely to insist that they are being singled out by power-hungry prosecutors and investigators.

An economic offender will rarely admit: "I was deliberately engaged in crooked business dealings. I was trying to do as much harm as possible."

Exploitation of Positions
Public and private officials sometime exploit their own power for personal gains through taking kickbacks and bribes. In the majority of cases, this type of offense occurs when the offender used power to ask for an additional payment for normal services.

GOVERNMENT CORRUPTION

Elected officials are in a unique position. These officials are in continuous contact with persons trying legitimately to influence policy and also dependent upon these same people for the financial support necessary to win reelection. A fact of political life is the lure of exchanging financial support for political favors. Often, the line between corruption and integrity is blurred. Government employees who do not run for office are in positions similar to their corporate counterparts. While much of the public scrutiny is directed towards elected representatives, the crimes of the bureaucrats are also significant. These employees cannot change laws, but they often determine how laws are carried out. Despite their lack of political influence, these government employees may be safer targets for corruption, because they are further from the public focus.

PUBLIC CORRUPTION

While a only a few public employees can offer contracts, other employees are vulnerable to corruption. The history of police corruption is long. Reports from the period of the Civil War indicate that bribery was widespread and problems such as assaulting superior officers, drunkenness, refusal to go on patrol, releasing prisoners from police custody, and extortion of prisoners were common. These offenses often occurred under the protection of the political overlord.

Investigative committees have uncovered corruption deeply rooted within police departments. The New York Police Department has been the target of three such investigations: by the Lexow Committee (1890s), the Seabury Commission (a generation later) and the Knapp Commission in the 1970s. Elsewhere, investigations of police misconduct include the Chicago City Council Commission of Crime (1915), the Senate Committee to Investigate Crime in Interstate Commerce (1950s) and the Pennsylvania Crime Commission's published report about the Philadelphia Police Department in the early 1970s. These committees all came to the conclusion that police corruption is a serious and widespread problem. One noted criminologist reported that investigative committees uncovered graft and corruption every time a commission looked for these problems.

Finding the cause of police corruption lies in understanding the number of opportunities police personnel have to receive payoffs and bribes. Police officers are in constant contact with people who desire that an officer "look the other way," and these people often have no qualms about breaking the law to achieve this end. Additionally, the unique social context of the police officer may encourage abuse. Despite the recognized need for protection and respect of officers, people also have considerable fear about their power and the potential for police misuse of power.

According to one criminologist, police personnel develop strong in-group attitudes, retreat from the public, and control behavior to serve the interest of the group. The need to depend on fellow officers in dangerous situations and inherent problems in police work itself operate to increase officer solidarity. This solidarity makes acceptance of traditions of corruption easier. Honest officers may be unwilling to report minor violations in such an organizational subculture, and these "minor" problems may expand into much more serious offenses.

CAMPAIGN CONTRIBUTIONS

While defenders of the current system argue that campaign contributions come with no strings attached, this argument ignores the fact that the large contributors' money puts those politician with whom they agree with into office. Politicians cannot totally ignore the money and the resulting influence of contributors.

The laws regarding campaign financing are frequently skirted if not completely broken. One case in which the campaign financing law was violated involved the activities of the American Shipbuilding Company. The charges, brought by a special prosecutor to the Watergate case, indicated that the American Shipbuilding Company gave employees bonuses. The expectation was clear that these bonuses would be contributed to President Nixon's reelection campaign in 1972. According to testimony, witnesses said that $25,000 (after taxes) was given in bonuses to eight employees. The employees in turn then wrote a personal check to the president's personal attorney. The attorney channeled these funds to the Committee to Re-Elect the President. Testimony indicated that bonuses had been received in 1970 and 1971 as well. As one witness stated: "I knew from those conversations with the company secretary that the bonuses I was to receive were for political contributions and weren't bonuses at all."

Regardless of the pressure candidates feel to raise money, the ability of campaign contributions to purchase political influence is limited. Often, the most important and powerful politicians have a easier time raising funds; they are less indebted to individual contributors. The financial power of some interest groups is neutralized by opposing interests with substantial financial means to promote their goals. Federal funds now help finance presidential elections. Thus, major party candidates are under less pressure to raise funds. Because of the limitations of campaign financing, influence seekers may try to garner influence with gifts, services, or directly giving money to government officials.

CRIMES AGAINST THE PUBLIC

Occupational crime victimizes not just the employers, but also the public. One example is the short-changing of consumers by sales clerks. An employee who lies to a consumer to sell a product also falls into this category, as long as these lies are not standard company policy. If they are company policy, these lies are organizational crime.

A very costly example is stockbrokers who lie to clients about a stock in which the stockbroker has a personal interest. These stockbrokers may be involved in a network of deceptive practices. Colleagues may issue deceptive news releases and market analyses for example. In one case, a client invested thousands of dollars for a company the broker said would be "the next IBM." After investing money, it came to light that the company in question was on the verge of bankruptcy and the stockbroker wanted unload the stock held by himself and friends before the firm failed.

EMBEZZLEMENT

Embezzlers are people in a position of trust who abuse their positions to appropriate someone else's assets for their own use. Because embezzlers have high incomes, the motives for committing their crimes may be unclear. According to research, embezzlers commit their activities because they are living beyond their means. Gambling, extravagant living, personal debt or a family emergency may prompt someone to embezzle.

The amount of money taken by computer literate embezzlers is still not as large as those of top management embezzlers. Because of their positions, members of top management are able to execute multimillion-dollar crimes that may loot an entire organization. One west Coast financier, C. Arnholt S., contributed to the bankruptcy of the U.S. National Bank of San Diego. He illegally diverted millions of dollars to fund other business ventures. The $143 million in losses and uncollectible loans on the bank's books when it closed were caused in large part by his operations. Mickey M. reportedly did the same thing in the 1990s by diverting millions to finance a basketball league, bankrupting the Phar Mor Corporation in the process.

Labor unions suffer the same embezzlement problems as businesses. Pension funds are usually the target of unscrupulous union officials. The International Brotherhood of Teamsters has a history of problems in this area. For a finder's fee, organized criminals offered to arrange loans from the Teamsters' pension fund. There is also ample evidence that the fund has financed underworld projects. Additionally, officials within the union have been convicted of cheating the fund.

EMPLOYEE THEFT AND FRAUD

Street crime is estimated to cost less than the losses caused by employee theft. Two to four percent is added to the cost of retail goods because of "inventory shrinkage." The bulk of inventory shrinkage may be caused by employee pilfering, not shoplifting. Both the consumer and businesses pay a price for inventory loss. The consumer pays for this theft in the increased cost of retail goods, and an estimated 1,000 businesses close their doors annually because of inventory loss.

Pilferage

Employee fraud can reach all levels of the organization. Pilferage is estimated to account for 30 to 75 percent of all shrinkage, making losses $10 billion to $20 billion annually. Some of the common techniques for pilferage include:

- Piece workers who steal garments and secret them inside their clothing
- Cashiers who ring up a sale at a lower price than the merchandise, and keep the difference
- Clerks who sell sale merchandise at regular prices and pocket the difference
- Receiving clerks who obtain duplicate keys to the warehouse and come back and steal merchandise
- Truck drivers who make fictitious purchases of fuel and split the difference with truck stop owners

- Employees who hide items in the trash and come back later and retrieve them

The magnitude of pilferage losses helps define the problem of employee theft, but other criminological issues are involved. Many managers see employee theft as a "fringe benefit" used to compensate for low wages or other work-related problems. If putting an end to employee theft meant raising wages and thus retail prices, perhaps the cost to the consumer is not as great as the numbers about employee theft would indicate. In fact, Gerald Mars, a Cambridge sociologist, argued that employee theft may help create a better economy by increasing employee satisfaction and productivity (!).

A popular myth is that employee theft is concentrated among lower-level employees. One study, conducted by a firm specializing in employee theft, headed by Norman Jaspan, found that sixty-two percent of inventory shrinkage caused by employees was committed by company supervisors. This does not make rank-and-file employees more honest; the losses caused by supervisors were just larger. In extreme cases, directors have been known to siphon assets, essentially bankrupting an organization. Lower-level employees simply do not have the power to cause this kind of damage.

Hollinger and Clark conducted one of the most extensive studies of employee theft. They found that of 9000 employees interviewed, one third admitted to stealing from an employer within the last year. Horning found that in a midwestern television plant, the workers had informal rules about what could legitimately be taken home. Power tools, heavy machinery, testing equipment, and other large, expensive items were clearly company property and could not be taken. Taking the personal belongings of others was also taboo. Light tools and small items such as nails and screws were of uncertain ownership and the theft of such items was seen to be a victimless crime.

Estimates of the amount of employee theft vary widely because no reliable empirical measurement by a governmental agency or other authority. Estimates of annual losses to employee theft have varied from as little as $6 billion to as much as $120 billion. Notwithstanding, losses from business crime are believed to total more than the dollar losses from street crime. Green reported on a survey by the U.S. Chamber of Commerce that asserted that about half the people who work in plants and offices steal to some extent. Broy reported that five to eight percent of employees steal in volume. Adler says that 30 percent of business failures can be traced to employee dishonesty.

The thefts can be simple, from the taking of supplies, paper clips and pencils, to the more complex and imaginative. Internal theft specialist Harvey Yaffee detailed one example of midwestern supermarket manager who had an extra checkout lane-with his own cash register--built at the store. Each day he would open up the store and collect the money paid into that register. He took some $70,000 in just a few months. Some employees steal in volume. A cleaning woman for Neiman Marcus stole 343 dresses valued at $686,000. And a warehouse employee stole 65,000 beer bottles he redeemed at a nickel each.

Computer-Related Employee Crime

No reliable statistics measure the extent of computer-related crime, which can be defined as an illegal act for which knowledge of computer technology is essential. The U.S. Army estimated the chances of being detected for computer crime is about one in a hundred, and being prosecuted for it is about one in 22,000. Typical computer-related crimes are not much different than more traditional means of employee fraud. Perhaps the most sinister aspect is the ease and speed with which they can be accomplished.

Some of the growth in contemporary crime may be caused by the increase in computer-related businesses. While the average bank robbery yield is relatively small, the average computer crime nets about $400,000. In one large case of computer embezzlement, $21 million was taken. Using electronic fund transfers, employees of the Wells Fargo Bank in California deposited funds in account held by boxing promoters. Because of amount of money involved, concealment was difficult and the perpetrators were eventually uncovered.

The public is intrigued by the image of the "whiz kid" with the ability to outsmart the legions of specialists employed by large bureaucracies. Computer crimes have off-beat names such as data diddler, Trojan horse, salami technique and super-zapping. The data diddler manipulates computer information to his own advantage. A "data diddler" might transfer funds electronically, erase debt, or reveal confidential information. A skilled programmer may place a "Trojan horse" in a program. This allows the programmer to enter the system later and conduct illegal transactions without the knowledge of the legitimate users.

In one intriguing case, the "salami technique" was employed. Taking "one thin slice at a time," two programmers at a New York garment firm instructed the computer to withhold two cents more from each employee's tax withholding account. The computer then deposited the money in the programmers' withholding accounts, so that they would each receive a large tax refund. These programmers were caught when the size of their withholding prompted an investigation by the IRS. "Superzapping" is another scheme in computer crime. Using this technique, special programs are employed to override security controls and access confidential information. "Trap doors," often used in security protected programs, allow a programmer to make changes within a program. Sometimes these "trap doors" are not removed and information can be obtained using them. A computer criminal can also "piggy back" a legitimate user, allowing the criminal to access information when the computer is tricked into thinking that the criminal has legitimate clearance.

New legislation has increased with the rise of "computer hackers" who break into private computers to steal data or create chaos within a system. From 1975 to 1985, the Federal government and forty-six states created legislation to prevent unauthorized access to computer systems. Yet, a study done by Pfuhl indicates that these laws are seldom enforced. Sometimes, the crimes are not reported, other times the perpetrator cannot be identified. The popular image of computer fraud being committed by bright young men as a playful activity, perpetuated against anonymous organizations, also affects the enforcement of criminal sanctions for computer crimes. Computer fraud is widely reported by the media, and in the opinion of one expert: "Computer fraud schemes are greatly over-reported and overblown."

FRAUD IN THE PROFESSIONS

Illegal activities involving respected professions have received far less attention and research than that of other offenses such as embezzlement, antitrust violations, theft, and political corruption. Crimes of professionals are also the least understood of white collar crime offenses.

The professions police themselves in professional self-regulatory organizations. Some professional organizations have power to regulate members because they control licensing. However, when the interest of the public does not agree with the interest of the professional associations, these organizations sometimes protect the profession and individual practitioners first. Professional practitioners who violate both public trust and criminal law rarely face sanctions from these self-regulating agencies.

Conflicts of interest are inherent in the relationship between professional practitioners and clients. Often, a fine line divides unethical and illegal behavior in such conflicts of interest. For self-employed professionals, a financial conflict exists between clients paying for services and professionals trying to maximize profits. Performing the largest number of the most expensive services, is one area where professionals have a direct financial interest. Conversely, clients are best served when only the necessary and most reasonably priced services are performed. While this conflict exists in many occupations, a client of the professionals is frequently unable to know whether the recommended services are essential.

Green believes crime in the professions is conceptually different from other occupational offenses. The difference arises because professions are distinctly characterized by self-regulation, and most professions require an oath or ethical commitment requiring members to have a special trust with persons who rely upon them. This trust means that the professional practitioner is expected to do what is best for the client, usually without regard to compensation to the professional.

Medical Professionals

Fraudulent acts by the medical profession include unnecessary surgery and treatment, fee splitting, false medical insurance claims, false expert testimony, and income tax evasion. On the latter score, Gross determined that physicians have been more than ten times as likely to be indicted for income tax evasion than the general population. How likely unnecessary surgery is motivated by fraud is difficult to estimate. Researchers at Cornell Medical School evaluated over 1,300 cases of major surgery and concluded that 25 percent were unnecessary.

Persuasive evidence that American physicians may allow financial interests to override medical necessity is apparent in research sponsored by the Department of Health, Education and Welfare. In one study, a group of government employees covered by Blue Cross health insurance (doctors paid on a fee-for-service basis) was compared to a health maintenance organization (doctors paid a flat salary). Twice as many surgical operations were performed and more days were lost from work when employees went to a private physician versus the HMO physician.

In studying Medicaid recipients, people who went to private doctors had more operations performed than those in a prepaid health plan. The obvious conclusion: the more money to be made from a procedure, the more doctors perform the procedure. While doctors will maintain that the procedure was medically necessary, there is an element of fraud to these claims. In the case of some doctors, financial interests clearly are a greater priority than the welfare of patients.

Fee splitting involves a kickback, usually to a general practitioner, who refers patients to a surgeon or specialist. The referral can be for either necessary or unnecessary treatment. "Pingponging" is the needless referral to another doctor for additional treatment. Sutherland estimated that two-thirds of surgeons in New York City had participated in fee splitting.

The Legal Profession
Offenses committed by lawyers include overbilling for time, embezzlement of trust funds, and fraud committed for the benefit of their clients (i.e., preparing false documents for admission in legal proceedings). The nebulous nature of many legal services makes fraud easy. As Blumberg theorized: Legal service lends itself particularly well to confidence games. Usually a plumber will be able to demonstrate that he has performed a service by clearing up a stuffed drain, repairing the leaky faucet or pipe--and therefore merits his fee. In the practice of law there is a special problem in this regard. Much legal work is intangible either because it is simply a few words of advice, some preventive action, a telephone call, negotiation of some kind, a form filled out and filed, a hurried conference with another attorney or an official of a government agency, a letter or opinion written, or a countless variety of seemingly innocuous and even prosaic procedures and actions.

INDIVIDUAL INCOME TAX EVASION

During one year, the following were convicted of criminal income tax fraud: 94 for fraudulent tax shelters, 275 for tax protesting, 116 for the bank secrecy act, and 1,391 convicted for "all other" violations. Green says the conviction rate is about one in 40,000 returns. However, the actual rate of income tax fraud may be much higher. Mason and Calvin sampled about 800 households in Oregon and almost a quarter admitted to some form of evasion. Tittle interviewed admitted tax evaders who had not been caught. Thirty-nine percent did not consider their fraud morally wrong, and 51 percent did not consider it a serious offense. Green says people commonly believe it is easier to justify fraud against the government because "they can afford it."

CONTROLLING OCCUPATIONAL CRIME

Control is difficult because the civil and criminal law enforcement process must reach individuals or small groups, one-by-one. No large organization is available as a target. Detection and prosecution encounter all the difficulties of evidence and due process characteristic of street crime enforcement. After conviction, problems remain about the nature of sanctions. Occupational violators are seldom jailed like violent criminals. Consider some of the possibilities in the sections below.

Restitution

Green and other criminologists advocate victim restitution for occupational criminals, in addition to other punishment. First, restitution helps the victim recover a financial loss. Second, it precludes perpetrators from using ill-gotten gains in further illegal activities. Green believes excessive amounts of restitution (i.e., double and treble damages) have little if any deterrent effects. He also advocates additional publicity for offenders who are punished, saying this is necessary to increase the perception of certain punishment.

Forfeiture

Forfeiture is government seizure of property derived from or used in criminal activity. Civil forfeiture is a proceeding against property used in criminal activity. Property subject to civil forfeiture often includes vehicles used to transport contraband, equipment used to manufacture and distribute drugs, cash used in illegal transactions, and property purchased with the proceeds of crime. No finding of criminal guilt is required in such proceedings. Criminal forfeiture is a part of the criminal action taken against a defendant upon conviction. It requires the defendant to forfeit various property rights and interests related to the violation. Most state forfeiture procedures appear in controlled substances or RICO laws. A few states provide for forfeiture in connection with the commission of any felony. Most state forfeiture provisions allow for civil rather than criminal forfeiture.

Occupational Disqualification

Two types of occupational disqualification are available. Selective incapacitation involves removing from occupations the persons who might commit additional offenses. The problem, of course, is predicting who will commit such offenses. Collective incapacitation involves removing all persons from occupations where an offense has occurred. The problem with this approach, however, is that it may unjustly punish those for whom deterrence is not a future problem. Selective incapacitation occurs frequently when state regulatory agencies revoke the licenses of doctors, lawyers, accountants, and others.

Green advocates the use of clearinghouses for professionals and others who have been convicted of past offenses. Someone seeking to employ or utilize the services of doctors, attorneys, and even clerical employees could check a data bank and see if the person had a past conviction. Green believes such sanctions have the advantage of being less expensive than incarceration, and potentially as effective.

Rehabilitation
The theory of rehabilitation is based on the medical model: a problem is diagnosed, treatment is prescribed, and a recovery follows. Unfortunately, when it comes to traditional criminals, rehabilitation appears to have been a costly failure. Although there are no conclusive studies, criminologists hypothesize that rehabilitation of white-collar offenders might be effective in some instances. One study found that companies convicted of the Australian Trade Practices Act made some strides toward self-correction. However, most of these improvements were voluntary, and there is no literature to suggest that mandated rehabilitation will work in the fraud area.

Perception of Detection
Employees are particularly influenced by the notion of being detected committing an offense. Internal accounting controls--while useful and necessary--must be combined with a proactive anti-fraud effort. Many companies manage the fraud risk by making the probability of detection known to employees. They organize the effort through units variously named "security department," "loss prevention department," and "internal audit department."

CONCLUDING REMARKS

The study of criminology and white-collar crime encompasses many areas. Criminology is not simply a description of the criminal justice system. It also includes theories of traditional crime, traditional economic crimes, and the differences between traditional economic crime and white-collar crimes. Examining white-collar crimes often involves raising the issue of ethical behavior. Common responses include reference to universal principles and rules and to the concept of action that produces the "greatest good." Unfortunately, circumstance and choices are frequently blurred and unclear in criminal justice and white-collar crime cases. If everyone could "do right," criminologists would need to find something else to do. This not being the case, fraud examiners and auditors need to be familiar with criminology.

CHAPTER 3
EMPLOYEE FRAUD

Employee fraud is a type of occupational crime. It is the use of fraudulent means to take money or other property from an employer. It usually involves falsification of some kind--false documents, lying, exceeding authority, or violating an employer's policies. It consists of three phases: (1) the fraudulent act, (2) the conversion of the money or property to the fraudster's use, and (3) the coverup. Most employee frauds can be placed in the legal categories of embezzlement and larceny. Sometimes, an employee fraud will result in misstated balance sheet accounts and financial statements.

This chapter deals with the characteristics of employees' fraudulent acts, conversions, and coverups. The focus is on schemes employees have used. Chapter 4 deals directly with misstated financial statements.

CASH SCHEMES

Cash on deposit in banks and petty cash can be misappropriated through on-book schemes (involving falsified accounting entries) or off-book schemes (no accounting entries in the books and records). Generally, cash schemes are smaller than other internal fraud schemes because companies have a tendency to use comprehensive internal controls over cash. Cash fraud schemes follow general basic patterns, including skimming, voids/under-rings, swapping checks for cash, alteration of cash receipt documentation, fictitious refunds and discounts, and kiting.

SKIMMING

Skimming involves removing cash from the business before the cash is recorded in the accounting system. This is an off-book scheme. Receipt of the cash is never reported to the business. A related type of scheme is to ring up a sale for less than the actual sale amount. (The difference between the actual sale and the amount on the cash register tape can then be diverted.) Skimming is of particular concern in retail operations (for example, fast food restaurants) where most of the daily sales are in cash and not by check or credit card.

Example of Cash Skimming

According to an investigation, fare revenues on the Chicago Transit Authority's (CTA) rail system allegedly were misappropriated by agency employees. The statistics indicate that the thefts were not confined to the one station that originally was suspected and that the fare-skimming by transit workers might have been reduced by news of the investigation. In the four days after reports of skimming surfaced, about $792,000 was turned in by station agents system wide. In a similar Monday through Friday period only $723,000 was turned in by station agents.

CTA officials estimated that a planned installation of a $38 million automated fare-collection system would eliminate $6.5 million annually in revenue "shrinkage," mostly from employee theft. At least 10 workers were investigated, including nine ticket agents and one supervisor. Early reports indicated that agents pocketed money after recording "transfer" or "monthly passes" as cash-paying customers passed through turnstiles.

Source: Urban Transport News

VOIDS/UNDER-RINGS

Three basic voids/under-ring schemes are common. The first is recording a sale/cash receipt and then voiding the same sale, thereby removing the cash from the register. The second, and more common variation, is purchasing merchandise at unauthorized discounts. The third scheme, which is a variation of the unauthorized discount, is selling merchandise to a friend or co-conspirator using the employee's discount. The co-conspirator then returns the merchandise for a full refund, disregarding the original discount.

Example of Voids/Under-Rings

Roberta F., a former Ball State University employee, was indicted on federal charges of stealing about $105,000 from the school's bookstore operations. She was charged with stealing the money over a 33-month period.

The thefts allegedly were from proceeds of the sales of books to students who took Ball State courses through an "off-campus" program at many cities around Indiana. Roberta F. was in charge of the sale of the books from the bookstore.

Roberta F. was accused of altering records and taking currency from a cash drawer. She was also charged with income tax violations for failing to report the stolen money on her federal tax returns.

Source: United Press International; Dateline: Indianapolis.

SWAPPING CHECKS FOR CASH

In a swapping scheme an employee's own check is exchanged for cash in the cash register or cash drawer. Periodically, a new check is written to replace the old check. This process can be continued so that on any given day, the cash drawer contains a current check for the cash removed. This is a form of unauthorized "borrowing" from the company. Obviously, if company policy is to reconcile cash drawers or registers at the conclusion of each day and turn the money over to a custodian, this fraud scheme is less likely to be committed. However, if personnel are allowed to keep their own cash drawers and only remit the day's receipts, this method of unauthorized borrowing can be more common.

Example of Swapping Checks

Lisa S., a Garfield High School fiscal clerk working in a central treasurer function allegedly "borrowed" $2,400 by placing 23 personal checks in deposits which were made from various student activities at decentralized locations. Ms. S. placed a personal check in each deposit as a method of keeping track of the amount of money which had been "borrowed." The deposits were inappropriately delayed for up to 5 months.

Auditors detected the delayed transactions during an unannounced cash count. On the day of the count, the fund custodian had only a few hundred dollars in the bank account. When all 23 personal checks were deposited in the district's account, several were returned as NSF. After payday, all NSF checks subsequently cleared the bank. The custodian's employment with the district was terminated.

Source: Seattle School District No. 1; King County, Washington, Audit Report No. 53464.

ALTERATION OF CASH RECEIPTS DOCUMENTATION

A lack of segregation of duties can create an opportunity for an employee to misappropriate company funds. For example, if the same person is responsible for both collecting and depositing the cash receipts, this person has the opportunity to remove funds from the business for personal use and conceal the theft through the deposits. This is often the case in small organizations where a few personnel divide the daily cash operations. A variation of this scheme is to mutilate or destroy the cash receipt documentation so that any attempt to reconcile the cash deposited with the cash receipts is thwarted.

Example of Document Alteration

An elected county treasurer allegedly stole $62,400 over a three-year period from property tax receipts. Every other day, after cash receipt transactions were batched and posted to the subsidiary accounting records, the treasurer altered the total cash receipt and the actual deposit. Therefore, the control account and the deposit were equal but that total did not match the total postings to the individual taxpayers' accounts. In each of the three years, the difference between the control account receivable and the summation of the individuals in the subsidiary accounts was written off. These were unsupported accounting adjustments.

Evidence was obtained by reconstructing the three years' cash receipts and matching the differences between the total cash receipts, control account, and the individual (subsidiary) accounts with the unsupported accounting adjustments.

Source: Asotin County, Washington; Special Examination Report No. 47242.

FICTITIOUS REFUNDS AND DISCOUNTS

Fictitious refunds occur when an employee enters a transaction as if a refund were given. However, no merchandise is returned, or no discount is approved to substantiates the refund or discount. The employee misappropriates funds equal to the fictitious refund or discount. This scheme is most prevalent in the retail industry. However, it can occur in any operation in which a refund or discount is given.

Example of Fictitious Refunds

Dora M., a former New York University student financial aid official, was charged along with her husband Salvatore with embezzling $4.1 million. The operation was carried out by falsifying more than a thousand tuition refund checks. The loss was described as one of the largest embezzlements ever uncovered at a U.S. university. The money was allegedly taken from the Tuition Assistance Program, operated by the New York State Higher Education Services Corporation to provide expense money to needy students. However, NYU officials assert that the funds came from a University account, not from State money.

Dora's job was to assure that students entitled to funds from the Corporation received their checks. According to the U.S. Attorney, she arranged for checks to be made out to hundreds of legitimate NYU students who were not entitled to receive any funds. These students were unaware because the checks were deposited into bank accounts in Manhattan and New Jersey that allegedly were controlled by the M's. These checks were made over to Elizabeth P. before being deposited into accounts in that name. Some other checks were made payable directly to P. The FBI was unable to locate Elizabeth P. and believes that such a person never existed.

Reportedly Dora and Salvatore spent $785,000 of the funds on expensive jewelry and $85,000 on Florida real estate.

Source: Predicasts, A Division of Ziff Communications Co./Elsevier Advanced Technology
Publications; Computer Fraud Security Bulletin.

KITING

Kiting is the process whereby cash is recorded in more than one bank account, but in reality, the cash is either nonexistent or is in transit. Kiting schemes can be perpetrated using one bank and more than one account or between several banks and several different accounts. Although banks generally have a daily report that indicates potential kiting schemes, experience has shown that they hesitate to report the scheme until the balance in the customer's account is zero.

To be successful banks must be willing to pay withdrawals on unfunded deposits. This is not to say that all payments on unfunded deposits are kiting schemes, but rather, that all kiting schemes require payments be made on unfunded deposits. When a bank allows its customers to withdraw funds on deposits for which the bank has not yet collected the cash, kiting schemes are possible. In today's environment, customers who use wire transfers can perpetrate kiting schemes very quickly and in very large numbers. (Additional discussion of kiting, with a numerical example and suggestions about auditing, is in chapter 8.)

Example of Kiting

Ronald S., 59, and his son-in-law, Philip G., 33, both of Dartmouth, admitted to participating in a check-kiting scheme that bilked the Bank of Boston out of $907,000. Philip, owner of two pharmacies in the New Bedford area, had cash-flow problems when Ronald, operator of two auto sales and leasing businesses, offered to write a check to cover some of his son-in-law's operating expenses. Philip repaid the $50,000 loan within a few days, but borrowed again and again "in ever-increasing amounts" to bring fresh infusions of cash into his faltering pharmacy businesses. An exchange of checks between Philip and Ronald eventually occurred daily until Ronald's bank caught on to the float scheme and froze Ronald's account.

Cut off from Ronald's supply of cash, Philip's account with the Bank of Boston was left overdrawn by $907,000. Philip was ordered to make restitution to the Bank of Boston.

ACCOUNTS RECEIVABLE SCHEMES

The basic schemes in accounts receivable are lapping, diversion of receipts on old written-off accounts, and fictitious sales with corresponding accounts receivable.

LAPPING

"Lapping" is the term used to describe a method of concealing a defalcation, wherein cash received from a customer is originally misappropriated by the employee, and, at a later date, cash received from another customer is credited to the first customer's account. The second customer's account is credited still later by cash received from a third customer, and so on. This delay of payment applications (credits) continues until it is detected, the cash is restored, or it is covered up by credit to the proper customer and a fictitious charge (write-off or return).

The basic lapping scheme operates - as follows: the employee misappropriates cash received on customer A's account. To conceal the misappropriation, the employee must now record receipts on customer A's account. When customer B makes a payment, the employee posts the cash receipt to customer A's account. When customer C makes a payment, the employee posts it to customer B's account, and so on. (A case example with discussion of audit procedures is in chapter 8.)

OLD OR WRITTEN-OFF ACCOUNTS RECEIVABLE

Another internal fraud scheme in accounts receivable is the diversion of cash received on old or slow-paying accounts. In this scheme, the employee has the opportunity to collect receivables that have been written off and keep the money. Companies typically do not keep track of old, written-off accounts receivable.

Often, old accounts receivable are assigned to a collection agency. These agencies typically are paid on a percentage of the collected amounts. Fraud schemes can be perpetrated by these collection agencies if the company does not monitor the method by which the agency receives old accounts and the collection process itself. The assignor company needs assurance that the collection agency is being assigned truly old accounts and not good accounts, which can reasonably be expected to pay within the normal course of business. Also, the company needs to be sure that the collection agency cannot compromise (settle) the indebtedness so that collections are not reported. This would allow the collection agency to compromise indebtedness for its own collection and not remit amounts owed the company.

FICTITIOUS ACCOUNTS RECEIVABLE

Generally, the motive for recording fictitious accounts receivable in the accounts is to disguise fictitious sales. This scheme is covered in more detail in chapter 4 under the heading of management fraud in financial statements. However, two employee fraud-related benefits also can be accomplished with fictitious accounts receivable and sales:
- Meet sales quotas
- Receive sales-based compensation

These two benefits enable employees to receive pay, promotion, and perhaps other rewards that seem to be based on merit.

Meet Sales Quotas
Establishing unobtainable sales quotas that employees think are arbitrary will increase the pressure to establish fictitious performance levels. If the pressure becomes significant, an employee may resort to recording fictitious sales and accounts receivable.

Example of Fictitious Receivables

The SEC filed a civil action against Coated Sales, Inc., alleging that some of the company officers were engaged in a scheme to inflate accounts receivable and inventory. The officers allegedly created phony sales invoices and recorded the corresponding accounts receivable. The purpose of the scheme was to make Coated appear to have more sales then it really did. Proceeds from the sale of common stock were used to reduce the accounts

---

receivable making it appear that the fictitious accounts receivable were being paid in a timely manner.

Source: The Associated Press; Byline: Dwight Oestricher, Associated Press Writer.

Receive Sales-Based Compensation

When a salesperson's primary compensation is based on sales, without regard to collection, the employee has an incentive to produce quantity rather than quality sales. Companies often push for higher sales levels to sustain growth. However, if the salespersons' compensation is based solely on quantity and not on a combination of quantity and quality, then the compensation incentive is misplaced. This may create an atmosphere which, if coupled with opportunity, will produce inflated or fictitious sales.

INVENTORY SCHEMES

Most fraud perpetrated in inventory and warehousing involves misappropriation for personal use, embezzlement of scrap proceeds, and false charges to inventory-related accounts. The most common inventory scheme is appropriating inventory for personal use. When this fraud is performed by a custodian, it is embezzlement; when performed by other employees, it is theft (larceny).

APPROPRIATING INVENTORY FOR PERSONAL USE

How many times have we heard someone say, "I'm just going to borrow this." Or "I took it home to work on the project over the weekend." In fact, a great deal of inventory is taken under the pretense that it is being borrowed. In actuality, the inventory is simply converted to personal use. Most personal thefts tend to be small. In other cases, theft rings can be operating.

Misappropriation can occur in many and varied forms. A common scheme requires collusion between delivery personnel and receiving personnel, where receiving personnel will sign for less merchandise than was actually received. The merchandise is then sold to fences. The delivery and the receiving personnel then divide the proceeds.

Example of Misappropriated Inventory

A former executive with the LTV Corporation who was convicted of taking more than $1.5 million in kickbacks and bribes was sentenced to four years and three months in prison and ordered to make full restitution. U.S. District Judge Sid Fitzwater handed Lewis B. the maximum prison sentence, with no provision for parole.

Lewis B. was indicted in a federal indictment charging him with 36 counts of fraud. He was in charge of buying and selling pipe, as well as billing for the purchased pipe. The indictments charged him with accepting tens of thousands of dollars in "commissions" from pipe supply companies. He also profited by selling pipe stolen from LTV's inventories.

Under an agreement with prosecutors, Lewis, 58, pleaded guilty to one count each of mail fraud, wire fraud, and tax evasion. Lewis worked for LTV for 37 years and used his illegal income to build and furnish a new home and purchase other luxuries

Source: United Press International; Dateline: Dallas, Texas.]

EMBEZZLEMENT OF SCRAP PROCEEDS

Misappropriation of scrap sale proceeds is a common practice. Because the amounts are generally insignificant to the financial statements of the company, scrap sales are usually not well controlled and good inventory records are not kept. However, when inventory is inappropriately designated as scrap, the proceeds of sale can be substantial.

FALSE CHARGES TO INVENTORY-RELATED ACCOUNTS

Since inventory accounts are generally not reconciled until the end of each year, it is a simple matter to charge embezzlements to these accounts. Embezzlements are often concealed through an expense or inventory account because at the conclusion of each fiscal year, the expense accounts are closed to retained earnings (or fund balance). Therefore, the audit trail becomes very obscure or even disappears at the conclusion of each year. Inventory accounts are often the concealment account for larger embezzlements because the account balances are large enough to accommodate the entries required to conceal large losses.

Example of False Inventory Entries

During the year a company can accumulate the effects of several payments to affiliated companies (real or not real) by charging cost of goods sold accounts. (Debit cost of goods sold; credit cash.) At the end of the year, the affiliated company payments can be reclassified as receivables. (Debit accounts receivable--affiliate; credit cost of goods sold.)

Unlike accounts receivable, the cost of goods sold are closed to retained earnings and, therefore, "go away" at the end of each year. If embezzlement losses have been charged to the expense accounts, then hidden in the accounts receivable, the audit trail will become obscured at the end of each year.

PURCHASING SCHEMES

The purchasing function of an enterprise involves the acquisition of goods and services. The only payment functions usually not included under purchasing are payroll and employee expense reimbursements. These two functions are discussed in more detail later. The acquisition function is especially vulnerable to fraudulent transactions because it involves payment of company funds--the point where most cash leaves the company. Purchasing fraud probably contributes the largest fraud risk to most enterprises.

The basic classifications of purchasing fraud schemes are: fictitious invoices, excess purchasing, over-billing, checks payable to employees, duplicate payments, and conflict of interest. Purchasing fraud does not necessarily require collusion with another employee or an outsider, although collusion often occurs.

FICTITIOUS INVOICES

A fictitious invoice is any invoice not represented by a legitimate sale and purchase. Fictitious invoices can take many forms, for example, the vendor may not exist.

Example of Fictitious Invoices

Harry S., 68, and Nicholas G., 51, were arrested on grand larceny charges for alleged submitting inflated and phony billings to National Westminster Bank in excess of $1.2 million. Allegedly, Nicholas, vice president of National Westminster for marketing and advertising, teamed up with Harry, owner of H.B. and Company, National Trading Co. and the Trade Union News, to defraud the bank while ostensibly providing advertising and marketing services. Simon's companies operated in Scarsdale, NY.

According to the prosecutor, Nicholas, while working in National Westminster's West Hempstead, N.Y. headquarters, would approve payment of invoices submitted by Harry and the two would then split the amount when it was paid by the bank. Reportedly, Harry billed the bank for $1.2 million worth of advertising that had purportedly been placed in the Trade Union News, a newspaper that does not exist. All the billings were paid by the bank upon Nicholas' approval.

Nicholas, who had worked for National Westminster for 19 years, was fired and the case turned over to the district attorney's Commercial Fraud Bureau.

Source: United Press International, Dateline: Muneola, N.Y.

EXCESS PURCHASING OF PROPERTY AND SERVICES

The fraudulent purchase of excess property is a variation of fictitious invoicing. Generally, excess purchasing takes one of three forms: excess supplies, excess inventory, or unnecessary services. With supplies, like inventory, the fraud offender must eventually convert the physical goods for his or her own benefit. This requires that the property be removed from the business premises or delivered to another site.

With services, the conversion is somewhat different. Services are deliverable in many forms, such as legal services, financial planning, and the like. It is much harder to detect excess purchase of services fraud because the documentation for receipt is not equivalent to the documents normally required for physical goods (i.e., no receiving report, bill of lading, or shipping charges for the purchase of services). Also, the invoices for services are often more brief and do not describe the exact nature of the services rendered (e.g., recipient, timing, or extent of the services). Therefore, it may be difficult to determine whether the services are for the business or for the personal benefit of the employees of the company.

Ordering excess inventory and then converting it for one's own personal benefit is a common form of inventory misappropriation. Often, the inventory is delivered directly to the perpetrator's home or other business.

Another type of fraudulent excess services purchasing involves the purchase of phantom services--the services are never rendered by the vendor. This type of scheme involves collusion with the vendor and purchasing or accounts payable personnel.

Example of False Purchase Payments

Scott S., 33, a former accounting manager for the Davis Company, was accused in a scheme to siphon funds from the District communications agency into his personal accounts at First Liberty National Bank. He pleaded guilty to one count of bank fraud.

In a strange twist, Scott S. allegedly used his brother Sean's identity when he applied for the Davis accounting job. Scott repeatedly circumvented the agency's accounting system and wrote company checks that he then cashed, deposited, or otherwise negotiated for his own personal benefit. Davis filed a $1.1 million civil suit against Scott, accusing him of altering company checks to make them payable to Sean S. or ABMI Joint Ventures, a company that never existed outside of Davis Companies' falsified purchase accounting records. The plea agreement called for Scott to repay $287,500 stolen from the Davis Co.

Source: News World Communications, Inc./The Washington Times; Byline: Phil Rabin and Carolyn Myles, The Washington Times.

OVER-BILLING

Over-billing is a method in which the fraud offender submits an artificially inflated invoice to the company for payment. Or, the offender alters existing documents requesting additional (fictitious) amounts be paid over to another. The amount of the overpayment is then diverted or paid to the employee or accomplice.

CHECKS PAYABLE TO EMPLOYEES

Employees can create payments to themselves by circumventing the control system so that company payments are diverted directly to themselves or to companies they control.

DUPLICATE PAYMENTS

Duplicate payments may occur anytime someone overrides the system, or an automated system does not "flag" duplicate payments. If an automated system is properly designed, it should recognize like-kind payments (e.g., same amount, same invoice number, same requisition number, same items purchased) and flag them for further investigation or prevent checks from being issued automatically. In these situations, collusion is probably necessary unless the individual intercepts the outgoing mail containing the payments.

Example of Duplicate Payments

Michael A., a former employee of the Museum of Fine Arts, was indicted on charges of embezzling more than $100,000 while he worked at the museum. Michael was charged with 13 counts of larceny over $250. He worked at the museum as a senior financial analyst whose responsibilities included overseeing the accounts of DAKA, a food service company that operated the museum restaurant. The state alleged that Michael embezzled the money by submitting duplicate requests for payments to DAKA, and then diverted the extra money into his personal bank accounts. The indictment alleged Michael stole a total of $108,888.48.

Source: United Press International; Dateline: Boston.]

CONFLICT OF INTEREST

A conflict of interest occurs when an employee, manager, or executive has an undisclosed economic interest in company transactions. For example, an employee may secretly own a business that supplies goods or services to his employer. It is not necessary that the company actually suffer damages in order for a conflict of interest violation to be sustained. The effect need only be potentially adverse.

Conflict of interest may be part of schemes wherein services are never rendered. This type of scheme requires the collusion of purchasing and/or accounts payable personnel with the supplier to not render the services requisitioned. The invoices are paid to the supplier and the proceeds divided among the co-conspirators.

Conflict of interest schemes are variations of the rule that a fiduciary, agent, or employee must act in good faith, with full disclosure, in the best interest of the principal or employer. Most schemes are a violation of the legal maxim that a person cannot serve "two masters." Some of the more common schemes involve an employee's, manager's, or executive's interest in a customer or supplier and receipt of gifts. Often, the employee, manager or executive is compensated in the form of "consulting fees."

Example of Conflict of Interest

Former Customs Service agent, Richard A., was convicted of conflict of interest for giving his wife four payments totaling $1,450 for drug information. Prosecutors alleged that he broke the law because Customs supervisors are not allowed to pay spouses for information.

A federal judge overruled the jury and threw out the conviction. The judge indicated that Richard was unintentionally entrapped because it was well-known among Customs officials that he was paying his wife but "it was never suggested that was improper or that he shouldn't do it."

Source: Phoenix Newspaper, Inc., The Arizona Republic; Byline: Susan Leonard

Example of Conflict of Interest

Former California state schools chief, Bill H., was convicted of felony conflict of interest in connection with $337,508 in state contracts. He paid four educators to set up parental involvement programs in local school districts. The Attorney General said the state contracts directly benefited his wife's nonprofit company, Quality Education Program.

Bill H. was sentenced to 1000 hours of community service and ordered to pay $10,800 in fines. He lost his post as superintendent of public instruction.

Source: The Times Mirror Company; Los Angeles Times; Dateline: Sacramento.

INVESTMENTS AND FIXED ASSETS SCHEMES

Company investments take many forms, including money market accounts, certificates of deposit, government securities, and other stocks and bonds. Internal fraud schemes using investment assets are generally perpetrated by employees who "borrow" or use the assets for personal benefit.

Fixed assets, on the other hand, can be misappropriated (theft). Fixed assets that are easily removed from the premises, such as tools, hand-held calculators, even computers, are especially subject to employee theft. Fixed assets that are either too cumbersome for employees to remove from the premises or are of no use to the employee are less likely to be misappropriated.

USE AS COLLATERAL

Employees who "use" company investments without detection, can "borrow" the asset for their own personal use. Sometimes, this borrowing results in pledging the asset as collateral for a loan or other financing arrangement. This is unauthorized use of a company asset for the personal benefit of an employee. If the lender or financier does not require physical possession of the asset (collateral), this type of fraud scheme may be difficult to detect.

BORROWING TO EARN INTEREST

Companies are often required to maintain compensating balances in financial institutions for various reasons, including the right to do business in the area (for example, for foreign corporations). If the controls over this kind of cash are inadequate, employees may have the opportunity to "borrow" the cash (or portion thereof) for a short period of time. Employees who can transfer funds to and from different institutions can conceal the "borrowing" over short periods of time.

The purpose of this type of fraud scheme is not to take the funds, but merely to use the earning ability of the funds for short periods of time. For example, interest on a $1 million compensating balance at 10% for one day is $274. On the surface this does not appear to be a great deal of money. However, a year's worth of interest is $100,000--a nice raise for any employee. The "borrowing" of investments is of particular concern to companies required to maintain deposits in other states or countries to conduct business in those geographic regions.

Example of Funds Diversion

Henry C., president and CEO of Managed Investments, Inc., a Pittsburgh investment manager was convicted on mail fraud charges in connection with embezzling funds from the Carnegie Firemen's Pension Fund and Relief Association, Carnegie, PA.

According to the Labor Department's Office of Inspector General and Office of Labor Racketeering, Henry defrauded the fund of four checks totaling $83,187 which were intended for investment in money market funds. The checks were deposited into accounts of Equity Management Associates Inc., an insolvent investment corporation Henry controlled. The money was used to make payments on options Equity held to purchase land and for other business expenses.

Source: The Bureau of National Affairs, Inc./Pension Reporter; Dateline: Pittsburgh.

FIXED ASSETS

Fixed assets are less subject to employee misappropriation than inventory and investments. Most fixed assets are of such a nature that either they are undesirable or they are of no use to the employees. However, employee theft of fixed assets does occur. In addition, the personal use of fixed assets by employees is a common form of fraud. This is especially true for fixed assets that are easily removed from the company premises.

Once a fixed asset has been fully depreciated and removed from service, the disposal of the asset should be monitored. Although the theft of a fully depreciated asset by an employee may have no economic impact on the company, it may represent a lost opportunity for capital gain and increased cash flow by the company through its eventual sale.

Example of Fixed Asset Theft

Robert O., the son of a Nassau county deputy executive was convicted of stealing equipment from a county building he was guarding. Within two weeks of the plea bargain that included a judge's ruling that he could no longer work in security, Robert O. got a new county job despite the conviction and a work record that included a reprimand, excessive absenteeism, and two suspensions. Robert was arrested in connection with the theft of two fax machines, allegedly stolen from the building he was assigned to guard. He cooperated with police, even returning the machines. Although charged with grand larceny, he pleaded guilty to a reduced misdemeanor charge of petty larceny, was fined $500 and got no jail time contingent on his staying out of trouble and out of county security work.

Source: Newsday, Inc./Newsday; Byline: Carol Eisenbery, Staff Writer.

PAYROLL SCHEMES

Like purchasing, payroll is a fruitful areas for fraudulent transactions. Although the payroll schemes are usually relatively smaller than other fraud schemes, they are no less important. An employee who helps conduct a payroll fraud is likely to commit other types of fraud schemes against the company. Three schemes are common in payroll fraud: ghost employees, overtime abuses, and withholding tax schemes.

GHOST EMPLOYEES

Placing a fictitious employee on the payroll is called a "ghost employee." No services are received in exchange for payment to the "ghost." Sometimes, the "ghost" is a real person who was once entitled to be paid, but who was retained on the payroll after being terminated.

Example of Ghost Employees

Mary L., a former employee of the Executive Office of Communities and Development, was accused of embezzling more than $300,000 earmarked for the needy. While working for the EOCD, Mary allegedly stole vouchers intended to help more than 5,000 needy people and deposited the checks in a personal banking account. During that time, Mary was a program director for an EOCD division know as the Commonwealth Services Corp., which provided financial assistance to general relief recipients who perform entry level tasks to gain job skills. Mary was responsible for preparing and distributing payment vouchers to the trainees.

Mary allegedly embezzled the funds by keeping the names of trainees on the program's voucher list after the trainees left the program. In addition to being indicted on five counts of larceny, she was indicted on five counts of filing false reports for allegedly submitting the falsified lists annually to the state treasurer's office. She was also charged with four counts of income tax evasion for allegedly failing to report the money in her state income tax returns.

Source: Globe Newspaper Company; The Boston Globe; Byline: Doris Sue Wong, Globe Staff.

OVERTIME ABUSES

Overtime abuse is a common form of payroll fraud, especially when employees are responsible for maintaining overtime pay timecards, and those timecards are not reviewed.

WITHHOLDING TAX (TRUST ACCOUNT TAXES) SCHEMES

It is not uncommon for employees to "borrow" (misappropriate) the trust account taxes from a company for the one or two days until they are required to be deposited. This scheme is similar to "borrowing" investment cash to earn the interest. Payroll employees may be able to deposit payroll tax and benefit funds to their own accounts until a later due date. Interest is earned on these funds during this interim period of time. Generally, this cash timing is not a problem until the trust account taxes are late or not paid at all. Some companies contract with service companies to perform the payroll function--preparation of the payroll checks and payment of the withholding taxes and benefits. A fraud on the company can be perpetrated if the payroll service "borrows" the funds.

Example of Employee Tax-Related Fraud

A husband and wife who served as top officials with the Massachusetts's state pension board were indicted on tax fraud and larceny charges. Paul Q., 50, the former executive director of the state Pension Reserves Investment Management Board, and his wife, Elizabeth, 31, the former finance director, were accused of stealing more than $20,000 by selling back to the state vacation time they had not actually accrued.

The grand jury also accused Elizabeth Q. of issuing W-2 forms to employees that under-reported the amount of state and federal taxes withheld, while over-reporting her own state and federal withholdings by the same amount. Allegedly, the scheme, which involved false W-2s issued to nine employees in one year, and three in another, netted Quirk $6,500.

In addition, Elizabeth Q. was charged with three counts of filing false state tax returns by under-reporting her income by nearly $36,000. Paul Q. was charged with two counts of filing false state tax returns by under-reporting his income by $16,000. Elizabeth Q. served as the director of finance until her resignation.

Paul Q. served as the $88,000-a-year executive director until he was ousted by the board. The body oversees nearly $3 billion in public employee pension money. At the time of his ouster, Paul was under fire for reportedly accepting $25,000 in cash and stock options from takeover specialist Carl Icahn to help mount a campaign against a company that Icahn wanted to acquire. It was also reported that he angered former Gov. Dukakis by ringing up hefty travel expenses at a time when the rest of the administration was taking across-the-board cuts.

Source: Globe Newspaper Company/The Boston Globe; Byline: Brian McGrory, Globe Staff.

PERSONAL EXPENSE
REIMBURSEMENT SCHEMES

Employees can submit inappropriate personal expenses for reimbursement. Probably the single most common area where this occurs is travel and entertainment. Personal expense reimbursement frauds have several variations, including: false mileage claims for the company use of a personal automobile, meals attended by family members but submitted as business lunches, golf with friends submitted as business associates, library materials for one's personal use under the ruse that the company needs them, and more.

Example of False Expense Reimbursement

A Los Angeles county community College District trustee and his wife were found guilty of stealing from the district by padding expense accounts, overestimating mileage, and misusing public funds for expensive clothing and fancy dinners. James E. was found guilty on 29 counts of fraud, embezzlement, and conspiracy. His wife, Ingrid E., was convicted on one count each of conspiracy, grand theft, and embezzlement

"As I see it," said jury foreman Chris Darwin, "they had no defense. They just had excuses. They didn't say `I didn't do it.' All they could say was, `I did it because.' I had a hard time accepting all those excuses." Darwin said he felt the couple "were probably good people. But they started doing this and it worked, so they did it again, and it worked, and the thing snow-balled."

The charges against the couple stemmed from eight trips they allegedly made together at district expense. At one point while in Vancouver, Canada, they allegedly spent $290 on sweaters in a gift shop at a hotel where they were staying at district expense. In Washington, D.C., they allegedly charged the district for nine meals in one day and billed the district for a play they attended at the Kennedy Center. And, while at a convention in Las Vegas, the couple was allegedly reimbursed for air fare and cabs, even though they had driven their car to the event.

Source: The Times Mirror Company/Los Angeles Times; Byline: Tina Daunt, Times Staff Writer.

INTERNAL FRAUD PREVENTION

Unofficial estimates of internal theft and fraud range from good, educated guesses to wild predictions. Some of the most intriguing estimates come from self-report surveys. In *The Day America Told the Truth*, researchers Paterson and Kim conducted anonymous surveys of 3,000 Americans on a variety of "hidden" topics. They claim their research accurately portrays what people think, do, and feel when no one is watching. They concluded that the following are the top five office "crimes":

- Taking office supplies and equipment
- Lying to a boss or co-worker
- Stealing company funds
- Taking credit for work not done

In addition, the survey revealed the following statistics about American workers:

- Workers admit that they spend more than 7 hours a week goofing off--20 percent of the work week
- Almost half the workers admit to chronic malingering, calling in sick when they are not, and doing it regularly
- One in six Americans surveyed used drugs or drank on the job
- Half the work force believes that one gets ahead on the basis of politics, rather than on hard work
- One-quarter of workers expect to compromise their beliefs to get ahead on the job
- Only one in five workers say they are "very satisfied" with their jobs
- Workers say they put in about 45 percent effort into their jobs.

PREVENTION VERSUS DETECTION

Most experts agree that it is much easier to prevent than detect fraud. Increasing the perception of detection may well be the most effective fraud prevention method. Controls, for example, do little good in forestalling theft and fraud if their presence is not known by those at risk. In the audit profession, this means letting employees, managers, and executives know that auditors are actively seeking out information concerning internal fraud. This can be accomplished in several ways.

Employee Education
Organizations should have a policy for educating managers, executives, and employees about fraud. This can be done as a part of employee orientation, or it can be accomplished through memoranda, training programs, and other intercompany communication methods. The goal is to make others within the company be the eyes and ears.

Education efforts should be positive and non-accusatory. Illegal conduct in any form eventually costs everyone in the company through lost profits, adverse publicity, and decreased morale and productivity. These facts should be emphasized in training.

Reporting Programs

Each employee in the company should know where to report suspicious, unethical, or illegal behavior. A reporting program should emphasize that:

- Fraud, waste and abuse occurs in nearly all companies
- Such conduct costs the company jobs and profits
- The company actively encourages any employee with information to be able to come forward
- The employee can come forward and provide information anonymously and without fear of recrimination for good faith reporting
- There is an exact method for reporting; i.e., a telephone number, name, or other information
- The report need not be made to one's immediate superiors

Hotlines

Hotlines have proved to be a very effective reporting mechanism. However, most hotline reports do not result in fraud cases. At the federal level, published reports indicate about five percent of hotline calls result in serious allegations. With careful screening of calls and proper handling, spurious complaints can be effectively weeded out. The advantages and disadvantages of three general types of hotlines are summarized next.

Part-time, In-house. These hotlines are assigned to an employee with other duties. The typical in-house hotline is manned by the audit or security department. When the employee is out, a recorder takes calls. The main advantage is cost. The main disadvantage is that the hotline is not staffed full-time, which can discourage calls. Also, some persons may be reluctant to report to the company.

Full-time, In-house. A full-time, in-house hotline may be feasible depending on the company size. The advantage is that persons can make reports at any time, day or night, and talk to a person. The disadvantage is cost, and like the part-time line, some persons may be reluctant to report directly to the company.

Third-Party. A third-party hotline is staffed by an outside company that typically provides services of this type as a specialty. The advantages are cost, efficiency, and anonymity. A few are staffed around the clock and will provide the information immediately to the client involved for the client to handle. They also provide anonymity to those who might be more comfortable with it. Their disadvantage is that the operation is beyond the company's control and sometimes the cost is high.

Rewards
Some companies have a policy of rewarding information that leads to the recovery of merchandise, property, or money. Others offer rewards upon the criminal conviction of the person(s) involved. If a reward policy exists, strict criteria should establish reward payments, and such proposed policies should be reviewed and approved by counsel. The amount of reward paid by companies varies from fixed fees to a percentage of the recovery. Studies indicate that rewards should not exceed a few thousand dollars. Crime Stoppers recommends rewards not over $1,000.

Proactive Audit Policies
Proactive fraud policies are generated from the top of the operation. A proactive policy simply means that a company will aggressively seek out possible fraudulent conduct instead of waiting for cases to come to attention. This can be accomplished by several means.

Increased Use of Analytical Review. Much internal fraud is discovered as a result of analytical review. To uncover such fraud and defalcations, they must materially affect the financial statements. Auditors should be especially mindful of the following trends:
- Increasing expenses
- Increasing cost of sales
- Increasing receivables/decreasing cash
- Increasing inventories
- Increasing sales/decreasing cash
- Increasing returns and allowances
- Increasing sales discounts

Fraud Assessment Questioning. Fraud assessment questioning is a non-accusatory interview technique used as a part of a normal audit. It operates on the theory that attitudes by employees are a good indicator of potential problems, and that one of the most effective ways to deal with fraud is to ask about it.

Enforcement of Mandatory Vacations. Much internal fraud requires manual intervention and is, therefore, discovered when the perpetrator is away on vacation. The enforcement of mandatory vacations will aid in the prevention of some fraud.

Surprise Audits. All too many fraud perpetrators are aware when auditors are coming and, therefore, have time to alter, destroy, or misplace records and other evidence. A proactive fraud policy involves using surprise audits as much as possible. It could have a significant deterrent effect.

FRAUD POLICY AND ETHICS POLICY

Companies often have an ethics policy that sets forth in detail the ethical expectations of the company. Still other companies have a fraud policy that specifically spells out who handles fraud matters under what circumstances. The components of a fraud policy will differ from company to company. Many fraud policies have some of the following elements.

Policy Statement
The policy sets forth that management is responsible for fraud, and each member of the management team should be familiar with the types of signals present within his or her scope of responsibilities. The policy statement also states who is in charge of investigating suspected irregularities.

Scope of Policy
This area of the fraud policy statement covers definitions of irregularities and the fact that the policy covers everyone from management to worker.

Actions Constituting Fraud

This area sets forth in detail the actions that constitute fraudulent conduct. This is important because it gives management and legal the grounds to investigate and punish violators. The actions listed can include:

- Any dishonest or fraudulent act
- Forgery or alteration of documents
- Misapplication of funds or assets
- Impropriety with respect to reporting financial transactions
- Profiting on insider knowledge
- Disclosing securities transactions to others
- Accepting gifts from vendors
- Destruction or disappearance of records or assets
- Any similar or related irregularity

Non-Fraud Irregularities

This section covers allegations of personal improprieties or irregularities and states that these should be resolved by management and not by the audit department.

Investigation Responsibilities

This part deals with who will investigate suspected irregularities as well as to whom these irregularities will be reported: management, law enforcement, and legal counsel.

Confidentiality

Under this section, the confidential nature of the investigation is set forth. It states that the investigation will not be disclosed to outsiders except as required.

Authorization for Investigation

This section delineates that whoever is in charge of the investigation has the authority to take control of and examine records.

Reporting Procedures

This part states that anyone suspecting fraud should report it and not attempt an investigation. It also states that management and others should not make statements regarding the alleged guilt of the perpetrator.

Termination
This section states that any recommendations to terminate employees should be reviewed by counsel and management.

COMMUNICATING THE FRAUD POLICY

It obviously does little good to have a fraud or ethics policy if it is not communicated to the employees. This communication can be accomplished in several ways. The communication of the policy should be presented in a positive, non-accusatory manner.

Orientation
During initial employee orientation, the fraud policy should be discussed. This is the first opportunity the company has to make its point, and it should be made thoroughly.

Memoranda
An interoffice memorandum from the chief executive officer detailing the fraud policy is a good idea. Once again, the policy should concentrate on the positive aspects of working for an ethical company.

Posters
Some companies may wish to use posters displayed in common areas. However, this should be carefully considered as some employees may object to such tactics.

Employee Morale
If an employee is properly instructed, communication of a fraud policy can have a positive impact on morale. Honest workers want to work for an honest company. A fraud policy helps set the proper tone.

LEGAL CONSIDERATIONS

Many companies have learned that it is best to spell out specific unacceptable conduct. If the type of conduct that is considered unacceptable is not accurately detailed, legal problems in discharging a dishonest employee may arise. Check with your counsel regarding any legal considerations with respect to a fraud policy. One of the most important legal considerations is to insure every person and every allegation is handled in a uniform manner.

SELLING FRAUD PREVENTION TO MANAGEMENT

Management usually does not support fraud prevention for one or more of several reasons.

- Management's concerns are often elsewhere than audit or fraud. Managers typically do not understand that fraud is hidden and that losses go on undetected without their knowledge. They might also refuse to believe that their own workers are capable of stealing even when studies suggest a third of employees might do such a thing.
- Because of the hidden nature of fraud, managers are understandably reluctant to believe the presence of fraud. And if one employee is caught committing fraud, management may claim that this is an isolated problem, and not worth additional consideration. Management must understand that when instances of fraud are detected, it is too late to do anything about it.
- Management sometimes unreasonably feels that by bringing up the issue, the work force will be alienated. This problem can be addressed by reminding management that the rank-and-file workers appreciate working for an honest company. It is also helpful to point out to management what the losses might be.

Many auditors complain that management does not adequately support fraud prevention efforts. Managers may believe that fraud is not really a problem in the company, or they may believe that even addressing the subject has a negative impact. In either scenario, it is difficult to break down management's built-in resistance to dealing with fraud prevention. The suggestions below may be helpful in "selling" fraud prevention to management.

The Impact on the Bottom Line ·
One of the best ways to sell management on fraud prevention is by showing the impact on the bottom line. Fraud reduces net sales more than dollar-for-dollar. For example, if a company nets 20 percent on sales, it must sell five

items at regular prices to recover losses from the theft of one item. Fraud can be very expensive.

Computing Fraud Losses

One of the problems in selling fraud prevention is convincing management that these hidden situations are costing the company money. Because fraud is hidden, the auditor can try to estimate losses.

In absence of good data, fraud examiners can use the "two percent rule" to compute potential fraud losses. This assumes that within a given population of people, at least two percent will steal in quantity. Or put another way, two percent of sales might be lost to fraud and other forms of dishonesty. This figure is an extrapolation and should be reasonably conservative for most companies. If it seems high, remember this: one percent of the population of the United States is under care of the courts for criminal offenses. These are the ones who are caught, prosecuted and convicted.

If the company has historical experience with fraud, the figures derived from past experience can be used to compute potential losses. However, the problem with this method is that it probably underestimates the amount of the losses.

The Impact of Publicity

Many corporate executives are more sensitive to adverse publicity than almost any other issue. Certainly, one way to convince management of the logic of fraud prevention is to point out that negative publicity, even in small cases, can have a devastating impact on the company's reputation. This negative impact can be eliminated or reduced by a proactive fraud prevention program.

One of the more significant examples of adverse publicity can be demonstrated in the E. F. Hutton case. About 20 executives of E.F. Hutton participated in a kiting scheme in the late 1980s. The publicity impact was devastating to Hutton, which eventually closed. This situation illustrates that fraud can have a very significant effect.

APPENDIX: SAMPLE FRAUD
POLICY STATEMENT POLICY

Management is responsible for detecting defalcation, misappropriation, and other irregularities. Each member of the management team should be familiar with the types of improprieties that might occur within his or her area of responsibility and be alert for any indication of irregularity.

Any irregularity detected or suspected must be reported immediately to the Fraud Examination Unit, which coordinates all investigations with the Legal Department and other affected areas, both internal and external.

SCOPE OF POLICY

The conditions of this policy apply to any irregularity, or suspected irregularity, involving not only employees but also shareholders, vendors, outside agencies doing business with employees of such agencies, and unknown parties.

Any investigative activity will be conducted without regard to the suspected wrong-doer's length of service, position/title, or relationship.

ACTIONS CONSTITUTING FRAUD

The terms defalcation, misappropriation, and other fiscal irregularities refer to, but are not limited to:
- Any dishonest or fraudulent act
- Forgery or alteration of any document or account belonging to a shareholder
- Forgery or alteration of a check, bank draft, or any other financial document
- Misappropriation of funds, securities, supplies, or other assets
- Impropriety in the handling or reporting of money or financial transactions
- Profiteering as a result of insider knowledge of securities activities
- Disclosing to other persons the securities activities engaged in, or contemplated by the company
- Accepting or seeking anything of [material] value from vendors or persons providing services/materials to the company [exception: perishable gift

less than [$50] in value intended for a group of employees, such as, [candy, flowers]
- Destruction or disappearance of records, furniture, fixtures, or equipment
- [similar or related irregularities unique to the company]

NON-FRAUD IRREGULARITIES

Identification or allegations of personal improprieties or irregularities whether moral, ethical, or behavioral, should be resolved by departmental management and the Employee Relations Unit of Human Resources rather than the Fraud Examination Unit.

Contact the Director of the Fraud Examination Unit for guidance if you have any question of whether an action constitutes fraud

INVESTIGATION RESPONSIBILITIES

The Fraud Examination Unit has the primary responsibility for investigations. If an investigation reveals that fraudulent activities have occurred, the Fraud Examination Unit will issue reports to the proper executives and, if appropriate, to the Board of Directors through its Audit Committee.

Decisions to prosecute or turn matters over to appropriate law enforcement and/or regulatory agencies for independent investigation will be made in conjunction with legal counsel and Senior Management, as will final decisions on disposition of cases.

CONFIDENTIALITY

The Fraud Examination Unit will accept relevant information on a confidential basis from an employee who suspects dishonest or fraudulent activity. Employees should contact the Fraud Examination Unit immediately, and should not attempt personally to conduct investigations or interviews/interrogations related to suspected frauds (see REPORTING PROCEDURE section below).

The results of investigations conducted by the Fraud Examination Unit will not be disclosed or discussed with anyone other than those persons associated with the company who have a legitimate need to know in order to perform their duties and responsibilities. This is important in order to avoid damaging the reputations of persons suspected, but subsequently found innocent of wrongful conduct, and to protect the company from potential civil liability.

AUTHORIZATION FOR INVESTIGATING SUSPECTED FRAUD

In those instances in which the Director of the Fraud Examination Unit believes it to be in the best interests, members of the Unit have the authority and duty, after consulting with appropriate executives, to:

- Take control of, and/or gain full access to, all Company premises, whether owned or rented
- Examine, copy, and/or remove all or any portion of the contents of files, desks, cabinets, and other storage facilities on the premises without prior knowledge or consent of any individual who may use or have custody of any such items or facilities.

REPORTING PROCEDURE

Great care must be taken in the investigation of suspected improprieties or irregularities to avoid mistaken accusations or alerting suspected individuals that an investigation is under way.

An employee who discovers or suspects fraudulent activity should contact the Fraud Examination Unit immediately. All inquiries from the suspected individual and his or her attorney or representative should be directed to the Fraud Examination Unit or Legal Department. Proper response to such an inquiry is: "I am not at liberty to discuss this matter." Under no circumstances should any reference be made to "what you did," "the crime," "the fraud," "the forgery," "the misappropriation," or any other specific reference.

The reporting individual must adhere to the following restrictions:

- Do not contact the suspected individual in an effort to determine facts or demand restitution.
- Do not discuss the case, facts, suspicions, or allegations with anyone outside unless specifically asked to do so by the Legal Department or Fraud Examination Unit.

• Do not discuss the case with anyone inside other than the Fraud Examination Unit, Legal, or individuals within the department who have a legitimate need to know.

TERMINATION

If an investigation results in a recommendation to terminate an individual, the recommendation will be reviewed for approval by the Vice President of Human Resources and, if necessary, by outside counsel before any such action is taken.

ADMINISTRATION

The Director of the Fraud Examination Unit is responsible for the administration, interpretation, and application of this policy.

CHAPTER 4
MANAGEMENT FRAUD

The terms "management fraud" and "fraudulent financial reporting" are synonymous. The production of financial statements is the responsibility of management. Therefore, financial statement fraud almost always occurs with the knowledge or consent of management. Victims can be persons either inside or outside the company. Insiders who are possible victims include directors, managers, and employees who may suffer a loss of position, reputation or standing. Outside victims include investors, creditors, depositors, suppliers, customers, partners, underwriters, attorneys, and independent auditors.

FINANCIAL STATEMENT (MANAGEMENT) FRAUD DEFINED

According to Elliott and Willingham, financial statement fraud is management fraud:

> "The deliberate fraud committed by management that injures investors and creditors through materially misleading financial statements."

The responsibility for detecting management fraud largely has fallen to the accounting profession. Since the early 1970's, this responsibility has gradually increased. Standards for independent auditors are set forth in Statements on Auditing Standards issued by the Auditing Standards Board of the American Institute of CPAs. These auditing standards deal almost exclusively with the problem of materially misleading financial statements (the organizational crime of management fraud) and very little with embezzlement and larceny (the occupational crime of employee fraud).

THE TREADWAY COMMISSION

The National Commission on Fraudulent Financial Reporting (chaired by James Treadway, former SEC commissioner) was formed in 1987 to define the responsibilities of managements and auditors for detecting and preventing fraud. Several professional accounting organizations--the American Institute of CPAs, the American Accounting Association, the Institute of Internal Auditors, the Institutee of Management Accountants, and the Financial Executives Institute established the Commission to undertake the study and make recommendations. The Commission defined fraudulent financial reporting as follows:

"Intentional or reckless conduct, whether [by] act or omission, that results in materially misleading financial statements."

WHY FINANCIAL STATEMENT FRAUD IS COMMITTED

False financial statements are used to make a company's earnings look better on paper. False statements sometimes cover up the embezzlement of company funds. Financial statement fraud occurs through a variety of methods, such as valuation judgments and fine points of timing the recording of transactions. These more subtle types of fraud are often dismissed as either mistakes or errors in judgment and estimation. Some of the more common reasons why people commit financial statement fraud include:
- To encourage investment through the sale of stock
- To demonstrate increased earnings per share or partnership profit interests, thus allowing increased dividend and distribution payouts
- To dispel negative market perceptions
- To obtain financing, or to obtain more favorable terms on existing financing
- To receive higher purchase prices for acquisitions
- To demonstrate compliance with financing covenants
- To meet company goals and objectives
- To receive performance-related bonuses

This limited list of reasons shows that the motivation for financial fraud does not always involve personal gain to the managers. According to the Treadway Commission, the cause of fraudulent financial reporting is the combination of situational pressures on either the company or the manager(s) and the opportunity to commit the fraud without the perception of being detected. These pressures defined by the Treadway Commission are known as "red flags." If red flags indicating situational pressures and opportunity are present, the risk of financial reporting fraud increases significantly. Examples of situational pressures include:

- Sudden decreases in revenue or market share experienced by a company or an industry
- Unrealistic budget pressures, particularly for short-term results
- Financial pressures resulting from bonus plans that depend on short-term economic performance

Opportunities to commit fraud generally arise from the lack of adequate oversight functions within the company. However, the existence of an oversight function does not, in and of itself, guarantee the detection of management fraud. The oversight functions must also respond effectively. The perception of detection is arguably the strongest deterrent to fraud. Some of the more obvious opportunities for management fraud are:

- The absence of, or improper oversight by, the board of directors or audit committee; or, the neglectful behavior of the board or committee
- Weak or non-existent internal controls, including an ineffective internal audit staff and a lack of external audits
- Unusual or complex transactions
- Financial estimates that require significant subjective judgment by management.

FINANCIAL STATEMENT SCHEMES

In general, financial statement fraud occurs through (1) the overstatement of assets and income, and (2) the understatement of liabilities and expenses. Misleading statements can also be caused by (3) false or omitted disclosures in notes to financial statements. These misstatements produce higher earnings or partnership profit interests or a more stable picture of the company's true situation.

To demonstrate these over/understatements, the typical schemes can be put in eight categories. Because the maintenance of financial records involves a double-entry system, fraudulent accounting entries always affect at least two accounts and, therefore, at least two categories on the financial statements. While the eight areas described below reflect their financial statement classifications, keep in mind that the other side of the fraudulent transaction exists elsewhere. It is common for schemes to involve a combination of several methods. The eight general classifications are:

1. Improper revenue recognition--form over substance
2. Revenue recognition in the wrong period
3. Improper sales accounting
4. Improper percentage-of-completion accounting

5. Inadequate disclosure of related-party transactions
6. Improper asset valuation
7. Improper deferral of costs and expenses
8. Inadequacies or omissions in disclosures

IMPROPER REVENUE RECOGNITION

Improper revenue recognition--form over substance--involves sham transactions made to enhance the reported income or per-share earnings. Two common schemes in this area are misclassification of gains and less-than-arm's-length transactions. Both will falsely enhance the ordinary earnings of a company. These schemes can occur in a single year or over several years.

MISCLASSIFICATION OF GAINS

According to generally accepted accounting principles (regarding disposal of a business segment and reporting extraordinary gains and losses), an extraordinary event is one in which the transaction is unusual and occurs infrequently relative to the environment in which the entity operates. Material events that are either unusual or occur infrequently--but not both--should be adequately disclosed, but they are not extraordinary events or transactions. These unusual or infrequent items should be reported as a separate component of income from continuing operations and not as an extraordinary item.

Unusual in Nature
The event or transaction should have a high degree of abnormality and be of a type clearly unrelated to, or only incidentally related to, the ordinary and typical activities of the entity. The unusual nature is not established by the fact that an event or transaction is beyond the control of management.

Infrequency of Occurrence
The event or transaction would not reasonably be expected to recur in the foreseeable future. The mere infrequent occurrence of a particular event or transaction does not alone imply that its effects should be classified as extraordinary. Certain gains and losses should not be reported as extraordinary items, such as:
- Write-down or write-off of receivables, inventory, equipment leased to others, deferred research and development costs
- Gains or losses from the exchange or translation of foreign currencies

- Gains or losses from the disposal of a business segment
- Other gains or losses from the sale or abandonment of property, plant, or equipment used in the business
- Effects of a strike
- Adjustment of accruals on long-term contracts

The criteria for extraordinary items is not always clear. A particular set of facts and circumstances may make an item an extraordinary item in one year, but the classification may become suspect in subsequent years with the occurrence of other events. The example below does not prove fraud, but rather illustrates the complexity of extraordinary items.

Example of Gain Misclassification

The Six Flags Over Texas amusement park was at one time owned by Great Southwest Corporation, which in turn was owned by the Penn Central railroad company. One year, Great Southwest sold the Six Flags Over Georgia amusement park, and the gain was recorded as an extraordinary item. The next year, the Company sold the Six Flags over Texas park and reasoned that the sale of two amusement parks placed the company in the business of constructing, operating, and selling amusement parks. Therefore, in the second year, the first year's statements were restated to show the sale of the Six Flags Over Georgia as an ordinary item, to coincide with the classification of the sale of the Six Flags Over Texas as ordinary operating income.

The financial statements for Great Southwest Corporation were consolidated with Penn Central, enabling Penn Central to show a consolidated net income from continuing operations of $5 million, rather than income from continuing operations of something less than $5 million and a gain from extraordinary transactions. In addition, the transaction was suspect because an investment limited partnership bought the Texas park as a tax shelter, in which Great Southwest Corporation was the general partner and operator of the park. The long-term note representing the purchase price was payable only from the income earned from the park operations.

Although the legal ownership of the Texas park changed, the substance of the transaction did not appear to be an actual sale (transfer of risk and reward) by Great Southwest Corporation. Great Southwest continued to be entitled to the income generated from the amusement park operations. However, was the Texas park sold to the partnership in an effort to justify the previous sale of the Georgia park as an item from continuing operations? Consider this question in light of the fact that Great Southwest retained all the functional ownership interests of the Texas park. This question remains unanswered, but it points out that one must look beyond the basic form of the transaction to seek the ultimate substance of the event. (Later, the SEC required Great Southwest to restate its financial statements and defer the gain on the "sale" of Six Flags Over Texas.)

Example of Income Manipulation

USF&G was in the business of writing property-casualty insurance and life insurance products. The Company established a subsidiary, LSIF, for the purpose of investing in corporate equity securities. The investment strategy used by LSIF, called "dividend capture" or "dividend rollover," worked basically this way: On the same day, LSIF purchased shares of XYZ Company at $105 per share, before the ex-dividend date, and it sells the shares of XYZ Company at $100 per share, with delivery to the purchaser sometime after the dividend date. Therefore, LSIF, as owner of record on the record date, would receive the dividend payment ($5) from XYZ Company. The selling price for the XYZ stock, with delivery after the record date was generally the original purchase price of $105, less the amount of the dividend.

The result of this investment strategy was that USF&G, through consolidated financial statements, was able to reflect $48 million in dividends as part of its investment income, a component of operating income. The approximate $48 million loss on the disposition of the stock was also included as part of net operating income, however, it was reported on a separate line. The net income of USF&G was unchanged. According to the SEC, however, the presentation of investment income and loss on sale of investments was substantially misleading.

In an enforcement action, the Securities and Exchange Commission found that although not proscribed by generally accepted accounting practices, LSIF did not hold the stock for a significant period or bear significant market risk to warrant recognition of the dividend income. The SEC claimed that dividend income should have offset the loss on sale of the stock, particularly in light of the fact that the purchase and sale were performed on the same day. The SEC contended this was a sham transaction. LSIF would have been entitled to the investment income (dividends) without offset if it had earned the dividends by holding the XYZ stock for sufficient time to warrant market risk. USF&G was required to restate the investment income (dividend) and loss on its financial statements.

Source: Securities Exchange Commission. Matter of USF&G Corp. and James M. Raley, Jr., Accounting and Auditing Enforcement Rel. No. 182, Exchange Act Rel. No. 25403.

LESS-THAN-ARM'S-LENGTH TRANSACTIONS

These transactions can be particularly difficult to detect because they generally require a co-conspirator's participation. Potential co-conspirators can be inside or outside the company, an affiliated or non-affiliated company, or a related or non-related-party. Generally, the co-conspirators receive some benefit from the less-than-arm's-length transaction.

Example of Disclosure Deficiency for Insider Benefit

Informix Corporation was in the business of developing and selling office automation and database software. Informix merged with Innovative Software ("Innovative") whereby Innovative became a wholly-owned subsidiary of Informix. In their complaint, Klein v. King, (D.C. Northern California, No. C-88-3141), the plaintiffs alleged that the officers and directors failed to disclose material adverse facts regarding the company's business operations, both prior to and following the merger, and that it failed to make full, complete and timely disclosure of problems affecting its management earnings, sales, marketing, product development, and financial controls. These non-disclosures adversely affected the potential success of the merger. As a result of the allegedly false and misleading statements prior to the merger, Informix common stock traded at artificially inflated prices.

The purpose of the inflated prices, as alleged, was to enable the officers and directors of Informix to sell substantial holdings (1.8 million shares) for proceeds in excess of $36 million and allow the merger to be accomplished. The plaintiffs further allege that subsequent to the merger, the two companies had difficulty integrating their operations, and management delays occurred in releasing new software programs.

REVENUE RECOGNITION IN WRONG PERIOD

Revenue recognition in improper periods typically involves (1) early booking, (2) holding the books open, and (3) untimely accounting for discounts and returns.

EARLY REVENUE RECOGNITION

Generally accepted accounting principles state that revenue should be recognized when the transaction is essentially complete. In the case of sales, the proper date is the one on which the risks and rewards of ownership pass to the purchaser. The risks and rewards include possession of an unrestricted right to the use of the property, title, assumption of liabilities, transferability of ownership, insurance coverage, and risk of loss.

In the case of services, revenue should be recognized when the services have been completed and the seller has incurred substantially all the costs. A buyer's acceptance of services rendered is not a requirement, unless the acceptance is a condition of the services themselves which would lead to the argument that the services are not "essentially complete." Therefore, a dispute regarding the quality of services, which arises after the services have been rendered, does not preclude the revenue recognition. However, a dispute may cause the recognition of a liability or reserve against the revenue.

EARLY BOOKING

Early booking of revenue can take several forms. A company may record anticipated sales and create invoices for the sales. Sometimes the schemes can be very sophisticated, as in the Time Energy Systems case.

Example of Early Revenue

Time Energy Systems, Inc. developed, promoted and marketed energy conservation systems--hardware and software for managing energy use in buildings. The company, in its capacity as general partner, formed limited partnerships to raise capital for its operations. The limited partnership interests were sold with the idea of using the funds to purchase equipment from Time Energy (the corporate general partner). However, Time Energy supposedly needed to show profitable operations for two reasons: (1) to induce investment in the limited partnerships, and (2) to obtain bank financing. Since the limited partnerships were Time Energy's primary customers, the company had few other sales to show for its profitability. Therefore, Time Energy charged management and incentive fees from research and development contracts to the limited partnerships, presumably for services rendered. Time Energy, however, recognized the fee income before performing the services and also failed to recognize an accrual for future costs of providing the services.

In addition, the limited partnerships borrowed money from outside lenders (banks) and from two of the officers of Time Energy. The borrowed funds were used to pay the management and incentive fees to Time Energy acting as the general partner. When limited partnership interests were purchased, the proceeds of those sales were used to repay the loans to both the banks and to the two officers. Therefore, Time Energy created income for itself through prepaid management and incentive fees (for services not yet rendered), using borrowed money which was later repaid by limited partners' capital contributions.

The SEC filed an enforcement action against both Time Energy and its accountants. The SEC said income was overstated because sales and fee revenues were recognized early, expenses were not accrued, and related-party transactions with the partnerships were not disclosed properly.

Source: Securities Exchange Commission, SEC v. Time Energy Systems, Inc., et al.., Civil Action No. 86-1370 (D.D.C.), Litigation Rel. No. 11106, Accounting and Auditing Enforcement Rel. No. 99

HOLDING THE BOOKS OPEN

Holding the books open occurs when sales made after the end of the accounting period are nevertheless recorded in the accounting period. In some cases, the sales are real; in others they are fabricated. In service industries, the services may be performed in the next period, or not at all.

Example of Early Booking

Electro-Catheter Corp. at one time had a normal accounting policy of recognizing sales revenue when merchandise was shipped. At the time the sale was recognized, the customer was billed, and inventory was relieved. The Company changed its policy and began recording sales and cost of sales when customers placed orders. For a two-year period, the Company allegedly overstated its income by approximately $4.5 million as a result of this new policy.

The company's policy was supposedly a "bill and hold scheme," whereby the Company recognized income in periods earlier than warranted. Sometimes the "bill and hold" policy was executed upon receipt of a distributor's order for a dollar amount of goods prior to the distributor identifying which merchandise was to be shipped. (Consequently, it was impossible to relieve inventory because the type of merchandise was not yet identified.) In some cases, shipment did not occur for over one year after the revenue was recognized.

Electro-Catheter Corp. had not passed any of the merchandise ownership rights after the institution of the new "bill and hold" policy. The company retained title to the merchandise, even commingling the goods with other inventory and allowing the customers the right of exchange. Electro-Catheter bore the storage and insurance expenses associated with the merchandise. The company maintained all the risk with respect to the decline in market value because the customers had merely identified a dollar amount and not the specific product mix in their orders.

Source: Securities Exchange Commission, Electro-Catheter Corp., Robert I. Bernstein and John J. Teryilan, Civil Action No. 87-0267 [NHJ] (D.D.C.), Litigation Rel. No. 11803, Accounting and Auditing Enforcement Rel. No. 196

UNTIMELY ACCOUNTING FOR DISCOUNTS AND RETURNS

Indirect methods can be used to overstate net sales. These methods do not involve the overstatement of gross sales, but instead an understatement in the accounts which reduce gross sales to net sales. For example, an understatement of discounts, returns, and allowances will artificially inflate net sales. The two basic schemes involve failing to mark down discounts on merchandise when sales are made and failing to record returns.

Example of Untimely Discounts

Endo-Lase Company competed well in the market for scientific products by offering discounts and credits to its customers. However, the company allegedly billed customers at list prices, taking off the discounts and credits when the customers paid the net amount due. No estimates of credits and allowances were booked prior to collection. Thus, receivables and sales were overstated until the receivables were collected. As business expanded, so did the overstatement.

Source: SEC v. Michael Clinger, Walter G. Solomon and Avi Oren, Accounting and Auditing Enforcement Rel. No 142

IMPROPER SALES ACCOUNTING

Classifying certain transactions as sales can take a wide variety of forms, from fictitious sales to booking loan proceeds as income. Any increase (credit) to sales can come from a legitimate as well as a non-legitimate source. Schemes involving the improper treatment of sales are designed to overstate or inflate sales.

FICTITIOUS SALES

Fictitious sales most often involve fake or phantom customers. However, fictitious sales can involve legitimate customers. For example, an invoice can be prepared for a legitimate customer with no shipment of goods. At the beginning of the next accounting period, the sale can be reversed. This is a fictitious sale coupled with a spurious bill and hold scheme. Another method of utilizing legitimate customers is to artificially inflate or alter an invoice to reflect higher prices or quantities.

Example of Fictitious Sales

The SEC filed a complaint against the Network Control Corporation for allegedly engaging in improper revenue recognition practices which led to the material understatement of losses reported in Network's first three quarterly Form 10-Qs. According to the complaint, the company employed fraudulent practices consisting of: (1) recording transactions as sales when customers had not agreed to purchase the equipment and the equipment had not been delivered; (2) recording a sales "prospect list" as sales transactions; and (3) removing inventory from Network's premises to simulate the delivery of goods sold to the customers, when no such delivery had occurred.

In the related class action lawsuit, the plaintiffs alleged that Network arbitrarily shipped unordered goods to potential customers, falsely recorded sales revenue from these shipments, and lost money when Network was either forced to accept the return of the unordered goods or to convince customers to keep excess shipments by providing substantial discounts and other costly incentives.

Source: Smith v. Network Equipment Technologies, Inc. et al., D.C. Northern District of California No. c-90-1138

As seen in the Network Control example, sales overstatement schemes can employ two or more schemes simultaneously to overstate sales. In this example, the company used fictitious sales, early recognition of revenue, and holding the books open. The company did not stop there. In addition to the three schemes, the company also entered into some fictitious related-party transactions which, when discovered, resulted in the revenue overstatement by an additional $240,500 and an asset overstatement of $184,000.

Example of Fictitious Sales

The SEC filed a civil action against Coated Sales, Inc., alleging that pursuant to a plan formulated by the former Chairman and CEO of the company, officers and employees of Coated engaged in a scheme to inflate accounts receivable and inventory. The complaint alleged that the employees and directors engaged in schemes designed to: (1) create phony invoices purporting to show sales of Coated; (2) record the phony invoices in the accounts receivable of Coated; and (3) in order to create the appearance that the phony invoices were being paid, apply proceeds from the sale of common stock.

Phillip K., former general counsel, assistant secretary, and director of Coated Sales, Inc., admitted to racketeering and securities fraud charges. He was the last of several officers to plead guilty to crimes contributing to Coated Sales' failure.

Coated Sales was one of the nation's fastest growing companies before it collapsed, robbing stockholders of more than $100 million and several banks of $52 million. Philip K. admitted he was paid $115,000 for legal work done for Coated Sales. He conspired with company executives to omit the payment from the company's annual report filed with the SEC.

Philip K. and other executives tried to persuade the company's external auditor to falsely state in an annual report that $6 million was used to buy machinery. The $6 million had been listed on bogus accounts receivable invoices, which were later used as collateral for about $52 million in bank loans.

When the external accountant resigned the Coated Sales account, the company's stock plummeted, and Coated Sales declared bankruptcy one month later.

Source: The Associated Press; Byline: Dwight Oestricher, Associated Press Writer.

SALES WITH CONDITIONS

Sales with conditions are sales that have not been completed and the risks and rewards of ownership have not passed to the purchaser. These types of sales are similar to schemes involving the recognition of revenue in improper periods, in particular the early recognition of revenue.

Example of Sales with Conditions

Automatix, Inc. sold products that required engineering and adapting work before they were acceptable to customers. However, the company recorded sales revenue before completing the engineering, testing, evaluation, and customer acceptance stages of production. In some cases, sales were to European subsidiaries and the final sales to user-customers did not takeplace for weeks or months. In other cases, sales were specifically contingent upon the customers' trial and acceptance of the product. To compound the problem, the company supposedly did not adequately record the progress of each order through the various stages of development, construction, testing, trial, and acceptance. The amount of the resulting overstatement was undisclosed in the SEC complaint, and the company was ordered to engage the services of an independent accountant to review and report on the procedures with respect to revenue recognition. The company was also ordered to implement any recommendations the independent accountant might make.

Source: Securities Exchange Commission, SEC v. Automatix Inc., Civil Action No. 86-1596 (D.D.C.); SEC v. John Dias, Civil Action No. 86-1597 (D.D.C.), Litigation Rel. No. 11121, Accounting and Auditing Enforcement Rel. No. 100

Example of Sales with Conditions

The SEC filed an enforcement action against Storage Technology Corporation, alleging material false statements and overstated revenues and accounts receivable. Storage Tech was engaged in the design, development, manufacture, marketing, and servicing of computer peripheral subsystems. The complaint alleged that Storage Tech recognized revenue before collection of the sales price was reasonably assured and before completion of the underlying sales transaction.

> Storage Tech's policy was to recognize revenue when the products were shipped. However, the sale was not complete as of the time of shipment because: (1) customers were not obligated to pay for the equipment until it had been installed, (2) Storage Tech had substantial obligations to the customers for installation and adjustments, and (3) major uncertainties concerning the customers' true willingness to complete the transaction remained because of the volatile nature of the high-tech product.
>
> Source: Securities Exchange Commission, SEC v. Storage Technology Corporation, Civil Action No 87-0175, Litigation Rel. No. 11340, Accounting and Auditing Enforcement Rel. No. 125.

CONSIGNMENT SALES

A consignment sale is not a completed sale with respect to the revenue recognition by the seller, until such time as the ultimate end-user (purchaser) accepts the product. For example, art galleries often accept artwork from artists on consignment. Once the artwork is sold to the gallery patron, the artist recognizes the revenue, but the artist cannot recognize the revenue upon delivery of the artwork to the gallery. Many other products ranging from books to fertilizers are "sold" on consignment.

> ### Example of Consignment Sales
>
> Edgar B., president of the Jacquard Division of AM International, Inc. allegedly "kept open" Jacquard's books routinely at the end of various months to record revenue for products which were shipped in subsequent months. Additionally, Jacquard officials, supposedly with Edgar B's knowledge, were said to have booked revenue upon shipment for sales which were, in substance, consignment sales.
>
> The result of the "open book" scheme was an overstatement of pre-tax income of approximately $500,000 and an overstatement of accounts receivable of approximately $6 million. The "consignment" scheme resulted in an overstatement of pre-tax income of $3 million. Consequently, the periodic reports containing these overstatements were alleged to be materially false and misleading.
>
> Source: Securities Exchange Commission, SEC v. Edgar Bolton, No. 85 Civ. 4787 (JES) (S.D.N.Y.), Litigation Rel. No. 11699, Accounting and Auditing Enforcement Rel. No. 185

IMPROPER PERCENTAGE-OF-COMPLETION ACCOUNTING

The percentage-of-completion method of accounting is a fertile area for financial statement fraud, even though it applies only to certain types of transactions. Percentage of completion schemes are often difficult to track because several estimates are involved in the accounting calculation. Percentage-of-completion was originally designed to account for long-term contracts in the construction industry. The method has been extended to contracts in many other industries, and the concept of "long term" has been shortened to be months instead of years.

Generally accepted accounting principles state that the percentage-of-completion method is preferred when both the costs and the extent of progress toward completion of the long-term contract are reasonably dependable. It is precisely these conditions that give rise to improper revenue recognition under the percentage-of-completion method. If management cannot make reasonably dependable estimates of a project's completion stage, the percentage of completion accounting method is not appropriate. If this method is used inappropriately, the financial statements can be materially misleading.

MISREPRESENTING PERCENTAGE OF COMPLETION

Revenue and the related expenses, using the percentage-of-completion method of accounting, are subject to misrepresentation. This commonly occurs when management knows the project is less complete than the amount declared on the financial statements. This scheme, in some instances, occurs with the production of fictitious documents.

Example of Percentage of Completion

George Risk Industries, Inc. ("GRI") designed, manufactured and marketed computer keyboards, push-button switches, and burglar alarm systems. GRI raised capital for its research and development projects by having investors sign contracts or "pledges." These contracts called for capital to be contributed 25% in cash with a promissory note for the balance. The promissory notes did not provide for payment of interest until the principal became due.

The SEC filed a civil action against GRI alleging that the company improperly used the percentage-of-completion method of accounting for its research and development project which caused an overstatement of revenues

---

for three years. Additionally, the SEC alleged that GRI overstated its working capital for the same three years. The complaint alleged that GRI lacked the ability to make reasonably dependable estimates of the stage of the project's completion and it could not be reasonably expected that the investors would fulfill their obligations on the long-term notes.

The alleged material overstatement of working capital was a result of GRI classifying accrued interest receivable on the promissory notes from the investors as a current asset. No payments of interest were made on these notes during the years that this accrued interest was reported as a current asset.

Source: Securities Exchange Commission, SEC v. George Risk Industries, Inc., Civil Action No. 88-2553 (D.D.C.), Litigation Rel. No. 11864, Accounting and Auditing Enforcement Rel. No. 199

Example of Percentage of Completion

Midwestern Companies, Inc. constructed ethanol plants for sale to customers. In its civil action against the company, the SEC alleged that Midwestern's reported revenues, net earnings, assets, and shareholders' equity were materially overstated, reflecting a false trend of increasingly favorable operating results when, in fact, Midwestern's financial condition had severely deteriorated. One of the reasons cited for the deterioration of Midwestern's financial condition was failure of the ethanol plants to operate after they were sold.

In one year, Midwestern reported over $23.2 million in revenues and approximately $9.5 million in pre-tax earnings and $44 million and $20.7 million in revenues and pre-tax earnings, respectively, in the first three quarters of the next year. The SEC alleged that Midwestern should have reported losses, not pre-tax income for these periods. This overstatement of income was the result of Midwestern's improper use of the percentage-of-completion method of accounting. The collection of the sales price for the sale of the ethanol plants was not reasonably assured and Midwestern was obligated to perform significant activities after the purported sale of the plants. Certain of the reported sales had not been consummated. The complaint further alleged that the company formed by Midwestern to purchase the ethanol plants was not independent, but was organized, controlled and financially supported by Midwestern.

The company supposedly manipulated and misrepresented the stage of completion of construction by falsifying some invoices for costs incurred, thus understating the estimated costs to complete. According to the SEC, when a cost-based percentage of completion method was applied to the manipulated data, Midwestern recognized more revenue than the facts warranted, and overstated the construction-in-progress inventory.

Source: SEC v. Ronald R. Walker, et al., Civil Action No. 86-523 (W.D. Mo.), Litigation Rel. No. 11071, Accounting and Auditing Enforcement Rel. No. 96. Litigation Rel. No. 11267

UNSUPPORTED ADJUSTMENTS

Unsupported adjustments occur when management estimates the percentage of completion of a particular project without proper basis or documentation. Although unsupported adjustments can be the cause of fraudulent financial reporting in any area of the financial statements, the percentage-of-completion accounting method is particularly vulnerable because of its dependence on estimates.

INADEQUATE DISCLOSURE OF RELATED-PARTY TRANSACTIONS

The inadequate disclosure of related-party transactions is a serious financial statement fraud. These transactions are susceptible to non-arm's-length manipulation. The Federal Deposit Insurance Corporation ("FDIC"), in an effort to curb some of this type of financial statement fraud, has issued proposed rules aimed at improving detection procedures and preventing losses in connection with fraud and abuse by bank officers and other insiders. According to the FDIC, significant insider abuse was identified in 42 percent of the 184 bank failures in 1987; 31 percent of the 200 bank failures in 1988; and 25 percent of the 206 bank failures in 1989.

Insider fraud accounts for more than half of all the financial institution fraud and embezzlement cases brought by the FBI, and total losses from these cases reaches several hundred million dollars. Inadequate disclosure of related-party transactions is not limited to any specific industry. It transcends all business types and relationships. Two of the most common areas of related-party transactions involve conflict of interest and sham transactions.

CONFLICT OF INTEREST

A conflict of interest occurs when a company official or insider has an undisclosed financial interest in a transaction. The financial interest of the company official is sometimes not immediately clear. For example, common directors of two companies doing business with each other, any corporate general partner and the partnerships with which it does business, any controlling shareholder and the corporation with which he or she does business are all illustrations of related parties. Family members can also be considered related parties. Related-party transactions are sometimes referred to as "self-dealing."

In some cases, the conflict of interest does little serious harm. In other cases, it is used to embezzle company funds. Several of the examples discussed previously have included fraud schemes that were partially a result of conflict of interest. In these, and the examples below, the conflicts of interest are not always easy to detect.

Example of Related-Party Conflict

American Biomaterials Corporation's (ABC) former chief executive officer and former chief financial officer formed a partnership called Kirkwood Associates. This partnership was formed as an executive search firm. ABC allegedly paid Kirkwood in excess of $410,000 for the location of 25 employees. These fees accrued for the benefit of the CEO and CFO of ABC, yet ABC failed to disclose this related-party transaction. Moreover, Kirkwood allegedly did not perform any substantial services in connection with ABC's hiring the 25 employees.

In addition to this failure to disclose the related-party transaction, ABC allegedly paid in excess of $65,000 in undisclosed perquisites for the benefit of one executive. These perquisites included: (1) the personal service of a carpenter, (2) personal jewelry, (3) use of the company credit card to purchase over $11,000 of personal items, (4) the use of company funds to purchase over $38,000 in personal items including clothes and furniture, and (5) reimbursement for business meals for which ABC had already paid.

Source: Securities Exchange Commission, American Biomaterials Corporation, Civil Action No. 88-1063 (D.D.C.), Litigation Rel. No. 11710, Accounting and Auditing Enforcement Rel. No. 187

SHAM TRANSACTIONS

Sham transactions are transactions with no economic substance or purpose. They are commonly used to inflate earnings or assets. In some cases, they hide the true nature of a transaction.

Example of Sham Transactions

G.C. Technologies, Inc. (GC) was controlled by Groover (an attorney) through nominee officers, directors, and shareholders. Groover acquired lease interests in producing oil wells located in Kansas at a cost of $63,150. These interests were "purchased" by GC for $180,000 shortly thereafter. About a month later, Groover acquired two mining leases on behalf of another nominee company for $550,000. This nominee company sold a 30% interest in the mining leases to GC for $1.5 million. Neither of these transactions was disclosed by GC as related-party transactions. Furthermore, even though GC purchased only a 30% interest in the two mining leases, it reported the entire, albeit inflated, purchase price of the entire lease interests.

Groover was convicted of using sham transactions and nominee officers, directors, and shareholders to create a misleading financial picture of GC. Groover hid his involvement in companies and caused related-party transactions to appear as if they were conducted at arm's length.

Source: United States of America v. Larry B. Groover. United States District Court for the District Court of Utah, Case No. 89-CR-02318. Accounting and Auditing Enforcement Rel. No. 285, Litigation Rel. No. 12724

Example of Related Party Transaction

American Saving and Loan Association of Florida (ASLA) entered into two repurchase transactions involving ESM Government Securities, Inc. (ESM), a broker-dealer in U.S. Government securities. ESM's principal and founder was on ASLA's board of directors. These repurchase agreements were, for all practical purposes, financing vehicles whereby ASLA purchased government securities, sold the government securities to third parties and agreed to repurchase the securities upon their maturities.

These repurchase transactions were substantially larger than any single previous ASLA securities transaction. They increased ASLA's assets and liabilities by approximately 33%. The alleged purpose of the repurchase transactions was to enable ASLA to recognize profit of $5.6 million, represented by the difference between the purchase and the repurchase price. The creditworthiness of some of the end-lenders in the repurchase transaction came under closer scrutiny by ASLA. This alerted ASLA to the potential risk of the transactions themselves and as a result, ASLA unwound the repurchase agreement transactions prior to their maturity dates. No disclosure was made of the premature unwinding of the transactions, the reasons for the unwinding, or the financial consequences. ASLA also did not disclose the fact that the substantial increase in its assets was essentially due to transactions with an affiliate of an ASLA director.

Source: Securities Exchange Commission, Matter of American Savings and Loan Association of Florida, FHLBB Enforcement Review Committee Resolution No. ERC 88-24; Exchange Act Rel. No. 34-25788, Accounting and Auditing Enforcement Rel. No. 194

IMPROPER ASSET VALUATION

Improper asset valuations involve a host of schemes because they involve estimates. According to SAS 57, an accounting estimate is "an approximation of a financial statement element, item or account." Examples of accounting estimates include:

- Net realizable value of accounts receivable
- Allowance for loan losses
- Net realizable value of inventory
- Valuation of securities
- Warranty expense and liability
- Percentage of completion revenue and construction-in-progress inventory
- Deferred revenue
- Probability and amount of contingent losses
- Fair value of non monetary exchanges
- Many others (listed in SAS 57).

Although management is responsible for making the accounting estimates, auditors are responsible for evaluating the reasonableness of those estimates in the context of the financial statements taken as a whole. In an effort to discharge those responsibilities, external auditors are supposed to:

- Keep track of the differences between management's estimates and the closest reasonable estimates supported by the audit evidence.

- Evaluate the differences taken altogether for indications of systematic bias and the combination of differences with other likely errors in the financial statements.

Most improper asset valuations involve the fraudulent overstatement of inventory and receivables. Other improper asset valuations can be purchase-versus-pooling accounting methods, misclassification of fixed and other assets, or improper capitalization of inventory or start-up costs.

INVENTORY

Inventory can be improperly valued through the manipulation of the percentage-of-completion accounting method, manipulation of the physical inventory count, failing to relieve inventory for costs of goods sold, and failing to make proper estimates for obsolete and unsalable goods. One of the most popular methods of overstating inventory is through fictitious (phantom) inventory.

Fictitious inventory schemes usually involve the creation of fake documents such as inventory count sheets, receiving reports, and even fake physical goods. In some instances, a friendly co-conspirator claims to be holding inventory for the company in question. Finally, it is also common to insert phony count sheets during the inventory observation or change the quantities on the count sheets.

Example of False Inventory

Former associate chairman of San Francisco-based Hambrecht & Quist (H&Q), Quentin W., was indicted by a federal grand jury for securities fraud and wire fraud. The indictment was for alleged illegal activities, including materially false and misleading financial statements, while he was chairman of Miniscribe Corporation.

H&Q, on behalf of a group of individuals and entities, made a venture capital investment of about $20 million in Miniscribe, gaining control of the company. Miniscribe, which made disk drives, filed for bankruptcy protection. According to an internal investigation report, the company inflated its inventory by packaging bricks as finished products. Scrap parts were also counted as inventory.

The indictment said Quentin W. and others engaged in an unlawful scheme to defraud by filing materially false and misleading financial statements with the SEC. The indictment said he ordered destroyed a memorandum that showed Miniscribe's reported inventory had a shortfall of millions of dollars.

The indictment also stated that during the period when the inventory was falsely represented, Quentin W. sold 150,000 shares of Miniscribe for about $1.7 million while having non-public information about the inventory shortfall.

Source: Reuters, Limited; Dateline: Denver.]

Example of False Inventory

Rocky Mount Undergarment Co., Inc. (RMU) manufactured and marketed women's, men's, and children's underwear. RMU, with its supplier as co-conspirator, allegedly overstated RMU's inventory. The supplier claimed to be holding inventories for RMU. In addition, three employees, allegedly at the direction of the former CEO, inflated quantity and cost figures on the inventory count sheets reflecting the year-end physical count of RMU's raw material inventory. These falsifications resulted in overstating inventory by 9% and net income by 134%.

Source: Rocky Mount Undergarment Co., Inc., et al.., Civil Action No. 89-014-5 (E.D.N.C.),
Litigation Rel. No. 11960 Accounting and Auditing Enforcement Rel. No. 212

INVENTORY VALUATION ISSUES

Inventory should be valued at the lower of cost or market, and obsolete inventory should be written down to its current value, or written off altogether if it has no value. Failing to write-down inventory results in overstated assets and the mismatching of revenues with cost of goods sold.

Example of False Inventory

The former president and chief executive officer and the former vice president of Saxon Industries, Inc. (Saxon) pleaded guilty to conspiracy and securities and mail fraud charges in connection with the falsification of Saxon's financial statements. These and other executives allegedly spent 14 years systematically defrauding shareholders and creditors of Saxon by adding more than $53 million in non-existent inventory to the books of various Saxon subsidiaries and divisions, creating an illusion of increased profits and assets. The SEC alleged that the "red flags," including the denial of access to the general ledger and other corporate records, was enough to put the independent auditors on notice that an intensified audit was necessary.

Source: SEC v. Arthur Rogovin and Albert DeBiccari, Civil Action No. 86-1740 (S.D.N.Y.), Litigation Rel. No. 11018

Example of False Inventory

A Long Island auto and motor home dealer with business holdings in Connecticut, Maryland, Florida, Georgia, and Nevada was charged with federal loan kiting charges while awaiting developments in another court case involving seizure of 700 new cars from his dealership.

Federal authorities described John M's get-rich scheme as the largest Ponzi-type kiting scheme ever conducted in the United States. It left General Motors with a $436 million loss.

John M., whose main car dealership was in Port Jefferson, New York, was charged with mail fraud, wire fraud, and money laundering. He defrauded GM by means of a phony auto-exporting scheme involving dummy companies he allegedly set up in Indiana and the island of Cyprus. His scheme went on for 10 years until GMAC auditors made a "routine visit" to his dealership. John M. allegedly borrowed $1.75 billion from GMAC to finance an inventory of tens of thousands of cars that did not exist.

John M's net worth was listed as $338 million. He was ordered by the court to sign over his $500,000 home, private jet, gold mine in Nevada, and the assets of 70 companies and 100 real estate holdings from Connecticut to Florida. In addition, he had to hand over a $200,000 cash bond and turn over his passport.

Reportedly, one of John M's bogus companies, Kay Industries, a van conversion company, was never registered with the U.S. Department of Transportation as required of all vehicle alteration companies. John M. was a major dealer in altered vehicles that are actually custom-made cars and vans built on standard chassis. The federal complaint charged him with using bogus invoices from Kay to obtain 30-day financing from GMAC for purchases of up to 17,000 vans a month.

Source: The New York Times Company/The New York Times; Byline: Jane Fritsch.]

ACCOUNTS RECEIVABLE

Accounts receivable are subject to manipulation in the same manner as sales and inventory. In many cases, the schemes are conducted together. The two most common schemes involving accounts receivable are fictitious receivables and the failure to write down or allow for uncollectible accounts receivable.

Fictitious Accounts Receivable

Fictitious accounts receivable is common among companies with financial problems, as well as with managers who receive a commission based on sales. The typical entry under fictitious accounts receivable is to debit (increase) accounts receivable and credit (increase) sales. These schemes tend to be timed around the end of accounting periods.

Example of Fictitious Sales and Receivables

The now-defunct Deerfield Beach, Florida company, Sahlen & Associates, was once the fifth-largest security service firm in the world, employing nearly 12,000 people at its peak. Sahlen & Associates provided security for President Bush's 1989 inauguration and for the 1988 Democratic and Republican Conventions. It also performed security work for AT&T, Delta Air Lines, Dow Chemical, and IBM. It serviced the DEA and guarded construction sites for 22 U.S. embassies.

Over a five-year period, reported company revenues grew from $459,000 to $54.9 million. The financial records made the company attractive to investors. However, these allegedly falsified records were used to create an "illusion of success." According to one expert, the firm was so broke it had to kite checks to create operating funds. The company even wrote reports to justify fake billings and mailed invoices to fake clients at post office boxes so the outside auditors would find convincing paper trails.

The company had 20 million outstanding shares when it collapsed, after directors announced it was under investigation by the Securities Exchange Commission. The portion of the business untainted by fraud was auctioned for $40 million. Harold S., the company founder, and six others were charged in a 28-count indictment which included conspiracy to defraud the SEC, securities fraud, bank fraud, and mail fraud.

Source: United Press International, 1993: Dateline: Ft. Lauderdale, FL.

Failure to Write Down

Companies should write off uncollectible receivables. The two methods for write-off include the allowance method and the direct charge method. Companies struggling for profits and income will often choose not to write off or allow for bad accounts receivable because of the negative effect on income.

Example of Failure to Write-Down Receivables

Allnet Communication Services, Inc. (Allnet), a publicly held company, was in the long-distance telephone business. Allnet had a problem with its computerized accounts-receivable system. The internal processing system lacked a balance-forward feature on generated bills. This led to an inability of customers to determine whether an unpaid balance existed or whether payments had been properly credited. As a result, Allnet accumulated a backlog of unaddressed or unresolved disputes. The problems with the billing system led to billing delays which decreased the ultimate collectibility of these accounts. In addition, the system failed to give Allnet's management complete and accurate aging data on accounts receivable.

As a result of the problems with the billing system, the $4 million annual income Allnet reported should have been reduced by a total of approximately $15 million in uncollectible accounts-receivable expense.

Source: In the Matter of Michael P. Richer, Melvyn J. Goodman and Robert S. Hardy, Exchange Act Rel. No. 25528, Accounting and Auditing Enforcement Rel. No. 184

Write-downs are also a consideration in the banking industry. A financial institution's accounts receivable are its loans, the same misrepresentations due to failure to write-down that are available to other companies are available to financial institutions.

Example of Overvalued Loan Receivables

In a class action suit, First American Bank and Trust v. Frogel, et al., (D.C. Southern District of Florida, Case No. 88-0638-CIV-HOEVELER), the plaintiffs alleged that the bank made large loans to present and former officers and directors. Loans were allegedly made in high-risk areas which carried higher interest rates. The bank recorded the loans at full value, but the plaintiffs allege that the bank officers knew that full payment was unlikely. The plaintiffs further allege that the bank failed to report an adequate allowance for loan losses. The FDIC later required the bank to record $50 million of the bank's loans as "loss," "doubtful" or "substandard."

BUSINESS COMBINATIONS

The two methods for accounting for business combinations are the purchase method and the pooling method. In general, the purchase method is used when cash or other assets are distributed as a result of the combination or if liabilities are incurred as a means of financing the purchase. On the other hand, if only voting common stock is issued to effect the business combination, the pooling-of-interest method is generally favored. Managers and auditors should look to the nature of the transaction to see if the primary purpose is to overstate assets or income. The Accounting Principles Board Opinion No. 16, "Business Combinations," contains the generally accepted accounting principles.

Example of Purchase Merger

For at least three and a half years, Lehman, Lucchesi & Walker (LLW) served as the auditors for Malibu Capital Corporation (Malibu). Malibu subsequently merged with Colstar Petroleum Corporation (Colstar). Prior to the combination with Colstar, Malibu supposedly had no business purpose other than to merge with or acquire one or a small number of private companies. LLW gave Malibu an unqualified opinion on the financial statements. These statements identified Colstar as the "acquired corporation." The combination was treated as a "purchase" of Colstar by Malibu, and Colstar's primary asset was adjusted from $11,055 to $1,342,600.

Under generally accepted accounting principles, the combination should have been treated as a "reverse purchase" with Colstar as the "acquiring corporation" and with no adjustment to Colstar's assets. As a result of the improper accounting treatment, Malibu allegedly overstated its assets by 102 percent.

MISCLASSIFICATION OF ASSETS

This scheme is used to inflate the current assets and understate long-term assets. The net effect is to improve the current ratio. The erroneous classification of long-term assets as current assets can be of critical concern to lending institutions that often require the maintenance of certain ratios. This is of particular concern when the loan covenants are on unsecured or under-secured lines of credit and other short-term borrowings. Sometimes these misclassifications are called "window dressing."

Example of False Assets

Two executives of a women's clothing and cosmetics store chain were indicted on charges of looting their company of about $30 million. Victor I., CEO of the Boca Raton, Florida-based Cascade International, and John S., were charged in a 14-count indictment on charges including grand larceny. The charges involved theft of money invested or loaned to the company based on false and inflated claims of its performance made to federal authorities. The alleged fraud was discovered when Incendy disappeared.

The company was formed as a shell company in Utah, filed for bankruptcy seven years later, and has since been liquidated. The bankruptcy court found $30 million missing and before it collapsed, investors and creditors may have lost as much as $100 million.

The defendants told federal securities officials that Cascade ran 150 cosmetics counters and 17 cosmetics retail outlets in five states. There were no counters and only one outlet, in Bridgeport, CT. But based on those numbers, Cascade claimed false profits of $3.66 million on sales of $7.76 million. Cascade also claimed it operated 21 women's clothing boutiques in New England, Florida, and California. Reportedly, Cascade ran only five stores--none of them in New England. Based on the alleged bogus filings, Cascade got $10 million in loans from the Bank of Scotland--money that John and Victor allegedly stole.

Source: The Associated Press; Byline: Samuel Maull, AP Writer.

FIXED ASSETS

Fixed assets are subject to manipulation through several different schemes. Some of the more common are:
- Booking fictitious assets
- Misrepresenting valuations of assets
- Improperly capitalizing inventory and start-up costs

Fictitious Fixed Assets

Fictitious assets can be created by a variety of methods. One of the most common is simply to create fictitious documents. In other instances, the equipment is leased and the fact is not disclosed when the transactions are recorded and reported.

Example of Fictitious Fixed Assets

During a three-year period, several senior officers of Flight Transportation Corporation (FTC) allegedly implemented a scheme to loot FTC through a variety of devices. Some of these devices included reporting non-existent assets, sales of a Cayman Island subsidiary, and undisclosed related-party transactions. The independent auditors gave unqualified opinions on FTC's financial statements.

The SEC found that the audits of these false financial statements had not been conducted in accordance with generally accepted auditing standards in that the auditing work performed provided an insufficient basis to support the unqualified opinions the CPAs issued. The auditors allegedly failed to obtain competent evidential matter to support the existence of reported material assets and the realization of reported revenues. The audits were not conducted with the degree of professional skepticism required of independent accountants.

Source: In the Matter of John E. Harrington and Gregory B. Arnott, Exchange Act Rel. No. 22686, Accounting and Auditing Enforcement Rel. No. 81

Fixed Asset Valuations

Generally, fixed assets should be recorded at the lower of cost or market. According to accounting principles, these assets (property, plant, and equipment) should not be written up to reflect appraisal, market, or current values that exceed cost. Write-up valuations can be of particular concern in mergers and acquisitions and, therefore, subject to much abuse. In some instances, such as the real estate market, the value of property is subject to wide interpretation and valuation. Often, schemes involving the valuation of fixed assets also involve related-party transactions.

Example of Overvalued Fixed Assets

Alta Gold Co. (Alta) was formed in part by the merger of Silver King Mines, Inc. (Silver) and Pacific Silver Corp. (Pacific), who were related parties to each other. Before the merger of these two related parties, Silver and Pacific exchanged mining properties at "fair values" rather than at historical costs.

Income and higher asset values were recognized by both Silver and Pacific on the exchange of these properties. The appraisals for the mining properties were performed by three individuals who were officers and directors of Silver and Pacific. Therefore, the appraisals were not prepared by independent parties. The inflated asset values and the false income resulting from the exchange of assets between Silver and Pacific were eventually reported on the financial statements of Alta. Therefore, the financial statements of Alta were materially misstated.

Source: Securities & Exchange Commission, Matter of the Registration Statement of Alta Gold Co., Securities Act Rel. No.6801, Accounting and Auditing Enforcement Rel. No. 203

IMPROPER CAPITALIZATION

The two most common areas for improper capitalization are inventory and start-up costs. Inventory is improperly capitalized on some occasions to improve the total assets picture and to hide obsolete inventory. Start-up costs my be improperly capitalized to hide losses.

Example of Improper Capitalization

For two years, U.S. Surgical Corporation (Surgical), a publicly held manufacturer of surgical staples and other medical devices, experienced for the first time sharply increased competition for its products. In an effort to meet these pressures, Surgical allegedly began a frenzied effort to develop, manufacture and market new products, which resulted in large production inefficiencies. Additionally, Surgical changed its accounting policy which resulted in the addition of over $5 million to a patent account which previously had only $1 million, and a 50% decrease in research and development expenditures.

Barden, a supplier of molds and dies to Surgical, conspired to assist Surgical in falsifying its financial statements. Surgical accounted for a large portion of Barden's total revenues (15%). Molds and dies supplied by Barden and used by Surgical in its manufacture of medical supplies were capitalized by Surgical, and parts were inventoried. The parts were eventually expensed through cost of goods sold. Barden allegedly falsified invoices to charge Surgical more for molds and dies and less for parts, thus enabling Surgical to overstate its fixed assets and understate its cost of goods sold. Barden falsified $1 million or more in this manner. A Barden official confirmed false information to Surgical's independent auditors, attesting to the false charges for dies.

Source: In the Matter of Michael S. Hope, et al., Exchange Act Rel., No. 23513, Securities Act Rel. No. 6655, Accounting and Auditing Enforcement Rel. No. 109

Example of Improper Capitalization

Savin, an office equipment manufacturer, was charged with materially overstating its assets and net worth and materially understating its losses by improperly classifying certain costs incurred in the research and development of a new line of photocopiers as "start-up" costs. As a result, Savin allegedly improperly capitalized more than $42 million as an asset.

Source: Securities Exchange Commission, Savin Corporation, Civil Action No. 85-3605 (D.D.C.), Litigation Rel. No. 10928, Accounting And Auditing Enforcement Rel. No. 80

IMPROPER DEFERRAL OF COSTS AND EXPENSES

Improper deferral of costs and expenses can be difficult to detect. Three common methods for improper deferral of costs and expenses are omissions of liabilities, capitalization of expenses, and failure to accrue enough warranty costs and liabilities.

OMISSION OF LIABILITIES

Liability omissions can take the form of simple failure to accrue expenses or more complex methods, such as the omission of contingent losses in accounting statements and note disclosures. Liability omissions are probably one of the hardest schemes of fraudulent financial reporting to discover. A thorough review of all post-balance sheet date transactions may go a long way toward discovery that management has omitted liabilities. Also, a review and analysis of all contractual obligations of the company may reveal unrecognized contingent liabilities.

Example of Omitted Liabilities

Because of inadequate internal controls, Marsh & McLennon (Marsh) allegedly allowed $1.2 billion in one year and $2.1 billion in the next year in undisclosed corporate liabilities to accumulate in the form of repurchase agreements. Marsh's books and records apparently did not accurately reflect the value, nature, terms, and profitability of its investments. Internal controls relating to investment activities were inadequate to ensure that investments were executed in accordance with management's authorization and that these investments were recorded to permit preparation of accurate financial statements.

Total liabilities and total assets were apparently understated, and income before taxes and earnings per share were overstated. Further, disclosures in the financial statements allegedly did not reflect that Marsh held a substantial position in intermediate and long-term marketable securities.

Source: Securities Exchange Commission, In the Matter of Marsh & Mclennan Companies, Inc., Exchange Act Rel. No. 24023, Accounting and Auditing Enforcement Rel. No. 124

CAPITALIZED EXPENSES

Capitalizing expenses is one of the more common forms of increasing income and assets. Abuses in this category often occur because generally accepted accounting principles are not always clear about rules for capitalizing costs. Fraud examiners and auditors should be diligent when determining the real reason for capitalization. For example, if a company capitalized the purchase of an eighteen-month supply of office supplies, because the supplies would last more than one year, is that an improper capitalization? Or is the company trying to manipulate the income by not reflecting the supplies as a current period expense? Are eighteen months of supplies actually available? Is this material?

Example of Improperly Capitalized Expenses

Computer Science Corporation (CSC) developed and sold computer-related services known as proprietary systems, one of which is known as "Computicket" (CT). Marx, an investor, availed himself of financial data of CSC. That financial data explained CSC's policy regarding capitalizing development expenses. The policy, in part, stated that CSC would initially capitalize development expenses rather than treat them as charges against current income. When a system (such as CT) became fully operational (defined as generating revenue in excess of expenses), CSC would begin to amortize the capitalized expenses over a specified period of time, presumably over the revenue-generating time period. At one point, CSC had approximately $6.8 million in capitalized costs for CT. In a registration statement filed with the SEC, CSC stated that it expected to begin amortizing CT's capitalized expenses later.

From its inception, CT had not met internal projections for market capture. CT supposedly experienced problems getting equipment installed, and it had been running deficits of $500,000 per month. In addition, CT lost one of its major contracts. Moreover, CSC had attempted, without success, to sell CT proprietary packages to various prospects for differing amounts. In October and November, CSC had gone so far as to discuss the abandonment of CT. The inference was clear: the likelihood of CT's commercial success became progressively more doubtful with the passage of time.

Marx sued CSC for violations of Rule 10b-5. The court in Marx v. Computer Sciences Corporation, 507 F.2d. 485, stated that the failure to disclose facts indicating that CT was in serious financial trouble was an omission "to state a material fact necessary in order to make the statements not misleading."

Example of Improper Cost Deferral

Cardillo Travel Systems, Inc. ("Cardillo") installed the Apollo computerized reservation system for United Airlines. In doing so, it incurred costs of $203,000 which, by arrangement, were to be reimbursed by United Airlines. When the reimbursement arrived, it was credited to revenue and the deferred costs were left in the asset account. Under the terms of the arrangement, the deferred costs were in the nature of an account receivable, and the reimbursement should have reduced this receivable and not increased income. Consequently, both assets and revenue were overstated.

Source: Securities Exchange Commission, SEC v. Cardillo Travel Systems, Inc. et al., Accounting and auditing Enforcement Rel. No. 143 (August 4, 1987); Litigation Rel. No. 11675

WARRANTY COST AND LIABILITY

Warranty expense understatement occurs when a company fails to accrue the proper expense and offsetting liability for returned or repaired products. The liability can be either omitted altogether or can be substantially understated. Another similar area is the liability resulting from defective products (product liability). Two of the most publicized examples of product liabilities are the Dalkon Shield and asbestos problems (Johns-Manville Corp.). The product liability may become so great and indeterminable as to render a company insolvent. For instance, Johns-Manville filed for protection in bankruptcy as a consequence of its asbestos products.

Example of Omitted Product Liability

In a class action suit against Pfizer, Inc. (Pfizer), a research-based company that deals in pharmaceuticals, medical devices, and surgical equipment, the plaintiffs alleged that Pfizer failed to disclose material information concerning the Shiley heart valve. This material information included the results of at least one product liability suit which Pfizer lost. Four years earlier, Pfizer reportedly knew the Shiley heart valve was troublesome, and it took the valve off the market. However, by that time, approximately 60,000 valves had been implanted. As of the date of the complaint, 389 fractures of the valve had been reported and the FDA reported that 248 deaths had been attributed to failed Shiley valves. Moreover, Pfizer maintained that surgery to replace the implanted valves would be more risky than leaving them in. Pfizer did not provide a reserve for this potential product liability.

Source: In re Pfizer, Inc. Securities Litigation, D.C. Southern District of New York No. 90 Civ. 1260

INADEQUACIES IN DISCLOSURES

Management has an obligation to disclose all significant information. If not measured quantitatively in the financial statements, disclosure should appear in the notes to financial statements or in management's discussion and analysis (MD&A). This information cannot be misleading. A general partner has a duty to disclose all material facts to its limited partners when soliciting the limited partner's consent to a partnership action, especially when a conflict of interest exists.

The court in Huddleston v. Herman & MacLean, 650 F.2d. 815 (5th Cir. 1981), held that "to warn that the untoward may occur when the event is contingent is prudent; to caution that it is only possible for the unfavorable events to happen when they have already occurred is deceit." In this case, a prospectus stated that "These securities involve a high degree of risk." The high degree of risk was due to the fact that proceeds from the stock sale were to be used for the construction of an automobile racetrack. However, at the time of the prospectus, management purportedly knew of understated construction costs and that the company's working capital position would not be as favorable as the prospectus reflected.

Management's discussion and analysis must be made with either a genuine belief or on a reasonable basis. If it is made without either a genuine belief or on a reasonable basis, then it is untrue. (See Eisenberg v. Gagnon, 776 F.2d. 770, 3rd Cir. 1985), cert. denied 474 U.S. 946 (1985) and Marx v. Computer Sciences Corp., 507 F.2d. 485 (9th Cir. 1974).) The most ordinary inadequacies in management's discussion and analyses involve one or more of the following: liability omissions, significant events, and management fraud.

LIABILITY OMISSIONS

Typical omissions include the failure to disclose loan covenants or contingent liabilities. As mentioned previously, another method of liability omission is failure to disclose product liability.

Example of Inadequate Disclosure

The Charter Company ("Charter"), a marketer of crude fuel oils, gasoline and related products, allegedly made material misstatements of fact in its annual report. Management's discussion and analysis omitted: (1) Charter's loss of trade credit, (2) a demand made by Charter's banks for new loan covenants as a condition for renewal of its $130 million credit line, which was scheduled to expire shortly after the report was issued, and (3) discussions with Charter's banks involving proposals which, if implemented, could have generated approximately $130 million in cash, but necessitated the sale of certain assets, the suspension of cash dividends, and the close of crude oil refining operations in Houston, Texas. Charter allegedly failed to disclose the effects of these developments on its operations, liquidity, and capital reserves.

Source: Securities Exchange Commission, SEC v. The Charter Co., Civil Action No. 86-713-CIV-J-12 (M.D. FL.), Litigation Rel. No. 11135, Accounting and Auditing Enforcement Rel. No. 104

Example of Inadequate Disclosure

Continental Illinois Corporation (Continental), the holding company of Continental Illinois National Bank and Trust Co. of Chicago, allegedly mischaracterized $425 million of the nearly $1 billion loan loss provision reported in its Form 10-Q. Continental characterized the $425 million as "loss on sale of loans subject to FDIC agreement." However, Continental allegedly did not disclose that the Office of the Comptroller of the Currency, after an examination, had directed Continental to record a $950 million provision for credit loss in the bank's portfolio before the loan sale. The Comptroller of the Currency concluded that splitting the provision and attributing $425 million thereof to the loss on sale was misleading.

Source: Securities Exchange Commission, In the Matter of Continental Illinois Corporation, Exchange Act Rel. No. 24142, Accounting and Auditing Enforcement Rel. No. 128

SIGNIFICANT EVENTS

Examples of significant events include new products or technology having an effect on sales, obsolescence of merchandise or manufacturing methods, lawsuits whose outcome is unknown, and any other significant event, that, if not disclosed, would mislead the financial statement users.

Example of Omitted Disclosure

E.F. Hutton Group, Inc. (Hutton) allegedly developed a cash management system for moving customer funds received by Hutton branch offices through bank accounts maintained at regional offices and to Hutton's corporate bank accounts located in New York City and Los Angeles. The system required the branch offices to calculate the daily net activity in their branch accounts and then to remove from the accounts all funds in excess of the required compensating balances. On certain days, the branches were alleged to have overdrafted their bank accounts to offset excess collected on other days. If, on the day after a branch over-drafted its bank account, insufficient funds were collected from customers to cover the overdraft, or if there was a delay in the check clearing process, the branch was to deposit a "branch reimbursement check " (BRC) in the branch bank account to make up the difference. BRCs were drawn on zero balance checking accounts which were funded at the end of each day.

Certain members of the senior management of Hutton supposedly encouraged greater use of the draw-down procedure, which increased the interest income and reduced the interest expense of Hutton. Net interest income was significant in Hutton's financial statements.

Hutton allegedly failed to disclose in its MD&A that the increased use of the over-drafting practices was a material cause of the significant increase in net interest income. The complaint also alleged that Hutton's MD&A failed to disclose that the reduced use of the bank over-drafting practices the next year was a material cause of the significant decrease in Hutton's net interest income that year.

Source: Securities Exchange Commission, Matter of E.F. Hutton Group, Inc., Exchange Act Rel. No. 25524; Accounting and Auditing Enforcement Rel. No. 183

Example of Omitted Disclosure

Fluid Corporation (Fluid), a business development company, allegedly failed to disclose a material unreported capital impairment condition which existed for about six months. Fluid owned two subsidiaries, Fluid Capital Corporation and Fluid Financial Corporation. Fluid's primary assets were the two wholly-owned subsidiaries, whose primary functions were to provide venture capital to small start-up companies through loans and equity investments. The two subsidiaries obtained their financing through the sale of debentures to the Small Business Administration (SBA). These debentures were subject to specific loan covenants, one of which was a capital impairment requirement. A capital impairment was deemed to exist when the undistributed-net-retained-earnings deficit exceeded 50% of private capital.

The SBA notified Fluid that a capital impairment condition existed at Fluid Capital Corporation. The condition would require a capital addition of at least $200,000. To cure the capital impairment condition, Fluid sold assets of Fluid Capital. The consolidated financial statements of Fluid allegedly failed to disclose that the original audit opinion on Fluid Capital's financial statements was qualified, but later reissued to reflect that no capital impairment existed.

A later report supposedly failed to disclose the SBA's written demand for payment of $1.9 million in debentures issued by Fluid Capital. This report failed to disclose that Fluid's, Fluid Capital's, and Fluid Financial's inability to meet this demand might result in the liquidation or receivership of the companies.

Source: Securities Exchange Commission, In the Matter of Fluid Corporation, Order Instituting Proceedings Pursuant to Section 12(j) of the Securities Exchange Act of 1934 and Section 54(c) of the Investment company Act of 1940, Findings, and Order of the Commission, Accounting and Auditing Enforcement Rel. No. 276, Investment Company Act Rel. No. IC-17756, Admin. Proc. File No. 307394.

MANAGEMENT FRAUD

Management has an obligation to disclose to the shareholders significant fraud committed by officers, executives, and others in important positions of trust. According to the court in Roeder v. Alpha Industries, Inc., 814 F.2d. 22, (1st Cir. 1987), management does not have the responsibility to disclose uncharged criminal conduct of its officers and executives. However, if and when officers, executives, or other persons in trusted positions become subjects of a criminal indictment, disclosure is required. In Roeder, the officers of the company bribed a defense contractor employee to obtain a subcontract. When the company learned that its officers were about to be indicted, the company released the information to the public. The court held that no liability can be imposed if there is no duty to disclose. The mere possession of non-public information also does not impose a duty to disclose; there must also be misrepresentation or misleading information as a result of the non-public information. See Backman v. Polaroid Corporation, 910 F.2d 10 (1st Cir. 1990).

Example of False Disclosure

Allegheny International, Inc. (AI) allegedly provided false and misleading information in its MD&A relating to a sale of real estate that constituted an unusual and infrequent event and which had a material impact on AI's pre-tax income.

Further, AI allegedly failed to maintain adequate records concerning the personal use of the corporate aircraft, the use of a condominium owned by AI but apparently used by the CEO and his family, a London townhouse purchased for the exclusive use of an AI subsidiary, use of 200 cases of wine purchased by AI for approximately $113,000, and resources devoted by AI to the structuring and administration of certain partnerships formed by AI officers for personal investment purposes.

Source: Securities Exchange Commission, SEC v. Allegheny International, Inc., Civil Action No. 87-2472, Litigation Rel. No. 11533, Accounting and Auditing Enforcement Rel. No. 151

Example of Omitted Disclosure

Wilfred Educational Corporation (Wilfred) owned and operated many "career" schools throughout the United States. Wilfred was a publicly traded company with over nine million shares outstanding. About 95% of Wilfred's students receive some form of government-sponsored financial aid and between 85% and 90% of Wilfred's revenues came from such aid.

In its complaint, the SEC alleged that Wilfred failed to disclose material facts regarding its compliance with the various governmental-sponsored financial aid programs. Allegedly, Wilfred flagrantly violated the regulations by encouraging students to submit false applications. The Department of Justice and the Education Department began investigations into the conduct of Wilfred. These investigations were not disclosed to the public through Wilfred's Annual Report or its press releases.

Source: Ballan v. Wilfred American Educational Corp.

OTHER DISCLOSURES

The total mix of information made available to the public must meet all the disclosure requirements for adequacy, accuracy, and inclusion. This means that disclosure requirements also apply to press releases and even oral statements.

Example of Misleading Press Release

The court in Columbia Securities v. Sony Corporation, District Court (Southern District of New York, 89 Civ 6821) held that Sony's press release was misleading when it falsely denied that merger negotiations were taking place. During the spring and summer 1989, Sony reportedly made statements to the press which falsely denied that merger negotiations were taking place, when in fact, several merger meetings had been held.

<u>Example of Misleading Oral Disclosure</u>

The primary assets of MHF and Mid-America Partnership consisted of livestock. Mid-America and several other investors purchased interests in the newly-formed partnership based on a multiple of the book value of the livestock, primarily horses. MHF management represented at the offering that the livestock was worth "substantially" more than the $1.6 million book value on the partnership books. In August, Mid-America sold substantially all of the partnership's livestock at auction for $750,000 (net). The partnership sustained a loss in excess of $710,000. The court held that the management of MHF had recklessly misrepresented the livestock's value in discussions at the offering.

Source: Kelly, et al. v. Mid-America Racing Stables, Inc. et al., D.C Oklahoma Western District No. 89-1362-A

CHAPTER 5
FRAUD EXAMINATION

Fraud examination is based in knowledge of law, criminology, and the various schemes employed by employees and organizations to commit fraud. The procedural and technical work of fraud examination is designed to resolve suspicions. The key element is suspicion, known to fraud examiners as "predication." Predication is the circumstance (tips, red flags, shortages, etc.) that lead professionally trained people to believe a fraud has occurred, is occurring, or will occur. Predication is the basis upon which an examination is commenced. Because they deal with the individual rights of people, fraud examinations must be conducted only with adequate predication.

Technical fraud examination consists of attempting to prove a case of fraud, in the course of which an examiner may find that a fraud has *not* occurred. Fraud examiners remain open-minded to both possibilities. The examination work consists of assembling evidence from documents and interviews, writing reports of the findings, and dealing with prosecutors and courts. The initial goal is to build a civil or criminal case file sufficient to support a prosecution.

This chapter provides an overview of the general fraud examination methodology and some insights into documentary and interview evidence.

FRAUD THEORY APPROACH

Every fraud examination begins with the prospect that the case will end in litigation or prosecution. Fraud examiners start with a "theory of the case." Like a scientist who postulates a theory based on observation and then tests it, the "theory of the case" begins with assumptions, based on initial facts or suspicions of the events that might have occurred. These assumptions are then tested to try to determine a provable truth. The fraud theory approach involves the following logical steps:
- Analyze available data
- Create a hypothesis
- Test the hypothesis
- Refine and amend the hypothesis
- Decide to accept or reject the hypothesis based on the evidence

Suppose the initial available data is a complaint from a vendor that the company's purchasing department is favoring other vendors, forgoing the vendor's low prices, and probably receiving kickbacks from a competitor. Fraud examiners know that purchase kickbacks and bribery happen frequently and can hypothesize: (1) purchasing is being shifted from long-time vendors to new ones, (2) bidding procedures are not being followed, (3) prices higher than those available from the aggrieved vendor are being paid, and (4) a purchasing agent is taking kickbacks or bribes. The test of these hypotheses lies in the evidence, some of which can be obtained from company document sources, some from interviews, and some from a suspect's public and nonpublic records. The fraud examination can find "no case" (refine and amend the hypotheses) if the evidence does not support these hypotheses and a suspect cannot be tentatively identified. The "suspect" (also known as the "target") is a key person. Without one, no litigation or prosecution is possible.

CHARACTERISTICS OF FRAUD EXAMINERS

Fraud examiners should have unique abilities. In addition to technical skills, successful examiners have the ability to elicit facts from numerous witnesses in a fair, impartial, lawful, and accurate manner. They can report the examination results accurately and completely. The ability to ascertain the facts and to report them accurately are of equal importance. Fraud examiners are part lawyer, part accountant, part criminologist, and part detective or investigator.

Allan Pinkerton, one of the first successful private investigators, stated the qualities a detective should possess:

> "The detective must possess certain qualifications of prudence, secrecy, inventiveness, persistency, personal courage, and above all other things, honesty; while he must add to these the same quality of reaching out and becoming possessed of that almost boundless information which will permit the immediate and effective application of his detective talent in whatever degree that may be possessed."

The ability to deal effectively with people is extremely important for fraud examiners. Examiners typically meet people for a short period of time and with a specific purpose--to obtain information. Ideally, examiners have the personality to attract and motivate people to be helpful.

Examiners' attitudes toward others affects their attitudes in return. A hostile attitude will create anxiety in others, thereby causing them to become withdrawn and protective, even if there is no reason to do so. Contrary to lore, successful investigators are rarely "tough," except when the need arises and toughness has been carefully planned and evaluated.

Buckwalter said, "The secret is for each private investigator to be the kind of person others will want to deal with." Examiners who mislead others will often themselves be misled. For each guilty person examiners encounter, they will deal with many innocent witnesses. Those innocent witnesses, and the examiners' ability to draw them out, are indispensable to fraud examination methodology. Because examiners deal with people from all walks of life, being able to establish rapport with strangers is vital.

Fraud examiners must have the technical ability to understand financial concepts and the ability to draw inferences from them. Examiners must be able to simplify financial concepts so that others comprehend them. Fraud cases often involve issues that appear complicated, but in reality most fraud is rather simple. The concealment methods make frauds appear complex.

A unique feature of fraud cases is that a suspect's identity is usually soon known, unlike traditional property crimes. In a bank robbery, for example, the question is not whether a crime was committed, but rather who committed the crime. In fraud cases, the issue usually is not the identity of the culprit, but whether the conduct constituted fraud.

EXAMINERS' BASIC SKILLS

Three essential skills are required of fraud examiners regardless of the nature of the examination.

Skills in examination of financial statements, books and records, and supporting documents are important in the beginning of an investigation. Fraud examiners must know the legal ramifications of evidence and how to maintain the chain of custody over documents. For example, checks and other financial records to prove the case must be lawfully obtained, analyzed, and used to draw conclusions. Knowledge of accounting systems and internal records and familiarity with numerous sources of individuals' public and nonpublic records are important.

Interviewing skills may be considered even more important than document examination skills. Interviewing is the process of obtaining relevant information about the case from people who may have direct or indirect knowledge. Interviews with co-workers, superiors, subordinates, and finally with the suspect are necessary. Prosecutions seldom proceed without direct testimony from the suspect.

The ability to conduct detective operations may be necessary in some cases. Fraud examiners may need to observe the suspect's behavior, search for displays of wealth, and in some instances, observe specific offenses. For example, examiners might recommend a video surveillance of a company's cashiers department to witness a defalcation being committed. Or, examiners might establish a visual surveillance in a public place to determine the patterns or activities of a suspect.

The fraud examination methodology gathers evidence from the general to the specific. Because of the legal ramifications of fraud examiners' actions, the rights of all individuals must be observed throughout.

THE FRAUD EXAMINATION TEAM

Fraud examiners do not operate as "Lone Rangers." Examinations usually require a cooperative effort among different disciplines. Typical investigation teams include personnel such as Certified Fraud Examiners trained to analyze a complex fraud case from inception to conclusion. Internal auditors often are used to review documentary evidence, evaluate tips or complaints, prepare estimates of losses, and provide assistance regarding technical areas of the company's operations. Security department investigators often conduct the "field work" stage of the investigation, interviewing outside witnesses, and obtaining public records and other documents from third parties.

Advice from a human resources specialist may also be sought, considering the protection of employee rights and the possibility of a wrongful discharge suit or other civil action by the employee. Normally this person will be an adviser and not participate directly in the investigation.

Attorneys may advise about the legal aspects of the examination. A representative of management, or in significant cases, the Board of Directors' audit committee, should be kept informed of the investigation's progress, and should be available to lend necessary assistance. A sensitive employee investigation has virtually no hope of success without strong management support.

In some cases, particularly when the suspect employee is powerful or popular, outside specialists are employed. They are relatively immune from company politics or threats of reprisals. Such experts may also have greater experience and investigative contacts than insiders.

DOCUMENT EXAMINATION

As a general rule, documents should be examined before interviews are conducted. An understanding of the potential evidentiary strength of the case must be obtained first, and the security of documents must be assured. The document examination is not limited to auditing. In the case of suspicious, altered, or forged documents, it may include forensics as well. If the fraud theory remains intact after analyzing the documents, the examiner proceeds to the next step--interviews of neutral third-party witnesses (discussed in next section on interviews).

Documents typically provide circumstantial--not direct--evidence. Circumstantial evidence means all proof other than direct admission of wrongdoing by the suspect or a co-conspirator. In a fraud case, documentary evidence is the proof of the suspect's representations, evidence of their falsity, and evidence of the suspect's intent to commit fraud. The circumstantial case may also include "similar act evidence" to show a common scheme or plan, lack of mistake or accident, modus operandi, and intent.

Circumstantial evidence may be the only evidence available. It must be complete with no gaps, consistent (tending to prove a single point), and must exclude all explanations other than guilt. Collecting this type of evidence can be very difficult. Many complex cases lose direction during the circumstantial stage when the examiner becomes overwhelmed by the mass of accumulated detail and documents. To avoid getting bogged down, examiners must: (1) keep in mind exactly what they are attempting to prove at all times, (2) break a complex case down to its essentials and make it as simple and clear as possible, and (3) keep the investigation focused on the fraud theory and not just gather information for the sake of gathering it.

THE VALUE OF DOCUMENTS

Documents can either help or hurt a case, depending on which ones are presented and how they are presented. The goal is to make certain that all relevant documents are included, and all irrelevant documents eliminated. Many examiners pay too much attention to documents. It is easy to get bogged down in detail when examining records and to lose sight of a simple fact: Documents do not make cases; witnesses make cases. The documents make or break the witness. So-called "paper cases" often confuse and bore a jury.

Basic procedures in handling evidence are required for acceptance by a court. Examiners must show that the evidence is relevant and material. Evidence must be properly identified, and examiners must show that the proper chain of custody was maintained. Here are a few general rules regarding the collection of documents:

- Obtain original documents where feasible. Make working copies for review, and keep the originals segregated.
- Do not touch originals any more than necessary. They may later undergo forensic fingerprint analysis.
- Maintain a good filing system for the documents. Filing is especially critical when large numbers of documents are obtained. Losing a key document is an unpardonable sin, and may damage the case. Documents can be stamped sequentially for easy reference.

CHAIN OF CUSTODY

From the moment evidence is received, its chain of custody must be maintained. A record must be made when the item is received or when it leaves the care, custody, or control of the fraud examiner. This is best handled by a memorandum of interview with the custodian of the records when the evidence is received. The memorandum should state:

- What items were received
- When they were received
- From whom they were received
- Where they are maintained

If a document item is later turned over to someone else, a record should be made--preferably in memorandum form. All evidence received should be uniquely marked so that it can be identified later. The preferable way is to initial and date the item. However, this can pose problems in the case of original business records furnished voluntarily. A small tick mark or other nondescript identifier can be used. If marking the original document is not practical, the document should be placed in a sealed envelope, which should then be initialed and dated.

A chronology of events should be commenced early in the case. The purpose is to establish the chain of events leading to the proof. The chronology may or may not be made a part of the formal report. Keep the chronology brief and include only information necessary to prove the case. The chronology should be revised as necessary, adding new information and deleting the irrelevant information.

OBTAINING DOCUMENTARY EVIDENCE

Documentary evidence is obtained by three methods. Subpoenas are ordinarily issued by a court or by a grand jury. A *subpoena duces tecum* calls for the production of documents and records, whereas a regular subpoena is used for witnesses. Obtaining documents by subpoena is not possible if the examiner is not an agent of the grand jury or the court. Subpoenas can call for the production of documents at a grand jury hearing or at a deposition at a specified time. A "forthwith subpoena" means that the records should be produced instantly. A forthwith subpoena is usually served by surprise and reserved for instances where the investigators think the records will be secreted, altered, or destroyed.

Search warrants are issued by a judge upon presentation of evidence of probable cause to believe the records are being used or have been used in the commission of a crime. An officer uses an affidavit to support the request for the search warrant. The affidavit must describe in detail the reason(s) the warrant is requested, along with the place the evidence is thought to be kept. Courts cannot issue search warrants without sufficient cause. The Fourth Amendment to the U.S. Constitution protects individuals against unreasonable searches and seizures. Search warrants are almost never used in civil cases. Although the law provides for warrantless searches, they should be avoided by fraud examiners at all costs.

The preferred method is to obtain documents by voluntary consent. The consent can be oral or written. In the cases of information obtained from possible adverse witnesses or the target of the examination, the consent should be in writing.

EXAMINING FRAUDULENT DOCUMENTS

Suspicious, forged, and altered documents are frequently found in fraud cases. Forensic document examination is the application of science to the resolution of fraud issues. Modern forensic science has definite limitations. Fraud examiners are not expected to be forensic document experts. However, they should have knowledge beyond that of a lay person. When a fraud examiner has reason to suspect the authenticity of documents or signatures, the services of a forensic document examiner should be obtained.

Forensic document examiners can be contacted through either of the following organizations:

> Forensic Document Examiners
> American Academy of Forensic Sciences
> P.O. Box 669
> Colorado Springs, CO 80901-0669
> (719) 836-1100
>
> American Board of Forensic Document Examiners
> 7887 San Felipe, Suite 122
> Houston, TX 77063
> (713) 784-9537

Because the physical evidence involving questioned documents is generally derived from the documents themselves, careful handling of such documents is imperative. When investigating document authenticity, consider the following circumstances:

- A signature that appears to be unnatural
- Paper that does not seem to be of the type customarily used for such documents
- Apparent differences in the types of ink used for its documents
- Use of more than one style of typewriting
- A questionable date of preparation

Documents contain a wide variety of identifiable characteristics that can be used to corroborate other evidence and associate a suspect with the fraud. Likewise, they can be used by a laboratory to clear a suspect of an offense.

INTERVIEWS

An interview is a question-and-answer session designed to elicit information. It differs from an ordinary conversation in that interviews are structured, not free-form. They are designed for a purpose. An interview may consist of only one question or a series of questions.

PREPARATION

Before embarking on an interview, an examiner should review the case file to learn the information probably known to the witness. The case hypothesis should be reviewed to make sure it reflects the information known to the interviewer from the document examination and other sources. Be prepared.

The examiner should consider the type of information that might be supplied by each of the potential witnesses. Generally, the most vulnerable witness should be interviewed after the more reluctant witnesses. This will provide the examiner a broader base of information that can be used to formulate later questions. However, the timing of interviews is at the discretion of the examination team.

INTERVIEW ORDER STRATEGY

Fraud examiners should not ordinarily interview the suspect first. Usually, interviews with other persons should be conducted with a view to gathering circumstantial or direct evidence that can make the interview with the suspect more effective.

Neutral Third-Party Witnesses
A neutral third-party witness is a person not involved in a specific instance of fraud. For example, if the fraud examination involves targeting a purchasing agent suspected of bid-rigging or kickback-taking, the first interview could be

with the company personnel officer (carefully gathering information about the suspect's personnel file). Though not strictly a neutral party, the tipster could be interviewed. If the case involves check-cashing, a bank teller could be interviewed.

Corroborative Witnesses

Corroborative witnesses are people who can corroborate facts relating to a specific offense. These witnesses may be cooperative or uncooperative, but they are not directly related to the offense involved. A suspect's coworkers or subordinates can be corroborative witnesses.

Co-Conspirators

If further work appears to be warranted after examining documents, neutral third-party witnesses, and corroborative witnesses, a fraud examiner typically interviews potential co-conspirators. In a case of suspected purchase kickbacks from a vendor, that vendor typically would be interviewed prior to contacting the suspect for an interview. Persons suspected of complicity are generally interviewed in the order of those thought to be least culpable to those thought to be most culpable.

In criminal cases, law enforcement officers and prosecutors can sometimes promise leniency to co-conspirators in return for their cooperation. These individuals are called "inside witnesses." They might confirm facts of improper payments and serve as witnesses for the prosecution. However, promises of leniency made by private sector fraud examiners are not permitted. Such promises might legally invalidate any admissions made by co-conspirators.

The Suspect

In general, the suspect (the "accused", the "target", the "subject") is interviewed last, after all the facts believed to implicate the person are in hand. The goal is to obtain a legal, admissible, and binding confession of guilt. This type of interview is an "admission-seeking interview" (in police parlance, an "interrogation"). In the event such an admission is not obtained, a fraud examiner's goal then is to identify the type of defenses the suspect might raise at trial or other formal proceedings.

An important part of the admission-seeking interview is to pose questions designed to elicit responses that can show the suspect's intent to defraud. The element of intent is crucial to proving a fraud allegation. Intent is rarely self-evident. However, it can be demonstrated by showing a pattern of activity. Some of the more common ways to show intent include proof that the suspect:

- Had no legitimate motive for the activities
- Repeatedly engaged in the same or similar activities
- Attempted to conceal the activities
- Made conflicting statements
- Acted to impede the investigation of the offense
- Knowingly made false statements
- Made admissions

CHARACTERISTICS OF A GOOD INTERVIEW

An interview should be of sufficient length and depth to uncover relevant facts. Most interviewers tend to get too little information rather than too much.

A good interview includes all pertinent questions and excludes irrelevant questions. At the outset, a fraud examiner should determine what information is relevant and seek that information. Extraneous or useless facts tends to complicate the analysis of the information.

Interviews should be conducted as closely as possible to the event in question. With the passage of time, memories of potential witnesses become faulty. Critical details can be lost or forgotten.

Interviews should progress smoothly without undue hesitation on the part of the interviewer. One hazard in interviews is the problem of recording the proceedings. Interviewees are usually inhibited by a tape recorder (even by the request to agree to use one), so some form of note-taking usually must take place. Interviewers should be careful not to let note-taking interfere with the flow of the interview. Do not try to write down all the information spoken during an interview, only the pertinent facts. Taking too many notes will make the interview process cumbersome and may inhibit the respondent. If a quote is particularly relevant, try to write it down verbatim. Enclose all direct quotes in quotation marks. Otherwise, just jot down key words or phrases, then go back over the details at the end of the interview. In general, interviewers should err on the side of taking too few notes rather than too many. Expand the interview notes immediately after the interview ends.

Avoid making notes regarding overall opinions or impressions of a witness. Such notes can cause problems with an interviewer's credibility if they are later produced in court. Be careful not to show excitement when note-taking. During interviews of targets and adverse witnesses, take notes in a manner that does not indicate the significance of the information. Never allow note-taking to "telegraph" emotions.

CHARACTERISTICS OF A GOOD INTERVIEWER

Good interviewers are "people persons." They have talents for human interaction. Successful interviewers are the type of people with whom others are willing to share information. Good interviewers do not interrupt the respondent with unnecessary questions. During the interview, much pertinent information results from volunteered information, as opposed to responses to specific questions. A good interviewer displays interest in the subject and in what is being said.

The respondent must be made to understand that the interviewer is attempting to obtain only the relevant facts and is not "out to get" someone. This can best be done by phrasing questions in a non-accusatory manner. Little is accomplished when the interviewer is formal, ostentatious, or attempts to impress the respondent with authority. Information gathering is best accomplished by approaching the interview in an informal and low-key fashion.

One of the most common errors made by novice interviewers is to yield to the temptation to impress the respondent with their knowledge of the subject of the interview. In doing so, interviewers run the risk of making the respondent feel threatened. Then, respondents tend to guard themselves and their responses rather than express their feelings frankly. Experienced interviewers will have the discipline to control their own responses.

If the respondent perceives that the interviewer is biased, or is attempting to confirm foregone conclusions, the respondent will be less likely to cooperate. Accordingly, the interviewer should make every effort to demonstrate a lack of bias.

Professionalism in the interview often involves a state of mind and a commitment to excellence. The interviewer should be on time, be professionally dressed (consistent with local custom), and be fair in all dealings with the respondent. The interviewer must not appear to be a threat. If persons perceive they are the target of an inquiry, they will be less likely to cooperate. However, at some critical stage, when admission of guilt is sought, the tenor of the interview will change.

QUESTION TYPOLOGY

The interviewer can ask five general types of questions--introductory, informational, assessment, closing, and admission-seeking. In routine interview situations, where the object is to gather information from neutral or corroborative witnesses, only three of the five types will normally be asked (introductory, informational, and closing questions). If the interviewer has reasonable cause to believe the respondent is not being truthful, assessment questions can be asked. Finally, if the interviewer has reason to believe the respondent is responsible for misdeeds, admission-seeking questions can be posed.

Introductory Questions
Getting started can be difficult. The interviewer must meet and greet the person, state a reason for the interview, establish necessary rapport and cooperation, then get the information. Introductory questions are used for two primary purposes: (1) to provide an introduction, and (2) to get the respondent to verbally agree to cooperate in the interview. This is done in a step-by-step procedure in which the interviewer briefly states the purpose for the contact, then poses a question designed to get the respondent to agree to talk further.

<u>Examples: Introductory Questions</u>

Wrong:
Interviewer: "Ms. Jones, I am Loren Bridges, a Certified Fraud Examiner with Bailey Books' fraud examination unit. I am investigating a case of suspected fraud, and you may know something about it. How long have you worked here at the company?"
Right:
Interviewer: "Ms. Jones, I am Loren Bridges. I work here at the company. Do you have a few minutes I can spend with you?"

Informational Questions
Once the proper format for the interview is set, an interviewer then turns to the fact-gathering portion. Three types of questions can be asked: open, closed, and leading. Each type is used in a logical sequence to maximize the development of information. If the interviewer has reason to believe the

respondent is being untruthful, followup assessment questions can be posed. Otherwise, the interview is ended with some closing questions.

Open Questions. Open questions are worded in a way to make it difficult to answer "yes" or "no." Also, the answer does not actually depend on the question. The typical open question calls for a monologue response, and it can be answered in several different ways. During the information phase of the interview, the interviewer should try to ask only open questions. This stimulates conversation. Some of the best open questions are subtle commands.

<u>Examples: Open Questions</u>

Interviewer: "Please tell me about your job."
      "Please tell me about the operation of your
      department."
      "Please describe the procedures to me."

Closed Questions. Closed questions require a precise answer--usually "yes" or "no." Closed questions also deal with specifics, such as amounts, dates, and times. As far as possible, closed questions should be avoided in the informational part of the interview. They are used extensively as closing questions.

<u>Examples: Closed Questions</u>

Interviewer: "Do you work here?"
      "What day of the week did it happen?"

Leading Questions. Leading questions contain the answer as a part of the question. They are used to confirm facts already known. Although leading questions are usually discouraged in court proceedings, they can be used effectively in interview situations.

Examples: Leading Questions

Interviewer: "So there have been no changes in the operation since last year?"
            "Are you still employed by the Bailey Book Corporation?"
            "You got promoted, right?"

Some Warnings. Double-negative questions are confusing and often suggest an answer opposite to the correct one. They should not be used. Avoid asking: "Didn't you suspect that something wasn't right?"

Complex questions may not be understood, cover more than one subject or topic, require more than one answer, or require a complicated answer. Avoid asking: "What are your duties here, and how long have you been employed, and do you like your job?"

As a general rule, questioning should proceed from the general to the specific. Seek general information before seeking details. A variation is to "reach backward" with the questions, by beginning with known information and working toward unknown areas. An efficient method of doing this is to recount the known information and then frame the next question as a logical continuation of the facts previously related. For example: "Earlier you said you were on duty that night; What did you see?"

In accounting and fraud-related matters, figures and numbers are often critical. Unfortunately, some witnesses are unable to recall specific amounts. The interviewer can jog the memory of the respondent by comparing unknown items with items of known quantity. Avoid asking: "Was the amount on the tax return $32,483.21?" Instead ask: "Was the amount on the tax return more than last year's figure?"

Questions that control the answer can be used to stimulate a desired answer or impression. For example, a person may admit knowledge of a matter by answering this question: "I understand you were present when the internal controls were developed, so would you please describe how they were constructed?" This phrasing provides a stronger incentive for the respondent to admit knowledge than does: "Were you present when the internal controls were developed?"

Questions that discourage cooperation must be avoided. Do not ask: "I don't guess you would mind answering a few questions?" Instead, try: "Because you are not involved in this matter, I am sure you would not mind discussing it with me?" This provides an incentive to cooperate.

Closing Questions

In routine interviews, certain questions are asked at closing for the purposes of reconfirming the facts, obtaining previously undiscovered information, seeking new evidence, and maintaining goodwill.

Informational interviews should be closed on a positive note. The closing serves several purposes. It is an opportunity for the interviewer to make sure of understanding the interviewee's responses. The interviewer should use short questions to go over key facts and make certain they have been comprehended.

The closing questions phase also seeks to obtain facts previously unknown. It provides the respondent further opportunity to say anything else about the matter at hand. If appropriate, the interviewer can ask whether the respondent knows other documents or witnesses that would be helpful to the case.

The interview can be closed, leaving an opening for another interview in the future. Ask: "May I call with any additional questions? Leave the respondent a business card or a telephone number. Invite the respondent to call about anything else relevant.

Private-sector interviewers should not promise confidentiality at the close. It is a promise difficult to keep. Instead, promise: "I'll keep your name as quiet as possible."

Examples: Closing Questions

Interviewer: "Ms. Jones, I want to make sure I have my information straight. Let me take a minute and summarize what we've discussed."

"You have known Linda (suspect) eight years, correct?"

"You knew Linda had some financial problems, is that right?"

"Ms. Jones, are you sure you suspected Linda falsified invoices?"

"If you were in my shoes, what would you do next?"

"Ms. Jones, this is just a standard question. Do you feel that I have treated you fairly in this interview?"

"Ms. Jones, I know you have given your time and effort to help me. I appreciate it. Good-bye.

Assessment Questions

Assessment questions seek to establish the credibility of the respondent. They are used only when the interviewer considers previous statements by the respondent to be inconsistent because of possible deception. A theme must be established to justify additional questions. This theme can ordinarily be put forth by saying, "I have a few additional questions." Do not indicate in any way that these questions are for a purpose other than seeking information. Assessment questions are generally hypothetical and non-accusatory. By observing the verbal and non-verbal responses to these questions, the interviewer can assess the respondent's credibility to some degree. This assessment will form the basis for an interviewer's decision about whether to pose admission-seeking questions to obtain a legal admission of wrongdoing.

Most assessment questions ask for agreement to matters that are against the principles of most honest people. Dishonest people are likely to agree with many of the statements, while honest people will not agree. Assessment questions are designed primarily to get a verbal or non-verbal reaction from the respondent. The interviewer will then carefully assess the respondent's reaction. Unfortunately, people demonstrate a variety of reactions to assessment-type questions. Hence, some norming (calibrating) is required.

Norming (calibrating) is the process of observing behavior before critical questions are asked, as opposed to doing so during questioning. Norming should be a routine part of all interviews. Persons with truthful attitudes will answer questions one way. Persons with untruthful attitudes will generally answer them differently. Suggestions for observing the verbal and physical behavior of the respondent include paying attention to all the verbal and non-verbal responses.

Speech Patterns. Deceptive persons often speed up, slow down, or speak louder. They may change their voice pitch. Tension tends to constrict the vocal chords. Deceptive persons also have a tendency to cough or clear their throats during times of deception.

Repetition. Liars will frequently repeat the interviewer's question to gain more time to think of what to say. The deceptive individual will say, "What was that again?" or use similar language.

Complaints. Deceptive persons will often complain about the physical environment of the interview room, such as, "It's cold in here." They will also sometimes ask how much longer the interview will take.

Selective Memory. In some cases, deceptive people have a fine memory for insignificant events, but when it comes to the important facts, "just can't seem to remember."

Excuses. Dishonest persons will frequently make excuses about things that look bad for them, such as, "I'm always nervous; don't pay any attention to that."

Oaths. Dishonest persons frequently will add comments they believe to add credibility to their lies by use of emphasis. Expressions such as "I swear to God," or "Honestly," or "Frankly," or "To tell the truth," are frequently used.

Character Testimony. A liar often will request that the interviewer, "Check with my wife," or "Talk to my minister." This is frequently done to add credibility to the false statement.

Answering with a Question. Rather than deny allegations outright, the liar may frequently answer with a question such as, "Why would I do something like that?" As a variation, the deceptive person will sometimes question the interview procedure by asking, "Why are you picking on me?"

Overuse of Respect. Some deceptive persons will go out of their way to be respectful and friendly. When accused of wrongdoing, it is unnatural for a person to react in a friendly and respectful manner.

Increasing Weaker Denials. An honest person will become angry or forceful in making denial when accused of something he or she did not do. The more the person is accused, the more forceful the denial becomes. The dishonest person, on the other hand, is likely to make a weak denial. Upon repeated accusations, the dishonest person's denials become weaker, to the point of becoming silent.

Qualified Denial. Dishonest persons are more likely than honest persons to deny an event specifically. An honest person may offer a simple and clear "no" while the dishonest person will qualify the denial: "No, I did not steal $43,500 from the Company on June 27." Other qualified denial phrases include, "To the best of my memory," and "As far as I recall," or similar language.

Avoidance of Emotive Words. A liar will often avoid emotionally provocative terms such as "steal," "lie," and "crime." Instead, the dishonest person frequently prefers "soft" words such as "borrow," and "it" (referring to the deed in question).

Refusal to Implicate Other Suspects. Both the honest respondent and the liar will have a natural reluctance to name others involved in misdeeds.

However, the liar will frequently refuse to implicate possible suspects, no matter how much pressure is applied by the interviewer. This is because the culpable person does not want the circle of suspicion to be narrowed.

Tolerant Attitudes. Dishonest persons typically have tolerant attitudes towards unethical and illegal conduct. The interviewer in an internal theft case may ask: "What should happen to this person when he is caught?" The honest person usually will say: "They should be fired/prosecuted." The dishonest individual, on the other hand, is much more likely to reply: "How should I know?" or, "Maybe she is a good employee who got into problems. Perhaps she should be given a second chance."

Reluctance to Terminate Interview. Dishonest persons generally will be more reluctant than honest ones to terminate the interview. The dishonest individual wants to convince the interviewer that he or she is not responsible, so the investigation can end. The honest person, on the other hand, generally has no such reluctance.

Feigned Unconcern. Dishonest persons will often try to appear casual and unconcerned and will frequently adopt an unnatural slouching posture. They may react to questions with nervous or false laughter or feeble attempts at humor. Honest persons, on the other hand, will typically be very concerned about being suspected of wrongdoing and will treat the interviewer's questions seriously.

Full Body Motions. When asked sensitive or emotive questions, dishonest persons will typically change posture completely--as if moving away from the interviewer. Honest persons will frequently lean forward toward the interviewer when questions are serious.

Hands Over the Mouth. Frequently, dishonest persons will cover their mouths with the hand or fingers during deception. This reaction goes back to childhood, when many children cover their mouths when telling a lie. Covering is done subconsciously to conceal the statement.

Manipulators. Manipulators are motions such as picking lint from clothing, playing with objects such as pencils, or holding one's hands while talking. Manipulators are displacement activities intended to reduce nervousness.

Fleeing Positions. During the interview, dishonest persons will often posture themselves in a "fleeing position." While the head and trunk may be facing the interviewer, the feet and lower portion of the body may be pointing toward the door in an unconscious effort to flee from the interviewer.

Crossing the Arms. Crossing one's arms over the middle zones of the body is a classic defensive reaction to difficult or uncomfortable questions. When the arms or hands are crossing the body, it is a defensive gesture, to protect the "soft underbelly." A variation is crossing the feet under the chair and locking them. These crossing motions occur mostly when being deceptive.

Reaction to Evidence. While trying to be outwardly concerned, a guilty person will have a keen interest in implicating evidence. A dishonest person will often look at documents presented by the interviewer, attempt to be casual about observing them, and then shove them away, as though wanting nothing to do with the evidence.

Smiles. Genuine smiles usually involve the whole mouth. False ones are confined to the upper half. Persons involved in deception tend to smirk rather than to smile.

Criminologists say that everyone will lie (at least occasionally) for one of two reasons: to receive rewards, or to avoid punishment. For most people, lying produces stress. The human body will attempt to relieve this stress (even in practiced liars) through verbal and nonverbal clues. However, conclusions concerning behavior must be tempered by a number of factors.

The physical environment in which the interview is conducted can affect behavior. If the respondent is comfortable, fewer behavior quirks may be exhibited.

The more intelligent the respondent, the more reliable verbal and nonverbal clues will be. If the respondent is biased toward the interviewer, or vice versa, behavior will be affected.

Persons who are mentally unstable or under the influence of drugs are unsuitable to interview.

Behavior symptoms of juveniles are generally unreliable.

Racial, ethnic, and economic factors should be carefully noted. Some cultures, for example, discourage looking directly at someone. Other cultures use certain body language that may be misinterpreted.

Professional pathological liars are often familiar with interview techniques. They are less likely to furnish observable behavioral clues.

<u>Examples: Assessment Questions</u>

Interviewer: "Most people who take things aren't criminals at all. A lot of times, they're just trying to save their jobs or just trying to get by because the company is so cheap that they won't pay people what they are worth. Do you know what I mean?"

Explanation: Although the honest person and the dishonest person will both probably answer "yes" to this question, the honest individual is less likely to accept the premise that these people are not wrongdoers. Many honest persons might reply, "Yes, I understand, but that doesn't justify stealing."

Interviewer: "Why do you think someone around here might be justified in taking company property?"

Explanation: Because fraud perpetrators frequently justify their acts, the dishonest individual is more likely than the honest person to attempt a justification, such as, "Everyone does it," or "The company should treat people better if they don't want them to steal." The honest person, on the other hand, is much more likely to say, "There is no justification for stealing from the company. It is dishonest."

* * * * *

Interviewer: "How do you think we should deal with someone who got in a bind and did something wrong in the eyes of the company?"

Explanation: Similar to other questions in this series, the honest person wants to "throw the book" at the miscreant; the culpable individual will typically say, "How should I know? It's not up to me," or, "If they were a good employee, maybe we should give them another chance."

On the basis of the respondent's reaction to the assessment questions, the interviewer then considers all the verbal and non-verbal responses together (not in isolation) to decide whether to proceed to the admission-seeking phase of the interview.

Admission-Seeking Questions

An interviewer should ask accusatory or admission-seeking questions only when there is a reasonable probability the respondent has committed the fraud under investigation. An assessment of culpability may be based on verbal and non-verbal responses to interview questions, as well as documents, physical evidence, and other interviews. The admission-seeking phase of an interview is used to (1) clear an innocent person, and (2) encourage a guilty person to confess. Admission-seeking questions must not violate the rights and privileges of the person being interviewed.

A transitional theme is necessary when proceeding from assessment-seeking questions to admission-seeking questions. Part of the purpose of this theme is to create in the mind of the miscreant that he or she has been caught. Under ideal circumstances, an interviewer will leave the room for just a few minutes, claiming to "check on something." If incriminating documents are available, copies can be placed inside a file folder and brought back to the interview. If no documents exist, the interviewer can fill a file folder with blank paper.

When the interviewer returns to the room, the file folder is placed on the desk, and the interviewer asks, "Is there something that you would like to tell me about_____?" Hand the documents to the respondent and ask for "comments." Do not introduce the evidence or explain it. In about 20 percent of the cases, the miscreant will admit to incriminating conduct. If not, proceed. Once the interviewer is reasonably convinced of guilt, the respondent can be confronted with an accusation.

Successful admission-seeking questions can produce a valid confession. Under the law, confessions must be voluntarily obtained. The importance of a valid and binding confession to wrongdoing cannot be overstated. An interviewer wants to obtain a signed, written statement acknowledging the facts. Although oral confessions are legally as binding as written ones, the written statement has greater credibility. It also discourages miscreants from later attempting to recant.

Arranging an Admission-Seeking Interview. Interviewers should control the situation. Hold the interview away from the accused's turf. If possible, make it a surprise. The location should be private. The door should be closed, but not locked. No physical barriers should prevent the target from leaving. Minimize distractions: no photographs on walls, no windows, or other objects in the room. The accused should not be permitted to sit (hide) behind a desk. Notes should be taken in a way that does not reveal their significance. (Ideally, a second interviewer can be present for the sole purpose of taking notes.)

Do not suggest a right to an attorney in a private interview. Of course, this right cannot be denied. However, if a target's attorney is present, the interview can be conducted only if the attorney will only observe, not ask questions or object. Other than the target and two examiners, no other observers should usually be permitted. If the target is in a union, a representative may have the right to attend. However, this may present legal problems in "broadcasting" the allegation to a third party. It is very difficult to obtain a confession with witnesses present. The examiner should therefore consider whether the case can be proved without the admission-seeking interview.

Miranda warnings are not required in a private interview. Police are required to use them only if an arrest is imminent following the interview. Confessions are admissible in court if they were (1) obtained voluntarily, and (2) the interviewer has a reasonable belief that the confession is true.

Getting To the Point. People rarely confess voluntarily. Guilty persons will confess to matters when they perceive that the benefits of confession outweigh the penalties. A good interviewer will be able to convince the respondent that confession is the best way to end the matter.

Persons generally will not confess if they believe an interviewer has some doubts about guilt. Interviewers must convey absolute confidence in the admission-seeking--even if not fully convinced. Interviewers must make the accusation in the form of a statement of fact. Accusatory questions do not ask: "Did you do it?" They ask: "Why did you do it?"

Emotive words such as "steal," "fraud," and "crime" should be avoided when making accusations. These words invite resistance. The accusation should be phrased so that the accused is psychologically "trapped," with no way out. The examples presented later are notable for not using these emotive words.

An innocent person generally will not accept the question's premise. Guilty persons, on the verge of confessing, need adequate time to come to terms with their guilt. Obtaining admissions and confessions takes patience. Therefore, admission-seeking interviews should be conducted under conditions of sufficient privacy when time is not a factor. Interviewers must not express disgust, outrage, or moral condemnation about the confessor's actions. To do so goes against the basic logic of obtaining confessions, which can be summarized as "maximize sympathy and minimize the perception of moral wrongdoing."

Interviewers must offer an acceptable reason for the confessor's behavior. The interviewer should not convey to the accused that he or she is a "bad person." Guilty persons will almost never confess under such conditions. To obtain a confession, interviewers must be firm, but must project compassion, understanding, and sympathy to obtain a confession. Interviewers must attempt to keep the confessor from voicing a denial. Denials should be interrupted before they become fixed in the target's testimony. Once the accused denies the act, overcoming that position will be very difficult.

It is generally legal to accuse innocent persons of misdeeds they did not commit as long as:

- The accuser has reasonable suspicion or predication to believe the accused has committed an offense.
- The accusation is made under conditions of privacy.
- The accuser does not take any action likely to make an innocent person confess.
- The accusation is presented under reasonable interview conditions.

Examples: Admission-Seeking Questions

Wrong:

Interviewer: "We have reason to believe that you...."

Right:

Interviewer: "Our investigation has clearly established that you made a false entry, took company assets without permission, took money from a vendor, and have not told the complete truth."

Right:

Interviewer: "As I said, Linda, our examination has concluded that you are the responsible person. It is not so much a question of what you did, but why you did it."

Wrong:

Interviewer: "Did you do this?"

Right:

Interviewer: "Why did you do this?"

Right:

Interviewer: "Linda, I have talked to many people before I sat down here with you. I am not asking you if you're responsible. I know you are. This is your opportunity to tell your side to someone who can understand."

Right:

Interviewer: "Linda, I feel like I know what makes you tick. And I know it isn't like you to do something like this without a reason. You have worked hard here to get a good reputation. I don't think the company has paid you what you're really worth. And that's the way you feel too, isn't it?"

Right:

Interviewer: "Linda, I know this is totally out of character for you. I know that this would never have happened if something wasn't going on in your life. Isn't that right, Linda?"

Once the confession is started, an interviewer should reinforce the confessor's decision by encouraging further incriminating statements. These include confession of the details of the scheme in the confessor's own words--details that may be known only by the confessor. An interviewer should work to let the confessor state knowledge that the act was wrong. Such a statement shows the element of intent that is crucial for a fraud charge. Other details can be obtained--the date the offense started and ended, the location of bank accounts or money still on hand, the disposition of the ill-gotten gains. The confession can also include written permission to obtain the confessor's bank records for examination. These types of information bring the admission-seeking interview to a close.

EMPLOYEES' RIGHTS DURING EXAMINATIONS

Fraud examiners must be careful not to violate persons' civil rights when obtaining and examining documents or when conducting interviews. Private examiners are not bound by all the rules applicable to law enforcement officers, but rules of civility still apply.

SEARCHES FOR DOCUMENTS

The Fourth Amendment to the U.S. Constitution protects people against unreasonable searches and seizures of property and papers. However, the letter of these rights is strictly applicable only in cases of government (e.g., police) action, in which case proper search warrants must be obtained from a judge. Searches conducted by private employers entirely on their own are not subject to the Fourth Amendment considerations. Nevertheless, searches conducted by employers at the suggestion of the state or federal authorities might be covered by the Fourth Amendment. Documents obtained in private searches and later turned over to state or federal authorities might be subject to the amendment. Fraud examiners must be very careful about being reasonable in searches for documents and probably should obtain an employee's permission to open desks, files, lockers, and similar personal areas.

Evidence seized illegally will be excluded in criminal proceedings. Such evidence may be used in civil proceedings, but it may be hotly contested by defense lawyers. The methods used to obtain evidence may give rise to counter-claims by an accused employee.

Non-discrimination statutes such as the federal Civil Rights Acts of 1866 and 1871, Title VII of the Civil Rights Act of 1964, and the Age Discrimination in Employment Act of 1970, as well as similar state statutes, protect employees from being singled out for searches on the basis of such characteristics as race, national origin, sex, religion, and age. These laws also protect employees against disparate discipline assessed as a result of a search.

A common law protection of privacy is recognized in most states. When employees expect privacy, a search without cause may give rise to a claim of invasion of privacy. Public (i.e., government) and private employers should use a "search policy" clause in employee contracts and handbooks to diminish or eliminate employees' expectation of strict privacy of work-related property and papers. Employers can retain keys to all desks, lockers, and similar places; require employees to provide keys to all personal locks; obtain consent to a search; and make consent to searches a condition of employment. The danger of not following an established "search policy" is that it may create an expectation of privacy where none is intended.

DISCLOSURE AND DEFAMATION

Another form of invasion of privacy involves public disclosure of private information, for example, an employer giving unreasonable publicity to true, but private, information about an employee. The balancing test weighs the employer's need to communicate the information (e.g., to internal auditors, fraud examiners, district attorney) against the intrusion into the employee's privacy.

Employers cannot engage in "outrageous conduct" intended to inflict emotional distress on a suspected or guilty employee. An aggrieved employee can sue, and courts can award civil damages both for pain and suffering and punishment.

Employers cannot engage in defamation of an employee's character. Four elements constitute defamation: (1) false statement of fact, (2) subject the person to ill will or disrepute, (3) published to one or more persons, and (4) made without privilege. Even a request to an employee to allow a search may border on defamation, depending on the manner and surroundings in which it is made. The greatest risk is voicing suspicion suggesting that the employee is engaged in wrongdoing where bystanders can hear.

Several states recognize a duty on the part of employers to deal with their employees fairly and in good faith. This duty may include abiding by all company policies and provisions in an employee handbook, including those relating to searches (e.g., how and when they may be conducted) and to expectations of privacy on the part of employees.

Many states now recognize an implied contract between employers and employees arising out of employee handbooks. An employer with an employee handbook containing provisions relating to searches and employee expectations of privacy may find itself contractually bound by those provisions and in breach of contract if the provisions are not followed to the letter.

FALSE IMPRISONMENT

False imprisonment is restraint by one person of the physical liberty of another without consent or legal justification. A claim of false imprisonment may be made if an employee is detained in any way during a search of the employee or of the employee's desk, locker, or other personal area. Generally, an employer is entitled to question an employee at work about a violation of company policy without incurring liability as long as the employee submits to the questioning voluntarily; that is, not as a result of threats or force. However, the length, nature, and manner of the interview will determine whether liability arises.

False imprisonment factors include: (1) size and nature of the room where an interview or search takes place (small, windowless, not easily accessible are negative), (2) lighting in the room--soft versus severe, (3) requiring the employee's presence or continued presence by any amount of force, including holding the employee's arm to escort from place to place, (4) violent behavior of any kind, including yelling, pounding on desk, kicking furniture or walls, (5) refusing to allow the employee to leave the room, such as by pushing the employee into a chair, locking the door, and (6) the number of people involved in the interview or search.

INTERVIEWS

In most cases, legal authority is not required to interview persons or to inquire into matters of suspected fraud. The U.S. Constitution permits any citizen the authority to inquire into virtually any subject area, as long as the rights of individuals are not transgressed in the process. Generally, no license is required to conduct interviews. However, some states require a license that permits an interviewer to represent himself or herself as an investigator.

Contrary to popular perception, deception sometimes can be legally employed to obtain information. The theory is that information can be obtained by nearly any means, with the exception of force or threats. However, the interviewer may not employ any deception likely to cause the innocent person to confess. The use of deception is not justified regarding promises of leniency, promises of confidentiality, or promises to obtain a monetary or business advantage.

The United State Supreme Court in Cupp vs. Frazier (394 U.S. 731) ruled that deception was not unlawful in this particular case. The police untruthfully told Subject A that Subject B had confessed to a crime and implicated Subject A. The court ruled that the deception alone was insufficient to invalidate the interview process.

The Fifth Amendment to the U.S. Constitution protects people from double jeopardy, from being a self-incriminating witness for a criminal offense, and from proceedings that lack due process of law. In the fraud examination context, the primary significance of the Fifth Amendment is protection against self-incrimination, which permits people to refuse to answer questions during an investigation. While this right is not strictly applicable to an private examiner's interview with an employee, nothing in criminal or civil law requires an employee to cooperate. However, public (i.e., government) employers cannot make employees choose between their Fifth Amendment rights and their jobs.

The Sixth Amendment to the U.S. Constitution (right to counsel, right to confront witnesses) is generally not applicable to private employers because standard practice calls for an employer to permit an employee to choose between having an attorney present or discontinuing an interview. The employee who insists on an attorney, thus cancelling an interview, cannot present his or her side of the story, and the employer can draw an inference of guilt from the employee's silence. The employer may be able to discipline the employee for refusing to cooperate in the investigation. However, government employees may have more protective rights under civil service rules.

VARIOUS FEDERAL STATUTES

The National Labor Relations Act prohibits any form of interrogation by employers that interferes with the rights of the employee to organize, bargain, or otherwise engage in concerted activities for the purpose of bargaining or other mutual aid or protection. An employer may not question an employee about any of these protected activities.

An employee represented by a union has the right to union representation during questioning by an employer only if the employee requests such representation; the employee reasonably believes that the investigation will result in disciplinary action; and the union representative acts as an observer and advises the employee of any rights under the bargaining agreement.

The Civil Rights Acts of 1866 and 1871, Title VII of the Civil Rights Act of 1964, and the Age Discrimination in Employment Act of 1970 prohibit singling out employees for investigation based on their race, national origin, religion, sex, or age.

The Fair Labor Standards Act requires an employer to pay an employee for time spent in an investigation.

The Employee Polygraph Protection Act prohibits the use of polygraphs by most private employers unless the employer is engaged in an ongoing investigation involving economic loss or injury to the employer with a reasonable suspicion that the employee is involved in the incident. Private employers may not use polygraphs to screen applicants for employment. Employers may not discharge an employee for refusing to take an exam. This act does not protect government employees. Other federal statutes do not address the use of polygraphs directly, but nonetheless may give rise to liability if a polygraph test is administered in a discriminatory fashion (e.g., based on race, sex, or some other prohibited factor), or used to ferret out union sympathies in connection with a union organizing campaign.

Several states have enacted laws addressing the use of polygraph examinations and some are more restrictive than the federal statute. Courts have recognized claims arising from unlawful administration of polygraph exams and wrongful discharge for refusal to take an exam after having been accused of fraud.   In common law, most courts have found that the circumstances surrounding polygraph exams do not in and of themselves rise to the level of outrageous conduct. In some states, courts have defined polygraph tests as invasions of privacy. Questions directly related to job performance or the incident under investigation are generally held not to be invasions of privacy.

LAWFUL SURVEILLANCE

Whether a particular form of surveillance is governed by the Fourth Amendment depends on the justified expectation of privacy and the reasonableness of the intrusion (assuming government action is involved). Wiretapping, eavesdropping, and surveillance by government agents at a non-public social gathering may violate the Constitution because the individual has a legitimate expectation of privacy.

The following do not constitute violations of most surveillance restrictions:

- Sensor tags placed on merchandise that alert store personnel to the removal of merchandise from the store without payment
- Pen registers for telephone numbers
- Examinations of the outside of items placed in the United States mail
- Cameras
- Supervisory surveillance, including from hidden catwalks and similar locations, particularly where employees are advised that such surveillance will occur
- Computer monitoring
- Surveillance of movements in public

The federal wiretapping statute allows interception of wire communications by:

- The operator of a switchboard or a common carrier as necessary for the rendition of service or for the protection of the carrier's rights or property
- An employee or agent of the Federal Communication Commission in the normal course of employment and in the discharge of statutory duties
- A party to a communication or a person to whom a party has given prior consent to the interception
- A person acting under the Foreign Intelligence Surveillance Act of 1978
- Law enforcement officials with a warrant
- A person using an extension telephone (with limitations)

The wiretapping statute also allows employers to monitor calls of their employees as part of a training program or an evaluation of service as long as employees are informed of this practice and only business calls are monitored. Monitoring personal calls is allowed only for so long as is needed to determine that the call is not a business call. Oral communications are judged as to the expectation of privacy under the specific circumstances.

The Electronic Communications Privacy Act of 1986 prohibits installation of pen registers (electronic devices that record numbers called) without court order, except in the following circumstances:

- Employers may use registers to monitor the use of their telephones. "Pen register" does not include "any device used by a ...customer of wire communication service for cost accounting or other like purposes in the ordinary course of its business"
- Providers of electronic or wire communication services may use a register to protect the users of the service from abuse or unlawful use of the service, or with the consent of the user of the service
- Employees are advised in advance of a plan to record numbers called

Statutes restrict surveillance of first class mail. A person may not knowingly and willfully obstruct the passage of the U.S. mail, take mail from any post office mailbox or mail carrier for the purpose of obstructing its passage, or pry into the business or secrets of another. Inspecting the outside of first class mail and the inside of lower class mail is lawful.

Many states have enacted statutes that restrict surveillance, including wiretapping or electronic surveillance, and the use of cameras, pen registers, two-way mirrors, or surveillance in particular areas, such as locker rooms, lounges, and rest areas. Under common law, gathering confidential information where the intrusion is unreasonable may be a tort. Privacy is not invaded if the information is open to public view or has been disclosed to others. However, unauthorized and secret surveillance may create liability for outrageous conduct. Trespass is the unauthorized, intentional, or negligent entry upon the property of others. Protection against trespass is particularly applicable to surveillance at an employee's home. Good faith and fair dealing is a matter of following company policies and procedures.

PUBLIC AND NONPUBLIC DOCUMENT SOURCES

The federal Privacy Act of 1974 restricts information that may be gathered by government agencies about individuals, both employees and non-employees. An agency may maintain records about a person containing information that is relevant and necessary to accomplish a purpose of the agency. This information may include a person's education, finances, medical history, criminal history, employment history, and identifying information (fingerprint, voice print, or photograph). The employee may have access to the information unless it is investigatory material compiled for law enforcement purposes, statistical records, or material compiled solely for determining suitability, eligibility, or qualification for federal service or promotion.

The Fair Credit Reporting Act regulates the use of credit reports to investigate employees. An employer may request a report when it is needed for a credit transaction, employment purposes, insurance purposes, governmental benefits, or other business transactions. These circumstances generally do not allow an employer to request a report for the purpose of an investigation into suspected fraud by an employee.

Consumer reports contain information concerning credit worthiness, standing or capacity, character, reputation, and personal characteristics. An employer must give a person written notice if a report was requested and was used as the basis for an adverse employment decision.

"Investigative" consumer reports are based on personal interviews with neighbors, friends, or associates concerning credit worthiness, character, general reputation, personal characteristics, and mode of living. Employers must disclose in writing each request for such a report even if no adverse employment action was based on it.

As in all matters relating to common law and statute, the best path is to obtain advice of counsel.

PUBLIC RECORD INFORMATION

Public record information can refer either to information developed about the public or information open to the public. In the United States, hundreds of data bases and information sources are open for legitimate access by fraud examiners. These data bases can be used to identify and locate people and assets. They are maintained in state (city, county, and state), federal, and local governmental agencies, in banks and financial institutions, in commercial and professional directories, and in the armed services. They are too numerous to list and describe in this book.

The following books are sources for an introduction to the use of public record information:

Pankau, Edmund J., *Check It Out* (Houston, TX: Cloak & Data Press, 1992).

Nossen, R.A., and J.W. Norvelle, *Detection, Investigation, and Prosecution of Financial Crimes* (Phoenix, AZ: Thoth Books, 1993).

Gunderson, Ted L., *How To Locate Anyone Anywhere* (New York, NY: E.P. Dutton, 1989).

Fraud examiners must be certain that information from public records is obtained legally. Records from confidential sources generally cannot be introduced as evidence. In criminal cases, illegally obtained documentary evidence can be excluded at trial. In civil cases, use of illegally obtained documentation may give rise to tort actions or other sanctions against the fraud examiner. Consult a lawyer before going to court.

FRAUD EXAMINATION REPORTS

Documenting results is a particularly important function in fraud examinations. In many instances, the written report is the only evidence that the work was performed. Cases can be won or lost on the strength of the written report. It conveys to the litigator all the evidence and provides credence to the fraud examination work. The requirement to write a report forces the examiner to consider carefully all actions during an investigation. A first-rate written report is based upon a first-rate examination.

ACCURACY

Each contact an examiner makes during the course of a fraud examination should be recorded on a timely basis in a memorandum of interview. Although there is no need to recapitulate testimony word for word, for accuracy's sake the fraud examiner should include all facts of possible relevance. An examiner should reconfirm dates and supporting information with the respondent. The facts should be reconfirmed before, not after, the report is written. Attachments to the report, if any, should be completely described. Inaccuracies and careless errors are inexcusable and can render a report useless.

CLARITY

Investigative reports on fraud examinations should convey pertinent information in the clearest possible language. If necessary, quote the respondent directly (provided the quotation does not distort the context). Convey only the facts. Do not editorialize or give judgments. Use complex or technical terms in their proper contexts, and where necessary, explain their meaning. Do not use jargon since the report may be used by persons who will not be familiar with esoteric or technical terminology.

IMPARTIALITY AND RELEVANCE

Report all facts without bias. Everything relevant should be included regardless of which side it favors or what it proves or disproves. At the outset of a fraud examination, the examiner should carefully determine the information that will be needed to prove the case and attempt to include only this information. A report should include only matters relevant to the examination. However, almost every investigation yields much information of which the relevance is not immediately known. In such cases, the examination report should be complete with the additional information.

TIMELINESS

Timeliness of reports enhances the accuracy of witness testimony. Another aim of timeliness is to preserve the examiner's memory of interview(s). All interviews should be transcribed as soon as possible after the questioning. Upon completing the examination, the examiner should prepare a final or interim report (whichever is appropriate) as soon as possible.

CONCLUSIONS AND OPINIONS

In a report-writing context, conclusions and opinions are similar, but are not identical. Conclusions are based upon observations of the evidence, whereas opinions call for an interpretation of the facts. The fraud examiner must be very circumspect about drawing conclusions. In most situations, the conclusions from the examination should be self-evident, and should not need to be pointed out in the report. If the conclusions are not obvious, the report may need to be clarified.

Fraud examiners must avoid stating opinions regarding the guilt or innocence of any person or party. (As a point of fact, the Certified Fraud Examiners Code of Professional ethics specifically prohibits such statements of opinion.) Opinions regarding technical matters are permitted if the fraud examiner is qualified in court as an expert in the matter being considered. For example, a permissible expert opinion may be in regard to the relative adequacy of an entity's internal controls or an opinion on whether financial accounting for transactions conforms to generally accepted accounting principles.

EVIDENCE

Strict legal guidelines determine how evidence is handled and its chain of custody. Fraud examiners can avoid evidence maintenance problems by simply documenting--in memorandum form--the receipt or release of all evidence.

COPY DOCUMENTS

Much fraud case evidence will be in document form. When operating under a lawful court order that compels a custodian to furnish original documents, the examiner should copy those documents (preferably in the presence of the custodian). Then the examiner should furnish the custodian with a receipt describing the documents copied or taken.

SAFEGUARDING AND MAINTAINING DOCUMENTS

After obtaining documents, the examiner should secure them for evidence. Be sure that only those persons with an absolute need for these documents can gain access to them. For practical purposes, all documents should be copied. (Original documents usually are not included in reports.) Mark all original documents in a unique manner, preferably by using initials and dates. To avoid defacing originals, use a small but distinctive tick mark or other form of identifier.

When documents are voluntarily furnished, leave the originals in place and work with the copies. If originals are later lost, stolen, or misplaced, the copies can normally be introduced in court under the "best evidence" rule. Do not take shortcuts with evidence, and certainly do not lose or misplace crucial documents. A fraud examiner cannot afford to mishandle evidence. Doing so will almost certainly compromise the case.

EFFECTIVE NOTE-TAKING

Note-taking is a demanding and necessary fraud examination skill. Good reports are based on good notes. Once the notes have helped the examiner prepare a memorandum of interview, they have fulfilled their essential purpose. However, some jurisdictions require that notes pertaining to criminal matters be retained for evidence.

The most common types of note-taking are manual, stenographic, and electronic. Manual note-taking is the most usual method. Its main advantage is that no extra persons are required to be present during the interview. However, manual note-taking can be obtrusive and distracting while questioning.

A stenographer may be present during the interview to take notes (rather than a verbatim transcript). This allows the interviewer to concentrate on the questioning. A potential disadvantage of this method is that the respondent may be inhibited by the presence of another individual.

Electronic note-taking commonly entails tape recording an interview, then summarizing the recording to reflect the most pertinent information. Its main advantages are increased accuracy and information-gathering efficiency. It can be especially helpful in complicated interview situations or in situations where terminology is defined or explained. Electronic note-taking has the disadvantage of requiring a duplication of effort. In some instances, an electronic recording device may be inhibiting. In a limited number of situations it may be illegal without the respondent's consent.

ORGANIZATION OF INFORMATION

Report information can be presented either in chronological order or in transaction order.

Chronological order presents facts in the order in which they were uncovered. For example, if an anonymous tip predicated the fraud examination, this information will be presented first in the report. Thereafter, the reader would follow the development of each step as the case progressed.

Transaction order involves presenting documentation organized by types of transactions. For example, in a case of internal fraud involving six different instances of embezzlement, the documents and the related interviews might best be understood if presented as each type. Chronological order within each type may enhance clarity.

ANALYZING THE READER

Be aware that the fraud examination report will probably be used by company executives and managers, directors, internal auditors, external auditors, media press reporters, attorneys, law enforcement officials, judges and jurors, and by the accused person. Under no circumstances should the examiner prepare a communication with the idea that the information will not be disclosed to adverse third parties. Write the report with this caveat in mind. A fraud examination should stand on its own. It should adequately answer the classic questions of who, what, why, where, when, and how. If the report is prepared properly, the reader should not need to refer to any other documents to understand the issues.

REPORT CONTENT

The basic report documents are:
- Cover page
- Transmittal letter
- Memoranda
- Exhibits, documents, or enclosures
- Indexes

A cover page summarizes the examination's salient points. The cover page should be direct and succinct. It may or may not include conclusions. If a report is submitted to an outside agency (such as law enforcement or outside counsel), a cover letter should accompany it. The cover letter should recapitulate and summarize information in the report. It is not necessary to list all witnesses, only those most valuable.

The heart of the report is the memoranda of interview. One memorandum should be prepared for each official contact. Once all the memoranda of interview are completed, they are typically assembled in chronological order and indexed. Use memoranda to document all interviews and other pertinent information discovered during the examination. Each memorandum should contain the following information where appropriate:
- Heading
- File number or control number
- Name of person reporting

- Case name or subject
- Subject of memorandum
- Date
- Interview was voluntary
- Indicate that you provided your identity
- The witness was informed of the nature of the inquiry
- Date of interview
- How the interview was conducted (in person, by telephone, etc.)
- Whether the interview was electronically recorded
- Facts learned during the interview

As a general rule, copies of exhibits should be included in the report and not attached separately. However, bulky files (including working papers and similar exhibits) may be attached separately and referred to in the body of the report. The chain of custody should be maintained over original documents.

A complete fraud examination report must document every step of the information-gathering process. Because the orderly and legal presentation of evidence requires examiners to organize a great deal of information, they should use forms available to facilitate this task. These forms usually are kept in the file and not included in the report unless necessary. These forms include the following:

- Consent to search
- Receipt for property
- Telephone recording consent
- Advice of rights (Miranda or other forms)
- Consent to record
- Customer consent and authorization for access to financial records (financial institutions)
- Evidence control log
- Signed statements of confession
- Visual aids
- Fraud examiner's engagement contract, if applicable

Clear, concise reports that present all the information necessary for others to reach conclusions and opinions are vital to end the fraud examination process. Keep reports simple, but make them complete. They are the only relevant record of the fraud examination, and the successful conclusion of the investigation rests on them.

CHAPTER 6
FRAUD AWARENESS AUDITING

Auditing for fraud can be very challenging. It has the aura of detective work--finding things people want to keep hidden. However, auditing and fraud examination are not easy. They should only be pursued by persons who have proper training and experience. Thus, fraud *awareness* for independent auditors and internal auditors is the focus of this chapter.

INTRODUCTION

This chapter is not intended to make you a fraud examiner or fraud auditor. Its purpose is to heighten your familiarity with the nature, signs, prevention, detection, and reaction to fraud that can enable you to perform financial statement audits with awareness of fraud possibilities.

Users of audited financial statements generally believe that one of the main objectives of audits is fraud detection. External auditors know the issue is very complex, and they fear the general view that their work should ferret out all manner of major and minor fraud and misstatement in financial statements. This difference in viewpoints is one of the chronic "expectation gaps" between external auditors and users of published financial statements.

Part of the gap arises from the ability and expertise needed to be a fraud examiner or fraud auditor. Most of the trained and experienced fraud examiners come from government agencies, such as the Internal Revenue Service (IRS), Federal Bureau of Investigation (FBI), U.S. General Accounting Office (GAO), U.S. Securities and Exchange Commission (SEC), U.S. Department of Justice, and various police departments. Alumni of these agencies often practice as consultants and fraud examiners, but few of them enter public accounting to become financial statement auditors. So, what are most financial statement auditors to do? One option is to become more aware of fraud possibilities so they can perform a limited set of procedures and determine when it is necessary to call upon people with greater fraud examination expertise. Financial statement auditors need to understand fraud and potential fraud situations, and they need to know how to ask the right kinds of questions during an audit.

DEFINITIONS RELATED TO FRAUD

Several kinds of "fraud" are defined in laws, while others are matters of general understanding. Exhibit 6-1 shows some acts and devices often involved in financial frauds. Collectively, these are known as **white-collar crime**--the misdeeds done by people who wear ties to work and steal with a pencil or a computer terminal. In white-collar crime, there are ink stains instead of bloodstains.

EXHIBIT 6-1   An Abundance of Frauds

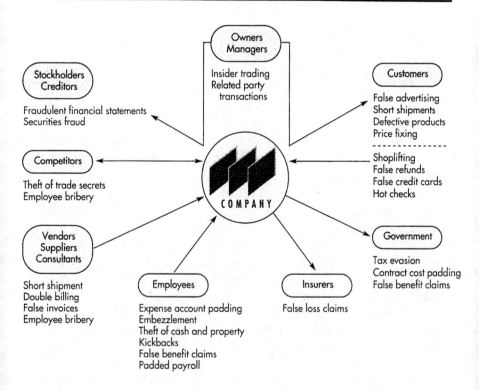

Fraud consists of knowingly making material misrepresentations of fact, with the intent of inducing someone to believe the falsehood and act upon it and, thus, suffer a loss or damage. This definition encompasses all the varieties by which people can lie, cheat, steal, and dupe other people.

Employee fraud is the use of fraudulent means to take money or other property from an employer. It usually involves falsifications of some kind--false documents, lying, exceeding authority, or violating an employer's policies. It consists of three phases: (1) the fraudulent act, (2) the conversion of the money or property to the fraudster's use, and (3) the coverup.

Embezzlement is a type of fraud involving employees' or nonemployees' wrongfully taking money or property entrusted to their care, custody, and control, often accompanied by false accounting entries and other forms of lying and coverup.

Larceny is simple theft--for example, an employee taking an employer's money or property that has not been entrusted to the custody of the employee.

Defalcation is another name for employee fraud, embezzlement, and larceny.

Management fraud is deliberate fraud committed by management that injures investors and creditors through materially misleading financial statements. The class of perpetrators is management; the class of victims is investors and creditors; and the instrument of perpetration is financial statements.[1] Sometimes management fraud is called "fraudulent financial reporting."

Fraudulent financial reporting was defined by the National Commission on Fraudulent Financial Reporting (1987) as *intentional or reckless conduct, whether by act or omission, that results in materially misleading financial statements.*
    The AICPA generally accepted auditing standards describe errors and fraud. **Errors** are unintentional misstatements or omissions of amounts or disclosures in financial statements.   **Fraud** involves intentional misstatements or omissions in financial statements, including fraudulent financial reporting to deceive financial statement users (management fraud)

and misappropriations of assets (defalcations) that cause material financial misstatements. **Direct-effect illegal acts** are violations of laws or government regulations by the company or its management or employees that produce direct and material effects on dollar amounts in financial statements.

Fraud auditing has been defined in courses conducted by the Association of Certified Fraud Examiners as: A proactive approach to detect financial frauds using accounting records and information, analytical relationships, and an awareness of fraud perpetration and concealment schemes.

CHARACTERISTICS OF FRAUDSTERS

White-collar criminals are not like typical bank robbers, who are often described as "young and dumb." Bank robbers and other strongarm artists often make comic mistakes like writing the holdup note on the back of a probation identification card, leaving the getaway car keys on the convenience store counter, using a zucchini as a holdup weapon, and timing the holdup to get stuck in rush hour traffic. Then there's the classic about the robber who ran into his own mother at the bank (she turned him in!).

Burglars and robbers average about $400-$500 for each hit. Employee frauds average $20,000, on up to $500,000 if a computer is used. Yet, employee frauds are not usually the intricate, well-disguised ploys you find in espionage novels. Who are these thieves wearing ties? What do they look like? Unfortunately, they "look like" most everybody else, including you and me. They have these characteristics:

- Likely to be married.
- Member of a church.
- Educated beyond high school.
- No arrest record.
- Range in age from teens to over 60.
- Socially conforming.
- Employment tenure from 1 to 20 or more years.
- Usually act alone (70 percent of incidents).

White-collar criminals do not make themselves obvious, although there may be tell-tale signs, which will be described later as "red flags." Unfortunately, the largest frauds are committed by people who hold high executive positions, have long tenure with an organization, and are respected and trusted employees. After all, these are the people who have access to the largest amounts of money and have the power to give orders and override controls.

THE ART OF FRAUD AWARENESS AUDITING

Fraud examination work combines the expertise of auditors and criminal investigators. Some fraud examiners are fond of saying that their successes are the result of accident, hunches, or luck. Nothing can be further from the reality. Successes come from experience, logic, and the ability to see things that are not obvious (as Sherlock Holmes noticed the dog that did not bark). Fraud awareness auditing, broadly speaking, involves familiarity with many elements: the human element, organizational behavior, knowledge of common fraud schemes, evidence and its sources, standards of proof, and sensitivity to red flags.[2]

WHO DOES IT?

Alex W was a 47-year-old treasurer of a credit union. Over a seven-year period, he stole $160,000. He was a good husband and the father of six children, and he was a highly reputed official of the credit union. His misappropriations came as a stunning surprise to his associates. He owed significant amounts on his home, cars, college for two children, two side investments, and five different credit cards. His monthly payments significantly exceeded his take-home pay.

Source: Association of Certified Fraud Examiners (ACFE), "Auditing for Fraud."

Independent auditors of financial statements and fraud examiners approach their work differently. While many differences exist, these are some of the most important and obvious ones:
- Financial auditors follow a program/procedural approach designed to accomplish a fairly standard job, while fraud examiners float in a mind-set of sensitivity to the unusual where nothing is standard.

- Financial auditors make note of errors and omissions, while fraud examiners focus as well on exceptions, oddities, and patterns of conduct.
- Financial auditors assess control risk in general and specific terms to design other audit procedures, while fraud examiners habitually "think like a crook" to imagine ways controls could be subverted for fraudulent purposes.
- Financial auditors use a concept of materiality (dollar size big enough to matter) that is usually much higher than the amounts that fraud examiners consider worth pursuing. Financial auditors use materiality as a measure of importance one year at a time, whereas fraud examiners think of a cumulative materiality. (Theft of $20,000 per year may not loom large each year, but after a 15-year fraud career, $300,000 is a considerable loss.)
- Financial audits are based on theories of financial accounting and auditing logic, while fraud examination has a theory of behavioral motive, opportunity, and integrity.

External and internal auditors get credit for finding about 20 percent of discovered frauds. Larger percentages are discovered by voluntary confessions, anonymous tips, and other haphazard means. Fraud examiners have a higher success rate because they are called in for a specific purpose when fraud is known or highly suspected.

Some aspects of audit methodology make a big difference in the fraud discovery success experience. Financial auditors often utilize inductive reasoning--that is, they sample accounting data, derive audit findings, and project ("induct") the finding to a conclusion about the population of data sampled. Fraud examiners often enjoy the expensive luxury of utilizing deductive reasoning--that is, after being tipped off that a certain type of loss occurred or probably occurred, they can identify the suspects, make observations (stakeouts), conduct interviews, eliminate dead-end results, and concentrate on running the fraudster to ground. They can conduct covert activities that usually are not in the financial auditors' tool kit. The "expensive luxury" of the deductive approach involves surveying a wide array of information and information sources, eliminating the extraneous, and retaining the selection that proves the fraud.

THE CASE OF THE EXTRA CHECKOUT

The district grocery store manager could not understand why receipts and profitability had fallen and inventory was hard to manage at one of the largest stores in her area. She hired an investigator who covertly observed the checkout clerks and reported that no one had shown suspicious behavior at any of the nine checkout counters. Nine? That store only has eight, she exclaimed! (The store manager had installed another checkout aisle, not connected to the cash receipts and inventory maintenance central computer, and was pocketing all the receipts from that register.)

Source: ACFE, "Auditing for Fraud."

CONDITIONS THAT MAKE FRAUD POSSIBLE, EVEN EASY

When can fraud occur? Imagine the probability of fraud being a function of three factors--motive, opportunity, and lack of integrity. When one or two of these factors weigh heavily in the direction of fraud, the probability increases. When three of them lean in the direction of fraud, it almost certainly will occur.[3] As Bologna and Lindquist put it: Some people are honest all the time, some people (fewer than the honest ones) are dishonest all the time, most people are honest all the time, and some people are honest most of the time.[4]

MOTIVE

A **motive** is some kind of pressure experienced by a person and believed unshareable with friends and confidants. Psychotic motivation is relatively rare; but it is characterized by the "habitual criminal," who steals simply for the sake of stealing. Egocentric motivations drive people to steal to achieve more personal prestige. Ideological motivations are held by people who think their cause is morally superior, and they are justified in making someone else a victim. However, economic motives are far more common in business frauds than the other three.

I COULDN'T TELL ANYONE

An unmarried young woman stole $300 from her employer to pay for an abortion. Coming from a family that strongly disdained premarital sex, she felt her only alternative was to have the secret abortion. Once she realized how easy it was to steal, however, she took another $86,000 before being caught.

Source: W. S. Albrecht, "How CPAs Can Help Clients Prevent Employee Fraud," *Journal of Accountancy*, December 1988, p. 113.

The economic motive is simply a need for money, and at times it can be intertwined with egocentric and ideological motivations. Ordinarily honest people can fall into circumstances where there is a new or unexpected need for money, and the normal options for talking about it or going through legitimate channels seem to be closed. Consider these needs to:

- Pay college tuition.
- Pay hospital bills for a parent with cancer.
- Pay gambling debts.
- Pay for drugs.
- Pay alimony and child support.
- Pay for high lifestyle (homes, cars, boats).
- Finance business or stock speculation losses.
- Report good financial results.

OPPORTUNITY

An **opportunity** is an open door for solving the unshareable problem in secret by violating a trust. The violation may be a circumvention of internal control policies and procedures, or it may be simply taking advantage of an absence or lapse of control in an organization. We have no police state where every person is shadowed by an armed guard. Everyone has some degree of trust conferred for a job, even if it is merely the trust not to shirk and procrastinate. The higher the position in an organization, the greater the degree of trust; and, hence, the greater the opportunity for larger frauds. Here are some examples:

- Nobody counts the inventory, so losses are not known.
- The petty cash box is often left unattended.
- Supervisors set a bad example by taking supplies home.

- Upper management considered a written statement of ethics but decided not to publish one.
- Another employee was caught and fired, but not prosecuted.
- The finance vice president has investment authority without any review.
- Frequent emergency jobs leave a lot of excess material just lying around.

SHE CAN DO EVERYTHING

Mrs. Lemon was the only bookkeeper for an electrical supply company. She wrote the checks and reconciled the bank account. In the cash disbursements journal, she coded some checks as inventory, but she wrote the checks to herself, using her own true name. When the checks were returned with the bank statement, she simply destroyed them. She stole $416,000 over five years. After being caught and sentenced to prison, she testified to having continuous guilt over doing something she knew was wrong.

Source: ACFE, "Auditing for Fraud."

LACK OF INTEGRITY

Practically everyone, even the most violent criminal, knows the difference between right and wrong. Unimpeachable **integrity** is the ability to act in accordance with the highest moral and ethical values all the time. Thus, it is the lapses and occasional lack of integrity that permit motive and opportunity to take form as fraud. But people normally do not make deliberate decisions to "lack integrity today while I steal some money." They find a way to describe (rationalize) the act in words that make it acceptable for their self-image. Here are some of these rationalizations:

- I need it more than the other person (Robin Hood theory).
- I'm borrowing the money and will pay it back.
- Nobody will get hurt.
- The company is big enough to afford it.
- A successful image is the name of the game.
- Everybody is doing it.

FRAUD PREVENTION

Accountants and auditors have often been exhorted to be the leaders in fraud prevention by employing their skills in designing "tight" control systems. This strategy is, at best, a short-run solution to a large and pervasive problem. Business activity is built on the trust that people at all levels will do their jobs properly. Control systems limit trust and, in the extreme, can strangle business in bureaucracy. Imagine street crime being "prevented" by enrolling half the population in the police force to control the other half! Managers and employees must have freedom to do business, which means giving them freedom to commit frauds as well.[5] Effective long-run prevention measures are complex and difficult, involving the elimination of the causes of fraud by mitigating the effect of motive, opportunity, and lack of integrity.

MANAGING PEOPLE PRESSURES IN THE WORKPLACE

From time to time, people will experience financial and other pressures. The pressures cannot be eliminated, but the facilities for *sharing* them can be created. Some companies have "ethics officers" to serve this purpose. Their job is to be available to talk over the ethical dilemmas faced in the workplace and help people adopt legitimate responses. However, the ethics officers are normally not psychological counselors.

THEY DESERVE EVERYTHING THEY GOT!

A controller of a small fruit packing company in California stole $112,000 from the company. When asked why, he said: "Nobody at the company, especially the owners, ever talked to me. They treated me unfairly, they talked down to me, and they were rude."

Source: ACFE, "Auditing for Fraud."

Many companies have "hot lines" for anonymous reporting of ethical problems. Reportedly, the best kind of hot line arrangement is to have the responding party be an agency outside the organization. In the United States, some organizations are in the business of being the recipients of hot line calls coordinating their activities with the management of the organization. The Association of Certified Fraud Examiners maintains a subscription hotline service called Ethics Line.

The most effective long-run prevention, however, lies in the practice of management by caring for people. Managers and supervisors at all levels can exhibit a genuine concern for the personal and professional needs of their subordinates and fellow managers, and subordinates can show the same concern for each other and their managers. Many companies facilitate this caring attitude with an organized Employee Assistance Program (EAP). EAPs operate in about 9 percent of small companies and in about 39 percent of medium-size companies. They offer a range of counseling referral services dealing with substance abuse, mental health, family problems, crisis help, legal matters, health education, retirement, career paths, job loss troubles, AIDS education, and family financial planning.

When external auditors are engaged in the audit of financial statements, they must obtain an understanding of the company's "control environment," which relates to the overall scheme of management activity in the company. Managements that consider carefully the people pressures in the workplace, using some of the devices mentioned above, have good control environment and the beginnings of a good control system.

HOW TO ENCOURAGE FRAUD

Practice autocratic management.

Manage by power with little trust in people.

Manage by crisis.

Centralize authority in top management.

Measure performance on a short-term basis.

Make profits the only criterion for success.

Make rewards punitive, stingy, and political.

Give feedback that is always critical and negative.

Create a highly hostile, competitive workplace.

Insist everything be documented with a rule for everything.

Source: Adapted from G. J. Bologna and R. J. Lindquist, *Fraud Auditing and Forensic Accounting* (New York: John Wiley & Sons, 1987), pp. 47-49.

CONTROL PROCEDURES AND EMPLOYEE MONITORING

Auditors would be aghast at an organization that had no control policies and procedures, and rightly so. Controls in the form of job descriptions and performance specifications are indeed needed to help people know the jobs they are supposed to accomplish. Almost all people need some structure for their working hours. An organization whose only control is "trustworthy employees" has no control.[6] Unfortunately, "getting caught" is an important consideration for many people when coping with their problems. Controls provide the opportunity to get caught. Even the perception of the possibility of being caught can prevent employee theft and embezzlement.

Without going into much detail about controls, let it be noted that procedures for recognizing and explaining red flags are important for nipping frauds in the bud before they get bigger. Controls that reveal the following kinds of symptoms are necessary:[7]

- Missing documents.
- Second endorsements on checks.
- Unusual endorsements.
- Unexplained adjustments to inventory balances.
- Unexplained adjustments to accounts receivable.
- Old items in bank reconciliations.
- Old outstanding checks.
- Customer complaints.
- Unusual patterns in deposits in transit.

WHEN A CUSTOMER COMPLAINS, LISTEN

A depositor told the S&L branch manager that there had been a $9,900 forged savings withdrawal from her account. She said she had recently made a $9,900 deposit at the branch and suspected the teller who had accepted the deposit. The teller was interviewed and admitted to forging and negotiating the savings withdrawal. He had obtained the depositor's mother's maiden name and birthplace (often used as identifier codes), fabricated a duplicate savings receipt book, and, posing as the depositor, went to another branch and made the withdrawal.

Source: ACFE, "Auditing for Fraud."

The problem with control systems is that they are essentially negative restrictions on people. The challenge is to have a bare minimum of useful controls and to avoid picky rules that are "fun to beat." The challenge of "beating the system," which can lead to bigger and better things, is an invitation to fraudulent types of behavior.

INTEGRITY BY EXAMPLE AND ENFORCEMENT

The key to integrity in business is "accountability"--that is, each person must be willing to put his or her decisions and actions in the sunshine. Many organizations begin by publishing codes of conduct. Some of these codes are simple, and some are very elaborate. Government agencies and defense contractors typically have the most elaborate rules for employee conduct. Sometimes they work, sometimes they do not. A code can be effective if the "tone at the top" supports it. When the chairman of the board and the president make themselves visible examples of the code, other people will then believe it is real. Subordinates tend to follow the boss's lead.

Hiring and firing are important. Background checks on prospective employees are advisable. A new employee who has been a fox in some other organization's hen house will probably be a fox in a new place. Organizations have been known to hire private investigators to make these background checks. Fraudsters should be fired and, in most cases, prosecuted. They have a low rate of recidivism (repeat offenses) if they are prosecuted, but they have a high rate if not.[8] Prosecution delivers the message that management does not believe that "occasional dishonesty" is acceptable.

WHERE DID HE COME FROM?

The controller defrauded the company for several million dollars. As it turned out, he was no controller at all. He didn't know a debit from a credit. The fraudster had been fired from five previous jobs where money had turned up missing. He was discovered one evening when the president showed up unexpectedly at the company and found a stranger in the office with the controller. The stranger was doing all of the accounting for the bogus controller.

Source: ACFE, "Auditing for Fraud."

FRAUD DETECTION

Since an organization cannot prevent all fraud, its auditors, accountants, and security personnel must be acquainted with some detection techniques. Frauds consist of the fraud act itself, the conversion of assets to the fraudster's use, and the coverup. Catching people in the fraud act is difficult and unusual. The act of conversion is equally difficult to observe, since it typically takes place in secret away from the organization's offices (e.g., fencing stolen inventory). Many frauds are investigated by noticing signs and signals of fraud, then following the trail of missing, mutilated, or false documents that are part of the accounting records coverup.

This chapter has already mentioned signs and signals in terms of red flags, oddities, and unusual events. Being able to notice them takes some experience, but this book can give some starting places.[9]

RED FLAGS

Employee Fraud
Employee fraud can involve high-level executives and people below the top executive levels. Observation of persons' habits and lifestyle and *changes* in habits and lifestyles may reveal some red flags. Fraudsters of the past have exhibited these characteristics:
- Lose sleep.
- Drink too much.
- Take drugs.
- Become irritable easily.
- Can't relax.
- Get defensive, argumentative.
- Can't look people in the eye.
- Sweat excessively.
- Go to confession (e.g., priest, psychiatrist).
- Find excuses and scapegoats for mistakes.
- Work standing up.
- Work alone, work late.

Personality red flags are difficult because (1) honest people sometimes show them and (2) they often are hidden from view. It is easier to notice *changes*, especially when a person changes his or her lifestyle or spends more money than the salary justifies--for example, on homes, furniture, jewelry, clothes, boats, autos, vacations, and the like.

HIGH STYLE IN THE MAILROOM

A female mailroom employee started wearing designer clothes (and making a big deal about it). She drove a new BMW to work. An observant manager, who had known her as an employee for seven years and knew she had no outside income, became suspicious. He asked the internal auditors to examine her responsibilities extra carefully. They discovered she had taken $97,000 over a two-year period.

Source: ACFE, "Auditing for Fraud."

Often, auditors can notice telltale hints of the coverup. These generally appear in the accounting records. The key is to notice exceptions and oddities, such as transactions that are: at odd times of the day, month, season; too many or too few; in the wrong branch location; in amounts too high, too low, too consistent, too different. Exceptions and oddities like these can appear:

- Missing documents.
- Cash shortages and overages.
- Excessive voids and credit memos.
- Customer complaints.
- Common names or addresses for refunds.
- Adjustments to receivables and payables.
- General ledger does not balance.
- Increased past due receivables.
- Inventory shortages.
- Increased scrap.
- Alterations on documents.
- Duplicate payments.
- Employees cannot be found.
- Second endorsements on checks.
- Documents photocopied.
- Dormant accounts become active.

A LARGE HOUSEHOLD

A benefit analyst with C. G. Insurance used her remote terminal in a Dade County, Florida, field claims office to defraud the company of $206,000 in 18 months. She used her position of trust and her knowledge of the claims system to execute the fraud by using false names to submit fictitious claims using the address of herself, her father, and her boyfriend. The repetition of the same claimant addresses eventually tipped off the insurance company's security department.

Source: G. J. Bologna and R. J. Lindquist, *Fraud Auditing and Forensic Accounting* (New York: John Wiley & Sons, 1987), p. 72.

Management Fraud (Fraudulent Financial Reporting)

Fraud that affects financial statements and causes them to be materially misleading often arises from the perceived need to "get through a difficult period." The difficult period may be characterized by cash shortage, increased competition, cost overruns, and similar events that cause financial difficulty. Managers usually view these conditions as "temporary," believing they can be overcome by getting a new loan, selling stock, or otherwise buying time to recover. In the meantime, falsified financial statements are used to "benefit the company." These conditions and circumstances have existed along with frauds in the past:

- Weak internal control environment.
- Management decisions dominated by an individual or a small group.
- Managers' attitudes very aggressive.
- Managers place much emphasis on earnings projections.
- Company profit lags the industry.
- Company is decentralized without much monitoring.
- Auditors have doubt about company as a going concern.
- Company has many difficult accounting measurement and presentation issues.
- Company has significant transactions or balances that are difficult to audit.
- Company has significant and unusual related-party transactions.
- Managers and employees tend to be evasive when responding to auditors' inquiries.

- Managers engage in frequent disputes with auditors.
- Company accounting personnel are lax or inexperienced in their duties.

By both fraud and "creative accounting," companies have caused financial statements to be materially misleading by (1) overstating revenues and assets, (2) understating expenses and liabilities, and (3) giving disclosures that are misleading or that omit important information. Generally, fraudulent financial statements show financial performance and ratios that are better than current industry experience or better than the company's own history. Sometimes the performance meets exactly the targets announced by management months earlier.

OVERSTATED REVENUE, RECEIVABLES, AND DEFERRED COSTS

Cali Computer Systems, Inc., sold franchises enabling local entrepreneurs to open stores and sell Cali products. The company granted territorial franchises; in one instance recording revenue of $800,000 and in another $580,000. Unfortunately, the first of these "contracts" for a territorial franchise simply did not exist, and the second was not executed and Cali had not performed its obligations by the time it was recorded. In both cases, the imaginary revenue was about 40 percent of reported revenues. These franchises were more in the nature of business hopes than completed transactions.

Cali was supposed to deliver computer software in connection with the contracts and had deferred $277,000 of software development cost in connection with the programs. However, this software did not work, and the contracts were fulfilled with software purchased from other suppliers.

Source: SEC Accounting and Auditing Enforcement Release 190, 1988.

Because of the double-entry bookkeeping system, fraudulent accounting entries always affect two accounts and two places in financial statements. Since many frauds involve improper recognition of assets, there is a theory of the "dangling debit," which is an asset amount that can be investigated and found to be false or questionable. Frauds may involve the omission of liabilities, but the matter of finding and investigating the "dangling credit" is normally very difficult. It "dangles" off the books. Misleading disclosures also present difficulty, mainly because they involve words and messages instead of numbers. Omissions may be hard to notice, and misleading inferences may be very subtle.

A client's far-removed illegal acts may cause financial statements to be misleading, and external auditors are advised to be aware of circumstances that might indicate them. The AICPA has given these signs and signals of the potential for illegal acts (SAS 54, AU 317):

- Unauthorized transactions.
- Government investigations.
- Regulatory reports of violations.
- Payments to consultants, affiliates, employees for unspecified services.
- Excessive sales commissions and agent's fees.
- Unusually large cash payments.
- Unexplained payments to government officials.
- Failure to file tax returns, to pay duties and fees.

INTERNAL CONTROL

An important feature of internal control is the separation of these duties and responsibilities: (1) transaction authorization, (2) recordkeeping, (3) custody of, or access to, assets, and (4) reconciliation of actual assets to the accounting records. Generally, a person who, acting alone or in a conspiracy, can perform two or more of these functions also can commit a fraud by taking assets, converting them, and covering up. (Other control features are explained in Chapter 7.)

Fraud awareness auditing involves perceptions of the controls installed (or not installed) by a company, plus "thinking like a crook" to imagine ways and means of stealing. When controls are absent, the ways and means may be obvious. Otherwise, it might take some scheming to figure out how to steal from an organization.

THE TRUSTED EMPLOYEE

A small business owner hired his best friend to work as his accountant. The friend was given full unlimited access to all aspects of the business and was completely responsible for the accounting. Five years later, the owner finally terminated the friend because the business was not profitable. Upon taking over the accounting, the owner's wife found that cash receipts from customers were twice the amounts formerly recorded by the accountant "friend." An investigation revealed that the friend had stolen $450,000 in cash sales receipts from the business, while the owner had never made more than $16,000 a year. (The friend had even used the stolen money to make loans to the owner and to keep the business going!)

NO LOCKS ON THE DOOR

Perini Corporation kept blank checks in an unlocked storeroom, where every clerk and secretary had access. Also in the storeroom was the automatic check signing machine. The prenumbered checks were not logged and restricted to one person. The bookkeeper was very surprised to open the bank statement one month and find that $1.5 million in stolen checks had been paid on the account.

Source: ACFE, "Auditing for Fraud."

SCHEMES AND DETECTION PROCEDURES

In this section of the chapter, we will try a new approach. Instead of discussing lists of schemes and detection procedures in the abstract, we will have a series of cases. They will follow a standard format in two major parts: (1) Case Situation, and (2) Audit Approach. Some problems at the end of the chapter will give the case situation, and you will be assigned to write the audit approach section. The first three cases deal with employee fraud, and the last two deal with management fraud. With the first three cases, you can practice on being able to: *Describe some common employee fraud schemes and explain some audit and investigation procedures for detecting them.* With the last two cases, you can practice on learning how to: *Describe some common financial reporting fraud features and explain some audit and investigation procedures for detecting them.*

CASE 6.1
CASE OF THE MISSING PETTY CASH

Problem
Petty cash embezzlement.

Method
The petty cash custodian (1) brought postage receipts from home and paid them from the fund, (2) persuaded the supervisor to sign blank authorization slips the custodian could use when the supervisor was away, and used these to pay for fictitious meals and minor supplies, (3) took cash to get through the weekend, replacing it the next week.

Paper Trail
Postage receipts were from a distant post office station the company did not use. The blank authorization slips were dated on days the supervisor was absent. The fund was cash short during the weekend and for a few days the following week.

Amount
The fund was small ($500), but the custodian replenished it about every two working days, stealing about $50 each time. With about 260 working days per year and 130 reimbursements, the custodian was stealing about $6,500 per year. The custodian was looking forward to getting promoted to general cashier and bigger and better things!

AUDIT APPROACH

Objective
Obtain evidence of the existence of the petty cash fund and validity of petty cash transactions.

Control
A supervisor is assigned to approve petty cash disbursements by examining them for validity and signing an authorization slip.

Test of Controls
Audit for transaction authorization and validity. Select a sample of petty cash reimbursement check copies with receipts and authorization slips attached; study them for evidence of authorization and validity (vouching procedure). Notice the nature and content of the receipts. Obtain supervisor's vacation schedule and compare dates to authorization slip dates.

Audit of Balance
On Friday, count the petty cash and receipts to see that they add up to $500. Then, count the fund again later in the afternoon. (Be sure the second count is a surprise and that the custodian and supervisor sign off on the count working paper so the auditor will not be accused of theft.)

Discovery Summary
Knowing the location of the nearby post office branch used by the company, the auditor noticed the pattern of many receipts from a distant branch, which was near the custodian's apartment. Several authorizations were dated during the supervisor's vacation, and he readily admitted signing the forms in blank so his own supervisor "wouldn't be bothered." The second count on the same day was a real surprise, and the fund was found $65 short.

CASE 6.2
THE LAUNDRY MONEY SKIM

Problem
Stolen cash receipts skimmed from collection.
   Albert owned and operated 40 coin laundries around town. As the business grew, he could no longer visit each one, empty the cash boxes, and deposit the receipts. Each location grossed about $140 to $160 per day, operating 365 days per year. (Gross income about $2 million per year.)

Method
Four part-time employees each visited 10 locations, collecting the cash boxes and delivering them to Albert's office, where he would count the coins and currency (from the change machine) and prepare a bank deposit. One of the employees skimmed $5 to $10 from each location visited each day.

Paper Trail
None, unfortunately. The first paper that gets produced is Albert's bank deposit, and the money is gone by then.

Amount
The daily theft does not seem like much, but at an average of $7.50 per day from each of 10 locations, it was about $27,000 per year. If all four of the employees had stolen the same amount, the loss could have been about $100,000 per year.

AUDIT APPROACH

Objective
Obtain evidence of the completeness of cash receipts--that is, that all the cash received is delivered to Albert for deposit.

Control
Controls over the part-time employees were nonexistent. There was no overt or covert surprise observation and no times when two people went to collect cash (thereby needing to agree, in collusion, to steal). There was no rotation of locations or other indications to the employees that Albert was concerned about control.

Test of Controls
With no controls, there are no test of control procedures. Obviously, however, "thinking like a crook" leads to the conclusion that the employees could simply pocket money.

Audit of Balance
The "balance" in this case is the total revenue that should have been deposited, and auditing for completeness is always difficult. Albert marked a quantity of coins with an etching tool and marked some $1 and $5 bills with ink. Unknown to the employees, he put these in all the locations, carefully noting the coins and bills in each.

Discovery Summary
Sure enough, a pattern of missing money emerged. When confronted, the employee confessed.

CASE 6.3
THE WELL-PADDED PAYROLL

Problem
Embezzlement with fictitious people on the payroll.

Method
Maybelle had responsibility for preparing personnel files for new hires, approval of wages, verification of time cards, and distribution of payroll checks. She "hired" fictitious employees, faked their records, and ordered checks through the payroll system. She deposited some checks in several personal bank accounts and cashed others, endorsing all of them with the names of the fictitious employees and her own.

Paper Trail
Payroll creates a large paper trail with individual earnings records, W-2 tax forms, payroll deductions for taxes and insurance, and Form 941 payroll tax reports. She mailed all the W-2 forms to the same post office box.

Amount

Maybelle stole $160,000 by creating some "ghosts," usually 3 to 5 out of 112 people on the payroll and paying them an average of $256 per week for three years. Sometimes the ghosts quit and were later replaced by others. But she stole "only" about 2 percent of the payroll funds during the period.

AUDIT APPROACH

Objective

Obtain evidence of the existence and validity of payroll transactions.

Control

Different people should be responsible for hiring (preparing personnel files), approving wages, and distributing payroll checks. "Thinking like a crook" leads an auditor to see that Maybelle could put people on the payroll and obtain their checks.

Test of Controls

Audit for transaction authorization and validity. Random sampling might not work because of the small number of ghosts. Look for the obvious. Select several weeks' check blocks, account for numerical sequence (to see whether any checks have been removed), and examine canceled checks for two endorsements.

Audit of Balance

There may be no "balance" to audit for existence/occurrence, other than the accumulated total of payroll transactions, and the total may not appear out of line with history because the fraud is small in relation to total payroll and has been going on for years. Conduct a surprise payroll distribution, follow up by examining prior canceled checks for the missing employees. Scan personnel files for common addresses.

Discovery Summary

Both the surprise distribution and the scan for common addresses provided the names of 2 or 3 exceptions. Both led to prior canceled checks (which Maybelle had not removed and the bank reconciler had not noticed), which carried Maybelle's own name as endorser. Confronted, she confessed.

CASE 6.4
FALSE SALES, ACCOUNTS RECEIVABLE, AND INVENTORY

Problem

Overstated sales and accounts receivable caused overstated net income, retained earnings, current assets, working capital, and total assets.

Method

Q. T. Wilson was a turnaround specialist who took the challenge at Mini Marc Corporation, a manufacturer of computer peripheral equipment. He set high goals for sales and profits. To meet these goals, managers shipped bricks to distributors and recorded some as sales of equipment to retail distributors and some as inventory out on consignment. No real products left the plant for these "sales." The theory was that actual sales would grow, and the bricks would be replaced later with real products. In the meantime, the distributors may have thought they were holding consignment inventory in the unopened cartons.

Paper Trail

All the paperwork was in order because the managers had falsified the sales and consignment invoices, but they did not have customer purchase orders for all the false sales. Shipping papers were in order, and several shipping employees knew the boxes did not contain disk drives.

Amount

Prior to the manipulation, annual sales were $135 million. During the two falsification years, sales were $185 million and $362 million. Net income went up from a loss of $20 million to $23 million (income), then to $31 million (income); and the gross margin percent went from 6 percent to 28 percent. The revenue and profit figures outpaced the industry performance. The accounts receivable collection period grew to 94 days, while it was 70 days elsewhere in the industry.

AUDIT APPROACH

Objective

Obtain evidence about the existence and valuation of sales, accounts receivable, and inventory.

Control

Company accounting and control procedures required customer purchase orders or contracts evidencing real orders. A sales invoice was supposed to indicate the products and their prices, and shipping documents were supposed to indicate actual shipment. Sales were always charged to a customer's account receivable.

Test of Controls

There were no glaring control omissions that "thinking like a crook" would have pointed to fraud possibilities. Sensitive auditors might have noticed the high tension created by concentration on meeting profit goals. Normal selection of sales transactions with vouching to customer orders and shipping documents might turn up a missing customer order. Otherwise, the paperwork would seem to be in order. The problem lay in the managers' power to override controls and instruct shipping people to send bricks. Most auditors do not ask the question: "Have you shipped anything, other than company products, this year?"

Audit of Balance
Confirmations of distributors' accounts receivable may have elicited exception responses. The problem was to have a large enough confirmation sample to pick up some of these distributors or to be skeptical enough to send a special sample of confirmations to distributors who took the "sales" near the end of the accounting period. Observation of inventory should include some inspection of goods not on the company's premises.

Discovery Summary
The overstatements were not detected. The confirmation sample was small and did not contain any of the false shipments. Tests of detail transactions did not turn up any missing customer orders. The inventory out on consignment was audited by obtaining a written confirmation from the holders, who apparently had not opened the boxes. The remarkable financial performance was attributed to good management.

CASE 6.5
OVERSTATE THE INVENTORY, UNDERSTATE THE
COST OF GOODS SOLD

Problem
Overstated inventory caused understated cost of goods sold; overstated net income and retained earnings; overstated current assets, working capital, and total assets.

Method
A division manager at Doughboy Foods wanted to meet his profit goals and simply submitted overstated quantities in inventory reports. The manager (a) inserted fictitious count sheets in the independent auditors' working papers, (b) handed additional count sheets to the independent auditors after the count was completed saying "these got left out of your set,

and (c) inserted false data into the computer system that produced a final inventory compilation (even though this ploy caused the computer-generated inventory not to match with the count sheets).

Paper Trail
In general, management reports should correspond to accounting records. The manager's inventory reports showed amounts larger than shown in the accounts. He fixed the problem by showing false inventory that was "not recorded on the books."

Amount
The food products inventory was overstated by $650,000. Through a two-year period, the false reports caused an income overstatement of 15 percent in the first year and would have caused a 39 percent overstatement the second year.

AUDIT APPROACH
Objective
Obtain evidence of the existence, completeness, and valuation of inventory.

Control
Inventory counts should be taken under controlled conditions, but not under the control of managers who might benefit from manipulation. (However, if these managers are present, auditors should nevertheless be prepared to perform the audit work.) Inventory-takers should be trained and follow instructions for recording quantities and condition.

Test of Controls
Auditors should attend the inventory-taker training sessions and study the instructions for adequacy. Observation of the inventory-taking should be conducted by managers and by auditors to ensure compliance with the instructions.

Audit of Balance

For evidence of existence, select a sample of inventory items from the perpetual records and test-count them in the warehouse. For evidence of completeness, select a sample of inventory items in the warehouse, test-count them, and trace them to the final inventory compilation. For evidence of valuation, find the proper prices of inventory for one or both of the samples, calculate the total cost for the items, and compare to their amounts recorded in the books. Compare book inventory amounts to management reports. Control the working papers so only members of the audit team have access.

Analytical procedures gave some signals. The particular manager's division had the lowest inventory turnover rate (6.3) among all the company divisions (comparable turnover about 11.1) and its inventory had consistently increased from year to year (227 percent over the two-year period).

Discovery Summary

In the second year, when the manager handed over the count sheets "that got left out of your set," the auditor thanked him, then went to the warehouse to check them out. Finding them inaccurate, she compared book inventories to his management reports and found an overstatement in the reports. This prompted further comparison of the computer-generated inventory with the count sheets and more evidence of overstated quantities on 22 of the 99 count sheets.

DOCUMENTS, SOURCES, AND "EXTENDED PROCEDURES"

References are often made in the auditing literature to "extended procedures," but they are rarely defined and listed. Authorities are afraid that a list will limit the range of such procedures, so "extended procedures" is generally left undefined as an open-ended set to refer vaguely to "whatever is necessary in the circumstances." This section describes some of the "extended procedures" and warns that (1) some auditors may consider them ordinary and (2) other auditors may consider them unnecessary in any circumstances. They are useful procedures in either event.

CONTENT OF COMMON DOCUMENTS

Auditing textbooks often advise beginner auditors to "examine checks," and to "check the employees on a payroll." It helps to know something about these common documents and the information that can be seen on them.

Information on a Check

Exhibit 6-2 describes the information found on a typical check. Knowledge of the codes for federal reserve districts, offices, states, and bank identification numbers could enable an auditor to spot a crude check forgery. Similarly, a forger's mistakes with the optional identification printing or the magnetic check number might supply a tipoff. If the amount of a check is altered after it has cleared the bank, the change would be noted by comparing the magnetic imprint of the amount paid to the amount written on the check face. The back of a check carries the endorsement(s) of the payees and holders in due course; the date and the name and routing number of the bank where the check was deposited; and the date, identification of the federal reserve office, and its routing number for the federal reserve check clearing. (Sometimes there is no federal reserve clearing identification when local checks are cleared locally without going through a federal reserve office.) Auditors can follow the path of a canceled check by following the banks where it was deposited and cleared. This route may or may not correspond with the characteristics of the payee. (For example, ask why a check to a local business in Texas was deposited in a small Missouri bank and cleared through the St. Louis federal reserve office.)

Information on a Bank Statement

Most of the information shown on the bank statement in Exhibit 6-3 is self-explanatory. However, auditors should not overlook the usefulness of some of the information: the bank's count and dollar amount of deposits and checks can be compared to the detail data on the statement; the account holder's federal business identification number is on the statement, and this can be used in other data bases (for individuals, this is a place to get a person's Social Security number); and the statement itself can be studied for alterations.

EXHIBIT 6-2   How to Read a Canceled Check and Endorsement

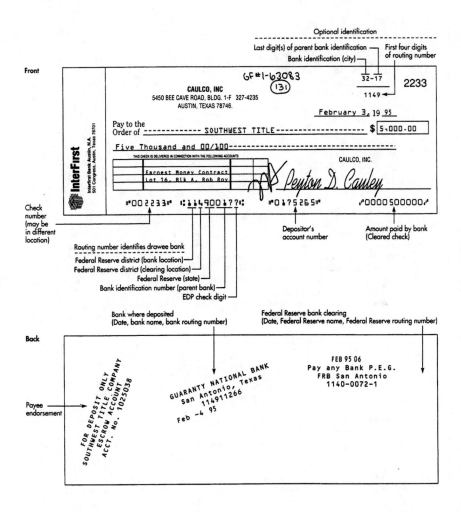

EXHIBIT 6-3   Small Business Bank Statement

```
                                                             27
  ⊠ First RepublicBank
     FIRST REPUBLICBANK AUSTIN, N.A.                    ACCOUNT
     P.O. BOX 908                      ---           604017-526-5
     AUSTIN, TEXAS  78781              ---  ---
                                       ---              PAGE
                                       ---               1

     CAULCO INC                                     SSN/TAX ID
     BLDG 1 OFFICE F                                74-2076251
     5450 BEE CAVE RD
     AUSTIN,  TX                                    CYC MC FREQ
     78746                                          01 01 M0000

     **  YOUR CHECKING ACCOUNT       01-29-95 THRU 02-29-95  **

  TO YOUR PREVIOUS BALANCE OF - - - - - - - - -      7,559.06
  YOU ADDED           1 DEPOSITS FOR  - - - - - -    5,654.16
  YOU SUBTRACTED    26 WITHDRAWALS FOR - - - - -    10,838.29
  GIVING YOU A CURRENT BALANCE OF - - - - - - -      7,374.93

  NUMBER OF DAYS USED FOR AVERAGES  - - - - - -            31
  YOUR AVERAGE LEDGER BALANCE - - - - - - - - -      4,014.67
  YOUR LOW BALANCE OCCURRED ON 02-22 AND WAS  -      2,374.93

              THANK YOU


  ------------------------------------------------------------
  ------------------------------------------------------------
              DEPOSITS AND OTHER ADDITIONS

       DATE    AMOUNT
       0204   5654.16 ✔
  ------------------------------------------------------------
              CHECKS AND OTHER WITHDRAWALS

  CHECK DATE    AMOUNT CHECK DATE    AMOUNT CHECK DATE    AMOUNT
  2201 0211     57.83✔ 2214 0203    403.92✔ 2225 0217   ✔182.77
   **                  2215 0203    135.59✔  **
  2205 0222     16.72✔ 2216 0216      6.16✔ 2231 0205   ✔254.37
  2206 0203    533.28✔ 2217 0217    138.43✔ 2232 0210   ✔ 60.61
  2207 0203   1312.15✔ 2218 0217    131.92✔
   **                  2219 0217     82.97✔ 2234 0217   ✔ 64.69
  2209 0203    247.10✔ 2220 0217     87.49✔ 2235 0218   ✔279.97
  2210 0203    249.98✔ 2221 0217     85.68✔  **
  2211 0203    255.26✔ 2222 0217     84.69✔ 2238 0219   ✔ 90.00
  2212 0203    242.09✔  **
  2213 0203    384.91✔ 2224 0217    449.71✔
```

Valid Social Security Numbers
In the United States, Social Security numbers have become a universal identification number. They can be useful to auditors when checking the personnel files and the validity of people on the payroll. Here are some characteristics of SSNs:[10]

- Every SSN consists of three groups of digits, three digits followed by two, followed by four (XXX-XX-XXXX). No group contains consecutive zeros, so 000-XX-XXXX, XXX-00-XXXX, and XXX-XX-0000 are not valid numbers.
- The first three digits gives the "area," indicating the state or territory where the number was issued. Numbers are usually issued at an early age, so the number might identify the state of birth. (Careful, however; the Social Security Administration may sometimes use numbers assigned to one geographic area for another.) By reference to the Social Security Number Table at the end of this chapter, you can see that certain three-digit area numbers have not been issued (as of 1990): 588, 627-699, and 729-999. The numbers from 700 to 728 were issued for the Railroad Retirement system years ago and probably belong to older workers. However, some of these numbers are issued as a courtesy to foreign visitors and foreign students.
- The middle two digits are the "group number," which could be from 01 to 99. However, many two-digit combinations have not been issued. By reference to the Social Security Number Table, you can see that the SSN numbers 001-76-9876, 001-08-9876, and 001-11-9876 are fictitious because the group numbers 76, 08, and 11 in combination with area 001 have not been used (as of 1990). (Levy pointed out that, in SSNs issued before 1965, group numbers of 10 or higher should be even numbers; and in SSNs issued in or after 1965, the group number can be odd or even. This feature can be correlated with a person's reported birthdate.)
- The last four digits can be 0001 to 9999. The only invalid one is 0000.

SOURCES OF INFORMATION

A wide variety of records and information is available for various kinds of investigations ranging from personal background checks to business inquiries. Our concern here is with public records and ways to get them. Only a few of the hundreds of sources are described briefly below.

General Business Sources

City and county tax assessor-collectors keep files on real property by address and legal description, owner, taxable value, improvements, amount of taxes and delinquencies. State (and some city) regulatory agencies have directories of liquor licenses, and various professionals (e.g., CPAs, dentists, doctors, plumbers, electricians). The U.S. Department of Housing and Urban Development (HUD) has a central index file of appraisers, real estate brokers, and most components of the building industry. The U.S. Department of State has data on companies that apply for import and export licenses. The Federal Aviation Administration maintains files on the chain of ownership of all civil aircraft in the United States. The U.S. Securities and Exchange Commission has extensive financial information on about 14,000 registered companies and their properties, principle officers, directors, and owners. Local Better Business Bureaus keep information about criminal rackets, cons, and their operators, and can provide information about the business reputation of local businesses. Standard & Poor's *Register of Corporations, Directors, and Executives* lists about 37,000 public and private companies and the names and titles of over 400,000 officials.[11]

Business and Asset Identification Sources

Each country and state has a system for registering businesses--corporations, joint ventures, sole proprietorships, partnerships. They keep files on registered "assumed names" (DBA, or "Doing Business As" names). Some businesses may be registered with a state and not a county, or with a county and not a state. All real corporations are chartered by a state, and each state's secretary of state keeps corporate record information, such as the date of registration and the initial officers and owners. (Using these sources, you can find the assets or business "hidden" in the spouse's name.) Crooks often work through a labyrinth of business entities, and you can find all the registered ones in these sources. You can find phony vendor companies created by real employees to bilk employers with false billings. Banks, finance companies, and other creditors often file Uniform Commercial Code (UCC) records to record the interest of the creditor in assets used as collateral for a loan, so other parties cannot claim interest in the assets (e.g., boats, business equipment, appliances). UCCs are found in county clerks' offices and in a state's office of the secretary of state or commercial department of the state records office. (They are also online in some commercial databases.)[12]

Federal and State Revenue Agencies

Ever wonder how revenue agents find tax evaders? One accountant described the following sources of tips for possible big audit findings. (1) Police and Drug Enforcement Agency arrest records point to people who may have illicit unreported income. (2) Real estate sales records may identify people who "forget" to put their sales in a tax return. (3) Auto registrations of expensive cars point to people who have a lot of money to spend, maybe some unreported income. (4) Comparison of state sales tax returns with income tax revenue amounts may reveal discrepancies (depending on which tax collector is feared the most). (5) Agents have used college-town newspaper rental ads to identify people who rent rooms, garage apartments, duplex halves, and the like, but forget to report the income.

EXTENDED PROCEDURES

The nature of extended procedures is limited only by an auditor's imagination and, sometimes, the willingness of management to cooperate in extraordinary audit activities. Next is a short series of extended procedures, with some brief explanations.[13]

Count the Petty Cash Twice in a Day

The second count is unexpected, and you might catch an embezzling custodian short.

Investigate Suppliers (Vendors)

Check the Better Business Bureau for reputation, the telephone book for a listing and address, the state and county corporation records for owners and assumed names. You may find fictitious vendors being used to make false billings or companies related to purchasing department employees.

Investigate Customers

As with vendors, investigation may reveal companies set up by insiders, with billings at below-list prices so the insiders can "buy" goods and resell them at a profit.

Examine Endorsements on Canceled Checks
Look for second endorsements, especially the name of employees. Most business payments are deposited with one endorsement. Be sure to include checks payable to "cash" or to a bank for purchase of cashiers' checks. The second endorsee indicates that the payee may not have received the benefit of the payment.

Add Up the Accounts Receivable Subsidiary
Cash payments on customer accounts have been stolen, with receipts given, credit entry to the customer account, but no cash deposit and no entry to the control account.

Audit General Journal Entries
Experience has shown that the largest number of accounting errors requiring adjustment are found in nonroutine, nonsystematic journal entries. (Systematic accounting is the processing of large volumes of day-to-day ordinary transactions.)

Match Payroll to Life and Medical Insurance Deductions
Ghosts on the payroll seldom elect these insurance coverages. Doing so reduces the embezzler's take and complicates the coverup.

Match Payroll to Social Security Numbers
Fictitious SSNs may be chosen at random, making the mistake of using an unissued number or one that does not match with the birthdate. Sort the payroll SSNs in numerical order and look for false, duplicate, or unlikely (e.g., consecutive) numbers.

Match Payroll with Addresses
Look for multiple persons at the same address.

Retrieve Customers' Checks
If an employee has diverted customer payments, the canceled checks showing endorsements and deposits to a bank where the company has no account are not available because they are returned to the issuing organization (customer). Ask the customer to give originals, copies, or provide access for examination.

Use Marked Coins and Currency

Plant marked money in locations where cash collections should be gathered and turned over for deposit.

Measure Deposit Lag Time

Compare the dates of cash debit recording and deposit slip dates to dates credited by the bank. Someone who takes cash, then holds the deposit for the next cash receipts to make up the difference, causes a delay between the date of recording and the bank's date of deposit.

Document Examination

Look for erasures, alterations, copies where originals should be filed, telltale lines from a copier when a document has been pieced together, handwriting, and other oddities. Auditors should always insist on seeing original documents instead of photocopies. Professional document examination is a technical activity that requires special training (e.g., IRS, FBI), but crude alterations may be observed, at least enough to bring them to specialists' attention.

WANT TO FUDGE YOUR TAX DEDUCTIONS?

Don't try to turn that $300 receipt into $800 with the stroke of a ballpoint pen. The IRS has ultraviolet scanners, ink chromatographers, densitometers, and argon-ion lasers that can identify the brand of pen, the age of the paper, and the source of the paper. Something printed on a laser printer is harder, but they're working on it.

Source: D. Churbuck, "Desktop Forgery," Forbes, November 27, 1989, p. 252.

Inquiry, Ask Questions

Be careful not to discuss fraud possibilities with the managers who might be involved. It gives them a chance to cover up or run. Wells described fraud assessment questioning (FAQ) as a nonaccusatory method of asking key questions of personnel during a regular audit to give them an opportunity to furnish information about possible misdeeds. Fraud possibilities are addressed in a direct manner, so the FAQ approach must have the support of management. Example questions are: "Do you think fraud is a problem for business in general?" "Do you think this company has any particular problem with fraud?" "In your department, who is beyond suspicion?" "Is there any information you would like to furnish regarding possible fraud within this organization?"[14]

Covert Surveillance
Observe activities while not being seen. External auditors might watch employees clocking onto a work shift, observing whether they use only one time card. Traveling hotel auditors may check in unannounced, use the restaurant and entertainment facilities, and watch the employees skimming receipts and tickets. (Trailing people on streets and maintaining a "stake-out" should be left to trained investigators.)

Horizontal and Vertical Analyses
This is analytical review ratio analysis and is very similar to preliminary analytical procedures. (A technical explanation is in Robertson, J.C., *Auditing*, eighth edition, Chapter 5, Richard D. Irwin, Inc., 1996.) Horizontal analysis refers to changes of financial statement numbers and ratios across several years. Vertical analysis refers to financial statement amounts expressed each year as proportions of a base, such as sales for the income statement accounts and total assets for the balance sheet accounts. Auditors look for relationships that do not make sense as indicators of potential large misstatement and fraud.

Net Worth Analysis
This is used when fraud has been discovered or strongly suspected, and the information to calculate a suspect's net worth can be obtained (e.g., asset and liability records, bank accounts). The method is to calculate the suspect's net worth (known assets minus known liabilities) at the beginning and end of a period (months or years), then try to account for the difference as (1) known income less living expenses and (2) unidentified difference. The unidentified difference may be the best available approximation of the amount of a theft.

Expenditure Analysis
This is similar to net worth analysis, except the data is the suspect's spending for all purposes compared to known income. If spending exceeds legitimate and explainable income, the difference may be the amount of a theft.

AFTER DISCOVERING A FRAUD

Building a case against a fraudster is a task for trained fraud examiners. Most internal and external auditors take roles as assistants to fraud examiners who know how to conduct interviews, perform surveillance, use informants, and obtain usable confessions. In almost all cases, the postdiscovery activity proceeds with a special prosecutorial assignment under the cooperation or leadership of management. A district attorney and police officials may be involved. Prosecution of fraudsters is advisable because, if left unpunished, they often go on to steal again. This is no place for "normal" auditing.

While engaged in audit work, auditors should know how to preserve the **chain of custody** of evidence. The chain of custody is the crucial link of the evidence to the suspect, called the "relevance" of evidence by attorneys and judges. If documents are lost, mutilated, coffee-soaked, compromised (so a defense attorney can argue that they were altered to frame the suspect), they can lose their effectiveness for the prosecution. Auditors should learn to mark the evidence, writing an identification of the location, condition, date, time, and circumstances as soon as it appears to be a signal of fraud. This marking should be on a separate tag or page, the original document should be put in a protective envelope (plastic) for preservation, and audit work should proceed with copies of the documents instead of originals.

A record should be made of the safekeeping and of all persons who use the original. Any eyewitness observations should be timely recorded in a memorandum or on tape (audio or video), with corroboration of colleagues, if possible. There are other features to the chain of custody relating to interviews, confessions, documents obtained by subpoena, and other matters, but these activities usually are not conducted by auditors.

Independent CPAs often accept engagements for litigation support and expert witnessing. This work is often called **forensic accounting,** which means the application of accounting and auditing skills to legal problems, both civil and criminal. **Litigation support** can take several forms, but it usually amounts to consulting in the capacity of helping attorneys document case evidence and determine damages. **Expert witness** work involves testifying to findings determined during litigation support and testifying about accounting principles and auditing standards applications.

SUMMARY

Fraud awareness auditing starts with knowledge of the types of errors, irregularities, illegal acts, and frauds that can be perpetrated. External, internal, and governmental auditors all have standards for care, attention, planning, detection, and reporting of some kinds of errors, irregularities, and illegal acts. The Association of Certified Fraud Examiners publishes standards for Certified Fraud Examiners.

Fraud may be contemplated when people have motives, usually financial needs, for stealing money or property. Motive, combined with perceived opportunity and a lapse of integrity, generally makes the probability of fraud or theft very high. Opportunities arise when an organization's management has lax attitudes about setting examples for good behavior and about maintenance of a supportive control environment. The fear of getting caught by control procedures is a strong deterrent for many would-be fraudsters. Otherwise, attentive management of personnel can ease the pressures people feel and, thus, reduce the incidence of fraud.

Auditors need to know about the red flags--the telltale signs and indications that have accompanied many frauds. When studying a business operation, auditors' ability to "think like a crook" to devise ways to steal can help in the planning of procedures designed to determine whether it happened. Often, imaginative "extended procedures" can be employed to unearth evidence of fraudulent activity. However, technical and personal care must always be exercised because accusations of fraud are always taken very seriously. For this reason, after preliminary findings indicate fraud possibilities, auditors should enlist the cooperation of management and assist fraud examination professionals in bringing an investigation to a conclusion.

PRACTICAL CASE PROBLEMS
INSTRUCTIONS FOR CASES

These cases are designed like the ones in the chapter. They give the problem, the method, the paper trail, and the amount. Your assignment is to write the "audit approach" portion of the case, organized around these sections:

Objective: Express the objective in terms of the facts supposedly asserted in financial records, accounts, and statements.

Control: Write a brief explanation of desirable controls, missing controls, and especially the kinds of "deviations" that might arise from the situation described in the case.

Test of controls: Write some procedures for getting evidence about existing controls, especially procedures that could discover deviations from controls. If there are no controls to test, then there are no procedures to perform; go then to the next section. A "procedure" should instruct someone about the source(s) of evidence to tap and the work to do.

Audit of balance: Write some procedures for getting evidence about the existence, completeness, valuation, ownership, or disclosure assertions identified in your *objective* section above.

Discovery summary: Write a short statement about the discovery you expect to accomplish with your procedures.

* * * * * * * * * *

CASE # 6.1: STEALING WAS EASY. Employee Embezzlement via Cash Disbursements and Inventory. Write the "audit approach" section like the cases in the chapter.

Problem: Cash embezzlement, inventory and expense overstatement.

Method: Lew Marcus was the only bookkeeper at the Ace Plumbing Supply Company. He ordered the supplies and inventory, paid the bills, collected the cash receipts and checks sent by customers, and reconciled the bank statements. The company had about $11 million in sales, inventory of $3 million, and expenses that generally ran about $6-7 million each year. Nobody checked Lew's work, so sometimes when he received a bill for goods from a supplier (say, for $8,000) he would make an accounting entry for $12,000 debit to inventory, write an $8,000 check to pay the bill, then write a $4,000 check to himself. The check to Lew was not recorded, and he removed it from the bank statement when he prepared the bank reconciliation. The owner of the business considered the monthly bank reconciliation a proper control activity.

Paper Trail: No perpetual inventory records were kept, and no periodic inventory count was taken. The general ledger contained an inventory control account balance that was reduced by 60 percent of the amount of each sale of plumbing fixtures (estimated cost of sales). The bank statements and reconciliations were in a file. The statements showed the check number and amount of Lew's checks to himself, but the checks themselves were missing. The checks to vendors were in the amounts of their bills, but the entries in the cash disbursements journal showed higher amounts.

Amount: Over an eight-year period, Lew embezzled $420,000.

CASE # 6.2: THE EXTRA BANK ACCOUNT. Employee Embezzlement via Cash Receipts and Payment of Personal Expenses. In this case, you can assume you have received the informant's message. Write the "audit approach" section like the cases in the chapter.

Problem: Cash receipts pocketed and personal expenses paid from business account.

Method: The Ourtown Independent School District, like all others, had red tape about school board approval of cash disbursements. To get around the rules, and to make timely payment of some bills possible, the superintendent of schools had a school bank account that was used in the manner of a petty cash fund. The board knew about it and had given blanket approval in advance for its use to make timely payment of minor school expenses. The board, however, never reviewed the activity in this account. The business manager had sole responsibility for the account, subject to the annual audit. The account got money from transfers from other school accounts and from deposit of cafeteria cash receipts. The superintendent did not like to be bothered with details, and he often signed blank checks so the business manager would not need to run in for a signature all the time. The business manager sometimes paid her personal American Express credit card bills, charged personal items to the school's VISA account, and pocketed some cafeteria cash receipts before deposit.

Paper Trail: An informant called the state education audit agency and told the story that this business manager had used school funds to buy hosiery. When told of this story, the superintendent told the auditor to place no credibility in the informant, who is "out to get us." The business manager had in fact used the account to write unauthorized checks to "cash," put her own American Express bills in the school files (the school district had a VISA card, not American Express), and signed on the school card for gasoline and auto repairs during periods of vacation and summer when school was not in session. (As for the hosiery, she purchased $700 worth with school funds one year.) The superintendent was genuinely unaware of the misuse of funds.

Amount: The business manager had been employed for six years, was trusted, and stole an estimated $25,000.

CASE #6.3: DOCTOR! DOCTOR? Employee Embezzlement: Medical Claims Fraud. Write the "audit approach" section like the cases in the chapter.
Problem: Fictitious medical benefit claims were paid by the company, which self-insured up to $50,000 per employee. The expense account that included legitimate and false charges was "employee medical benefits."

Method: As manager of the claims payment department, Martha Lee was considered one of Beta Magnetic's best employees. She never missed a day of work in 10 years, and her department had one of the company's best efficiency ratings. Controls were considered good, including the verification by a claims processor that: (1) the patient was a Beta employee, (2) medical treatments were covered in the plan, (3) the charges were within approved guidelines, (4) the cumulative claims for the employee did not exceed $50,000 (if over $50,000 a claim was submitted to an insurance company), and (5) the calculation for payment was correct. After verification processing, claims were sent to the claims payment department to pay the doctor directly. No payments ever went directly to employees. Martha Lee prepared false claims on real employees, forging the signature of various claims processors, adding her own review approval, naming bogus doctors who would be paid by the payment department. The payments were mailed to various post office box addresses and to her husband's business address.

Nobody ever verified claims information with the employees. The employees received no reports of medical benefits paid on their behalf. While the department had performance reports by claims processors, these reports did not show claim-by-claim details. No one verified the credentials of the doctors.

Paper Trail: The falsified claims forms were in Beta's files, containing all the fictitious data on employee names, processor signatures, doctors' bills, and phony doctors and addresses. The canceled checks were returned by the bank and were kept in Beta's files, containing "endorsements" by the doctors. Martha Lee and her husband were somewhat clever: They deposited the checks in various banks in accounts opened in the names and identification of the "doctors."

Martha Lee did not stumble on the paper trail. She drew the attention of an auditor who saw her take her 24 claims processing employees out to an annual staff appreciation luncheon in a fleet of stretch limousines.

Amount: Over the last seven years, Martha Lee and her husband stole $3.5 million, and, until the last, no one noticed anything unusual about the total amount of claims paid.

CASE #6.4: THANK GOODNESS IT'S FRIDAY. Financial Reporting: Overstated Sales and Profits. Write the "audit approach" section like the cases in the chapter. For this case, give the recommended adjusting journal entry as well as the audit approach.

Problem: Overstated sales caused overstated net income, retained earnings, current assets, working capital, and total assets. Overstated cash collections did not change the total current assets or total assets, but it increased the amount of cash and decreased the amount of accounts receivable.

Method: Alpha Brewery Corporation has generally good control policies and procedures related to authorization of transactions for accounting entry, and the accounting manual has instructions for recording sales transactions in the proper accounting period. The company regularly closes the accounting process each Friday at 5 p.m. to prepare weekly management reports. The year-end date (cutoff date) is December 31 and, in 1990, December 31, was a Monday. However, the accounting was performed through Friday as usual, and the accounts were closed for the year on January 4.

Paper Trail: All the entries were properly dated after December 31, including the sales invoices, cash receipts, and shipping documents. However, the trial balance from which the financial statements were prepared was dated December 31, 1990. Nobody noticed the slip of a few days because the Friday closing was normal.

Amount: Alpha recorded sales of $672,000 and gross profit of $268,800 over the January 1-4 period. Cash collections on customers' accounts came in the amount of $800,000.

CASE #6.5: THE PHANTOM OF THE INVENTORY. Financial Reporting: Overstated Inventory and Profits.

Write the "audit approach" section like the cases in the chapter, and also recalculate the income (loss) before taxes using the correct inventory figures. (Assume the correct beginning inventory two years ago was $5.5 million.)

Problem: Overstated physical inventory caused understated cost of goods sold and overstated net income, current assets, total assets, and retained earnings.

Method: All Bright Company manufactured lamps. Paul M, manager of the State Street plant, was under pressure to produce profits so the company could maintain its loans at the bank. The loans were secured by the inventory of 1,500 types of finished goods, work in process, and parts used for making lamps (bases, shades, wire, nuts, bolts, and so on). Paul arranged the physical inventory counting procedures and accompanied the external audit team while the external auditors observed the count and made test counts after the company personnel had recorded their counts on tags attached to the inventory locations. At the auditors' request, Paul directed them to the "most valuable" inventory for their test counts, although he did not show them all of the most valuable types. When the auditors were looking the other way, Paul raised the physical count on inventory tags the auditors did not include in their test counts. When everyone had finished each floor of the multistory warehouse, all the tags were gathered and sent to data processing for computer compilation and pricing at FIFO cost.

Paper Trail: All Bright had no perpetual inventory records. All the record of the inventory quantity and pricing was in the count tags and the priced compilation, which was produced by the data processing department six weeks later. The auditors traced their test counts to the compilation and did not notice the raised physical quantities on the inventory types they did not test count. They also did not notice some extra (fictitious) tags Paul had handed over to data processing.

Amount: Paul falsified the inventory for three years before the company declared bankruptcy. Over that period, the inventory was overstated by $1 million (17 percent, two years ago), $2.5 million (31 percent, one year ago), and $3 million (29 percent, current year). The financial statements showed the following (dollars in 000):

	Two Years Ago	One Year Ago	Current Year
Sales	$25,000	$29,000	$40,500
Cost of goods sold	(20,000)	(22,000)	(29,000)
Expenses	(5,000)	(8,000)	(9,000)
Income (loss) before taxes	0	$(1,000)	$ 2,500
Ending inventory	$ 6,000	$ 8,000	$10,200
Other current assets	9,000	8,500	17,500
Total assets	21,000	21,600	34,300
Current liabilities	5,000	5,500	13,000
Long-term debt *	5,500	6,600	9,300
Stockholder equity	10,500	9,500	12,000

* Secured by inventory pledged to the bank.

CASE #6.6: IS THIS THE PERFECT CRIME? Embezzlers often try to cover up by removing canceled checks they made payable to themselves or endorsed on the back with their own names. Missing canceled checks are a signal (red flag). However, people who reconcile bank accounts may not notice missing checks if the bank reconciliation is performed using only the numerical listing printed in the bank statement. Now consider the case of *truncated bank statements*, when the bank does not even return the canceled checks to the payor. *All* the checks are "missing," and the bank reconciler has no opportunity to notice anything about canceled checks.

Required:
Consider the following story of a real enbezzlement. List and explain the ways and means you believe someone might detect the embezzlement. Think first about the ordinary everyday control activities. Then, think about extensive detection efforts assuming a tip or indication of a possible fraud has been received. Is this a "perfect crime?"

This was the ingenious embezzler's scheme: (a) He hired a print shop to print a private stock of Ajax Company checks in the company's numerical sequence. (b) In his job as an accounts payable clerk, he intercepted legitimate checks written by the accounts payable department and signed by the Ajax treasurer, then destroyed them. (c) He substituted the same-numbered check from the private stock, payable to himself in the same amount as the legitimate check, and he "signed" it with a rubber stamp that looked enough like the Ajax Company treasurer's signature to fool the paying bank. (d) He deposited the money in his own bank account. The bank statement reconciler (a different person) was able to correspond the check numbers and amounts listed in the cleared items in the bank statement to the recorded cash disbursement (check number and amount), thus did not notice the trick. The embezzler was able to process the vendor's "past due" notice and next month statement with complete documentation, enabling the Ajax treasurer to sign another check the next month paying both the past due balance and current charges. The embezzler was careful to scatter the double-expense payments among numerous accounts (telephone, office supplies, inventory, etc.), so the double-paid expenses did not distort any accounts very much. As time passed, the embezzler was able to recommend budget figures that allowed a large enough budget so his double-paid expenses in various categories did not often pop up as large variances from the budget.

CASE #6.7: EXAMINE THE BANK STATEMENT IN EXHIBIT 6-3.
Is anything suspicious?

FOOTNOTES

[1]   R. K. Elliott and J. J. Willingham, *Management Fraud: Detection and Deterrence* (New York: Petrocelli Books, Inc., 1980), p. 4.

[2]   These and other aspects of the art of fraud auditing are more fully developed in: G. J. Bologna and R. J. Lindquist, *Fraud Auditing and Forensic Accounting* (New York: John Wiley & Sons, 1987), pp. 27-42; W. S. Albrecht, M. B. Romney, D. J. Cherrington, I. R. Payne, and A. J. Roe, *How to Detect and Prevent Business Fraud* (New York: Prentice Hall, 1982); R. White and W. G. Bishop, III, *The Role of the Internal Auditor in the Deterrence, Detection, and Reporting of Fraudulent Financial Reporting* (The Institute of Internal Auditors); M. J. Barrett and R. N. Carolus, *Control and Internal Auditing* (The Institute of Internal Auditors); and W. S. Albrecht, G. W. Wernz, and T. L. Williams, *Fraud--Bringing Light to the Dark Side of Business* (Burr Ridge, IL.: Richard D. Irwin, Inc., 1995).

[3]   For further reference, see: D. R. Cressey, "Management Fraud, Accounting Controls, and Criminological Theory," pp. 117-47, and Albrecht et al., "Auditor Involvement in the Detection of Fraud," pp. 207-61, both in R. K. Elliott and J. J. Willingham, *Management Fraud: Detection and Deterrence* (New York: Petrocelli Books, Inc., 1980).; J. K. Loebbecke; M. M. Eining; and J. J. Willingham, "Auditors' Experience with Material Irregularities: Frequency, Nature, and Detectability," *Auditing: A Journal of Practice and Theory*, Fall 1989, pp. 1-28.

[4]   Bologna and Lindquist, *Fraud Auditing*, p. 8.

[5]   Cressey, "Management Fraud," p. 124.

[6]   W. S. Albrecht, "How CPAs Can Help Clients Prevent Employee Fraud," *Journal of Accountancy*, December 1988, pp. 110-14.

[7]   Ibid., p. 113-14.

[8]   Ibid., p. 114.

[9]   Long lists of red flags can be found in Bologna and Lindquist, *Fraud Auditing*, pp. 49-56; Albrecht et. al., in *Management Fraud*, pp. 223-26; *Statements on Auditing Standards* 82 and 54; "Auditing for Fraud" courses of the Association of Certified Fraud Examiners; courses offered

by other organizations, such as the AICPA and The Institute of Internal Auditors.

[10] Caution: The Social Security Administration periodically adds numbers that have been issued and may use numbers assigned to one geographic area for another. If the validity of a SSN becomes important in an audit, check with the Social Security Administration to ascertain the current status of numbers issued. For further reference, see M. L. Levy, "Financial Fraud: Schemes and Indicia," *Journal of Accountancy*, August 1985, p. 85; E. J. Pankau, *Check It Out* (Houston: Cloak & Data Press, 1990), pp. 20-27.

[11] Hundreds of sources and directories under the categories of business, finance, people, property, and electronic data bases are listed and described in the U.S. General Accounting Office publication entitled *Investigators' Guide to Sources of Information* (GAO/OSI-88-1, March 1988, updated periodically).

[12] These and other sources of business and personal information are described in Pankau, *Check It Out*.

[13] Further explanation of these and other procedures can be found in the books and articles cited in preceding footnotes and in these sources: AICPA *Technical Practice Aids* (TPA 8200.02); D. Churbuck, "Desktop Forgery," *Forbes*, November 27, 1989, pp. 246-54; O. Hilton, *Scientific Examination of Questioned Documents*, rev. ed. (New York: Elsevier North Holland, 1982); A. C. Levinston, "40 Years of Embezzlement Tracking," *Internal Auditor*, April 1991, pp. 51-55.

[14] Joseph T. Wells, "From the Chairman: Fraud Assessment Questioning," *The White Paper*, Association of Certified Fraud Examiners, May-June 1991), p. 2. This technique must be used with extreme care and practice.

SOCIAL SECURITY NUMBER TABLE

(1)	(2)	(3)	(4)	(5)	(6)
	Highest Group Numbers				
	Odd	Even	Even	Odd	State
Area	less	10 and	less	greater	or
Number	than 10	above	than 10	than 10	Territory
000	None	None	None	None	Unassigned
001	09	74	None	None	New Hampshire
002-003	09	72	None	None	New Hampshire
004	09	86	None	None	Maine
005-007	09	84	None	None	Maine
008	09	70	None	None	Vermont
009	09	68	None	None	Vermont
010-029	09	68	None	None	Massachusetts
030-034	09	66	None	None	Massachusetts
035-037	09	56	None	None	Rhode Island
038-039	09	54	None	None	Rhode Island
040-041	09	82	None	None	Connecticut
042-049	09	80	None	None	Connecticut
050-119	09	72	None	None	New York
120-134	09	70	None	None	New York
135-152	09	82	None	None	New Jersey
153-158	09	80	None	None	New Jersey
159-184	09	68	None	None	Pennsylvania
185-211	09	66	None	None	Pennsylvania
212-216	09	98	08	17	Maryland
217-220	09	98	08	15	Maryland
221-222	09	72	None	None	Delaware
223-228	09	98	08	45	Virginia
229-231	09	98	08	43	Virginia
232	09	98	08	33	North Carolina West Virginia
233-234	09	98	08	33	West Virginia
235-236	09	98	08	31	West Virginia
237-246	09	98	08	55	North Carolina
247-248	09	98	08	71	South Carolina

SOCIAL SECURITY NUMBER TABLE CONTINUED

(1)	(2)	(3)	(4)	(5)	(6)
	Highest Group Numbers				
Area Number	Odd less than 10	Even 10 and above	Even less than 10	Odd greater than 10	State or Territory
249-251	09	98	08	69	South Carolina
252-258	09	98	08	61	Georgia
259-260	09	98	08	59	Georgia
261-267	09	98	08	99	Florida
268-272	09	88	None	None	Ohio
273-302	09	86	None	None	Ohio
303-309	09	98	02	None	Indiana
310-317	09	98	None	None	Indiana
318	09	80	None	None	Illinois
319-361	09	78	None	None	Illinois
362-367	09	98	04	None	Michigan
368-386	09	98	02	None	Michigan
387-397	09	98	None	None	Wisconsin
398-399	09	96	None	None	Wisconsin
400-406	09	98	08	33	Kentucky
407	09	98	08	31	Kentucky
408	09	98	08	57	Tennessee
409-415	09	98	08	55	Tennessee
416-424	09	98	08	27	Alabama
425-428	09	98	08	59	Mississippi
429-431	09	98	08	67	Arkansas
432	09	98	08	65	Arkansas
433-438	09	98	08	67	Louisiana
439	09	98	08	65	Louisiana
440-441	09	92	None	None	Oklahoma
442-448	09	90	None	None	Oklahoma
449-463	09	98	08	91	Texas
464-467	09	98	08	89	Texas
468-472	09	98	08	13	Minnesota
473-477	09	98	08	11	Minnesota
478-481	09	98	08	13	Iowa

SOCIAL SECURITY NUMBER TABLE CONTINUED

(1)	(2)	(3)	(4)	(5)	(6)
	Highest Group Numbers				
	Odd	Even	Even	Odd	State
Area	less	10 and	less	greater	or
Number	than 10	above	than 10	than 10	Territory
482-485	09	98	08	11	Iowa
486-490	09	96	None	None	Missouri
491-500	09	94	None	None	Missouri
501	09	98	08	11	North Dakota
502	09	98	08	None	North Dakota
503	09	98	08	13	South Dakota
504	09	98	08	11	South Dakota
505	09	98	08	21	Nebraska
506-508	09	98	08	19	Nebraska
509-515	09	94	None	None	Kansas
516	09	98	08	15	Montana
517	09	98	08	13	Montana
518-519	09	98	08	23	Idaho
520	09	98	08	15	Wyoming
521-524	09	98	08	59	Colorado
525	09	98	08	69	New Mexico
526-527	09	98	08	99	Arizona
528	09	98	08	75	Utah
529	09	98	08	73	Utah
530	09	98	08	27	Nevada
531	09	98	08	None	Washington
532-539	09	98	06	None	Washington
540-544	09	98	08	21	Oregon
545-573	09	98	08	99	California
574*	09	92	None	None	Alaska
575-576	09	98	08	39	Hawaii
577	09	98	08	15	District of Columbia
578-579	09	98	08	13	District of Columbia

SOCIAL SECURITY NUMBER TABLE CONTINUED

(1)	(2)	(3)	(4)	(5)	(6)
	Highest Group Numbers				
Area Number	Odd less than 10	Even 10 and above	Even less than 10	Odd greater than 10	State or Territory
580*	09	98	08	21	Puerto Rico Virgin Islands
581-584	09	98	08	99	Puerto Rico
585	09	98	08	67	New Mexico
586*	09	84	None	None	Guam Amer. Samoa N. Mariana Is. Philippines
587	09	98	08	59	Mississippi
588	None	None	None	None	Mississippi
589-591	09	60	None	None	Florida
592-595	09	58	None	None	Florida
596-597	09	14	None	None	Puerto Rico
598-599	09	12	None	None	Puerto Rico
600	09	50	None	None	Arizona
601	09	48	None	None	Arizona
602-620	03	None	None	None	California
621-626	01	None	None	None	California
627-699	None	None	None	None	Unassigned
700-723	09	18	None	None	RR Retirement†
724	09	28	None	None	RR Retirement†
725-726	09	18	None	None	RR Retirement†
727	09	10	None	None	RR Retirement†
728	09	14	None	None	RR Retirement†
729-999	None	None	None	None	Unassigned

* SSNs in these areas also assigned to Southeast Asian refugees during period from April 1975 through November 1979.

† No longer issued.

Source: Edmund J. Pankau, [it]Check It Out (Houston: Cloak & Data Press, 1990), pp. 24-27. Reprinted with permission.

CHAPTER 7
OVERVIEW OF
INTERNAL CONTROL

This chapter defines and explains internal controls as they affect financial recordkeeping and reporting. Controls help prevent and detect errors, irregularities, and frauds, although they cannot guarantee prevention and detection of all types of frauds. Management is responsible for designing, implementing, and monitoring internal controls. Internal and external auditors are concerned with internal controls in connection with planning audit procedures and making reports of control weaknesses. This chapter provides an overview of internal control theory mainly from the perspective of external auditors.

INTRODUCTION

Internal control evaluation and control risk assessment is a very important part of the work in every audit of financial statements. Generally accepted auditing standards (GAAS) emphasize internal control in the second field work standard:

> A sufficient understanding of the internal control structure is to be obtained to plan the audit and to determine the nature, timing, and extent of tests to be performed (SAS 1, AU 150; SAS 55, AU 319).

The key idea in the audit standard is "to plan the audit" (i.e., determine the nature, timing, and extent of subsequent audit procedures). The "understanding of a client's internal control" need be only *sufficient* to accomplish this purpose. The audit standard does not require auditors to evaluate controls exhaustively in every audit. However, as you study this chapter, you will encounter aspects of auditors' involvement with controls that go beyond this limited purpose.

This chapter presents a general introduction to the theory and definitions you will find useful for internal control evaluation and control risk assessment.

Chapters 8-12 explain internal control considerations in the context of specific accounts and classes of transaction.

INTRODUCTION--THE COSO REPORT

Through 1995, the auditing standard on internal control in a financial statement audit was SAS 55, AU 319. In 1996, the AICPA Auditing Standards Board issued SAS 78 to amend SAS 55 to make it consistent with a popular report on internal control known under the title of *Internal Control--Integrated Framework* produced in 1992 by the Committee of Sponsoring Organizations of the Treadway Commission (hereafter abbreviated as the "COSO Report").[1] This chapter incorporates SAS 78 and the COSO Report and uses them to explain independent auditors' responsibilities for internal control evaluation and control risk assessment.

DEFINITION

The COSO Report defined internal control as follows:

> Internal control is a process, effected by an entity's board of directors, management and other personnel, designed to provide reasonable assurance regarding the achievement of objectives in the following three *categories*:
> *   Reliability of financial reporting.
> *   Compliance with applicable laws and regulations.
> *   Effectiveness and efficiency of operations.

FUNDAMENTAL CONCEPTS

COSO stated that this definition reflects four fundamental concepts--*process, people, reasonable assurance,* and *category objectives.*

Internal control is a *process*, not an end in itself, but a means to ends (i.e., the category objectives). SAS 78and the second standard of GAAS field work (SAS 1, AU 150) use the term *structure* to describe internal control. The semantic distinction of process versus structure is not especially important, as long as you understand that internal control is a dynamic function (process) operating every day within a company's framework (structure). Internal control is operated by *people*. A company may have policy manuals, procedures, forms, computer-controlled information and accounting, and other features of control, but people make the system work at every level of company management. People establish the objectives, put control mechanisms in place, and operate them.

Internal control provides *reasonable assurance*, not absolute assurance, that category control objectives will be achieved. Since people operate the controls, breakdowns can occur. Human error, deliberate circumvention, management override, and improper collusion among people who are supposed to act independently can cause failure to achieve objectives. Internal control can help prevent and detect these people-caused failures, but it cannot guarantee that they will never happen. In auditing standards, the concept of reasonable assurance recognizes that the costs of controls should not exceed the benefits that are expected from the controls (SAS 78, AU 319). Hence, a company can decide that certain controls are too costly in light of the risk of loss that may occur.

Internal control is designed to achieve *objectives in three categories*. In the operations category, some examples of objectives are: good business reputation, return on investment, market share, new product introduction, and safeguarding assets in the context of their effective and efficient use. The operations control objectives cover business strategy and tactics. In the financial reporting category, the objectives are: reliable published financial reports (e.g., annual financial statements, interim financial reports), and safeguarding assets from unauthorized use (e.g., embezzlement, theft, damage, unauthorized purchase or disposition), including the accounting-reporting of lapses in asset safeguarding. The financial reporting objectives are of most direct concern to internal and external auditors. In the compliance category, the broad objective is compliance with laws and regulations that affect the company. Internal and external auditors are also concerned with evaluation of compliance objective controls.

INTERNAL CONTROL COMPONENTS

The COSO Report and SAS 78 state that internal control consists of five interrelated *components* (Exhibit 7-1)--management's control environment, management's risk assessment, management's control activities, management's monitoring, and the management information and communication systems that link all the components. COSO wrote the report to be a guide for managements of organizations (directors, officers, internal auditors, and employees). Hence, *management* is used to describe all the components. The COSO Report is not a guide for external auditors' procedural control evaluation and control risk assessment responsibilities. However, the components provide the focus for auditors' attention. Exhibit 7-1 shows the interrelated control components.

The control components are relevant for each of the control objectives categories. The COSO Report defined each of the three categories and stated that management should enact the five components in each of them. Exhibit 7-2 diagrams this scheme.

The foregoing description of the COSO Report briefly explains the entire integrated framework and places the reliable financial reporting category in perspective. The remainder of this chapter deals with the objectives of financial reporting controls and the auditors' work in evaluating them. The chapter concentrates on the components as they apply to financial reporting. The auditors' task is to evaluate internal control based on evidence that these five components are (1) properly designed and specified, (2) placed in operation, and (3) functioning effectively. Thus, the five components are prerequisite criteria for effective internal control.

EXHIBIT 7 -1 Interrelated Internal Control Components

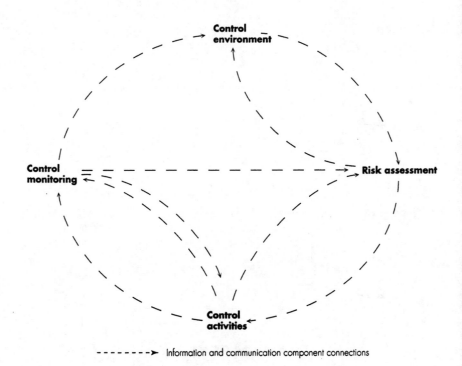

Information and communication component connections

EXHIBIT 7-2   Internal Control-Integrated Framwork (COSO)

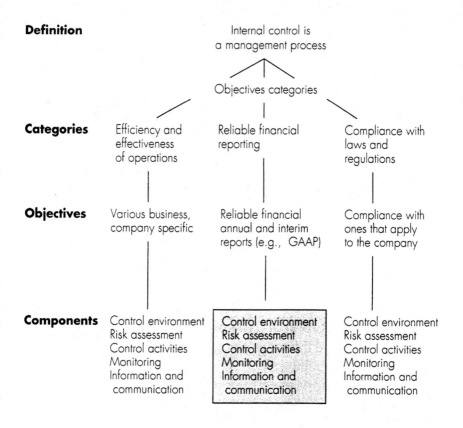

Definition   Internal control is
                                        a management process

                                        Objectives categories

Categories   Efficiency and   Reliable financial   Compliance with
                 effectiveness   reporting   laws and
                 of operations   regulations

Objectives   Various business,   Reliable financial   Compliance with
                 company specific   annual and interim   ones that apply
                                        reports (e.g., GAAP)   to the company

Components   Control environment   Control environment   Control environment
                 Risk assessment   Risk assessment   Risk assessment
                 Control activities   Control activities   Control activities
                 Monitoring   Monitoring   Monitoring
                 Information and   Information and   Information and
                 communication   communication   communication

MANAGEMENT VERSUS
AUDITOR RESPONSIBILITY

A company's management is responsible for the components of its internal control. Management establishes a control environment, assesses risks it wishes to control, specifies information and communication channels and content (including the accounting system and its reports), designs and implements control activities, and monitors, supervises, and maintains the controls.

External auditors are not responsible for designing effective controls for audit clients. They are responsible for *evaluating* existing internal controls and *assessing* the control risk in them. "Designing control" refers to management's responsibility for the five components. However, accounting firms undertake control design as consulting engagements and consider such work to be separate and apart from the audit engagement responsibility.

External auditors often provide information useful to management and directors for carrying out the company's control mission. Auditors' communications of reportable conditions and material weaknesses are intended to help management carry out its responsibilities for internal control monitoring and change. However, external auditors' observations and recommendations are usually limited to external financial reporting matters.

External auditors' basis for knowing about reportable conditions and material weaknesses is found in their familiarity with the types of errors, irregularities, frauds, and misstatements that can occur in any account balance or class of transactions. Clearly, hundreds of innocent errors and not-so-innocent fraud schemes are possible. (Many of these are discussed in Chapter 6, Fraud Awareness Auditing.) Instead of trying to learn hundreds of possible errors and irregularities, it is better to start with seven general categories of them. Exhibit 7-3 shows a typology of seven categories, with some examples. The external auditors' task of control risk assessment starts with learning about a company's controls designed to prevent, detect, and correct these potential errors and irregularities.

EXHIBIT 7-3 General Categories and Examples of Errors and Irregularities (Misstatements)

1. *Invalid transactions are recorded*: Fictitious sales are recorded and charged to nonexistent customers.
2. *Valid transactions are omitted from the accounts*: Shipments to customers never get recorded.
3. *Unauthorized transactions are executed and recorded*: A customer's order is not approved for credit, yet the goods are shipped, billed, and charged to the customer without requiring payment in advance.
4. *Transaction amounts are inaccurate*: A customer is billed and the sale is recorded in the wrong amount because the quantity shipped and the quantity billed are not the same and the unit price is for a different product.
5. *Transactions are classified in the wrong accounts*: Sales to a subsidiary company are recorded as sales to outsiders instead of intercompany sales, or the amount is charged to the wrong customer account receivable record.
6. *Transaction accounting and posting is incorrect*: Sales are posted in total to the accounts receivable control account, but some are not posted to individual customer account records.
7. *Transactions are recorded in the wrong period*: shipments made in January (next year) are backdated and recorded as sales and charges to customers in December. Shipments in December are recorded as sales and charges to customers in January.

REASONS FOR INTERNAL CONTROL EVALUATION

A useful, though unofficial, definition of internal control related to a company's financial reporting objectives is: "All the policies and procedures a company uses to prevent, detect, and correct errors, irregularities, and frauds that might get into financial statements." You can properly infer that such control enables a company to safeguard its assets from unauthorized disposition and prepare financial statements in conformity with generally accepted accounting principles.

The auditors' task is to assess the control risk associated with the controls management designed and implemented for the period under audit. **Control**

risk is the probability that a company's controls will fail to detect errors, irregularities, and frauds, provided any enter the accounting system in the first place. Control risk is a characteristic of the client's controls. The auditors' assessment task is to assign an evaluation to the control risk. Many auditors conclude the internal control risk assessment decision with a descriptive assessment (e.g., maximum, slightly below maximum, high, moderate, low), and some auditors put probability numbers on it (e.g., 1.0, 0.90, 0.70, 0.50, 0.30).

PLANNING THE SUBSTANTIVE AUDIT PROGRAM

The primary reason under GAAS for conducting an evaluation of a company's internal control and assessing control risk is to give the auditors a basis for planning the audit and determining the nature, timing, and extent of audit procedures for the account balance (substantive) audit program. The presumption is that the auditors have prepared a preliminary audit program and have ideas about the work they want to do. This preliminary program might be last year's audit program or an off-the-shelf "standard program."

An **account balance (substantive) audit program** is a specification (list) of procedures designed to produce evidence about the *assertions* in financial statements. Each procedure should have identifiable characteristics of nature, timing, and extent, as well as a direct association with one or more financial statement assertions. The **nature** of procedures refers to the seven general procedures: recalculation, physical observation, confirmation, verbal inquiry, document examination, scanning, and analytical procedures. The **timing** of procedures is a matter of *when* they are performed: at "interim" before the balance sheet date, or at "year-end" shortly before and after the balance sheet date. The **extent** of procedures refers to the *amount* of work done when the procedures are performed.

If auditors assess control risk as "maximum" (i.e., poor control), they will tend to perform a great deal of substantive balance-audit work with large sample sizes (extent), at or near the company's fiscal year-end (timing), using procedures designed to obtain high-quality external evidence (nature). On the other hand, if auditors assess control risk as "low" (i.e., effective control), they can perform a lesser quantity of substantive balance-audit work with small sample sizes (extent), at an interim date before the company's fiscal year-end (timing), using a mixture of procedures designed to obtain high-quality external evidence and lower quality internal evidence (nature). Of course, auditors may assess control risk between "low" and "maximum" (e.g., "moderate," "high," or "slightly below maximum") and adjust the substantive audit work accordingly.

COMMUNICATING INTERNAL CONTROL DEFICIENCIES

A secondary reason for evaluating internal control is to provide a basis for communicating to a client's management and directors any *reportable conditions* regarding internal control problems. **Reportable conditions** are defined as *matters the auditors believe should be communicated to the client's audit committee because they represent significant deficiencies in the design or operation of the internal controls that could adversely affect the organization's ability to record, process, summarize, and report financial data in the financial statements* (SAS 60, AU 325). Examples include:

- Absence of appropriate segregation of duties.
- Absence of appropriate reviews and approvals of transactions.
- Evidence of failure of control procedures.
- Evidence of intentional management override of control procedures by persons in authority to the detriment of control objectives.
- Evidence of willful wrongdoing by employees or management, including manipulation, falsification, or alteration of accounting records.

REPORT OF MATERIAL WEAKNESS

Reportable conditions include the more serious condition called a **material weakness in internal control**, which is defined as a *condition in which the design or operation of internal control does not reduce to a relatively low level the risk that errors or irregularities in amounts that would be material to the financial statements being audited may occur and may not be detected within a timely period by employees in the normal course of performing their assigned functions.* This long and involved definition describes a more serious version of a reportable condition.

  Although auditors are not obligated to search for or identify reportable conditions and material weaknesses, they must communicate ones that come to their attention in the normal performance of the audit. Written communications are preferred, but auditing standards permit auditors to communicate reportable conditions orally, in which case a memorandum of the oral report should be placed in the working papers (SAS 60, AU 325). However, because the potential for misinterpretation is great, auditors should not issue reports stating that no reportable conditions were noted during an audit (AU 9325). A manager receiving such a report could conclude (incorrectly) that the auditors are stating positively that the company has no internal control problems.

FINANCIAL REPORTING CONTROL--THE AUDITORS' EVALUATION PROCESS

The five components of internal control are considered to be criteria for evaluating a company's financial reporting controls and the bases for auditors' assessment of control risk as it relates to financial statements. Thus, auditors must consider the five components in terms of (1) understanding a client's financial reporting controls, (2) documenting the understanding, (3) assessing the control risk, and (4) using the control risk assessment to plan the remainder of the audit work (Exhibit 7-4).

EXHIBIT 7-4   Auditors' Work on Internal Control

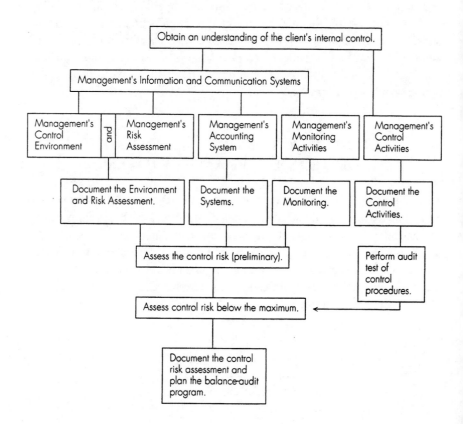

CONTROL ENVIRONMENT AND
RISK ASSESSMENT

The control environment sets the tone of the organization. It is the foundation for all other components of internal control. It provides discipline and structure. Control environment factors include the integrity, ethical values, and competence of the company's people. The following are general elements of an internal control environment:

- Management's philosophy and operating style
- Management and employee integrity and ethical values
- Company organization structure
- Company commitment to competence--job skills and knowledge
- Functioning of the board of directors, particularly its audit committee
- Methods of assigning authority and responsibility
- Human resource policies and practices

Management should assess the risks present in the financial reporting category. The production of reliable financial reports is the general objective. All companies face the risk that their financial statements may be unreliable. They may report assets that do not exist or ones that are not owned by the company. Asset and liability amounts may be improperly valued. They may fail to report liabilities and expenses. They may present information that does not conform to GAAP. The risk of producing unreliable financial reports arises from control breakdowns. The types of errors and irregularities shown in Exhibit 7-3 are manifestations of these breakdowns.

Management needs to assess financial reporting risks in terms of its own business. Financial accounting and reporting problems are different for manufacturers, banks, insurance companies, hospitals, churches, charities, and a wide range of other organizations.

Since management fraud in financial statements became a topic for acceptable discussion in the late 1980s, the "tone at the top" has become a buzzword for the necessary condition for good internal control. The "tone" is virtually identical to the control environment component. Likewise, the financial reporting risk assessment component is an integral part of the effort to avoid fraudulent financial reports.

INFORMATION AND COMMUNICATION--
THE ACCOUNTING SYSTEM

We all live in an "information age." The "information highway" is a national obsession. Likewise, the information and communication component of internal control is a necessary prerequisite for establishing, maintaining, and changing control features in a company. While a wide range of communication channels is important for control, this section concentrates on the accounting system. It is an integral part of the monitoring and control activities in companies.

An **accounting system** processes transactions, records them in journals and ledgers (either computerized or manual), and produces financial statements without necessarily guaranteeing their accuracy. Nevertheless, the accounting policies and procedures often contain important elements of control. The accounting instruction: "Prepare sales invoices only when shipment has been made," is a control so long as the people performing the work follow the instruction. The control part of this policy could be expressed: "Prepare sales invoices and record them only when a shipping document is matched."

All accounting systems, whether computerized or manual, consist of four essential functions--data identification, data entry, transaction processing, and report production and distribution.

Data identification is the analysis of transactions and their "capture" for accounting purposes. The "capture" amounts to creation of source documents, such as sales invoices, credit memos, cash receipts listings, purchase orders, receiving reports, negotiable checks, and the like. These source documents provide the information for data entry. However, in some computerized accounting systems, the paper source documents are not produced first. Transactions may be entered directly on a keyboard, or electronic equipment may capture the transaction information. Your long-distance telephone charges are initially captured by the telephone company's computers using your telephone number, the location called, and the duration of the call.

Data description and entry often consists of accounting personnel using a batch of source documents to enter transaction information on a keyboard into an accounting software program. This process may produce a "book of original entry," another name for a *journal*, such as the sales journal, purchases journal, cash receipts journal, cash disbursements journal, general journal, and others. In advanced paperless systems, electronic equipment may enter the accounting information automatically without producing an intermediate journal. Your long-distance telephone call is entered automatically into the telephone company's revenue and receivable accounts. Your monthly telephone bill is later produced from the accounting information.

Transaction measurement and processing usually refers to posting the journals to the general ledger accounts. The posting operation updates the account balances. When all data are entered and processed, the account balances are ready for placement in reports.

Report production and distribution is the object of the accounting system. The account balances are put into internal management reports and external financial statements. The internal reports are management's feedback for monitoring operations. The external reports are the financial information for outside investors, creditors, and others.

The accounting system produces a trail of accounting operations, from data identification to reports. Often, this is called the *audit trail.* You can visualize that it starts with the source documents and proceeds through to the financial reports. Auditors often follow this trail frontwards and backwards! They will follow it backwards from the financial reports to the source documents to determine whether everything in the financial reports is supported by appropriate source documents. They will follow it forward from source documents to reports to determine that everything that happened (transactions) was recorded in the accounts and reported in the financial statements.

MONITORING

Internal control systems need to be monitored. Management should assess the quality of its control performance on a timely basis. Monitoring includes regular management and supervisory activities and other actions personnel take in performing their duties. Errors, irregularities, and internal control deficiencies should be reported to top management and to the audit committee of the board of directors.

Monitoring helps ensure that internal control continues to operate effectively. Everyday monitoring of the types shown below are part of the internal control process:

- Operating managers compare internal reports and published financial statements with their knowledge of the business.
- Customer complaints of amounts billed are analyzed.
- Vendor complaints of amounts paid are analyzed.
- Regulators report to the company on compliance with laws and regulations (e.g., bank examiners' reports, IRS audits).
- Accounting managers supervise the accuracy and completeness of transaction processing.
- Recorded amounts are periodically compared to actual assets and liabilities (e.g., internal auditors' inventory counts, receivables and payables confirmations, bank reconciliations).
- External auditors report on control performance and give recommendations for improvement.
- Training sessions for management and employees heighten awareness of the importance of controls.

These elements of the monitoring component have a great deal in common with the controls included in the control activities component. Indeed, some of the control activities explained later in this chapter are monitoring activities as well (e.g., periodic comparison).

CONTROL ACTIVITIES

Control activities are the policies and procedures that help ensure that management directives are carried out. They include: (1) *Performance reviews*--for example, study of budget variances with follow-up action, (2) *Information processing*, including approvals, authorizations, verifications, and reconciliations, (3) *Physical controls* designed to ensure safeguarding and security of assets and records, and (4) *Segregation of duties* designed to reduce opportunities for a person to be in a position to perpetrate and conceal errors and irregularities when performing normal duties.

Control activities are actions taken by a client's management and employees. You should be careful to distinguish the "client's control activities" from the "auditors' test of control procedures." Control activities are part of the internal control designed and operated by the company. The auditors' procedures are the auditors' own evidence-gathering work performed to obtain evidence about the client's control activities.

Control activities (both computerized and manual) are imposed on the accounting system for the purpose of preventing, detecting, and correcting errors and irregularities that might enter and flow through to the financial statements. For example, a control activity related to the accounting policy cited earlier would be: "At the end of each day, the billing supervisor reviews all the sales invoices to see that the file copy has a bill of lading copy attached."

Minimum requirements for a good control-oriented accounting system include a chart of accounts and some written definitions and instructions about measuring and classifying transactions. In most organizations, such material is incorporated in computer systems documentation, computer program documentation, systems and procedures manuals, flowcharts of transaction processing, and various paper forms. A company's internal auditors and systems staff often review and evaluate this documentation. Independent auditors may review and study their work instead of doing the same tasks over again.

Accounting manuals should contain statements of objectives, policies, and procedures. Management should approve statements of specific accounting and control objectives and assure that appropriate steps are taken to accomplish them. In general, the overriding objective of an accounting system is to produce financial statement assertions that are correct. An accounting system cannot accomplish this objective without an integrated set of control activities.

TRANSACTION PROCESSING CONTROL OBJECTIVES AND ACTIVITIES

While the objective of the control system is to produce reliable financial statement assertions, principally in account *balances*, the overriding objective of control activities is to process *transactions* correctly. Correctly processed transactions produce correct account balances, which in turn help produce accurate and reliable assertions in the financial statements.

CONTROL ACTIVITIES

Companies use numerous detailed accounting and control activities designed to achieve the control objectives. These detail activities are directed, one way or another, toward preventing, detecting, or correcting the seven general kinds of errors, irregularities, frauds, and misstatements that can occur. Control activities can be complicated. Exhibit 7-5 presents an overview of the organization of the discussion that follows. The discussion is organized under the headings of general controls, segregation of technical responsibilities, and application controls (error-checking activities).

GENERAL CONTROL ACTIVITIES

While the "tone at the top" (control environment) is pervasive, the control activities of capable personnel, segregation of responsibilities, controlled access, and periodic comparison are always important in a company's control process.

Capable Personnel

The most important feature of control is the people who make the system work. A company's personnel problems sometimes create internal control problems. High turnover in accounting jobs means that inexperienced people are doing the accounting and control tasks, and they generally make more mistakes than experienced people. New accounting officers and managers (financial vice president, controller, chief accountant, plant accountant, data processing manager) may not be familiar enough with company accounting and may make technical and judgmental errors. Sometimes, accounting officers and employees are fired because they refuse to go along with improper accounting procedures desired by a higher level of management. In general, accounting personnel changes *may* be a warning signal.

EXHIBIT 7-5 Overview of Transaction Processing Control Activities

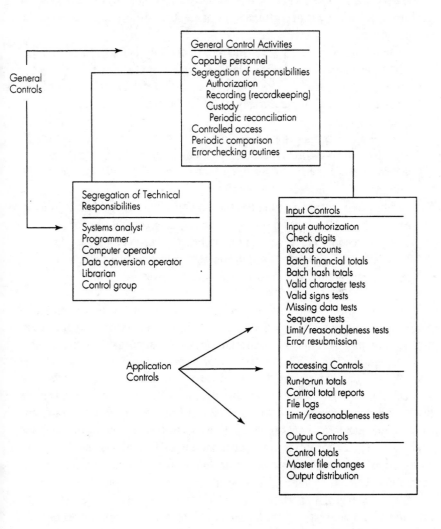

Segregation of Responsibilities

A very important characteristic of effective internal control is an *appropriate segregation of functional responsibilities*. Sometimes this characteristic is called *division of duties*. Four kinds of functional responsibilities should be performed by different departments, or at least by different persons on the company's accounting staff:

1. Authorization to execute transactions. This duty belongs to people who have authority and responsibility for initiating the recordkeeping for transactions. Authorization may be general, referring to a class of transactions (e.g., all purchases), or it may be specific (e.g., sale of a major asset).
2. Recording of transactions. This duty refers to the accounting and recordkeeping function (bookkeeping) which, in most organizations, is delegated to a computer system. (People who control the computer processing are the recordkeepers.)
3. Custody of assets involved in the transactions. This duty refers to the actual physical possession or effective physical control of property.
4. Periodic reconciliation of existing assets to recorded amounts. This duty refers to making comparisons at regular intervals and taking appropriate action with respect to any differences.

Incompatible responsibilities are combinations of responsibilities that place a person alone in a position to create and conceal errors, irregularities, and misstatements in his or her normal job. Duties should be so divided that no one person can control two or more of these responsibilities. If different departments or persons are forced to deal with these different facets of transactions, then two benefits are obtained: (1) Irregularities are made more difficult because they would require collusion of two or more persons, and most people hesitate to seek the help of others to conduct wrongful acts, and (2) by acting in a coordinated manner (handling different aspects of the same transaction), innocent errors are more likely to be found and flagged for correction. The old saying is: "Two heads are better than one."

Supervision is an important element of control activities. You can readily imagine a company having clerks and computers to carry out the accounting and control. Equally important is management's provision for supervision of the work. A supervisor could, for example, oversee the credit manager's performance or could periodically compare the sum of customers' balances to the accounts receivable control account total. Supervisors or department heads can correct errors found by the clerical staff and make or approve accounting decisions. Supervision is important as management's means of monitoring and maintaining a system of internal control.

Controlled Access

Physical access to assets and important records, documents, and blank forms should be limited to authorized personnel. Such assets as inventory and securities should not be available to persons who have no need to handle them. Likewise, access to cost records and accounts receivable records should be denied to people who do not have a recordkeeping responsibility for them.

Some blank forms are very important for accounting and control, and their availability should be restricted. Someone not involved in accounting for sales should not be able to pick up blank sales invoices and blank shipping orders. A person should not be able to obtain blank checks (including computer-paper blank checks) unless he or she is involved in cash disbursement activities. Sometimes, access to blank forms is the equivalent of access to, or custody of, an important asset. For example, someone who has access to blank checks has a measure of actual custody and access to cash.

Periodic Comparison

Management has responsibility for the *recorded accountability* for assets and liabilities. Managers should provide for periodic comparison of the recorded amounts with independent evidence of existence and valuation. Internal auditors and other people on an accounting staff can perform periodic comparison on a regular basis. However, the people who perform these periodic comparisons should not also have responsibility for authorization of related transactions, accounting or recordkeeping, or custodial responsibility for the assets.

Periodic comparisons may include counts of cash on hand, reconciliation of bank statements, counts of securities, inventory counting, confirmation of accounts receivable and accounts payable, and other such comparison operations undertaken to determine whether accounting records--the *recorded accountability*--represent real assets and liabilities. A management that performs frequent periodic comparisons has more opportunities to detect errors in the records than a management that does not. The frequency, of course, is governed by the costs and benefits. One should not try to count, compare, or confirm assets with great frequency (say, weekly) unless they are especially susceptible to loss or error or unless they are unusually valuable.

Subsequent action to correct differences is also important. Periodic comparison and action to correct errors lowers the risk that material misstatements remain in the accounts. Such comparisons are frequently assigned to internal auditors and other employees. Research has shown that companies with active internal auditors have fewer account errors.

SEGREGATION OF TECHNICAL RESPONSIBILITIES

Most companies use computer-based accounting and control systems. In large companies, the essential separation of responsibilities involves the duties of analysts, programmers, and operators. The duties associated with these and other important roles are defined as follow:

Systems Analyst. Analyzes requirements for information. Evaluates the existing system and designs new or improved data processing. Outlines the system and prepares specifications that guide the programmers. Prepares documentation of the application system. Acquires suitable commercial software.

Programmer. Flowcharts the logic of the computer programs required by the overall system designed by the systems analyst. Codes the logic in the computer program. Prepares documentation of the program.

Computer Operator. Operates the computer for each accounting application system according to written operating procedures found in the computer operation instructions.

Data Conversion Operator. Prepares data for machine processing. Previously these individuals operated keypunch machines and produced punched cards; now these operators usually convert visible source data to magnetic tape or disk, use optical-character reading equipment, or use data transmission terminals. In advanced computer systems, the data conversion operators will likely be accounting clerks entering transactions from the accounting department into remote terminals.

Librarian. Two types of librarian functions may be found in a computer facility--one for system and program documentation and the other for the actual programs and data files. The purpose of the system/program documentation library is to maintain control over documentation of the design and operation stages of computer information systems. The purpose of the program/data library is to maintain control over the data files and programs actually used from day to day. In many systems, this second library function is done automatically with software.

Control Group. The control group receives input from user departments, logs the input and transfers it to data conversion, reviews documentation sequence numbers, reviews and processes error messages, monitors actual processing, compares control totals to computer output, and distributes output.

Separation of the duties performed by analysts, programmers, and operators is important. The general idea is that anyone who designs a processing system should not do the technical programming work, and anyone who performs either of these tasks should not be the computer operator when "live" data is processed. Persons performing each function should not have access to each other's work, and only the computer operators should have access to the equipment. Computer systems are susceptible to manipulative handling, and the lack of separation of duties along the lines described should be considered a serious weakness in general control.

PROGRAMMER AND OPERATOR COMBINED

A programmer employed by a large savings and loan association wrote a special subroutine that could be activated by a command from the computer console. The computation of interest on deposits and certificates was programmed to truncate calculations at the third decimal place. The special subroutine instructed the program to accumulate the truncated mills, and, when processing was complete, to credit the amount to the programmer-operator's savings account. Whenever this person was on duty for the interest calculation run, she could "make" several hundred dollars! She had to be on duty to manipulate the control figures "properly" so the error of overpaying interest on her account would not be detected by the control group. She was a programmer with computer operation duties.

APPLICATION CONTROLS (Error-Checking Routines)

Numerous techniques used to check for errors in accounting data can be categorized as (1) input controls, (2) processing controls, and (3) output controls. The weakest point in computer systems is input--the point at which transaction data are transformed from hard-copy source documents into machine-readable tape or disk, or when direct entry is made with a communication device such as a remote terminal. When undetected errors are entered originally, they may not be detected during processing, and, if detected, they are troublesome to correct. Processing control refers to error-condition check routines written into the computer program. Output control refers primarily to control over the distribution of reports, but feedback on errors and comparison of input totals to output totals also are part of this "last chance" control point.

Input Control Activities. Input controls are designed to provide reasonable assurance that data received for processing by the computer department have been authorized properly and converted into machine-sensible form, and that data have not been lost, suppressed, added, duplicated, or otherwise improperly changed. These controls also apply to correction and resubmission of data initially rejected as erroneous. The following control areas are particularly important:

Input Authorized and Approved. Only properly authorized and approved input should be accepted for processing by the computer center. Authorization usually is a clerical (noncomputer) procedure involving a person's signature or stamp on a transaction document. However, some authorizations can be general (e.g., a management policy of automatic approval for sales under $500), and some authorizations can be computer controlled (e.g., automatic production of a purchase order when an inventory item reaches a predetermined reorder point).

Check Digits. Numbers often are used in computer systems in lieu of customer names, vendor names, and so forth. One common type of number validation procedure is the calculation of a *check digit*. A **check digit** is an extra number, precisely calculated, that is tagged onto the end of a basic identification number such as an employee number. The basic code with its check digit sometimes is called a **self-checking number.** An electronic device can be installed on a data input device or the calculation can be programmed. The device or the program calculates the correct check digit and compares it to the one on the input data. When the digits do not match, an error message is indicated on the device or printed out on an input error report. Check digits are used only on identification numbers (not quantity or value fields) to detect coding errors or keying errors such as the transposition of digits (e.g., coding 387 as 837).[2]

Data Conversion. Conversion of data into machine-sensible form is a source of many errors. Controls include the following:

- *Record counts.* Counts of records are tallies of the number of transaction documents submitted for data conversion. The known number submitted can be compared to the count of records produced by the data-conversion device (e.g., the number of sales transactions or count of magnetic records coded). A count mismatch indicates a lost item or one converted twice. Record counts are used as **batch control totals** and also are used during processing and at the output stage--whenever the comparison of a known count can be made with a computer-generated count.
- *Batch financial totals.* These totals are used in the same way as record counts, except the batch total is the sum of some important quantity or amount (e.g., the total sales dollars in a batch of invoices). Batch totals are also useful during processing and at the output stage.
- *Batch hash totals.* These totals are similar to batch number totals, except the hash total is not meaningful for accounting records (e.g., the sum of all the invoice numbers on invoices submitted to the data input operator).

Edit or Validation Routines. Various computer-programmed editing or validation routines can be used to detect data conversion errors. Some of these are listed below:

- *Valid character tests.* These tests are used to check input data fields to see if they contain numbers where they are supposed to have numbers and alphabetic letters where they are supposed to have letters.
- *Valid sign tests.* Sign tests check data fields for appropriate plus or minus signs.

- *Missing data tests.* These edit tests check data fields to see if any are blank when they must contain data for the record entry to be correct.
- *Sequence tests.* These test the input data for numerical sequence of documents when sequence is important for processing, as in batch processing. This validation routine also can check for missing documents in a prenumbered series.
- *Limit or reasonableness tests.* These tests are computerized checks to see whether data values exceed or fall below some predetermined limit. For example, a payroll application may have a limit test to flag or reject any weekly payroll time record of 50 or more hours. The limit tests are a computerized version of scanning--the general audit procedure of reviewing data for indication of anything unusual that might turn out to be an error.

Error Correction and Resubmission. Errors should be subject to special controls. Usually, the computer department itself is responsible only for correcting its own errors (data conversion errors, for example). Other kinds of errors, such as those due to improper coding, should be referred to and handled by the user departments. It is a good idea to have a control group log the contents of error reports in order to monitor the nature, disposition, and proper correction of rejected data. Unless properly supervised and monitored, the error-correction process itself can become a source of data input errors.

Processing Control Activities. Processing controls are designed to provide reasonable assurance that data processing has been performed as intended without any omission or double-counting of transactions. Many of the processing controls are the same as the input controls, but they are used in the actual processing phases, rather than at the time input is checked. Other important controls are the following:

  Run-to-Run Totals. Movement of data from one department to another or one processing program to another should be controlled. One useful control is run-to-run totals. **Run-to-run** refers to sequential processing operations--*runs*--on the same data. These totals may be batch record counts, financial totals, and/or hash totals obtained at the end of one processing run. The totals are passed to the next run and compared to corresponding totals produced at the end of the second run.

Control Total Reports. Control totals--record counts, financial totals, hash totals, and run-to-run totals--should be produced during processing operations and printed out on a report. Someone (the control group, for example) should have the responsibility for comparing and/or reconciling them to input totals or totals from earlier processing runs. Loss or duplication of data thus may be detected. For example, the total of the balances in the accounts receivable master file from the last update run, plus the total of the credit sales from the current update transactions, should equal the total of the balances at the end of the current processing.

File and Operator Controls. External and internal labels are means of assuring that the proper files are used in applications. The systems software should produce a log to identify instructions entered by the operator and to make a record of time and use statistics for application runs. These logs should be reviewed by supervisory personnel.

Limit and Reasonableness Tests. These tests should be programmed to ensure that illogical conditions do not occur; for example, depreciating an asset below zero or calculating a negative inventory quantity. These conditions, and others considered important, should generate error reports for supervisory review. Other logic and validation checks, described earlier under the heading of input edit checks, also can be used during processing.

Output Control Activities. Output controls are the final check on the accuracy of the results of computer processing. These controls also should be designed to ensure that only authorized persons receive reports or have access to files produced by the system. Typical output controls are the following:

Control Totals. Control totals produced as output should be compared and/or reconciled to input and run-to-run control totals produced during processing. An independent control group should be responsible for the review of output control totals and investigation of differences.

Master File Changes. These changes should be reported in detail back to the user department from which the request for change originated because an error can be pervasive. For example, changing selling prices incorrectly can cause all sales to be priced wrong. Someone should compare computer-generated change reports to original source documents for assurance that the data are correct.

Output Distribution. Systems output should be distributed only to persons authorized to receive it. A distribution list should be maintained and used to deliver report copies. The number of copies produced should be restricted to the number needed.

Auditors need to be aware of the transaction processing controls and the failures that can lead to accounting errors. The box below summarizes some research findings about the relation of controls and accounting errors.

RELATIONS OF CONTROLS AND ACCOUNTING ERRORS

Causes of Errors:

Incorrect computations	35%
Management (mis)judgment	25%
Faulty transaction processing	16%
Overworked accounting personnel	11%
Omission of transactions	5%
Incorrect computer input	3%

Control Problems:

Missing controls	21%
Poor hiring and training of personnel	21%
Controls applied incorrectly	17%
Poorly designed controls	10%
Poor segregation of duties	1%

Frequent Error Accounts:
(1 = most frequent, 6 = least frequent)

	Rank
Inventory	1 (tie)
Accrued expenses	1 (tie)

Accounts receivable	3
Accounts payable	4 (tie)
Fixed assets	4 (tie)
Other current assets	6

Source: Bell, T., W. R. Knechel, and J. Willingham. "An Empirical Investigation of the Relationship Between Selected Attributes of Accounting Systems and the Incidence of Audit Differences." Survey of 242 audits of an international accounting firm.

PERFORMING TEST OF CONTROLS AUDIT PROCEDURES

To reduce a final control risk assessment to a low level, auditors must determine (1) the required degree of company compliance with the control policies and procedures and (2) the actual degree of company compliance. The **required degree of compliance** is the auditors' decision criterion for good control performance. Knowing that compliance cannot realistically be expected to be perfect, auditors might decide, for example, that evidence of using bills of lading (shipping documents) to validate sales invoice recordings 96 percent of the time is sufficient to assess a low control risk for the audit of accounts receivable (looking for overstatement in receivables and sales).

Now the auditors can perform **test of controls procedures** to determine how well the company's controls actually functioned during the period under audit. A test of controls audit procedure is a two-part statement. Part one is an *identification of the data population* from which a sample of items will be selected for audit. Part two is an expression of an *action* taken to produce relevant evidence. In general, the action is: (1) determine whether the selected items correspond to a standard (e.g., mathematical accuracy), and (2) determine whether the selected items agree with information in another data population. Here is an example of a test of control procedure:

Select a sample of recorded sales invoices; look for proper credit approval; find the related shipping document and compare it for the corresponding date and quantity.

One other important aspect of these audit procedures is known as *the direction of the test*. The procedure illustrated above can provide evidence about control over the *validity* of sales transactions. However, it does not provide evidence about control over *completeness* of recording all shipments. Another data population--the shipping documents--can be sampled to provide evidence about completeness. The direction of the test idea is illustrated in Exhibit 7-6.

TEST OF CONTROLS NECESSARY FOR
ASSESSING LOW CONTROL RISK

Inquiry alone generally will not provide sufficient evidential matter to support a conclusion about the effectiveness of design or operation of a specific [client] control. When the auditor determines that a specific [client] control may have a significant effect in reducing control risk to a low level for a specific assertion, he ordinarily needs to perform additional tests [of controls] to obtain sufficient evidential matter to support the conclusion about the effectiveness of the design or operation of that [client] control.

Source: SAS 55, AU 319.51.

EXHIBIT 7-6   Direction of the Test of Controls Audit Procedures

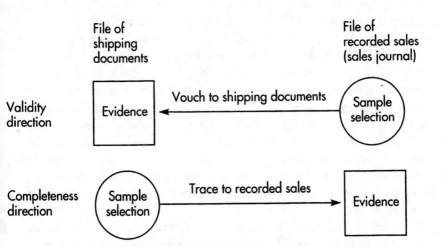

Some test of controls procedures involve **reperformance**--the auditors perform again the arithmetic calculations and the comparisons the company people were supposed to have performed. Some accountants, however, believe mere **inspection** is enough--the auditors just look to see whether the documents were marked with an initial, signature, or stamp to indicate they had been checked. They maintain that reperformance is not necessary.

Some test of controls procedures depend on *documentary evidence*, like a sales entry supported by a bill of lading. Documentary evidence in the form of signatures, initials, checklists, reconciliation working papers, and the like provides better evidence than procedures that leave no documentary tracks. Some controls, such as segregation of employees' duties, may leave no documents behind. In this case, the best kind of procedures--reperformance of control activities--cannot be done, and the second procedure--observation--must be used. This procedure amounts to an auditor's unobtrusive eyewitness observation of employees at their jobs performing control activities.

Test of controls procedures, when performed, should be applied to samples of transactions and control activities executed throughout the period under audit. The reason for this requirement is that the conclusions about controls will be generalized to the whole period under audit.

CONTROL EVALUATION AND COST-BENEFIT

An assessment of control risk should be coordinated with the final audit plan. The final account balance audit plan includes the specification (list) of **substantive audit procedures**, which are defined as the detail audit and analytical procedures designed to detect material misstatements in account balances and footnote disclosures.

Control systems are subject to cost-benefit considerations. Controls possibly could be made perfect, or nearly so, at great expense. An inventory could be left unlocked and unguarded (no control against theft and no control expenses), or a fence could be used; locks could be installed; lighting could be used at night; television monitors could be put in place; armed guards could be hired. Each of these successive safeguards costs money, as does extensive supervision of clerical personnel in an office. At some point, the cost of protecting the inventory from theft (or of supervisors' catching every clerical error) exceeds the benefit of control. Hence, control systems generally do not provide absolute assurance that the objectives of internal control are satisfied. **Reasonable assurance** is thought to be enough, and has been defined: "The concept of reasonable assurance recognizes that the cost of an entity's internal control should not exceed the benefits that are expected to be derived" (SAS 55, AU 319).

Notwithstanding the common sense of the concept of reasonable assurance, auditors must be careful to determine whether a system contains any internal control weakness. Business managers can make estimates of benefits to be derived from controls and weigh them against the cost. Managers are perfectly free to make their own judgments about the necessary extent of controls. Managers can decide the degree of control risk they are willing to accept. However, auditors should be aware that the "cost-benefit" and "reasonable assurance" concepts can sometimes be used loosely by a management to tolerate control deficiencies.

Since preparation of the final account balance audit plan is the primary aim and purpose, the evaluation of internal control must be documented in audit working papers. Documentation of the understanding of the internal control structure and the control risk assessment is required. These audit working papers can include internal control questionnaires, narrative descriptions, flowcharts, specifications of controls and compliance criteria, and the evidence produced by test of controls audit procedures.

INTERNAL CONTROL IN SMALL AND MIDSIZED ENTITIES

The foregoing explanations of control characteristics contain an underlying thread of bureaucratic organization theory and a large-business orientation. A company must be large and employ several people (about 10 or more) to have a theoretically appropriate segregation of functional responsibilities and its accompanying high degree of specialization of work. Supervision requires people. The paperwork and computer control necessary in most large systems is extensive. Control theory also suggests that people perform in accounting and control *roles* and do not engage in frequent personal interaction across functional responsibility boundaries. None of these theoretical dimensions fit small and midsized businesses very well.

Auditors should be careful to recognize the bureaucratic, large-business orientation of internal control theory. When the business under audit is small, allowances must be made for (1) the number of people employed, and (2) the control attitude of important managers and owners. Indeed, as you study the following aspects of small-business control, notice the important role of managers and owners dealing with their employees in an informal manner.

CONTROL ENVIRONMENT

Instead of having a formal, written code of conduct, small business managers may develop an exemplary corporate culture that emphasizes integrity and ethical behavior. They may use oral communication and personal example to carry the message. Small businesses may not have outside (nonemployee) members on the board of directors and its audit committee. While outside members are required by the stock exchanges, the lack of them may not be an impediment in a company that otherwise conducts its affairs with integrity.

RISK ASSESSMENT

The risk assessment process may be informal and less structured in a small business. Recognition of financial reporting objectives may be generally understood by accounting personnel instead of written in a large manual. Managers can deal with financial reporting risks through direct personal involvement instead of through a chain of complicated reporting paths of communication involving numerous lower-level executives.

CONTROL ACTIVITIES

Detail control activities may not need to be highly formal because managers and owners can be personally involved. They may themselves approve routine transactions (e.g., credit sales, purchases, loans) and check the accuracy of recording them in the accounts. When the company has too few people to segregate duties to a high degree, the owner-manager may conduct personal reviews.

However, as a small business begins to grow (say, from 4 people to 10 or 15), the transition to more formalized internal control tends to lag behind. The owner-manager may become overburdened with control duties and may tacitly delegate these to others. The intermediate-size stage represents a turning point where both owner-manager and auditor need to be very careful. At this point, such measures as limited specialization and surety bonding of employees may help make the transition, and an auditor may offer many suggestions to the owner-manager as an added service.

INFORMATION AND COMMUNICATION

Small businesses have less formal systems. They may not have a written credit policy, extensive security over records and files, a competitive bidding policy for purchases, or elaborate error-checking control activities (application controls). The availability of management for consultation and the ability of employees to reach a small number of colleagues and co-workers easily makes communication quick and effective.

MONITORING

Managers' and owners' direct day-to-day involvement enables them to notice problems such as erroneous journal entries, budget variances, unreconciled differences in accounts (e.g., comparing recorded amounts to other information as accomplished with a bank reconciliation), and the like. The managers themselves may conduct the monitoring as part of their risk assessment, communication, and detail control duties.

SUMMARY

The key person in internal control in a small business with few employees is the owner-manager. A diligent owner-manager may be able to oversee and supervise all the important authorization, record keeping, and custodial functions. He or she also may be able to assure satisfactory transaction processing accuracy. Thus, an auditor evaluating control risk will study the extent of the owner-manager's involvement in the operation of the accounting and control system and evaluate the owner-manager's competence and integrity.

SUMMARY

This chapter explains the theory and practice of auditors' involvement with a client's control process. The purposes of auditor involvement are to assess the control risk in order to plan the substantive audit program and to report control deficiencies to management and the board of directors.

In theory, a financial reporting control system consists of five components--management's control environment, management's risk assessment, management's information and communication (accounting) system, management's control activities, and management's monitoring of the control system. Each of these is evaluated and documented in the audit working papers. The control environment and management's risk assessment is explained in terms of understanding the client's business. Elements of the accounting system are explained in conjunction with control activities designed to prevent, detect, and correct misstatements that occur in transactions. These misstatements are systematized in a set of seven categories of errors and irregularities that can occur.

Control procedures are covered extensively. They are organized under the headings of general control activities (i.e., capable personnel, segregation of responsibilities, controlled access, periodic comparison, and error-checking routines), segregation of technical responsibilities (computer-related jobs), and error-checking routine detail (11 input controls, 4 processing controls, and 3 output controls). The explanations of these controls integrate computerized accounting systems with control practice.

The chapter closes with sections on cost-benefit and reasonable assurance considerations and on adaptation of control theory to small businesses.

FOOTNOTES

¹ The National Commission on Fraudulent Financial Reporting (Treadway Commission) produced a 1987 report on problems in financial reporting. The sponsoring organizations (COSO) of the Treadway Commission were: the American Institute of CPAs, the American Accounting Association, the Institute of Internal Auditors, the Institute of Management Accountants, and the Financial Executives Institute.

² One check digit algorithm is the "Modulus 11 Prime Number" method:
a. Begin with a basic number: 814973.
b. Multiply consecutive prime number weights of 19, 17, 13, 7, 5, 3 to each digit in the basic code number:

8	1	4	9	7	3	
x19	x17	x13	x7	x5	x3	
=152	+17	+52	+63	+35	+9	= 328

Note: The sequence of weights is the same for all codes in a given system.
c. Add the result of the multiplication = 328.
d. Determine the next higher multiple of 11, which is 330.
e. Subtract the sum of the multiplication (330 - 328 = 2). This is the check digit.
f. New account number: 8149732. Now if this number is entered incorrectly, say it is keypunched as 8419732, the check digit will not equal 2 and an error will be indicated. [See J. G. Burch, Jr., F. R. Strater, Jr., and G. Grudnitski, *Information Systems: Theory and Practice*, 5th ed. (New York: John Wiley & Sons, 1989), pp. 191-93.]

CHAPTER 8
CASH COLLECTIONS AND
RECEIVABLES

The revenue and collection accounting cycle covers sales, sales returns, accounts receivable, account write-offs, and cash collections. This chapter contains sections on (1) typical control activities in the cycle, (2) the audit evidence available in management reports and data files, (3) control risk assessment (including detail test of controls procedures), and (4) case story-style explanations concerning discovery of errors, irregularities, and frauds. Special notes in the chapter cover (1) the existence assertion, (2) using confirmations, (3) bank reconciliation with attention to lapping and kiting, and (4) bank transfer and proof of cash analyses.

REVENUE AND COLLECTION CYCLE:
TYPICAL ACTIVITIES

The basic activities in the revenue and collection cycle are: (1) receiving and processing customer orders, including credit granting; (2) delivering goods and services to customers; (3) billing customers and accounting for accounts receivable; (4) collecting and depositing cash received from customers; and (5) reconciling bank statements. Exhibit 8-1 shows the activities and transactions involved in a revenue and collection cycle. As you follow the exhibit, you can track some of the highlighted elements of a control system.

EXHIBIT 8-1 Revenue and Collection Cycle

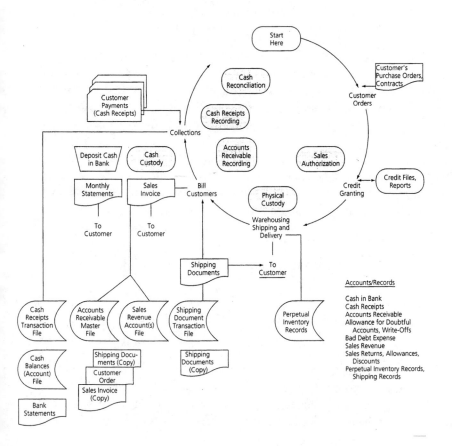

SALES AND ACCOUNTS RECEIVABLE

Authorization

Exhibit 8-2 represents a computerized system for processing customer orders. Company personnel receive the customer's purchase order and create a sales order, entering it in a computer terminal. The computer system then performs automatic authorization procedures--determining whether the customer is a "regular" or a new customer, approving credit, and checking the availability of inventory to fill the order. (If inventory is short, a back order is entered.) When these authorizations are imbedded in a computer system, access to the master files for additions, deletions, and other changes must be limited to responsible persons. If these controls fail, orders might be processed for fictitious customers, credit might be approved for bad credit risks, and packing slips might be created for goods that do not exist in the inventory.

When a customer order passes these authorizations, the system: (1) creates a record in the pending order master file, (2) produces a packing slip that is transmitted to the stockroom and shipping department, and (3) updates the inventory master file to show the commitment (removal) of the inventory. At this stage, the pending order and the packing slip should be numbered in a numerical sequence so the system can determine later whether any transactions have not been completed (completeness objective of control). The packing slip is the storekeeper's authorization to release goods to the shipping department and the shipping department's authorization to release goods to a trucker or to the customer.

Another authorization in the system is the price list master file. It contains the product unit prices for billing customers. Persons who have power to alter this file have the power to authorize price changes and customer billings.

EXHIBIT 8-2   Sales and Accounts Receivable: Computer Processing

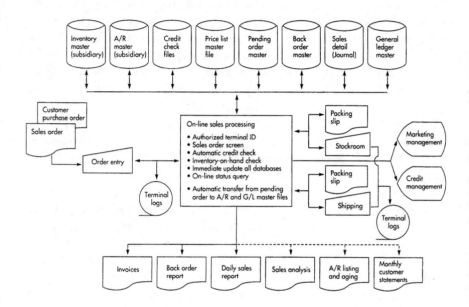

PRICE MANIPULATION

The company's computer programmer was paid off by a customer to cause the company to bill the customer at prices lower than list prices. The programmer wrote a subroutine that was invoked when the billing system detected the customer's regular code number. This subroutine instructed the computer billing system to reduce all unit prices 9.5 percent. The company relied on the computer billing system, and nobody ever rechecked the actual prices billed.

Custody

Physical custody of goods starts with the storeroom or warehouse where inventory is kept. Custody is transferred to the shipping department upon the authorization of the packing slip that orders storeskeepers to release goods to the shipping area. As long as the system works, custody is under accountability control. However, if the storeskeepers or the shipping department personnel have the power to change the quantity shown on the packing slip, they can cause errors in the system by billing the customer for too small or too large a quantity. (This power combines custody with a recording function. A computer record or "log" of such changes will create an electronic paper trail.)

"Custody" of accounts receivable records themselves implies the power to alter them directly or enter transactions to alter them (e.g., transfers, returns and allowance credits, write-offs). Personnel with this power have a combination of authorization and recording responsibility. (A computer "log" of such entries will create an electronic paper trail.)

Recording

When delivery or shipment is complete, the shipping personnel enter the completion of the transaction in a terminal, and the system (1) produces a bill of lading shipping document, which is evidence of an actual delivery/shipment; (2) removes the order from the pending order master file; and (3) produces a sales invoice (prenumbered the same as the order and packing slip) that bills the customer for the quantity shipped, according to the bill of lading. Any personnel who have the power to enter or alter these transactions or to intercept the invoice that is supposed to be mailed to the customer have undesirable combinations of authorization, custody, and recording responsibilities; they can "authorize" transaction changes and record them by making entries in systems under their control.

SHIPPING EMPLOYEE CAUGHT BY COMPUTER!

A customer paid off a shipping department employee to enter smaller quantities than actually shipped on the packing slip and bill of lading. This caused the customer's invoices to be understated. Unknown to the employee, a computer log recorded all the entries that altered the original packing slip record. An alert internal auditor noticed the pattern of "corrections" made by the shipping employee. A trap was laid by initiating fictitious orders for this customer, and the employee was observed making the alterations.

Periodic Reconciliation
The most frequent reconciliation is the comparison of the sum of customers' unpaid balances with the accounts receivable control account total. Usually, this reconciliation is done with an aged trial balance. An aged trial balance is a list of the customers and their balances, with the balances classified in columns headed for different age categories (e.g., current, 10-30 days past due, 31-60 days past due, 61-90 days past due, over 90 days past due). Internal auditors can perform periodic comparison of the customers' obligations (according to the customers) with the recorded amount by sending confirmations to the customers. (Refer to the special note on confirmations later in this chapter.)

CASH RECEIPTS AND CASH BALANCES

Authorization
Cash can be received in several ways--over the counter, through the mail, by electronic funds transfer, and by receipt in a "lockbox." In a lockbox arrangement, a fiduciary (e.g., a bank) opens the box, lists the receipts, deposits the money, and sends the remittance advices (stubs showing the amount received from each customer) to the company. Most companies need little "authorization" to accept a payment from a customer! However, authorization is important for approving customers' discounts and allowances taken, claiming to pay the bill in full. Exhibit 8-3 shows some cash receipts processing procedures in a manual accounting setting. (It is easier to describe these procedures as manual ones instead of as computerized procedures.) You can see the "approval of discounts" noted in Exhibit 8-3.

Custody
Someone always gets the cash and checks in hand and thus has custody of the physical cash for a time. Control over this custody can vary. Companies can rotate people through the custody responsibility so one person does not have this custody all the time; they can have rotating teams of two or more people so they would need to collude with one another to steal money; they can make arrangements outside the company for actual cash custody (e.g., the lockbox arrangement). Since this initial custody cannot be avoided, it is always good control to prepare a list of the cash receipts as early in the process as possible, then separate the actual cash from the bookkeeping documents. The cash goes to the cashier or treasurer's office, where a bank deposit is prepared and the money is sent to the bank. The list goes to the accountants, who record the cash receipts. (This list may be only a stack of the remittance advices received with the customers' payments. You yourself prepare a "remittance advice" each time you write the "amount enclosed" on the top part of your credit card billing, tear it off, and enclose it with your check.)

Recording
The accountants who record cash receipts and credits to customer accounts should not handle the cash. They should use the remittance list to make entries to the cash and accounts receivable control accounts and to the customers' accounts receivable subsidiary account records. In fact, a good error-checking activity is to have control account and subsidiary account entries made by different people, then later the accounts receivable entries and balances can be compared (reconciled) to determine whether the proper source documents (remittance lists) were used to make error-free accounting entries. Some computerized accounting programs post the customers' accounts automatically by keying on the customer identification number.

EXHIBIT 8-3 Cash Receipts Processing

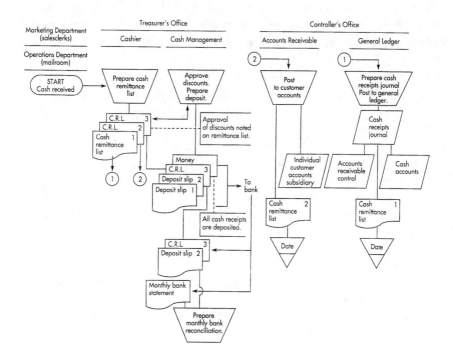

Periodic Reconciliation

Bank account reconciliations should be prepared carefully. Deposit slips should be compared to the details on cash remittance lists, and the total should be traced to the general ledger entries. Likewise, paid checks should be traced to the cash disbursements listing (journal). This care is required to establish that all the receipts recorded in the books were deposited and that credit was given to the right customer. (Refer to the special note on auditing bank reconciliations later in this chapter.)

CAREFUL RECONCILIATION
(Refer to Exhibit 8-3)

Suppose the cashier who prepares the remittance list had stolen and converted Customer A's checks to personal use. It might work for a short time until Customer A complained that the company had not given credit for payments. The cashier knows this. So, the cashier later puts Customer B's check in the bank deposit, but shows Customer A on the remittance list; thus, the accountants give Customer A credit. So far, so good for preventing Customer A's complaint. But now Customer B needs to be covered. This "lapping" of customer payments to hide an embezzlement can be detected by a bank reconciliation comparison of the checks deposited (Customer B) with the remittance credit recorded (Customer A).

AUDIT EVIDENCE IN MANAGEMENT REPORTS AND DATA FILES

Computer processing of revenue and cash receipts transactions makes it possible for management to generate several reports that can provide important audit evidence. Auditors should obtain and use these reports.

ENDING ORDER MASTER FILE

This file contains sales transactions that were started in the system but are not yet completed, thus not recorded as sales and accounts receivable. Old orders may represent shipments that actually were made, but for some reason the shipping department did not enter the shipping information (or entered an incorrect code that did not match the pending order file). The pending orders can be reviewed for evidence of the *completeness* of recorded sales and accounts receivable.

CREDIT CHECK FILES

The computer system may make automatic credit checks, but up-to-date maintenance of the credit information is very important. Credit checks on old or incomplete information are not good credit checks. A sample of the files can be tested for current status. Alternatively, the company's records on updating the files can be reviewed for evidence of updating operations.

PRICE LIST MASTER FILE

The computer system may produce customer invoices automatically; but, if the master price list is wrong, the billings will be wrong. The computer file can be compared to an official price source for accuracy. (The company should perform this comparison every time the prices are changed.)

SALES DETAIL (SALES JOURNAL) FILE

This file should contain the detail sales entries, including the shipping references and dates. The file can be scanned for entries without shipping references (fictitious sales?) and for match of recording dates with shipment dates (sales recorded before shipment?). This file contains the population of debit entries to the accounts receivable.

SALES ANALYSIS REPORTS

A variety of sales analyses may be produced. Sales classified by product lines is information for the business segment disclosures. Sales classified by sales employee or region can show unusually high or low volume that might bear further investigation if error is suspected.

ACCOUNTS RECEIVABLE AGED TRIAL BALANCE

This list of customers' accounts receivable balances is the accounts receivable. If the control account total is larger than the sum in the trial balance, too bad. A receivable amount that cannot be identified with a customer cannot be collected! The trial balance is used as the population for selecting accounts for confirmation. (See the special note on the existence assertion and the special note on using confirmations later in this chapter.) The aging information is used in connection with assessing the allowance for doubtful accounts. (An aged trial balance is in Exhibit 8-8.)

CASH RECEIPTS JOURNAL

The cash receipts journal contains all the detail entries for cash deposits and credits to various accounts. It contains the population of credit entries that should be reflected in the credits to accounts receivable for customer payments. It also contains the adjusting and correcting entries that can result from the bank account reconciliation. These entries are important because they may signal the types of accounting errors or manipulations that happen in the cash receipts accounting.

PEAKS AND VALLEYS

During the year-end audit, the independent auditors reviewed the weekly sales volume reports classified by region. They noticed that sales volume was very high in Region 2 the last two weeks of March, June, September, and December. The volume was unusually low in the first two weeks of April, July, October, and January. In fact, the peaks far exceeded the volume in all the other six regions. Further investigation revealed that the manager in Region 2 was holding open the sales recording at the end of each quarterly reporting period in an attempt to make the quarterly reports look good.

CONTROL RISK ASSESSMENT

Control risk assessment is important because it governs the nature, timing, and extent of substantive audit procedures that will be applied in the audit of

account balances in the revenue and collection cycle. These account balances
(listed in the corner of Exhibit 8-1) include:
- Cash in bank.
- Accounts receivable.
- Allowance for doubtful accounts.
- Bad debt expense.
- Sales revenue.
- Sales returns, allowances, discounts.

GENERAL CONTROL CONSIDERATIONS

Control procedures for proper segregation of responsibilities should be in
place and operating. By referring to Exhibit 8-1, you can see that proper
segregation involves authorization of sales and credit by persons who do not
have custody, recording, or reconciliation duties. Custody of inventory and
cash is in persons who do not directly authorize credit, record the accounting
entries, or reconcile the bank account. Recording (accounting) is performed by
persons who do not authorize sales or credit, handle the inventory or cash, or
perform reconciliations. Periodic reconciliations should be performed by
people who do not have authorization, custody, or recording duties related to
the same assets. Combinations of two or more of these responsibilities in one
person, one office, or one computerized system may open the door for errors,
irregularities, and frauds.

A common feature of cash management is to require that persons who
handle cash be insured under a fidelity bond. A **fidelity bond** is an insurance
policy that covers most kinds of cash embezzlement losses. Fidelity bonds do
not prevent or detect embezzlement, but the failure to carry the insurance
exposes the company to complete loss when embezzlement occurs. Auditors
may recommend fidelity bonding to companies that do not know about its
coverage.

In addition, the control system should provide for detail error-checking
activities. For example: (1) policy should provide that no sales order should
be entered without a customer order; (2) a credit-check code or manual
signature should be recorded by an authorized means; (3) access to inventory
and the shipping area should be restricted to authorized persons; (4) access to
billing terminals and blank invoice forms should be restricted to authorized
personnel; (5) accountants should be under orders to record sales and accounts

receivable when all the supporting documentation of shipment is in order, and care should be taken to record sales and receivables as of the date the goods and services were shipped and the cash receipts on the date the payments were received; (6) customer invoices should be compared with bills of lading and customer orders to determine that the customer is sent the goods ordered at the proper location for the proper prices, and that the quantity being billed is the same as the quantity shipped; (7) pending order files should be reviewed frequently to avoid failure to bill and record shipments; and (8) bank statements should be reconciled in detail monthly.

FICTITIOUS REVENUE

A San Antonio computer peripheral equipment company was experiencing slow sales, so the sales manager entered some sales orders for customers who had not ordered anything. The invoices were marked "hold," while the delivery was to a warehouse owned by the company. The rationale was that these customers would buy the equipment eventually, so why not anticipate the orders! (However, it's a good idea not to send them the invoices until they actually make the orders, hence the "hold.") The "sales" and "receivables" were recorded in the accounts, and the financial statements contained overstated revenue and assets.

Information about a company's controls often is gathered by completing an internal control questionnaire. Auditors use extensive questionnaires on every audit.

Another way to obtain general information about controls is called a "walk-through," or a "sample of one." In this work, the auditors take a single example of a transaction and "walk it through" from its initiation to its recording in the accounting records. The revenue and collection cycle walk-through involves following a sale from the initial customer order through credit approval, billing, and delivery of goods, to the entry in the sales journal and subsidiary accounts receivable records, then its subsequent collection and cash deposit. Sample documents are collected, and employees in each department are questioned about their specific duties. The purposes of a walk-through are to: (1) verify or update the auditors' understanding of the client's sales/accounts receivable accounting system and control activities and (2) learn whether the controls the client reported in the internal control questionnaire are actually in place. The walk-through, combined with inquiries, can contribute evidence about appropriate separation of duties, which might be a sufficient basis for assessing control risk slightly below the maximum. However, a walk-through is too limited in scope to provide evidence of whether the client's control activities were operating effectively during the period under audit. Usually, a larger sample of transactions for detail testing of control performance is necessary to justify a low control risk assessment based on actual control performance evidence.

DETAIL TEST OF CONTROLS AUDIT PROCEDURES

An organization should have input, processing, and output control activities in place and operating to prevent, detect, and correct accounting errors. The general control objectives are: validity, completeness, authorization, accuracy, classification, accounting/posting, and proper period recording. Exhibit 8-4 puts these in the perspective of revenue cycle activity with examples of specific objectives. This exhibit takes control objectives out of the abstract and expresses them in specific examples related to controlling sales accounting.

EXHIBIT 8-4 Internal Control Objectives: Revenue Cycle (Sales)

General Objectives	Examples of Specific Objectives
1. Recorded sales are *valid* and documented.	Customer purchase orders support invoices. Bills of lading or other shipping documentation exist for all invoices. Recorded sales in sales journal supported by invoices.
2. Valid sales transactions are *recorded* and none omitted.	Invoices, shipping documents, and sales orders are prenumbered and the numerical sequence is checked. Overall comparisons of sales are made periodically by a statistical or product-line analysis.

**EXHIBIT 8-4 Internal Control Objectives: Revenue Cycle (Sales)
Continued**

General Objectives	Examples of Specific Objectives
3. Sales are *authorized* according to company policy.	Credit sales approved by credit department. Prices used in preparing invoices are from authorized price schedule.
4. Sales invoices are *accurately* prepared.	Invoice quantities compared to shipment and customer order quantities. Prices checked and mathematical accuracy independently checked after invoice prepared.
5. Sales transactions are properly *classified*.	Sales to subsidiaries and affiliates classified as intercompany sales and receivables. Sales returns and allowances properly classified.
6. Sales transaction *accounting and posting* is proper.	Credit sales posted to customers' individual accounts. Sales journal posted to general ledger account. Sales recognized in accordance with generally accepted accounting principles.
7. Sales transactions are recorded in the *proper period*.	Sales invoices recorded on shipment date.

Auditors can perform detail test of controls audit procedures to determine whether controls that are said to be in place and operating actually are being performed properly by company personnel. A **detail test of control procedure** consists of (1) identification of the data population from which a sample of items will be selected for audit and (2) an expression of the action that will be taken to produce relevant evidence. In general, the *actions* in detail test of control audit procedures involve vouching, tracing, observing, scanning, and recalculating. A specification of such procedures is part of an audit program for obtaining evidence useful in a final control risk assessment. If personnel in the organization are not performing their control activities very well, auditors will need to design substantive audit procedures to try to detect whether control failures have produced materially misleading account balances.

Test of controls audit procedures can be used to audit the accounting for transactions in two directions. This dual-direction testing involves samples selected to obtain evidence about control over *completeness* in one direction and control over *validity* in the other direction. The completeness direction determines whether all transactions that occurred were recorded (none omitted), and the validity direction determines whether recorded transactions actually occurred (were valid). An example of the first direction is the examination of a sample of shipping documents (from the file of all shipping documents) to determine whether invoices were prepared and recorded. An example of the second direction is the examination of a sample of sales invoices (from the file representing all recorded sales) to determine whether supporting shipping documents exist to verify the fact of an actual shipment. The content of each file is compared with the other. The example is illustrated in Exhibit 8-5. (The A-2-a and A-1-a codes correspond to the test of controls procedures in Exhibit 8-6.)

EXHIBIT 8-5 Dual Direction of Test Audit Samples

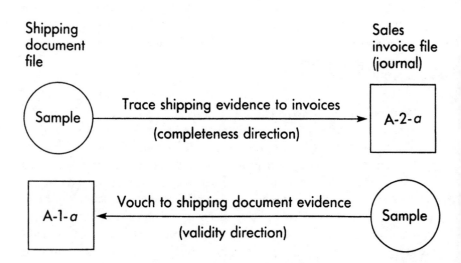

Exhibit 8-6 contains a selection of test of controls audit procedures. Many of these procedures can be characterized as steps taken to verify the content and character of sample documents from one file with the content and character of documents in another file. These steps are designed to enable the audit team to obtain objective evidence about the effectiveness of controls and about the reliability of accounting records.

EXHIBIT 8-6 Test of Controls Audit Procedures for Sales, Cash Receipts and Receivables

	ControlObjective
A. Sales	
1. Select a sample of recorded sales invoices from the sales journal.	
a. Vouch to support shipping documents	Validity
b. Determine whether credit was approved	Authorization
c. Vouch prices to the approved price list	Authorization Accuracy
d. Compare the quantity billed to the quantity shipped	Accuracy
e. Recalculate the invoice arithmetic	Accuracy
f. Compare the shipment date with the invoice record date	Proper period
g. Trace the invoice to posting in the general ledger control account and in the correct customer's account	Acctg/posting
h. Note the type of product shipped and determine proper classification in the right product-line revenue account	Classification
2. Select a sample of shipping documents from the shipping department file.	
a. Trace shipments to recorded sales invoices	Completeness

EXHIBIT 8-6   Test of Controls Audit Procedures for Sales, Cash Receipts and Receivables Continued

	ControlObjective
3. Scan recorded sales invoices for missing numbers in sequence.	Completeness
B. Cash Receipts	
1. Select a sample of recorded cash receipts.	
a. Vouch them to deposits in the bank statement	Validity
b. Vouch discounts taken by customers to proper approval or policy, recalculate discounts	Authorization Accuracy
c. Recalculate the cash summarized for a daily deposit or posting	Accuracy
d. Trace the deposit to the right cash account	Classification
e. Compare the date of receipt to the recording date	Proper period
f. Trace the receipts to postings in the correct customers' accounts	Acctg/posting
2. Select a sample of daily cash reports or another source of original cash records.	
a. Trace to the case receipts journal	Completeness
C. Accounts Receivable	
1. Select a sample of customers' accounts.	
a. Vouch debits in them to supporting sales invoices	Validity
b. Vouch credits in them to supporting cash receipts documents and approved credit memos	Validity
2. Select a sample of credit memos.	
a. Review for proper approval	Authorization
b. Trace to posting in customers' accounts	Acctg/posting

EXHIBIT 8-6   Test of Controls Audit Procedures for Sales, Cash Receipts and Receivables Continued

	ControlObjective
3. Scan the accounts receivable control account for postings from sources other than the sales and cash receipts journals (e.g., general journal adjusting entries, credit memos). Vouch a sample of such entries to supporting documents.	Validity Authorization Accuracy Proper Period Classification

Exhibit 8-6 shows the control objectives tested by the audit procedures. Thus, the test of controls procedures produce evidence that helps auditors determine whether the specific control objectives listed in Exhibit 8-4 were achieved.

SUMMARY: CONTROL RISK ASSESSMENT

The audit manager must evaluate the evidence obtained from an understanding of the internal control structure and from test of controls audit procedures. The initial process of obtaining an understanding of the company's controls and the later process of obtaining evidence from actual test of controls are two of the phases of control risk assessment work.

If the control risk is assessed very low, the substantive audit procedures on the account balances can be limited in cost-saving ways. For example, the accounts receivable confirmations can be sent on a date prior to the year-end, and the sample size can be fairly small.

On the other hand, if tests of controls reveal weaknesses (such as posting sales without shipping documents, charging customers the wrong prices, and recording credits to customers without supporting credit memos), the substantive procedures will need to be designed to lower the risk of failing to detect material error in the account balances. For example, the confirmation procedure may need to be scheduled on the year-end date with a large sample of customer accounts. Descriptions of major deficiencies, control weaknesses, and inefficiencies may be incorporated in a letter to the client describing "reportable conditions."

SPECIAL NOTE: THE EXISTENCE ASSERTION

When considering assertions and obtaining evidence about accounts receivable and other assets, auditors must put emphasis on the existence and rights (ownership) assertions. (For liability accounts, the emphasis is on the completeness and obligations assertions, as explained in Chapter 9.) This emphasis on existence is rightly placed because companies and auditors often have gotten into malpractice trouble by giving unqualified reports on financial statements that overstated assets and revenues and understated expenses. For example, credit sales recorded too early (fictitious sales?) result in overstated accounts receivable and overstated sales revenue; failure to amortize prepaid expense results in understated expenses and overstated prepaid expenses (current assets).

Discerning the population of assets to audit for existence and ownership is easy because the company has *asserted* their existence by putting them on the balance sheet. The audit procedures described in the following sections can be used to obtain evidence about the existence and ownership of accounts receivable and other assets.

RECALCULATION

Think about the assets that depend largely on calculations. They are amenable to auditors' recalculation procedures. Expired prepaid expenses are recalculated, using auditors' vouching of basic documents, such as loan agreements (prepaid interest), rent contracts (prepaid rent), and insurance policies (prepaid insurance). Goodwill and deferred expenses are recalculated by using original acquisition and payment document information and term (useful life) estimates. A bank reconciliation is a special kind of calculation, and the company's reconciliation can be audited. (See the special note on auditing a bank reconciliation later in this chapter.)

PHYSICAL OBSERVATION

Inventories and fixed assets can be inspected and counted (more on inventory observation is in Chapter 9). Titles to autos, land, and buildings can be vouched, sometimes using public records in the county clerk's office. Petty cash and undeposited receipts can be observed and counted, but the cash in the bank cannot. Securities held as investments can be inspected if held by the company.

CONFIRMATION

Letters of confirmation can be sent to banks and customers, asking for a report of the balances owed the company. Likewise, if securities held as investments are in the custody of banks or brokerage houses, the custodians can be asked to report the names, numbers, and quantity of the securities held for the company. In some cases, inventories held in public warehouses or out on consignment can be confirmed with the other party. (Refer to the special note on confirmations later in this chapter.)

VERBAL INQUIRY

Inquiries to management usually do not provide very convincing evidence about existence and ownership. However, inquiries always should be made about the company's agreements to maintain compensating cash balances (may not be classifiable as "cash" among the current assets), about pledge or sale of accounts receivable with recourse in connection with financings, and about pledge of other assets as collateral for loans.

EXAMINATION OF DOCUMENTS (VOUCHING)

Evidence of ownership can be obtained by studying the title documents for assets. Examination of loan documents may yield evidence of the need to disclose assets pledged as loan collateral.

SCANNING

Assets are supposed to have debit balances. A computer can be used to scan large files of accounts receivable, inventory, and fixed assets for uncharacteristic credit balances. Usually, such credit balances reflect errors in the recordkeeping--customer overpayments, failure to post purchases of inventory, depreciation of assets more than cost. The names of debtors can be scanned for officers, directors, and related parties, amounts which need to be reported separately or disclosed in the financial statements.

ANALYTICAL PROCEDURES

A variety of analytical comparisons might be employed, depending on the circumstances and the nature of the business. Comparisons of asset and revenue balances with recent history might help detect overstatements. Such relationships as receivables turnover, gross margin ratio, and sales/asset ratios can be compared to historical data and industry statistics for evidence of overall reasonableness. Account interrelationships also can be used in analytical review. For example, sales returns and allowances and sales commissions generally vary directly with dollar sales volume, bad debt expense usually varies directly with credit sales volume, and freight expense varies with the physical sales volume. Accounts receivable write-offs should be compared with earlier estimates of doubtful accounts.

SIMPLE ANALYTICAL COMPARISON

The auditors prepared a schedule of the monthly credit sales totals for the current and prior years. They noticed several variations, but one, in November of the current year, stood out in particular. The current-year credit sales were almost twice as large as any prior November. Further investigation showed that a computer error had caused the November credit sales to be recorded twice in the control accounts. The accounts receivable and sales revenue were materially overstated as a result.

SPECIAL NOTE: USING CONFIRMATIONS

This special note gives some details about using confirmations in the audit of cash and accounts receivable. In general, the use of confirmations for cash balances and trade accounts receivable is considered a required generally accepted audit procedure (SAS 67, AU 330). However, auditors may decide not to use them if suitable alternative procedures are available and applicable in particular circumstances. Auditors should document justifications for the decision not to use confirmations for trade accounts receivable in a particular audit. Justifications include: (1) receivables are not material; (2) confirmations would be ineffective, based on prior years' experience or knowledge that responses could be unreliable; and (3) analytical procedures and other substantive test of details procedures provide sufficient, competent evidence.

A DECISION NOT TO USE ACCOUNTS RECEIVABLE CONFIRMATIONS

Sureparts Manufacturing Company sold all its production to three auto manufacturers and six aftermarket distributors. All nine of these customers typically paid their accounts in full by the 10th of each following month. The auditors were able to vouch the cash receipts for the full amount of the accounts receivable in the bank statements and cash receipts records in the month following the Surepart year-end. Confirmation evidence was not considered necessary in these circumstances.

CONFIRMATION OF CASH AND LOAN BALANCES

The standard bank confirmation form, approved by the AICPA, the American Bankers Association, and the Bank Administration Institute, is shown in Exhibit 8-7. This form is used to obtain bank confirmation of deposit and loan balances. (Other confirmation letters are used to obtain confirmation of contingent liabilities, endorsements, compensating balance agreements, lines of credit, and other financial instruments and transactions. The standard form and illustrative letters are reproduced in the AICPA *Audit and Accounting Manual*.) A word of caution is in order: While financial institutions may note exceptions to the information typed in a confirmation and may confirm items omitted from it, the AICPA warns auditors that sole reliance on the form to satisfy the completeness assertion, insofar as cash and loan balances are concerned, is unwarranted. Officers and employees of financial institutions cannot be expected to search their information systems for balances and loans that may not be immediately evident as assets and liabilities of the client company. However, it is a good idea to send confirmations on accounts the company represents as closed during the year to get the bank to confirm zero balances. (If a nonzero balance is confirmed by a bank, the auditors have evidence that some asset accounting is omitted in the company records.)

EXHIBIT 8-7 Bank Confirmation

C-22	**STANDARD FORM TO CONFIRM ACCOUNT** **BALANCE INFORMATION WITH FINANCIAL INSTITUTIONS**		

Kingston Company

FINANCIAL INSTITUTION'S NAME AND ADDRESS — CUSTOMER NAME

First National Bank
Main Street
Chicago, Illinois

We have provided to our accountants the following information as of the close of business on

Dec. 31, 19 95

regarding our deposit and loan balances. Please confirm the accuracy of the information, noting any exceptions to the information provided. If the balances have been left blank, please complete this form by furnishing the balance in the appropriate space below.* Although we do not request nor expect you to conduct a comprehensive, detailed search of your records, if during the process of completing this confirmation additional information about other deposit and loan accounts we may have with you comes to your attention, please include such information below. Please use the enclosed envelope to return the form directly to our accountants.

1. At the close of business on the date listed above, our records indicated the following deposit balance(s):

ACCOUNT NAME	ACCOUNT NO.	INTEREST RATE	BALANCE*
Kingston Company	146-2013	none	$506,100

2. We were directly liable to the financial institution for loans at the close of business on the date listed above as follows:

ACCOUNT NO./ DESCRIPTION	BALANCE*	DATE DUE	INTEREST RATE	DATE THROUGH WHICH INTEREST IS PAID	DESCRIPTION OF COLLATERAL
042743	$750,000	6-30-96	11%	NA	Unsecured

Larry Lancaster   December 29, 1995
(Customer's Authorized Signature)   (Date)

The information presented above by the customer is in agreement with our records. Although we have not conducted a comprehensive, detailed search of our records, no other deposit or loan accounts have come to our attention except as noted below.

Alfred E. Neuman   January 15, 1996
(Financial Institution Authorized Signature)   (Date)

Assistant Vice President
(Title)

EXCEPTIONS AND OR COMMENTS

PLEASE RETURN THIS FORM DIRECTLY TO OUR ACCOUNTANTS: Anderson, Olds, Watershed
Rush Street
Chicago, Illinois

* Ordinarily, balances are intentionally left blank if they are not available at the time the form is prepared.

Approved 1990 by American Bankers Association, American Institute of Certified Public Accountants, and Bank Administration Institute. Additional forms available from: AICPA—Order Department, P.O. Box 1003, NY, NY 10108-1003   D451 5951

CONFIRMATION OF ACCOUNTS AND NOTES RECEIVABLE

Confirmations provide evidence of existence and, to a limited extent, of valuation of accounts and notes receivable. The accounts and notes to be confirmed should be documented in the working papers with an aged trial balance. (An aged trial balance is shown in Exhibit 8-8, annotated to show the auditors' work.) Accounts for confirmation can be selected at random or in accordance with another plan consistent with the audit objectives. Statistical methods may be useful for determining the sample size. Generalized audit software to access computerized receivables files may be utilized to select and even to print the confirmations.

EXHIBIT 8-8 Accounts Receivable Aged Trial Balance

```
D-2                    KINGSTON COMPANY           Prepared  Ҁ
PG. 1 OF 15           ACCOUNTS RECEIVABLE         Date      1-12-96
                      December 31, 1995           Reviewed  Terri Tough
                                                  Date      1-17-96

------------------------------------------------------------------------
                  ---------- -------- Aged --------   Jan. 1996 Collection
                            30-60   61-90  Over 90                    Past
                  Current   Days    Days   Days   Total  Current      Due
------------------------------------------------------------------------
Able Hardware     12,337 X                        12,337 XPCu 12,337
Baker Supply         712                             712         712
Charley Company    1,486 X    420 X                1,906 XPC   1,486      420
Dogg General Store                          755      755

Welsch Windows                      531 X          531 X NC           531
Zlat Stuff Place                           214      214              214
------------------------------------------------------------------------
Balance per books 335,000 30,000 20,000 15,000 400,000 320,000   25,000
                                                    (7)
Billing errors    (11,000)       (1,000)       (12,000)(7)        · ·
------------------------------------------------------------------------
Adjusted balance  324,000 30,000 19,000 15,000 388,000
------------------------------------------------------------------------

X  Traced to accounts receivable subsidiary ledger.
PC Positive confirmation mailed Jan. 4. Replies D-2.3
NC Negative confirmation mailed Jan. 4. Replies D-2.4
u  No reply to positive confirmation, vouched charges to invoices.
9  Traced to general ledger control account.
(7) Billing error adjustment explained on working paper D-2.2
Note: See D-2.2 for analysis of doubtful accounts and our test
      of reasonableness
```

Two widely used confirmation forms are *positive confirmations* and *negative confirmations*. An example of a positive confirmation is shown in Exhibit 8-9. A variation of the positive confirmation is the *blank form*. A blank confirmation does not contain the balance; customers are asked to fill it in themselves. The blank positive confirmation may produce better evidence because the recipients need to get the information directly from their own records instead of just signing the form and returning it with no exceptions noted. (However, the effort involved may cause a lower response rate.)

The negative confirmation form for the same request shown in Exhibit 8-9 is in Exhibit 8-10. The positive form asks for a response. The negative form asks for a response *only if something is wrong with the balance*; thus, lack of response to negative confirmations is considered evidence of propriety.

The positive form is used when individual balances are relatively large or when accounts are in dispute. Positive confirmations may ask for information about either the account balance or specific invoices, depending on knowledge about how customers maintain their accounting records. The negative form is used mostly when inherent risk and control risk are considered low, when a large number of small balances is involved, and when the client's customers can be expected to consider the confirmations properly. Frequently, both forms are used by sending positive confirmations on some customers' accounts and negative confirmations on others.

Getting confirmations delivered to the intended recipient is a problem that requires auditors' careful attention. Auditors need to control the confirmations, including the addresses to which they are sent. Experience is full of cases where confirmations were mailed to company accomplices, who provided false responses. The auditors should carefully consider features of the reply, such as postmarks, fax and telegraph responses, letterhead, electronic mail, telephone, or other characteristics that may give clues to indicate false responses. Auditors should follow up electronic and telephone responses to determine their origin (e.g., returning the telephone call to a known number, looking up telephone numbers to determine addresses, or using a criss-cross directory to determine the location of a respondent). Furthermore, the lack of response to a negative confirmation is no guarantee that the intended recipient received it unless the auditor carefully controlled the mailing.

EXHIBIT 8-9 Positive Confirmation Letter

D-2.3

KINGSTON COMPANY
Chicago, Illinois

January 5, 1996

Charley Company
Lake and Adams
Chicago, Illinois

Gentlemen:

Our auditors, Anderson, Olds, and Watershed, are making their regular audit of our financial statements. Part of this audit includes direct verification of customer balances.

PLEASE EXAMINE THE DATA BELOW CAREFULLY AND EITHER CONFIRM ITS ACCURACY OR REPORT ANY DIFFERENCES DIRECTLY TO OUR AUDITORS USING THE ENCLOSED REPLY ENVELOPE.

This is not a request for payment. Please do not send your remittance to our auditors.

Your prompt attention to this confirmation request will be appreciated.

Samuel Carboy

Samuel Carboy, Controller

The balance due Kingston Company as of December 31, **1995,** is $1,906. This balance is correct except as noted below:

It's correct. Will send payment as soon

as possible

Date: *Jan. 7, 1996*   By: *P. "Charley" O'Quirk*

Title: *President*

EXHIBIT 8-10 Negative Confirmation Letter

KINGSTON COMPANY
Chicago, Illinois

January 5, 1996

Charley Company
Lake and Adams
Chicago, Illinois

Gentlemen:

Our auditors, Anderson, Olds, and Watershed, are making their regular audit of our financial statements. Part of this audit includes direct verification of customer balances.

PLEASE EXAMINE THE DATA BELOW CAREFULLY AND COMPARE THEM TO YOUR RECORDS OF YOUR ACCOUNT WITH US. IF OUR INFORMATION IS NOT IN AGREEMENT WITH YOUR RECORDS, PLEASE STATE ANY DIFFERENCES ON THE REVERSE SIDE OF THIS PAGE, AND RETURN DIRECTLY TO OUR AUDITORS IN THE RETURN ENVELOPE PROVIDED. IF THE INFORMATION IS CORRECT, NO REPLY IS NECESSARY.

This is not a request for payment. Please do not send your remittance to our auditors.

Your prompt attention to this confirmation request will be appreciated.

Samuel Carboy
_____
Samuel Carboy, Controller

As of December 31, **1995,** balance due to Kingston Company: $1,906
Date of Origination: November and December, **1995**
Type: Open trade account

The **response rate** for positive confirmations is the proportion of the number of confirmations returned to the number sent, generally after the audit team prompts recipients with second and third requests. Research studies have shown response rates ranging from 66 to 96 percent. Recipients seem to be able to detect account misstatements to varying degrees. Studies have shown **detection rates** (the ratio of the number of exceptions reported to auditors to the number of account errors intentionally reported to customers) ranging from 20 to 100 percent. Negative confirmations seem to have lower detection rates than positive confirmations. Also, studies show somewhat lower detection rates for misstatements favorable to recipients (i.e., an accounts receivable understatement). Overall, positive confirmations appear to be more effective than negative confirmations; but results depend on the type of recipients, the size of the account, and the type of account being confirmed. Effective confirmation practices depend on attention to these factors and on prior years' experience with confirmation results on a particular client's accounts.

Effective confirmation also depends on using a "bag of tricks" to boost the response rate. Often, auditors merely send out a cold, official-looking request in a metered mail envelope and expect customers to be happy to respond. However, the response rate can be increased by using: (1) a postcard sent in advance, notifying that a confirmation is coming; (2) special delivery mail; (3) first-class stamp postage (not metered); and (4) an envelope imprinted "Confirmation Enclosed: Please Examine Carefully." These devices increase the cost of the confirmation procedure, but the benefit is a better response rate.[1]

The audit team should try to obtain replies to all positive confirmations by sending second and third requests to nonrespondents. If there is no response or if the response specifies an exception to the client's records, the auditors should carry out document vouching procedures to audit the account. These alternative procedures include the *vouching direction* of finding sales invoice copies, shipping documents, and customer orders that signal the existence of sales charges. They also are used to find evidence of customers' payments in subsequent cash receipts.

When sampling is used, all accounts in the sample should be audited. It is improper to substitute an easy-to-audit customer account not in the sample for one that does not respond to a confirmation request.

Confirmation of receivables may be performed at a date other than the year-end. When confirmation is done at an interim date, the audit firm is able to spread work throughout the year and avoid the pressures of overtime that typically occur around December 31. Also, the audit can be completed sooner after the year-end date if confirmation has been done earlier. The primary consideration when planning confirmation of accounts before the balance sheet date is the client's internal control over transactions affecting receivables. When confirmation is performed at an interim date, the following additional procedures should be considered:

1. Obtain a summary of receivables transactions from the interim date to the year-end date.
2. Obtain a year-end trial balance of receivables, compare it to the interim trial balance, and obtain evidence and explanations for large variations.
3. Consider the necessity for additional confirmations as of the balance sheet date if balances have increased materially.

One final note about confirmations: Confirmations of accounts, loans, and notes receivable may not produce sufficient evidence of ownership by the client. Debtors may not be aware that the auditor's client has sold their accounts, notes, or loans receivable to financial institutions or to the public (collateralized securities). Auditors need to perform additional inquiry and detail procedures to get evidence of the ownership of the receivables and the appropriateness of disclosures related to financing transactions secured by receivables.

SUMMARY: CONFIRMATIONS

Confirmations of cash balances, loans, accounts receivable, and notes receivable are required, unless auditors can justify substituting other procedures in the circumstances of a particular audit. The bank confirmation is a standard positive form. Confirmations for accounts and notes receivable can be in positive or negative form, and the positive form may be a blank confirmation.

Auditors must take care to control confirmations to ensure that responses are received from the real debtors and not from persons who can intercept the confirmations to give false responses. Responses by fax, telegraph, electronic mail, telephone, or other means not written and signed by a recipient should be followed up to determine their genuine origins. Second and third requests should be sent to prompt responses to positive confirmations, and auditors should audit nonresponding customers by alternative procedures. Accounts in a sample should not be left unaudited (e.g., "They didn't respond"), and easy-to-audit accounts should not be substituted for hard-to-audit ones in a sample. Various "tricks" can be used to raise the response rate.

Confirmations yield evidence about existence and gross valuation. However, the fact that a debtor admits to owing the debt does not mean the debtor can pay. Other procedures must be undertaken to audit the collectibility of the accounts. Nevertheless, confirmations can give some clues about collectibility when customers tell about balances in dispute. Confirmations of accounts, notes, and loans receivable should not be used as the only evidence of the ownership of these financial assets.

SPECIAL NOTE: AUDIT OF BANK RECONCILIATIONS WITH ATTENTION TO LAPPING AND KITING

The company's bank reconciliation is the primary means of valuing cash in the financial statements. The amount of cash in the bank is almost always different from the amount in the general ledger (financial statements), and the reconciliation purports to explain the difference. The normal procedure is to obtain the company-prepared bank reconciliation and audit it. Auditors should not perform the company's control function of preparing the reconciliation.

A client-prepared bank reconciliation is shown in Exhibit 8-11. The bank balance is confirmed and cross-referenced to the bank confirmation working paper (Exhibit 8-7). The reconciliation is recalculated, the outstanding checks and deposits in transit are footed, and the book balance is traced to the trial balance (which has been traced to the general ledger). The reconciling items should be vouched to determine whether outstanding checks really were not paid and that deposits in transit actually were mailed before the reconciliation date. The auditors' information source for vouching the bank reconciliation items is a **cutoff bank statement**, which is a complete bank statement including all paid checks and deposits slips. The client requests the bank to send this bank statement directly to the auditor. It is usually for a 10- to 20-day period following the reconciliation date. (It also can be the next regular monthly statement, received directly by the auditors.)

The vouching of outstanding checks and deposits in transit is a matter of comparing checks that cleared in the cutoff bank statement with the list of outstanding checks for evidence that all checks that were written prior to the reconciliation date were on the list of outstanding checks. The deposits shown in transit should be recorded by the bank in the first business days of the cutoff period. If recorded later, the inference is that the deposit may have been made up from receipts of the period after the reconciliation date. For large outstanding checks not clearing in the cutoff period, vouching may be extended to other documentation supporting the disbursement. These procedures are keyed and described by tickmarks in Exhibit 8-11.

ACCOUNTS RECEIVABLE LAPPING

When the business receives many payments from customers, a detailed audit should include comparison of the checks listed on a sample of deposit slips (from the reconciliation month and other months) to the detail of customer credits listed on the day's posting to customer accounts receivable (daily remittance list or other record of detail postings). This procedure is a test for accounts receivable lapping. It is an attempt to find credits given to customers for whom no payments were received on the day in question. An example of this type of comparison is in the discovery summary section of Case 8.1 (The Canny Cashier) later in this chapter.

EXHIBIT 8-11 Bank Reconciliation

```
                      KINGSTON COMPANY
C-2         BANK RECONCILIATION-FIRST NATIONAL BANK      Prepared  9.D. 1/10/96
                     General Account                     Reviewed  JRA 1/10/96
                        12/31/95
                   (Prepared by client)

Balance per bank statement                          506,100  c
Add:
   Deposit in transit as of 12/31/95                 51,240  n
Deduct outstanding checks:                          557,340
        Date     No.    Payee
       --------  ----   ------------------------
       12/10/94  842    Ace Supply Company            500  X
       11/31/95  1280   Ace Supply Company          1,800  ✓
       12/15/95  1372   Northwest Lumber Co.        30,760  ✓
       12/28/95  1412   Gibson & Johnson             7,270  X
       12/30/95  1417   First National payroll      20,000  ✓
       12/30/95  1418   Ace Supply Company           2,820  ✓
       12/30/95  1419   Windy City Utilities         2,030  ✓
       12/30/95  1420   Howard Hardware Supply       8,160  ✓
                                                   -------
Balance per book                                    73,340

                                                   484,000  f
```

Note: *Obtained cutoff bank statement 1/9/96* (C-23) (TIB-1)

f *Footed*

c *Confirmed by bank, standard bank confirmation* (C-22)

n *Vouched to cutoff bank statement, deposit recorded by bank on 1/3/96. Vouched to duplicate deposit slip validaged 1/3/96*

✓ *Vouched to paid check cleared with cutoff bank statement.*

X *Vouched to statement from attorneys.*

X *Amount in dispute per controller.*

CHECK KITING

Auditors also should be alert to the possibility of a company's practice of illegal "kiting." **Check kiting** is the practice of building up balances in one or more bank accounts based on uncollected (float) checks drawn against similar accounts in other banks. Kiting involves depositing money from one bank account to another, using a hot check. The depository bank does not know the check is on insufficient funds, but the deficiency is covered by another hot check from another bank account before the first check clears. Kiting is the deliberate floating of funds between two or more bank accounts. By this method, a bank customer uses the time required for checks to clear to obtain an unauthorized loan without any interest charge.

Professional money managers working for cash-conscious businesses try to have minimal unused balances in their accounts, and their efforts sometimes can look like check kites. Tight cash flows initiate kites, and *intent to kite* is the key for criminal charges. Kites evolve to include numerous banks and numerous checks. The more banks and broader geographical distance, the harder a perpetrator finds it to control a kite scheme.

The transactions described below illustrate a simple kite scheme. The transactions are shown in Exhibit 8-12.

Start with no money in the First National Bank and none in the Last National Bank. Run the kite quickly from July 3 (Monday) through July 12 (next Wednesday)--taking advantage of the holiday and the weekend to float the hot checks.

A. Deposit a $15,000 check drawn on First National Bank to the Last National account. Simultaneously, deposit a $10,000 check drawn on Last National Bank to the First National account. Do not record the deposits and disbursements in the general ledger.

B. Deposit an $11,000 check drawn on First National Bank to the Last National account. Simultaneously, deposit a $13,000 check drawn on Last National Bank to the First National account. Do not record the deposits and disbursements in the general ledger.

C. Purchase an $8,000 certified check from First National Bank to make a down payment on a Mercedes automobile. Record the check in the general ledger.

D. The first transfer checks (part A) clear each bank.

E. Deposit a $16,000 check drawn on First National Bank to the Last National account. Simultaneously, deposit a $14,000 check drawn on Last National Bank to the First National account. Do not record the deposits and disbursements in the general ledger.

F. Write checks for $14,000 drawn on First National Bank and $32,000 drawn on Last National Bank payable to a travel agent, and take a long trip (preferably to a country with no extradition treaty!).

G. When the checks are presented to the banks for payment, the accounts are empty. A total of $79,000 was kited, of which $25,000 cleared during the kite period (the first transfers in **A**), so the "take" was $54,000. The criminals got the Mercedes ($8,000) and the vacation funds ($46,000).

These are some characteristic signs of check kiting schemes:

- Frequent deposits and checks in same amounts.
- Frequent deposits and checks in round amounts.
- Frequent deposits with checks written on the same (other) banks.
- Short time lag between deposits and withdrawals.
- Frequent ATM account balance inquiries.
- Many large deposits made on Thursday or Friday to take advantage of the weekend.
- Large periodic balances in individual accounts with no apparent business explanation.
- Low average balance compared to high level of deposits.
- Many checks made payable to other banks.
- Bank willingness to pay against uncollected funds.
- "Cash" withdrawals with deposit checks drawn on another bank.
- Checks drawn on foreign banks with lax banking laws and regulations.

EXHIBIT 8-12 Illustrative Check Kiting Transactions

Index	Date	Transaction	First National Bank At Bank (1)	First National Bank Actual (2)	Last National Bank At Bank (1)	Last National Bank Actual (2)
A	July 3	1st transfer	------	($15,000)	$15,000	$15,000
A	July 3	1st transfer	$10,000	$10,000	------	($10,000)
		Balances	$10,000	($5,000)	$15,000	$5,000
B	July 5	2nd transfer	------	($11,000)	$11,000	$11,000
B	July 5	2nd transfer	$13,000	$13,000	------	($13,000)
		Balances	$23,000	($3,000)	$26,000	$3,000
C	July 6	Mercedes	($8,000)	($8,000)		
		Balances	$15,000	($11,000)	$26,000	$3,000
D	July 7	1st trf clear	($15,000)		($10,000)	
E	July 7	3rd transfer	------	($16,000)	$16,000	$16,000
E	July 7	3rd transfer	$14,000	$14,000	------	($14,000)
		Balances	$14,000	($13,000)	$32,000	$5,000
F	July 8	Pay travel	------	($14,000)	------	($32,000)
		Balances	$14,000	($27,000)	$32,000	($27,000)
G	July 10	2nd trf clear	($11,000)		($13,000)	
G	July 12	3rd trf clear	($16,000)		($14,000)	
G	July 12	Travel clear	($14,000)		($32,000)	
			($27,000)		($27,000)	

(1) "At Bank" means the bank's records of deposits received and checks paid (cleared).
(2) "Actual" means the amounts the general ledger would have shown had the transfers been recorded.

Auditors can detect the above signs of check kiting by reviewing bank account activity. The only trouble is that criminal check kiters often destroy the banking documents. If a company cannot or will not produce its bank statements, with all deposit slips and canceled checks, the auditors should be wary.

If these cash transfers are recorded in the books, a company will show the negative balances that result from checks drawn on insufficient funds. However, perpetrators may try to hide the kiting by not recording the deposits and checks. Such maneuvers may be detectable in a bank reconciliation audit.

SUMMARY: BANK RECONCILIATIONS, LAPPING AND KITING

The combination of all the procedures performed on the bank reconciliation provides evidence of existence, valuation, and proper cutoff of the bank cash balances. Auditors use a cutoff bank statement to obtain independent evidence of the proper listing of outstanding checks and deposits in transit on a bank reconciliation.

Additional procedures can be performed to try to detect attempts at lapping accounts receivable collections and kiting checks. For lapping, these procedures include auditing the details of customer payments listed in bank deposits in comparison to details of customer payment postings (remittance lists). For kiting, these procedures include being alert to the signs of kites and preparing a schedule of interbank transfers and a proof of cash.

BANK TRANSFER SCHEDULE
AND "PROOF OF CASH"

Auditors usually prepare a schedule of interbank transfers to determine whether transfers of cash from one bank to another were recorded properly (correct amount and correct date). Assume the facts given in the preceding kiting illustration, and the following: (1) the First National Bank account is the company's general bank account, and the Last National Bank account is the payroll account, (2) the company pays its payroll on the 15th and 30th days of each month, and (3) the company transfers the net amount of each payroll from the general account to the payroll account. A "schedule of interbank transfers" prepared from the recorded entries in the general ledger would look like the one in Panel A in Exhibit 8-13.

However, we know that the managers performed a check kite and did not record several transfers between these accounts. Auditors should review the bank statements, and find the other transfers, and put them on the schedule (shown in Panel B in Exhibit 8-13). Panel B shows how the auditors can document the unrecorded transfers.

EXHIBIT 8-13 Illustration of Interbank Transfer Schedule

			Disbursing Account		Receiving Account		
Check			Date per	Date per		Date Per	Date per
Number	Bank	Amount	Books	Bank	Bank	Books	Bank
PANEL A							
7602	1st Nat'l	$24,331	Jul 14	Jul 18	Last Nat'l	Jul 14	Jul 14
8411	1st Nat'l	$36,462	Jul 28	Aug 1	Last Nat'l	Jul 28	Jul 28
PANEL B							
6722	1st Nat'l	$15,000	none	July 7	Last Nat'l	none	July 3
11062	Last Nat'l	$10,000	none	July 7	1st Nat'l	none	July 3
6793	1st Nat'l	$11,000	none	July 10	Last Nat'l	none	July 5
11097	Last Nat'l	$13,000	none	July 10	1stNat'l	none	July 5
6853	1st Nat'l	$16,000	none	July 12	Last Nat'l	none	July 7
11106	Last Nat'l	$14,000	none	July 12	1stNat'l	none	July 7

Auditors can use another method to discover unrecorded cash transactions. It is called a "proof of cash." You may know this method under the name of "four-column bank reconciliation." The proof of cash is a reconciliation in which the bank balance, the bank report of cash deposited, and the bank report of cash paid are all reconciled to the company's general ledger. Exhibit 8-14 illustrates a proof of cash. The illustration assumes some bank reconciliation information, some transaction activity, and the unrecorded transfers for the First National Bank account used in the previous illustrations of kiting and interbank transfers. (Changing the kiting illustration: the bank accounts did not start with zero balances.)

The proof of cash attempt to reconcile the deposits and payments reported by the bank to the deposits and payments recorded in the general ledger will reveal the unrecorded transfers. The amounts will not reconcile until the auditors inspect the bank statement and find the bank amounts that are not in the general ledger. (Likewise, the attempt to reconcile the July 31 bank balance will show a $5,000 difference, which is explained by the $37,000 unrecorded deposits and the $42,000 unrecorded payments.).

EXHIBIT 8-14 Illustration of Proof of Cash--First National Bank

	Balance June 30	Deposits	Payments	Balance July 31
		Month of July		
Bank statement amounts	$264,322	$398,406	$390,442	$272,286
Deposits in transit				
June 30	76,501	(76,501)		
July 31		79,721		79,721
Outstanding checks				
June 30	(89,734)		(89,734)	
July 31			62,958	(62,958)
Unrecorded bank interest				
(recorded in the next month)				
June 30	(162)	162		
July 31		(155)		(155)
Unrecorded service charges				
(recorded in the next month)				
June 30	118		118	
July 31			(129)	129
Unrecorded transfers received from Last National Bank		(37,000)		(37,000)
Unrecorded transfers to Last National Bank			(42,000)	42,000
General ledger amounts	$251,045	$364,633	$321,655	$294,023

AUDIT CASES: SUBSTANTIVE
AUDIT PROCEDURES

The audit procedures to gather evidence on account balances are called "substantive procedures." Some amount of substantive audit procedures must be performed in all audits. Auditors should not place total reliance on controls to the exclusion of other procedures. Substantive audit procedures differ from test of controls audit procedures in their basic purpose. Substantive procedures are designed to obtain direct evidence about the dollar amounts in account balances, while test of controls procedures are designed to obtain evidence about the company's performance of its own control activities. Sometimes an audit procedure can be used for both purposes simultaneously, and then it is called a **dual-purpose procedure**.

DUAL-PURPOSE NATURE OF ACCOUNTS
RECEIVABLE CONFIRMATIONS

Accounts receivable confirmation is a substantive procedure designed to obtain evidence of the existence and gross amount (valuation) of customers' balances directly from the customer. If such confirmations show numerous exceptions, auditors would be concerned with the controls over the details of sales and cash receipts transactions even if previous control evaluations seemed to show little control risk.

The goal in performing substantive procedures is to detect evidence of errors, irregularities, and frauds, if any exist in the accounts as material overstatements or understatements of account balances. In the remainder of this part of the chapter, the approach is to use a set of cases which contain specific examples of test of controls and substantive audit procedures (recalculation, observation, confirmation, inquiry, vouching, tracing, scanning, and analysis). The case stories are used instead of listing schemes and detection procedures in the abstract.

The cases follow a standard format, which first tells about an error, irregularity, or fraud situation. This part is followed by an "audit approach" section that tells about the audit objective (assertion), controls, test of controls, and audit of balances (substantive procedures) that could be considered in an approach to the situation. The audit approach section presumes that the auditors do not know everything about the situation. (As a student of the case, you have "inside information.")

These are the parts of the case situation description for each one:

Method: A cause of the misstatement (accidental error, intentional irregularity, or fraud attempt), which usually is made easier by some kind of failure of controls.

Paper trail: A set of telltale signs of erroneous accounting, missing or altered documents, or a "dangling debit" (the false or erroneous debit that results from an overstatement of assets).

Amount: The dollar amount of overstated assets and revenue, or understated liabilities and expenses.

The audit approach section contains these parts:

Audit objective: A recognition of a financial statement *assertion* for which evidence needs to be obtained. The assertions are about existence of assets, liabilities, revenues, and expenses; their valuation; their complete inclusion in the account balances; the rights and obligations inherent in them; and their proper presentation and disclosure in the financial statements.

Control: A recognition of the control activities that *should* be used in an organization to prevent and detect errors and irregularities.

Test of controls: Ordinary and extended procedures *designed to produce evidence about the effectiveness of the controls* that should be in operation.

Audit of balances: Ordinary and extended *substantive procedures designed to find signs* of errors, irregularities, and frauds in account balances and classes of transactions.

At the end of the chapter, some similar discussion cases are presented, and you can write the audit approach to test your ability to design audit procedures for the detection of errors, irregularities, and frauds.

CASE 8.1
THE CANNY CASHIER

Problem

Cash embezzlement caused overstated accounts receivable, overstated customer discounts expense, and understated cash sales. Company failed to earn interest income on funds "borrowed."

Method

D. Bakel was the assistant controller of Sports Equipment, Inc. (SEI), an equipment retailer. SEI maintained accounts receivable for school districts in the region, otherwise customers received credit by using their own credit cards.

Bakel's duties included being the company cashier, who received all the incoming mail payments on school accounts and the credit card account and all the cash and checks taken over the counter. Bakel prepared the bank deposit (and delivered the deposit to the bank), listing all the checks and currency, and also prepared a remittance worksheet (daily cash report) that showed amounts received, discounts allowed on school accounts, and amounts to credit to the accounts receivable. The remittance worksheet was used by another accountant to post credits to the accounts receivable. Bakel also reconciled the bank statement. No one else reviewed the deposits or the bank statements except the independent auditors.

Bakel opened a bank account in the name of Sport Equipment Company (SEC), after properly incorporating the company in the secretary of state's office. Over-the-counter cash and checks and school district payments were taken from the SEI receipts and deposited in the SEC account. (None of the customers noticed the difference between the rubber stamp endorsements for the two similarly named corporations, and neither did the bank.) SEC kept the money awhile, earning interest, then Bakel wrote SEC checks to SEI to replace the "borrowed" funds, in the meantime taking new SEI receipts for deposit to SEC. Bakel also stole payments made by the school districts, depositing them to SEC. Later, Bakel deposited SEC checks in SEI, giving the schools credit, but approved an additional 2 percent discount in the process. Thus, the schools received proper credit later, and SEC paid in less by the amount of the extra discounts.

Paper Trail
SEI's bank deposits systematically showed fairly small currency deposits. Bakel was nervous about taking too many checks, so cash was preferred. The deposit slips also listed the SEC checks because bank tellers always compare the deposit slip listing to the checks submitted. The remittance worksheet showed different details: Instead of showing SEC checks, it showed receipts from school districts and currency, but not many over-the-counter checks from customers.

The transactions became complicated enough that Bakel had to use the microcomputer in the office to keep track of the school districts that needed to get credit. There were no vacations for this hard-working cashier because the discrepancies might be noticed by a substitute, and Bakel needed to give the districts credit later.

Amount
Over a six-year period, Bakel built up a $150,000 average balance in the Sport Equipment Company (SEC) account, which earned a total of $67,500 interest that should have been earned by Sports Equipment, Inc. (SEI). By approving the "extra" discounts, Bakel skimmed 2 percent of $1 million in annual sales, for a total of $120,000. Since SEI would have had net income before taxes of about $1.6 million over this six years (about 9 percent on the sales dollar), Bakel's embezzlement took about 12.5 percent of the income.

AUDIT APPROACH

Objective

Obtain evidence to determine whether the accounts receivable recorded on the books represent claims against real customers in the gross amounts recorded.

Control

Authorization related to cash receipts, custody of cash, recording cash transactions, and bank statement reconciliation should be separate duties designed to *prevent* errors, irregularities, and frauds. Some supervision and detail review of one or more of these duties should be performed as a next-level control designed to *detect* errors, irregularities, and frauds, if they have occurred. For example, the remittance worksheet should be prepared by someone else, or at least the discounts should be approved by the controller; the bank reconciliation should be prepared by someone else.

Bakel had all the duties. (While recording was not actually performed, Bakel provided the source document--the remittance worksheet--the other accountant used to make the cash and accounts receivable entries.) According to the company president, the "control" was the diligence of "our" long-time, trusted, hard-working assistant controller. *Note*: An auditor who "thinks like a crook" to imagine ways Bakel could commit errors, irregularities, or fraud could think of this scheme for cash embezzlement and accounts receivable lapping.

Test of Controls

Since the "control" purports to be Bakel's honest and diligent performance of the accounting and control activities that might have been performed by two or more people, the test of controls is an audit of cash receipts transactions as they relate to accounts receivable credit. The dual-direction samples and procedures are these:

Validity direction: Select a sample of customer accounts receivable, and vouch payment credits to remittance worksheets and bank deposits, including recalculation of discounts allowed in comparison to sales terms (2 percent), classification (customer name) identification, and correspondence of receipt date to recording date. *Completeness direction*: Select a sample of remittance worksheets (or bank deposits), vouch details to bank deposit slips (trace details to remittance worksheets if the sample is bank deposits), and trace forward to complete accounting posting in customer accounts receivable.

Audit of Balance
Since there is a control risk of incorrect accounting, perform the accounts receivable confirmation as of the year-end date. Confirm a sample of school district accounts, using positive confirmations. Blank confirmations may be used. Since there is a control risk, the "sample" may be all the accounts, if the number is not too large.

As prompted by notice of an oddity (noted in the discovery summary below), use the telephone book, chamber of commerce directory, local criss-cross directory, and a visit to the secretary of state's office to determine the location and identity of Sport Equipment Company.

Discovery Summary
The test of controls samples showed four cases of discrepancy, one of which is shown below.

The auditors sent positive confirmations on all 72 school district accounts. Three of the responses stated the districts had paid the balances before the confirmation date. Follow-up procedures on their accounts receivable credit in the next period showed they had received credit in remittance reports, and the bank deposits had shown no checks from the districts but had contained a check from Sports Equipment Company. Investigation of SEC revealed the connection of Bakel, who was confronted and then confessed.

Bank Deposit Slip

Jones	25
Smith	35
Hill District	980
Sport Equipment	1,563
Currency	540
Deposit	3,143

Cash Remittance Report

Name	Amount	Discount	AR	Sales
Jones	25	0	0	25
Smith	35	0	0	35
Hill Dist.	980	20	1,000	0
Marlin Dist.	480	20	500	0
Waco Dist.	768	32	800	0
Currency	855	0	0	855
Totals	3,143	72	2,300	915

CASE 8.2
THE TAXMAN ALWAYS RINGS TWICE

Problem

Overstated receivables for property taxes in a school district because the tax assessor stole some taxpayers' payments.

Method

J. Shelstad was the tax assessor-collector in the Ridge School District, serving a large metropolitan area. The staff processed tax notices on a computer system and generated 450,000 tax notices each October. An office copy was printed and used to check off "paid" when payments were received. Payments were processed by computer, and a master file of "accounts receivable" records (tax assessments, payments) was kept on the computer hard disk.

Shelstad was a good personnel manager, who often took over the front desk at lunchtime so the teller staff could enjoy lunch together. During these times, Shelstad took payments over the counter, gave the taxpayers a counter receipt, and pocketed some of the money, which was never entered in the computer system.

Shelstad resigned when he was elected to the Ridge school board. The district's assessor-collector office was eliminated upon the creation of a new countywide tax agency.

Paper Trail
The computer records showed balances due from many taxpayers who had actually paid their taxes. The book of printed notices was not marked "paid" for many taxpayers who had received counter receipts. These records and the daily cash receipts reports (cash receipts journal) were available at the time the independent auditors performed the most recent annual audit in April. When Shelstad resigned in August, a power surge permanently destroyed the hard disk receivables file, and the cash receipts journals could not be found.

The new county agency managers noticed that the total of delinquent taxes disclosed in the audited financial statements was much larger than the total turned over to the country attorney for collection and foreclosure.

Amount
Shelstad had been the assessor-collector for 15 years. The "good personnel manager" pocketed 100-150 counter payments each year, in amounts of $500-$2,500, stealing about $200,000 a year for a total of approximately $2.5 million. The district had assessed about $800-$900 million per year, so the annual theft was less than 1 percent. Nevertheless, the taxpayers got mad.

AUDIT APPROACH

Objective
Obtain evidence to determine whether the receivables for taxes (delinquent taxes) represent genuine claims collectible from the taxpayers.

Control
The school district had a respectable system for establishing the initial amounts of taxes receivable. The professional staff of appraisers and the independent appraisal review board established the tax base for each property. The school board set the price (tax rate). The computer system authorization for billing was validated on these two inputs.

The cash receipts system was well designed, calling for preparation of a daily cash receipts report (cash receipts journal that served as a source input for computer entry). This report was always reviewed by the "boss," Shelstad.

Unfortunately, Shelstad had the opportunity and power to override the controls and become both cash handler and supervisor. Shelstad made the decisions about sending delinquent taxes to the county attorney for collection, and the ones known to have been paid but stolen were withheld.

Test of Controls
The auditors performed dual-direction sampling to test the processing of cash receipts.
Validity direction: Select a sample of receivables from the computer hard disk, and vouch (1) charges to the appraisal record, recalculating the amount using the authorized tax rate and (2) payments, if any, to the cash receipts journal and bank deposits. (The auditors found no exceptions.) *Completeness direction*: Select a sample of properties from the appraisal rolls, and determine that tax notices had been sent and tax receivables (charges) recorded in the computer file. Select a sample of cash receipts reports, vouch them to bank deposits of the same amount and date, and trace the payments forward to credits to taxpayers' accounts.

Select a sample of bank deposits, and trace them to cash receipts reports of the same amount and date. In one of these latter two samples, compare the details on bank deposits to the details on the cash receipts reports to determine whether the same taxpayers appear on both documents. (The auditors found no exceptions.)

Audit of Balance
Confirm a sample of unpaid tax balances with taxpayers. Response rates may not be high, and follow-up procedures determining the ownership (county title files) may need to be performed, and new confirmations may need to be sent.

Determine that proper disclosure is made of the total of delinquent taxes and the total of delinquencies turned over to the county attorney for collection proceedings.

Discovery Summary
Shelstad persuaded the auditors that the true "receivables" were the delinquencies turned over to the county attorney. The confirmation sample and other work was based on this population. Thus, confirmations were not sent to fictitious balances that Shelstad knew had been paid, and the auditors never had the opportunity to receive "I paid" complaints from taxpayers.

The new managers of the countywide tax district were not influenced by Shelstad. They questioned the discrepancy between the delinquent taxes in the audit report and the lower amount turned over for collection. Since the computer file was not usable, the managers had to use the printed book of tax notices, where paid accounts had been marked "paid." (Shelstad had not marked the stolen ones "paid" so the printed book would agree with the computer file.) Tax due notices were sent to the taxpayers with unpaid balances, and they began to show up bringing their counter receipts and loud complaints.

In a fit of audit overkill, the independent auditors had earlier photocopied the entire set of cash receipts reports (cash journal), and they were then able to determine that the counter receipts (all signed by Shelstad) had not been deposited or entered.

CASE 8.3
BILL OFTEN, BILL EARLY

Problem
Overstated sales and receivables, understated discounts expense, and overstated net income resulted from recording sales too early and failure to account for customer discounts taken.

Method
McGossage Company experienced profit pressures for two years in a row. Actual profits were squeezed in a recessionary economy, but the company reported net income decreases that were not as severe as other companies in the industry.

Sales were recorded in the grocery products division for orders that had been prepared for shipment but not actually shipped until later. Employees backdated the shipping documents. Gross profit on these "sales" was about 30 percent. Customers took discounts on payments, but the company did not record them, leaving the debit balances in the customers' accounts receivable instead of charging them to discounts and allowances expense. Company accountants were instructed to wait 60 days before recording discounts taken.

The division vice president and general manager knew about these accounting practices, as did a significant number of the 2,500 employees in the division. The division managers were under orders from headquarters to achieve profit objectives they considered unrealistic.

Paper Trail
The customers' accounts receivable balances contained amounts due for discounts the customers already had taken. The cash receipts records showed payments received without credit for discounts. Discounts were entered monthly by a special journal entry.

The unshipped goods were on the shipping dock at year-end with papers showing earlier shipping dates.

Amount

As misstatements go, some of these were on the materiality borderline. Sales were overstated 0.3 percent and 0.5 percent in the prior and current year, respectively. Accounts receivable were overstated 4 percent and 8 percent. But the combined effect was to overstate the division's net income by 6 percent and 17 percent. Selected data were:

	One Year Ago*		Current Year*	
	Reported	Actual	Reported	Actual
Sales	$330.0	$329.0	$350.0	$348.0
Discounts expense	1.7	1.8	1.8	2.0
Net income	6.7	6.3	5.4	4.6

*Dollars in millions.

AUDIT APPROACH

Objective

Obtain evidence to determine whether sales were recorded in the proper period and whether gross accounts receivable represented the amounts due from customers at year-end. Obtain evidence to determine whether discounts expense was recognized in the proper amount in the proper period.

Control

The accounting manual should provide instructions to record sales on the date of shipment (or when title passes, if later). Management subverted this control procedure by having shipping employees date the shipping papers incorrectly.

Cash receipts procedures should provide for authorizing and recording discounts when they are taken by customers. Management overrode this control instruction by giving instructions to delay the recording.

Test of Controls

Questionnaires and inquiries should be used to determine the Company's accounting policies. It is possible that employees and managers would lie to the auditors to conceal the policies. It is also possible that pointed questions about revenue recognition and discount recording policies would elicit answers to reveal the practices.

For detail procedures: Select a sample of cash receipts, examine them for authorization, recalculate the customer discounts, trace them to accounts receivable input for recording of the proper amount on the proper date. Select a sample of shipping documents and vouch them to customer orders, then trace them to invoices and to recording in the accounts receivable input with proper amounts on the proper date. These tests follow the *tracing direction*--starting with data that represent the beginning of transactions (cash receipts, shipping) and tracing them through the company's accounting process.

Audit of Balance
Confirm a sample of customer accounts. Use analytical relationships of past years' discount expense to a relevant base (sales, sales volume) to calculate an overall test of the discounts expense.

Discovery Summary
The managers lied to the auditors about their revenue and expense timing policies. The sample of shipping documents showed no dating discrepancies because the employees had inserted incorrect dates. The analytical procedures on discounts did not show the misstatement because the historical relationships were too erratic to show a deficient number (outlier). However, the sample of cash receipts transactions showed that discounts were not calculated and recorded at time of receipt. Additional inquiry led to discovery of the special journal entries and knowledge of the recording delay. Two customers in the sample of 65 confirmations responded with exceptions that turned out to be unrecorded discounts.

Two other customers in the confirmation sample complained that they did not owe for late invoices on December 31. Follow-up showed the shipments were goods noticed on the shipping dock. Auditors taking the physical inventory noticed the goods on the shipping dock during the December 31 inventory-taking. Inspection revealed the shipping documents dated December 26. When the auditors traced these shipments to the sales recording, they found them recorded "bill and hold" on December 29. (These procedures were performed and the results obtained by a successor audit firm in the third year!)

CASE 8.4
THANK GOODNESS IT'S FRIDAY

Problem
Overstated sales caused overstated net income, retained earnings, current assets, working capital, and total assets. Overstated cash collections did not change the total current assets or total assets, but it increased the amount of cash and decreased the amount of accounts receivable.

Method
Alpha Brewery Corporation generally has good control policies and procedures related to authorization of transactions for accounting entry, and the accounting manual has instructions for recording sales transactions in the proper accounting period. The company regularly closes the accounting process each Friday at 5 P.M. to prepare weekly management reports. The year-end date (cutoff date is December 31, and, in 1990, December 31 was a Monday. However, the accounting was performed through Friday as usual, and the accounts were closed for the year on January 4.

Paper Trail
All the entries were properly dated after December 31, including the sales invoices, cash receipts, and shipping documents.

However, the trial balance from which the financial statements were prepared was dated December 31, 1990. Nobody noticed the slip of a few days because the Friday closing was normal.

Amount
Alpha recorded sales of $672,000 and gross profit of $268,800 over the January 1-4 period. Cash collections on customers' accounts were recorded in the amount of $800,000.

AUDIT APPROACH

Objective
Obtain evidence to determine the existence, completeness, and valuation of sales for the year ended December 31, 1990, and cash and accounts receivable as of December 31, 1990.

Control
The company had in place the proper instructions to people to date transactions on the actual date on which they occurred and to enter sales and cost of goods sold on the day of shipment and to enter cash receipts on the day received in the company offices. An accounting supervisor should have checked the entries through Friday to make sure the dates corresponded with the actual events, and that the accounts for the year were closed with Monday's transactions.

Test of Controls
In this case, the auditors need to be aware of the company's weekly routine closing and the possibility that the intervention of the December 31 date might cause a problem. Asking the question: "Did you cut off the accounting on Monday night this week?" might elicit the "Oh, we forgot!" response. Otherwise, it is normal to sample transactions around the year-end date to determine whether they were recorded in the proper accounting period.
The procedure: Select transactions 7-10 days before and after the year-end date, and inspect the dates on supporting documentation for evidence of accounting in the proper period.

Audit of Balance
The audit for sales overstatement is partly accomplished by auditing the cash and accounts receivable at December 31 for overstatement (the dangling debit location). Confirm a sample

Audit of Balance

The audit for sales overstatement is partly accomplished by auditing the cash and accounts receivable at December 31 for overstatement (the dangling debit location). Confirm a sample of accounts receivable. If the accounts are too large, the auditors expect the debtors to say so, thus leading to detection of sales overstatements.

Cash overstatement is audited by auditing the bank reconciliation to see whether deposits in transit (the deposits sent late in December) actually cleared the bank early in January. Obviously, the January 4 cash collections could not reach the bank until at least Monday, January 7. That's too long for a December 31 deposit to be in transit to a local bank.

The completeness of sales recordings is audited by selecting a sample of sales transactions (and supporting shipping documents) in the early part of the next accounting period (January 1991). One way that sales of 1990 could be incomplete would be to postpone recording December shipments until January, and this procedure will detect them if the shipping documents are dated properly.

The completeness of cash collections (and accounts receivable credits) are audited by auditing the cash deposits early in January to see whether there is any sign of holding cash without entry until January.

In this case, the existence objective is more significant for discovery of the problem than the completeness objective. After all, the January 1-4 sales, shipments, and cash collections did not "exist" in December 1990.

Discovery Summary

The test of controls sample from the days before and after December 31 quickly revealed the problem. Company accounting personnel were embarrassed, but there was no effort to misstate the financial statements. This was a simple error. The company readily made the following adjustment:

	Debit	Credit
Sales	$672,000	
Inventory	$403,200	
Accounts receivable	$800,000	
Accounts receivable		$672,000
Cost of goods sold		$403,200
Cash		$800.000

SUMMARY

The revenue and collection cycle consists of customer order processing, credit checking, shipping goods, billing customers and accounting for accounts receivable, and collecting and accounting for cash receipts. Companies reduce control risk by having a suitable separation of authorization, custody, recording, and periodic reconciliation duties. Error-checking activities of comparing customer orders and shipping documents are important for billing customers the right prices for the delivered quantities. Otherwise, many things could go wrong--ranging from making sales to fictitious customers or customers with bad credit to erroneous billings for the wrong quantities at the wrong prices at the wrong time.

Cash collection is a critical point for asset control. Many cases of embezzlement occur in this process. Illustrative cases in the chapter tell the stories of some of these cash embezzlement schemes, including the practice of "lapping" accounts receivable.

Three topics have special technical notes in the chapter. The *existence assertion* is very important in the audit of cash and receivables assets because misleading financial statements often have contained overstated assets and revenue. The *use of confirmations* gets a special section because confirmation is frequently used to obtain evidence of asset existence from outside parties, such as customers who owe on accounts receivable. The *audit of bank reconciliations* is covered in the context of an audit opportunity to recalculate the amount of cash for the financial statements and to look for signs of accounts receivable lapping and check kiting. The *schedule of interbank transfers* and the *proof of cash* methods are tools auditors can use to find unrecorded cash transactions.

PRACTICAL CASE PROBLEMS

CASE # 8.1: INTERBANK TRANSFERS AND CHECK KITING

EverReady Corporation is in the home building and repair business. Construction business has been in a slump, and the company has experienced financial difficulty over the past two years. Part of the problem lies in the company's desire to avoid laying off its skilled crews of bricklayers and cabinetmakers. Meeting the payroll has been a problem. The auditors are engaged to audit the 1995 financial statements. Knowing of EverReady's financial difficulty and its business policy, the auditors decided to prepare a schedule of interbank transfers covering the 10 days before and after December 31, which is the company's balance sheet date.

First, the auditors used the cash receipts and disbursements journals to prepare part of the schedule shown in Exhibit 8.1-1. They obtained the information for everything except the dates of deposit and payment in the bank statements (disbursing date per bank, and receiving date per bank). They learned that EverReady always transferred money to the payroll account at 1st National Bank from the general account at 1st National Bank. This transfer enabled the bank to clear the payroll checks without delay. The only bank accounts in the EverReady financial statements are the two at 1st National Bank.

Next, the auditors obtained the December 1995 and January 1996 bank statements for the general and payroll accounts at 1st National Bank. They recorded the bank disbursement and receipt dates in the schedule of interbank transfers. For each transfer, these dates are identical because the accounts are in the same bank. An alert auditor noticed that the 1st National Bank general account bank statement also contains deposits received from Citizen National Bank and canceled check number 1799 dated January 5 payable to Citizen National Bank. This check cleared the 1st National Bank account on January 8 and was marked "transfer of funds." This led to new information.

EXHIBIT 8.1-1 Schedule of Interbank Transfers

C-5

EVERREADY CORPORATION
Schedule of Interbank Transfers
December 31, 1995

Prepared _____
Date _____
Reviewed _____
Date _____

	Disbursing Account				Receiving Account		
Check #	Bank	Amount	Date per Books	Date per Bank	Bank	Date per Books	Date per Bank
1417	1st Nat'l	9,463✓	24-Dec	24-Decμ	1st Nat payroll	24-Decλ	24-Decν
1601	1st Nat'l	11,593✓	31-Dec✓X	31-Decμ	1st Nat payroll	31-Decλ	31-Decν
1982	1st Nat'l	9,971✓	08-Jan	08-Janμ	1st Nat payroll	08-Janλ	08-Jan ν

✓   Traced from cash disbursements journal.
✓X   Check properly listed as outstanding on bank reconciliation.
μ Vouched to check cleared in bank statement.
λ Traced from cash receipts journal.
ν Vouched deposit cleared in bank statement.
Note: We scanned the cash disbursements and cash receipts journals for checks to and deposits from other bank accounts.

NEW INFORMATION

Asked about the Citizen National Bank transactions, EverReady's chief financial officer readily admitted the existence of an off-books bank account. He explained that it was used for financing transactions in keeping with normal practice in the construction industry. He gave the auditors the December and January bank statements for the account at Citizen National Bank. In it, the auditors found the following:

CASE #8.1-1 Bank Statements

Citizen National Bank

Check #	Payable to	Amount	Dated	Cleared Bank
4050	1st National	10,000	23-Dec	29-Dec
4051	Chase Bank	12,000	28-Dec	31-Dec
4052	1st National	12,000	30-Dec	05-Jan
4053	Chase Bank	14,000	04-Jan	07-Jan
4054	1st National	20,000	07-Jan	13-Jan

Deposits

Received from	Amount	Dated
Chase Bank	11,000	22-Dec
Chase Bank	15,000	30-Dec
1st National	10,000	05-Jan
Chase Bank	12,000	07-Jan

Chase Bank

Check #	Payable to	Amount	Dated	Cleared Bank
2220	Citizen Bank	11,000	22-Dec	28-Dec
2221	Citizen Bank	15,000	30-Dec	05-Jan
2222	Citizen Bank	12,000	7-Jan	12-Jan

Deposits

Received from	Amount	Dated
Citizen Bank	12,000	28-Dec
Citizen Bank	14,000	04-Jan

When asked about the Chase Bank transactions, EverReady's chief financial officer admitted the existence of another off-books bank account, which he said was the personal account of the principal stockholder. He explained that the stockholder often used it to finance EverReady's operations.

He gave the auditors the December and January bank statements for this account at Chase Bank; in it, the auditors found the information above:
An abbreviated calendar for the period is in Exhibit 8.1-2.

EXHIBIT 8.1-2 Calendar

	S	M	T	W	T	F	S
December	20	21	22	23	24	25	26
1995	27	28	29	30	31		
January						1	2
1996	3	4	5	6	7	8	9
	10	11	12	13	14	15	16

Required:
a. Complete the Schedule of Interbank Transfers (working paper C-5, Exhibit 8.1-1) by entering the new information.
b. What is the actual cash balance for the four bank accounts combined, considering only the amounts given in this case information, as of December 31, 1995 (before any of the December 31 payroll checks are cashed by employees)? As of January 8, 1996 (before any of the January 8 payroll checks are cashed by employees)? (*Hint*: Prepare a schedule of bank and actual balances like the one illustrated in Chapter 8 to explain check kiting.)

INSTRUCTIONS FOR DISCUSSION CASES

The next two cases are designed like the ones in the chapter. They give the problem, the method, the paper trail, and the amount. Your assignment is to write the "audit approach" portion of the case, organized around these sections:

Objective: Express the objective in terms of the facts supposedly asserted in financial records, accounts, and statements.

Control: Write a brief explanation of desirable controls, missing controls, and especially the kinds of "deviations" that might arise from the situation described in the case.

Test of controls: Write some procedures for getting evidence about existing controls, especially procedures that could discover deviations from controls. If there are no controls to test, then there are no procedures to perform; go then to the next section. A "procedure" should instruct someone about the source(s) of evidence to tap and the work to do.

Audit of balance: Write some procedures for getting evidence about the existence, completeness, valuation, ownership, or disclosure assertions identified in your *objective* section above.

Discovery summary: Write a short statement about the discovery you expect to accomplish with your procedures.

CASE #8.2: THE EXTRA BANK ACCOUNT-- Employee Embezzlement via Cash Receipts and Payment of Personal Expenses. This case is the same as CASE #6.2 in Chapter 6. Write the "audit approach section" like the cases in the chapter.

CASE #8.3: RING AROUND THE REVENUE--Overstated Sales and Accounts Receivable. Write the audit approach section like the cases in the chapter.

Problem: Sales were recorded early, sometimes at fictitiously high prices, overstating sales revenue, accounts receivable, and income.

Method: Mattox Toy Manufacturing Company had experienced several years of good business. Income had increased steadily, and the common stock was a favorite among investors. Management had confidently predicted continued growth and prosperity. But business turned worse instead of better. Competition became fierce.

In earlier years, Mattox had accommodated a few large retail customers with the practice of field warehousing coupled with a "bill and hold" accounting procedure. These large retail customers executed noncancellable written agreements, asserting their purchase of toys and their obligation to pay. The toys were not actually shipped because the customers did not have available warehouse space. They were set aside in segregated areas on the

Mattox premises and identified as the customers' property. Mattox would later drop-ship the toys to various retail locations upon instructions from the customers. The "field warehousing" was explained as Mattox serving as a temporary warehouse and storage location for the customers' toys. In the related bill and hold accounting procedure, Mattox prepared invoices billing the customers, mailed the invoices to the customers, and recorded the sales and accounts receivable.

When business took the recent downturn, Mattox expanded its field warehousing and its bill and hold accounting practices. Invoices were recorded for customers who did not execute the written agreements used in previous arrangements. Some customers signed the noncancellable written agreements with clauses permitting subsequent inspection, acceptance, and determination of discounted prices. The toys were not always set aside in separate areas, and this failure later gave shipping employees problems with identifying shipments of toys that had been "sold" earlier and those that had not.

Mattox also engaged in overbilling. Customers who ordered close-out toys at discounted prices were billed at regular prices, even though the customers' orders showed the discounted prices agreed by Mattox sales representatives.

In a few cases, the bill and hold invoices and the close-out sales were billed and recorded in duplicate. In most cases, the customers' invoices were addressed and mailed to specific individuals in the customers' management instead of the routine mailing to the customers' accounts payable departments.

Paper trail: The field warehousing arrangements were well known and acknowledged in the Mattox accounting manual. Related invoices were stamped "bill and hold." Customer orders and agreements were attached in a document file. Sales of close-out toys also were stamped "close-out," indicating the regular prices (basis for salespersons' commissions) and the invoice prices. Otherwise, the accounting for sales and accounts receivable was unexceptionable. Efforts to record these sales in January (last month of the fiscal year) caused the month's sales revenue to be 35 percent higher than the January of the previous year.

In the early years of the practice, inventory sold under the field warehousing arrangements (both regular and close-out toys) was segregated and identified. The shipping orders for these toys left the "carrier name" and "shipping date" blank, even though they were signed and dated by a company employee in the spaces for the company representative and the carrier representative signature.

The lack of inventory segregation caused problems for the company. After the fiscal year-end, Mattox solved the problem by reversing $6.9 million of the $14 million bill and hold sales. This caused another problem because the reversal was larger than the month's sales, causing the sales revenue for first month of the next year to be a negative number!

Amount: Company officials' reasons for the validity of recognizing sales revenue and receivables on the bill and hold procedure and field warehousing were persuasive. After due consideration of the facts and circumstances, the company's own accountants agreed that the accounting practices appropriately accounted for revenue and receivables.

It was Mattox's abuse of the practices that caused financial statements to be materially misstated. In January of the year in question, the company overstated sales by about $14 million, or 5 percent of the sales that should have been recorded. The gross profit of $7 million on these sales caused the income to be overstated by about 40 percent.

FOOTNOTE

[1] AICPA, *Confirmation of Accounts Receivable*, Auditing Procedures
Study (New York, 1984), chap. 4. See also: Paul Caster, "The Role of
Confirmations as Audit Evidence," *Journal of Accountancy*, February
1992, pp. 73-76.

CHAPTER 9
CASH DISBURSEMENTS
AND PAYABLES

The acquisition and expenditure accounting cycle covers purchasing, receiving, accounts payable, and cash disbursements. This chapter contains sections on (1) typical control activities in the cycle, (2) the audit evidence available in management reports and data files, (3) control risk assessment (including detail test of controls procedures), and (4) case story-style explanations concerning discovery of errors, irregularities, and frauds. Special notes in the chapter cover (1) the completeness assertion, and (2) physical inventory observation.

ACQUISITION AND EXPENDITURE CYCLE:
TYPICAL ACTIVITIES

The basic acquisition and expenditure activities are (1) purchasing goods and services and (2) paying the bills. Exhibit 9-1 shows the activities and transactions involved in an acquisitions and expenditure cycle. The exhibit also lists the accounts and records typically found in this cycle. As you follow the exhibit, you can track the elements of a control system described in the sections below.

AUTHORIZATION

Purchases are requested (requisitioned) by people who know the needs of the organization. A purchasing department seeks the best prices and quality and issues a purchase order to a selected vendor. Obtaining competitive bids is a good practice because it tends to produce the best prices and involves several legitimate suppliers in the process.

Cash disbursements are authorized by an accounts payable department's assembly of purchase orders, vendor invoices, and internal receiving reports to show a valid obligation to pay. This assembly of supporting documents is called a **voucher** (illustrated in Exhibit 9-1). Accounts payable obligations usually are recorded when the purchaser receives the goods or services ordered.

EXHIBIT 9-1   Acquisition and Expenditure Cycle

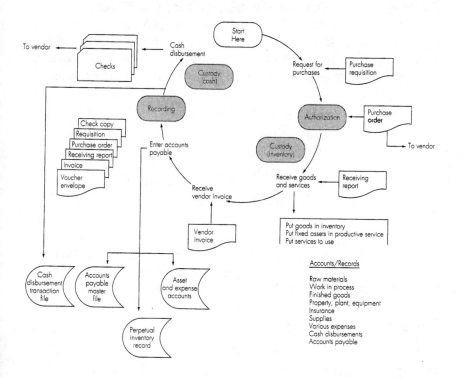

Checks are signed by a person authorized by the management or the board of directors. A company may have a policy to require two signatures on checks over a certain amount (e.g., $1,000). Vouchers should be marked "paid" or otherwise stamped to show that they have been processed completely so they cannot be paid a second time.

TOO MUCH TROUBLE

A trucking company self-insured claims of damage to goods in transit, processed claims vouchers, and paid customers from its own bank accounts. Several persons were authorized to sign checks. One person thought it "too much trouble" to stamp the vouchers PAID and said: "That's textbook stuff anyway." Numerous claims were recycled to other check signers, and $80,000 in claims were paid in duplicate before the problem was discovered.

CUSTODY

A receiving department inspects the goods received for quantity and quality (producing a *receiving report*), then puts them in the hands of other responsible persons (e.g., inventory warehousing, fixed asset installation). Services are not "received" in this manner, but they are accepted by responsible persons. Cash "custody" rests largely in the hands of the person or persons authorized to sign checks.

Another aspect of "custody" involves access to blank documents, such as purchase orders, receiving reports, and blank checks. If unauthorized persons can obtain blank copies of these internal business documents, they can forge a false purchase order to a fictitious vendor, forge a false receiving report, send a false invoice from a fictitious supplier, and prepare a company check to the fictitious supplier, thereby accomplishing an embezzlement.

RECORDING

When the purchase order, vendor's invoice, and receiving report are in hand, accountants enter the accounts payable, with debits to proper inventory, fixed asset, and expense accounts and with a credit to accounts payable. When checks are prepared, entries are made to debit the accounts payable and credit cash.

PERIODIC RECONCILIATION

A periodic comparison or reconciliation of existing assets to recorded amounts is not shown in Exhibit 9-1, but it occurs in several ways, including: physical inventory-taking to compare inventory on hand to perpetual inventory records, bank account reconciliation to compare book cash balances to bank cash balances, inspection of fixed assets to compare to detail fixed asset records, preparation of an accounts payable trial balance to compare the detail of accounts payable to the control account, and internal audit confirmation of accounts payable to compare vendors' reports and monthly statements to recorded liabilities.

CLASSIFY THE DEBITS CORRECTLY

Invoices for expensive repairs were not clearly identified, so the accounts payable accountants entered the debits that should have been repairs and maintenance expense as capitalized fixed assets. This initially understated expenses and overstated income by $125,000 one year, although the incorrectly capitalized expenses were written off as depreciation in later years.

AUDIT EVIDENCE IN MANAGEMENT REPORTS

Computer processing of acquisition and payment transactions enables management to generate several reports that can provide important audit evidence. Auditors should obtain and use these reports.

OPEN PURCHASE ORDERS

Purchase orders are "open" from the time they are issued until the goods and services are received. They are held in an "open purchase order" file. Generally, no liability exists to be recorded until the transactions are complete. However, auditors may find evidence of losses on purchase commitments in this file, if market prices have fallen below the purchase price shown in purchase orders.

THINKING AHEAD

Lone Moon Brewing purchased bulk aluminum sheets and manufactured its own cans. To assure a source of raw materials supply, the company entered into a long-term purchase agreement for 6 million pounds of aluminum sheeting at 40 cents per pound. At the end of this year, 1.5 million pounds had been purchased and used, but the market price had fallen to 32 cents per pound. Lone Moon was on the hook for a $360,000 (4.5 million pounds x 8 cents) purchase commitment in excess of current market prices.

UNMATCHED RECEIVING REPORTS

Liabilities should be recorded on the date the goods and services are received and accepted by the receiving department or by another responsible person. Sometimes, however, vendor invoices arrive later. In the meantime, the accounts payable department holds the receiving reports "unmatched" with invoices, awaiting enough information to record an accounting entry. Auditors can inspect the "unmatched receiving report" file report to determine whether the company has material unrecorded liabilities on the financial statement date.

UNMATCHED VENDOR INVOICES

Sometimes, vendor invoices arrive in the accounts payable department before the receiving activity is complete. Such invoices are held "unmatched" with receiving reports, awaiting information that the goods and services were actually received and accepted. Auditors can inspect the "unmatched invoice file" and compare it to the "unmatched receiving report" file to determine whether liabilities are unrecorded. Systems failures and human coding errors can cause "unmatched" invoices and related "unmatched" receiving reports to sit around unnoticed when all the information for recording a liability is actually in hand.

ACCOUNTS PAYABLE TRIAL BALANCE

This trial balance is a list of payable amounts by vendor, and the sum should agree with the accounts payable control account. (Some organizations keep records by individual invoices instead of vendor names, so the trial balance is a list of unpaid invoices. The sum still should agree with the control account balance.) The best kind of trial balance for audit purposes is one that contains the names of all the vendors with whom the organization has done business, even if their balances are zero. The audit "search for unrecorded liabilities" should emphasize the small and zero balances, especially for regular vendors, because these may be the places where liabilities are unrecorded.

All paid and unpaid accounts payable should be supported by a "voucher" or similar document. A "voucher" is a cover sheet, folder, or envelope that contains all the supporting documents--purchase requisition (if any), purchase order (if any), vendor invoice, receiving report (if any), and check copy (or notation of check number, date, and amount), as shown in Exhibit 9-1.

PURCHASES JOURNAL

A listing of all purchases may or may not be printed out. It may exist only in a computer transaction file. In either event, it provides raw material for (1) computer-audit analysis of purchasing patterns, which may exhibit characteristics of errors and irregularities, and (2) sample selection of transactions for detail test of controls audit of supporting documents for validity, authorization, accuracy, classification, accounting/posting, and proper period recording. (A company may have already performed analyses of purchases, and auditors can use these for analytical evidence, provided the analyses are produced under reliable control conditions.)

INVENTORY REPORTS (TRIAL BALANCE)

Companies can produce a wide variety of inventory reports useful for analytical evidence. One is an item-by-item trial balance that should agree with a control account (if balances are kept in dollars). Auditors can use such a trial balance (1) to scan for unusual conditions (e.g., negative item balances, overstocking, and valuation problems) and (2) as a population for sample selection for a physical inventory observation (audit procedures to obtain evidence about the existence of inventory shown in the account). The scanning and sample selection may be computer-audit applications on a computer-based inventory report file.

THE SIGN OF THE CREDIT BALANCE

Auto Parts & Repair, Inc., kept perpetual inventory records and fixed assets records on a computer system. Because of the size of the files (8,000 parts in various locations and 1,500 asset records), the company never printed reports for visual inspection. Auditors ran a computer-audit "sign test" on inventory balances and fixed asset net book balances. The test called for a printed report for all balances less than zero. The auditors discovered 320 negative inventory balances caused by failure to record purchases and 125 negative net asset balances caused by depreciating assets more than their cost.

FIXED ASSET REPORTS

These reports are similar to inventory reports because they show the details of fixed assets in control accounts. They can be used for scanning and sample selection, much like the inventory reports. The information for depreciation calculation (cost, useful life, method, salvage) can be used for the audit of depreciation on a sample basis or by computer applications to recalculate all the depreciation.

CASH DISBURSEMENTS REPORTS

The cash disbursements process will produce a cash disbursements journal, sometimes printed out, sometimes maintained only on a computer file. This journal should contain the date, check number, payee, amount, account debited for each cash disbursement, and a cross-reference to the voucher number (usually the same as the check number). This journal is a population of cash disbursement transactions available for sample selection for detail test of controls audit of supporting documents in the voucher for validity, authorization, accuracy, classification, accounting/posting, and proper period recording.

CONTROL RISK ASSESSMENT

Control risk assessment is important because it governs the nature, timing, and extent of substantive audit procedures that will be applied in the audit of account balances in the acquisition and expenditure cycle. These account balances include:

- Inventory.
- Fixed assets.
- Depreciation expense.
- Accumulated depreciation.
- Accounts and notes payable.
- Cash disbursements part of cash balance auditing.
- Various expenses:
  Administrative: supplies, legal fees, audit fees, taxes.
  Selling: commissions, travel, delivery, repairs, advertising.
  Manufacturing: maintenance, freight in, utilities.

GENERAL CONTROL CONSIDERATIONS

Control procedures for proper segregation of responsibilities should be in place and operating. By referring to Exhibit 9-1, you can see that proper segregation involves authorization (requisitioning, purchase ordering) by persons who do not have custody, recording, or reconciliation duties. Custody of inventory, fixed assets, and cash is given to persons who do not directly authorize purchases or cash payments, record the accounting entries, or reconcile physical assets and cash to recorded amounts. Recording (accounting) is performed by persons who do not authorize transactions or have custody of assets or perform reconciliations. Periodic reconciliations should be performed by people who do not have authorization, custody, or recording duties related to the same assets. Combinations of two or more of these responsibilities in one person, one office, or one computerized system may open the door for errors, irregularities, and frauds.

In addition, the control system should provide for detail control checking activities. For example: (1) Purchase requisitions and purchase orders should be signed or initialed by authorized personnel. (Computer-produced purchase orders should come from a system whose master file specifications for reordering and vendor identification are restricted to changes only by authorized persons.) (2) Inventory warehouses and fixed asset locations should be under adequate physical security (storerooms, fences, locks, and the like). (3) Accountants should be under orders to record accounts payable only when all the supporting documentation is in order; and care should be taken to record purchases and payables as of the date goods and services were received, and to record cash disbursements on the date the check leaves the control of the organization. (4) Vendor invoices should be compared to purchase orders and receiving reports to determine that the vendor is charging the approved price and that the quantity being billed is the same as the quantity received.

Information about the control system often is gathered initially by completing an Internal Control Questionnaire. Auditor use extensive questionnaires on every audit.

PURCHASE ORDER SPLITTING

The school district authorized its purchasing agent to buy supplies in amounts of $1,000 or less without getting competitive bids for the best price. The purchasing agent wanted to favor local businesses instead of large chain stores, so she broke up the year's $350,000 supplies order into numerous $900-$950 orders, paying about 12 percent more to local stores than would have been paid to the large chains.

DETAIL TEST OF CONTROLS AUDIT PROCEDURES

An organization should have detail controls in place and operating to prevent, detect, and correct accounting errors by accomplishing the control objectives of validity, completeness, authorization, accuracy, classification, accounting/posting, and proper period recording. Exhibit 9-2 expresses the general control objectives in specific examples related to purchasing.

Auditors can perform detail test of controls audit procedures to determine whether controls that are said to be in place and operating actually are being performed properly by company personnel. A **detail test of control procedure** consists of (1) identification of the data population from which a sample of items will be selected for audit and (2) an expression of the action that will be taken to produce relevant evidence. In general, the *actions* in detail test of control audit procedures involve vouching, tracing, observing, scanning, and recalculating. A specification of such procedures is part of an audit program for obtaining evidence useful in a final control risk assessment. If personnel in the organization are not performing their control activities very well, auditors will need to design substantive audit procedures to try to detect whether control failures have produced materially misleading account balances.

EXHIBIT 9-2 Internal Control Objectives (Purchases)

General Objectives	Examples of Specific Objectives
1. Recorded purchases are *valid* and documented.	Recorded vouchers in the voucher register supported by completed vouchers.
	Voucher for purchases of inventory (or fixed assets) supported by vendor invoices, receiving reports, purchase orders, and requisitions (or approved capital budget).
2. Valid purchase transactions are *recorded* and none omitted.	Requisitions, purchase orders, receiving reports, and vouchers are prenumbered and numerical sequence is checked.
	Overall comparisons of purchases are made periodically by statistical or product-line analysis.
3. Purchases are *authorized* according to company policy.	All purchase orders are supported by requisitions from proper persons (or approved capital budgets).
	Purchase made from approved vendors or only after bids are received and evaluated.
4. Purchase orders are *accurately* prepared.	Completed purchase order quantities and descriptions independently compared to requisitions and vendors' catalogs.

EXHIBIT 9-2   Internal Control Objectives (Purchases) (Continued)

General Objectives	Examples of Specific Objectives
5. Purchase transactions are properly *classified*.	Purchase from subsidiaries and affiliates classified as intercompany purchases and payables. Purchase returns and allowances properly classified. Purchases for repairs and maintenance segregated from purchases of fixed assets.
6. Purchase transaction *accounting and posting* is complete and proper.	Account distribution on vouchers proper and reviewed independent of preparation. Freight-in included as part of purchase and added to inventory (or fixed assets) costs.
7. Purchase transactions are recorded in the *proper period*.	Perpetual inventory and fixed asset records updated as of date goods are received.

Exhibit 9-3 contains a selection of detail test of controls audit procedures for controls over purchase, cash disbursement, and accounts payable transactions. The samples are usually attribute samples. On the right, the exhibit shows the control objectives tested by the audit procedures.

EXHIBIT 9-3   Test of Controls Audit Procedures for Purchases, Cash Disbursements, and Accounts Payable

	Control Objective
A. Purchases	
1. Select a sample of receiving reports:	
a. Vouch to related purchase orders.	Authorization
b. Trace to inventory record posting of additions.	Completeness

**EXHIBIT 9-3   Test of Controls Audit Procedures for Purchases, Cash
                Disbursements, and Accounts Payable (Continued)**

	Control Objective
B. Cash Disbursements and Other Expenses	
1. Select a sample of vouchers recorded in a purchase journal and cash disbursements in a cash journal.	
a. Vouch supporting documentation for evidence of accurate mathematics, correct classification, proper approval, and proper date of entry.	Accuracy Classification Authorization Proper Period
b. Trace recorded debits to general and subsidiary ledger accounts.	Acctg/posting
2. Select a sample of recorded expenses from various accounts and vouch them to (a) canceled checks, and (b) supporting documentation.	Validity Classification

DETAIL TEST OF CONTROLS FOR INVENTORY RECORDS

Many organizations have material investments in inventories. In many engagements, auditors need to determine whether they can rely on the accuracy of perpetual inventory records. Tests of controls over accuracy involve tests of the additions (purchases) to the inventory detail balances and tests of the reductions (issues) of the item balances. Exhibit 9-4 pictures the "direction of the test" for detail test of controls audit procedures. The samples from the source documents (receiving reports, issues documents) meet the completeness direction requirement to determine whether everything received was recorded as an addition, and whether everything issued was recorded as a reduction of the balance. The sample from the perpetual inventory records meets the validity direction requirement to determine whether everything recorded as an addition or reduction is supported by receiving reports and issue documents. (The symbols A-1-a, A-2-a, A-3-a, and A-3-b are cross-references to the procedures in Exhibit 9-5).

EXHIBIT 9-4   Dual Direction of Test Audit Samples

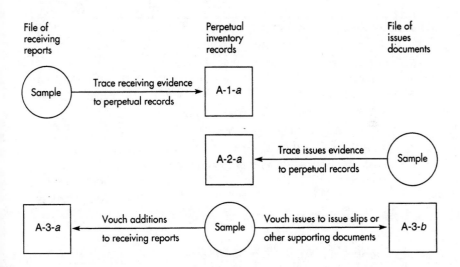

EXHIBIT 9-5   Test of Controls Audit Procedures for Inventory Records

	Control Objective
A. Inventory Receipts and Issues	
1. Select a sample of receiving reports:	
a.Trace to perpetual inventory record entry of receipt.	Authorization Completeness
2. Select a sample of sales invoices, bills of lading or other shipping documents, or production requisitions:	
a. Trace to perpetual inventory record entry of issue.	Authorization Completeness
3. Select a sample of inventory item perpetual records:	
a. Vouch additions to receiving reports.	Validity
b. Vouch issues to invoices, bills of lading or other shipping documents, or production requisitions.	Validity
B. Cost of Sales	
1. With the sample of issues in A-2 above:	
a. Review the accounting summary of quantities and prices for mathematical accuracy.	Accuracy
b. Trace posting of amounts to general ledger.	Completeness
2. Obtain a sample of cost of goods sold entries in the general ledger and vouch to supporting summaries of finished goods issues.	Validity
3. Review (recalculate) the appropriateness of standard costs, if used, to price inventory issues and cost of goods sold. Review the disposition of variances from standard costs.	Accuracy

Exhibit 9-5 is similar to Exhibit 9-3 in that it contains a selection of detail test of controls audit procedures. As before, the samples are usually attribute samples. On the right, the exhibit shows the control objectives tested by the audit procedures.

SUMMARY: CONTROL RISK ASSESSMENT

The audit manager or senior accountant in charge of the audit should evaluate the evidence obtained from an understanding of the internal control system and from the test of controls audit procedures. If the control risk is assessed very low, the substantive audit procedures on the account balances can be limited in cost-saving ways. For example, the inventory observation test-counts can be performed on a date prior to the year-end, and the sample size can be fairly small. On the other hand, if tests of controls reveal weaknesses, the substantive procedures will need to be designed to lower the risk of failing to detect material error in the account balances. For example, the inventory observation may need to be scheduled on the year-end date with the audit team making a large number of test counts. Descriptions of major deficiencies, control weaknesses, and inefficiencies may be incorporated in a letter to the client describing "reportable conditions."

SPECIAL NOTE: THE COMPLETENESS ASSERTION --SEARCH FOR UNRECORDED LIABILITIES

When considering assertions and obtaining evidence about accounts payable and other liabilities, auditors must put emphasis on the completeness assertion. (For asset accounts, the emphasis is on the existence assertion.) This emphasis on completeness is rightly placed because companies typically are less concerned about timely recording of expenses and liabilities than they are about timely recording of revenues and assets. Of course, generally accepted accounting principles require timely recording of liabilities and their associated expenses.

Evidence is much more difficult to obtain to verify the completeness assertion than the existence assertion. Auditors cannot rely entirely on a management assertion of completeness, even in combination with a favorable assessment of control risk (AU 9326). Substantive procedures--tests of details or analytical procedures--ought to be performed. The **search for unrecorded liabilities** is the set of procedures designed to yield audit evidence of liabilities that were not recorded in the reporting period. Such a search ought normally to be performed up to the report date in the period following the audit client's balance sheet date.

The following is a list of procedures useful in the search for unrecorded liabilities. The audit objective is to search all the places where evidence of them might exist. If these procedures reveal none, the auditors can conclude that all material liabilities are recorded.

1. Scan the open purchase order file at year-end for indications of material purchase commitments at fixed prices. Obtain current prices and determine whether any adjustments for loss and liability for purchase commitments are needed.
2. List the unmatched vendor invoices and determine when the goods were received, looking to the unmatched receiving report file and receiving reports prepared after the year-end. Determine which invoices, if any, should be recorded.
3. Trace the unmatched receiving reports to accounts payable entries, and determine whether ones recorded in the next accounting period need to be adjusted to report them in the current accounting period under audit.
4. Select a sample of cash disbursements from the accounting period following the balance sheet date. Vouch them to supporting documents (invoice, receiving report) to determine whether the related liabilities were recorded in the proper accounting period.
5. Trace the liabilities reported by financial institutions to the accounts. (See the Bank Confirmation in Exhibit 8-7, Chapter 8. However, a bank really is not expected to search all its files to report all client liabilities to auditors, so the bank confirmation is not the best source of evidence of unrecorded debts.)
6. Study IRS examination reports for evidence of income or other taxes in dispute, and decide whether actual or estimated liabilities need to be recorded.
7. Confirm accounts payable with vendors, especially regular suppliers showing small or zero balances in the year-end accounts payable. These are the ones most likely to be understated. (Vendors' monthly statements controlled by the auditors also may be used for this procedure.) Be sure to verify the vendors' addresses so confirmations will not be misdirected, perhaps to conspirators in a scheme to understate liabilities.

8. Study the accounts payable trial balance for indications of dates showing fewer payables than usual recorded near the year-end. (A financial officer may be stashing vendor invoices in a desk drawer instead of recording them.)

9. Review the lawyers' responses to requests for information about pending or threatened litigation, and for unasserted claims and assessments. The lawyers' information may signal the need for contingent liability accruals or disclosures.

10. Use a checklist of accrued expenses to determine whether the company has been conscientious about expense and liability accruals; including accruals for wages, interest, utilities, sales and excise taxes, payroll taxes, income taxes, real property taxes, rent, sales commissions, royalties, and warranty and guarantee expense.

11. When auditing the details of sales revenue, pay attention to the terms of sales to determine whether any amounts should be deferred as unearned revenue. Inquiries directed to management about terms of sales can be used to obtain initial information, such as inquiries about customers' rights of cancellation or return. (See the box below.)

ADVERTISED SALES RETURN PRIVILEGE

This advertisement appeared in popular magazines.

THE 1956 THUNDERBIRD--authentic die-cast replica of the classic T-Bird described as America's finest production sports car ever! Send no money now. You will be billed for a deposit of $24 and four equal monthly installments of $24 each.

RETURN ASSURANCE POLICY: If you wish to return any Franklin Mint Precision Models purchase, you may do so within 30 days of your receipt of that purchase for replacement, credit, or refund.

---

12. Prepare or obtain a schedule of casualty insurance on fixed assets, and determine the adequacy of insurance in relation to asset market values. Inadequate insurance and self-insurance should be disclosed in the notes to the financial statements.

13. Confirm life insurance policies with insurance companies to ask whether the company has any loans against the cash value of the insurance. In this confirmation, request the names of the beneficiaries of the policies. If the insurance is for the benefit of a party other than the company, the beneficiaries may be creditors on unrecorded loans. Make inquiries about the business purpose of making insurance proceeds payable to other parties.

14. Review the terms of debt due within one year but classified long-term because the company plans to refinance it on a long-term basis. Holders of the debt or financial institutions must have shown (preferably in writing) a willingness to refinance the debt before it can be classified long-term. Classification cannot be based solely on management's expressed intent to seek long-term financing.

15. Apply analytical procedures appropriate in the circumstances. In general, accounts payable volume and period-end balances should increase when the company experiences increases in physical production volume or engages in inventory stockpiling. Some liabilities may be functionally related to other activities; for example, sales taxes are functionally related to sales dollar totals, payroll taxes to payroll totals, excise taxes to sales dollars or volume, income taxes to income.

SPECIAL NOTE: PHYSICAL INVENTORY OBSERVATION

The audit procedures for inventory and related cost of sales accounts frequently are extensive in an audit engagement. A 96-page AICPA auditing procedure study entitled *Audit of Inventories* (AICPA, 1986) describes many facets of inherent risk, control risk, and the process of obtaining evidence about inventory financial statement assertions. Inventories often are the largest current asset.

A material error or irregularity in inventory has a pervasive effect on financial statements. Errors in inventory cause misstatements in current assets, working capital, total assets, cost of sales, gross margin, and net income. While analytical procedures can help indicate inventory presentation problems, the auditors' best opportunity to detect inventory errors and irregularities is during the physical observation of the client's inventory count taken by company personnel. (Auditors *observe* the inventory-taking and make *test counts*, but they seldom actually *take* (count) the entire inventory.) Auditing standards express the requirement for inventory observation in SAS 1, AU 331:

> Observation of inventories is a generally accepted auditing procedure. . . . When inventory quantities are determined solely by means of a physical count . . . it is ordinarily necessary for the independent auditor to be present at the time of count and, by suitable observations, tests, and inquiries, satisfy himself respecting the methods of inventory-taking and the reliance which may be placed upon the client's representation about the quantities and physical condition of the inventories.

The remainder of this special note gives details about auditors' observation of physical inventory-taking. The first task is to review the client's inventory-taking instructions. The instructions should include the following:

1. Names of client personnel responsible for the count.
2. Dates and times of inventory-taking.
3. Names of client personnel who will participate in the inventory-taking.
4. Instructions for recording accurate descriptions of inventory items, for count and double-count, and for measuring or translating physical quantities (such as counting by measures of gallons, barrels, feet, dozens).
5. Instructions for making notes of obsolete or worn items.
6. Instructions for the use of tags, punched cards, count sheets, computers, or other media devices and for their collection and control.
7. Plans for shutting down plant operations or for taking inventory after store closing hours, and plans for having goods in proper places (such as on store shelves instead of on the floor, or of raw materials in a warehouse rather than in transit to a job).
8. Plans for counting or controlling movement of goods in receiving and shipping areas if those operations are not shut down during the count.
9. Instructions for computer compilation of the count media (such as tags, count sheets) into final inventory listings or summaries.
10. Instructions for pricing the inventory items.
11. Instructions for review and approval of the inventory count; notations of obsolescence or other matters by supervisory personnel.

These instructions characterize a well-planned counting operation. As the plan is carried out, the independent auditors should be present to hear the count instructions being given to the client's count teams and to observe the instructions being followed.

Many physical inventories are counted at the year-end when the auditor is present to observe. The auditors can perform dual-direction testing by (1) selecting inventory items from a perpetual inventory master file, going to the location, and obtaining a test count, which produces evidence for the *existence assertion*; and (2) selecting inventory from locations on the warehouse floor, obtaining a test count, and tracing the count to the final inventory compilation, which produces evidence for the *completeness assertion*. If the company does not have perpetual records and a file to test for existence, the auditors must be careful to obtain a record of all the counts and use it for the existence-direction tests.

However, the following other situations frequently occur.

PHYSICAL INVENTORY NOT ON YEAR-END DATE

Clients sometimes count the inventory before or after the balance sheet date. When the auditors are present to make their physical observation, they follow the procedures outlined above for observation of the physical count. However, with a time period intervening between the count date and the year-end, additional roll-forward or rollback auditing procedures must be performed on purchase, inventory addition, and issue transactions during that period. The inventory on the count date is reconciled to the year-end inventory by appropriate addition or subtraction of the intervening receiving and issue transactions.

CYCLE INVENTORY COUNTING

Some companies count inventory on a cycle basis or use a statistical counting plan but never take a complete count on a single date. In these circumstances, the auditors must understand the cycle or sampling plan and evaluate its appropriateness. In this type of situation, the auditors are present for some counting operations. Only under unusual circumstances and as an "extended procedure" are auditors present every month (or more frequently) to observe all counts. Businesses that count inventory in this manner purport to have accurate perpetual records and carry out the counting as a means of testing the records and maintaining their accuracy.

The auditors must be present during some counting operations to evaluate the counting plans and their execution. The procedures for an annual count enumerated above are utilized, test counts are made, and the audit team is responsible for a conclusion concerning the accuracy (control) of perpetual records.

AUDITORS NOT PRESENT AT CLIENT'S INVENTORY COUNT

This situation can arise on a first audit when the audit firm is appointed after the beginning inventory already has been counted. The auditors must review the client's plan for the already completed count as before. Some test counts of current inventory should be made and traced to current records to make a conclusion about the reliability of perpetual records. If the actual count was recent, intervening transaction activity might be reconciled back to the beginning inventory.

However, the reconciliation of more than a few months' transactions to unobserved beginning inventories may be very difficult. The auditors may employ procedures utilizing such interrelationships as sales activity, physical volume, price variation, standard costs, and gross profit margins for the decision about beginning inventory reasonableness. Nevertheless, much care must be exercised in "backing into" the audit of a previous inventory.

INVENTORIES LOCATED OFF THE CLIENT'S PREMISES

The auditors must determine where and in what dollar amounts inventories are located off the client's premises, in the custody of consignees, or in public warehouses. If amounts are material and if control is not exceptionally strong, the audit team may wish to visit these locations and conduct on-site test counts. However, if amounts are not material and/or if related evidence is adequate (such as periodic reports, cash receipts, receivables records, shipping records) and if control risk is low, then direct confirmation with the custodian may be considered sufficient competent evidence of the existence of quantities (SAS 1, AU 901).

INVENTORY COUNT AND MEASUREMENT CHALLENGES

Examples	Challenges
Lumber.	Problem identifying quality or grade.
Piles of sugar, coal, scrap steel.	Geometric computations, aerial photos.
Items weighed on scales.	Check scales for accuracy.
Bulk materials (oil, grain, liquids in storage tanks).	Climb the tanks. Dip measuring rods. Sample for assay or chemical analysis.
Diamonds, jewelry.	Identification and quality determination problems. Ask a specialist.
Pulp wood.	Quantity measurement estimation. Aerial photos.
Livestock.	Movement not controllable. Count critter's legs and divide by four (two, for chickens).

Source (adapted): AICPA, *Audit of Inventories*, Auditing Procedure Study (1986), p. 28.

INVENTORY EXISTENCE AND COMPLETENESS

The physical observation procedures are designed to audit for existence and completeness (physical quantities) and valuation (recalculation of appropriate FIFO, LIFO, or other pricing at cost, and lower-of-cost-or-market write-down of obsolete or worn inventory). After the observation is complete, auditors should have sufficient competent evidence of the following physical quantities and valuations:

• Goods in the perpetual records but not owned were excluded from the inventory compilation.
• Goods on hand were counted and included in the inventory compilation.
• Goods consigned-out or stored in outside warehouses (goods owned but not on hand) were included in the inventory compilation.

- Goods in transit (goods actually purchased and recorded but not yet received) were added to the inventory count and included in the inventory compilation.
- Goods on hand already sold (but not yet delivered) were not counted and were excluded from the inventory compilation.
- Goods consigned-in (goods on hand but not owned) were excluded from the inventory compilation.

INVENTORY--A RIPE FIELD FOR FRAUD

These problems have arisen in companies' inventory frauds:
- Auditors were fooled as a result of taking a small sample for test-counting, thus missing important information.
- Companies included inventory they pretended to have ordered.
- Auditors permitted company officials to follow them and notice their test counts. Then the managers falsified counts for inventory the auditors did not count.
- Shipments between plants (transfers) were reported as inventory at both plant locations.
- Auditors spotted a barrel whose contents management had valued at thousands of dollars, but it was filled with sawdust. The auditors required management to exclude the value from the inventory, but it never occurred to them that they had found one instance in an intentional and pervasive overstatement fraud.
- Auditors observed inventory at five store locations and told the management in advance of the specific stores. Management took care not to make fraudulent entries in these five stores, instead making fraudulent adjustments in many of the other 236 stores.
- After counting an inventory of computer chips, the auditors received a call from the client's controller: "Just hours after you left the plant, 2,500 chips arrived in a shipment in transit." The auditors included them in inventory but never checked to see whether the chips were real.

An accounting firm advised its audit personnel:
- Focus test counts on high-value items, and sample lower-value items. Test-count a sufficient dollar amount of the inventory.

- If all locations will not be observed, do not follow an easily predictable pattern. Advise client personnel as late as possible of the locations we will visit.

- Be skeptical of large and unusual test count differences or of client personnel making notes or displaying particular interest in our procedures and test counts.

- Be alert for inventory not used for some time, stored in unusual locations, showing signs of damage, obsolescence, or excess quantities.

- Ensure that interplant movements (transfers) are kept to an absolute minimum. Obtain evidence that any items added to inventory after the count is completed are proper and reasonable (i.e., exist in stated quality and quantity).

Source: *The Wall Street Journal* and Grant Thornton.

AUDIT CASES: SUBSTANTIVE AUDIT PROCEDURES

The audit of account balances consists of procedural efforts to detect errors, irregularities, and frauds that might exist in the balances, thus making them misleading in financial statements. If such misstatements exist, they are characterized by the following features:

Method: A cause of the misstatement (accidental error, intentional irregularity, or fraud attempt), which usually is made easier by some kind of failure of controls.

Paper trail: A set of telltale signs of erroneous accounting, missing or altered documents, or a "dangling debit" (the false or erroneous debit that results from an overstatement of assets).

Amount: The dollar amount of overstated assets and revenue, or understated liabilities and expenses.

The cases in this section tell about an error, irregularity, or fraud situation in terms of the method, the paper trail, and the amount. The first part of each case gives you the "inside story" that auditors seldom know before they perform the audit work. The next part is an "audit approach" section, which tells about the audit objective (assertion), controls, test of controls, and test of balances (substantive procedures) that could be considered in an approach to the situation. The "audit approach" section presumes that the auditors do not know everything about the situation. The audit approach part of each case contains the following parts:

Audit objective: A recognition of a financial statement *assertion* for which evidence needs to be obtained. The assertions are about existence of assets, liabilities, revenues, and expenses; their valuation; their complete inclusion in the account balances; the rights and obligations inherent in them; and their proper presentation and disclosure in the financial statements.

Control: A recognition of the control activities that *should be* used in an organization to prevent and detect errors and irregularities.

Test of controls: Ordinary and extended procedures *designed to produce evidence about the effectiveness of the controls* that should be in operation.

Audit of balance: Ordinary and extended *substantive procedures designed to find signs* of errors, irregularities, and frauds in account balances and classes of transactions.

At the end of the chapter, some similar discussion cases are presented, and you can write the audit approach to test your ability to design audit procedures for the detection of errors, irregularities, and frauds.

CASE 9.1
PRINTING (COPYING) MONEY

Problem

Improper expenditures for copy services charged to motion picture production costs.

Method

Argus Productions, Inc., a motion picture and commercial production company, assigned M. Welby the authority and responsibility for obtaining copies of scripts used in production. Established procedures permitted Welby to arrange for outside script copying services, receive the copies, and approve the bills for payment. In effect, Welby was the "purchasing department" and the "receiving department" for this particular service. To a certain extent, Welby was also the "accounting department" by virtue of approving bills for payment and coding them for assignment to projects. Welby did not make the actual accounting entries or sign the checks.

M. Welby set up a fictitious company under the registered name of Quickprint Company with himself as the incorporator and stockholder, complete with a post office box number, letterhead stationery, and nicely printed invoices, but no printing equipment. Legitimate copy services were "subcontracted" by Quickprint with real printing businesses, which billed Quickprint. Welby then prepared Quickprint invoices billing Argus, usually at the legitimate shop's rate, but for a few extra copies each time. Welby also submitted Quickprint bills to Argus for fictitious copying jobs on scripts for movies and commercials that never went into production. As the owner of Quickprint, Welby endorsed Argus's checks with a rubber stamp and deposited the money in the business bank account, paid the legitimate printing bills, and took the rest for personal use.

Paper Trail
Argus's production cost files contained all the Quickprint bills, sorted under the names of the movie and commercial production projects. Welby even created files for proposed films that never went into full production, and thus should not have had script copying costs. There were no copying service bills from any shop other than Quickprint Company.

Amount
M. Welby conducted this fraud for five years, stealing $475,000 in false and inflated billings. (Argus's net income was overstated a modest amount because copying costs were capitalized as part of production cost, then amortized over a 2-3 year period.)

AUDIT APPROACH

Objective
Obtain evidence of the valid existence (occurrence) and valuation of copying charges capitalized as film production cost.

Control
Management should assign the authority to request copies and the purchasing authority to different responsible employees. The accounting, including coding cost assignments to projects, also should be performed by other persons. Managerial review of production results could result in notice of excess costs.

The request for the quantity (number) of copies of a script should come from a person involved in production who knows the number needed. This person also should sign off for the receipt (or approve the bill) for this requested number of copies, thus acting as the "receiving department." This procedure could prevent waste (excess cost), especially if the requesting person were also held responsible for the profitability of the project.

Actual purchasing always is performed by a company agent, and in this case, the agent was M. Welby. Purchasing agents generally have latitude to seek the best service at the best price, with or without bids from competitors. Requirements to obtain bids is usually a good idea, but much legitimate purchasing is done with sole-source suppliers without bid.

Someone in the accounting department should be responsible for coding invoices for charges to authorized projects, thus making it possible to detect costs charged to projects not actually in production.

Someone with managerial responsibility should review project costs and the purchasing practices. However, this is an expensive use of executive time. It was not spent in the Argus case. Too bad.

Test of Controls
In gaining an understanding of the control structure, auditors could learn of the trust and responsibility vested in M. Welby. Since the embezzlement was about $95,000 per year, the total copying cost under Welby's control must have been around $1 million or more. (It might attract unwanted attention to inflate a cost more than 10 percent.)

Controls were very weak, especially in the combination of duties performed by Welby and in the lack of managerial review. For all practical purposes, there were no controls to test, other than to see whether Welby had approved the copying cost bills and coded them to active projects. This provides an opportunity, since proper classification is a control objective.

Procedures: Select a sample of project files, and vouch costs charged to them to support in source documents (validity direction of the test). Select a sample of expenditures, and trace them to the project cost records shown coded on the expenditures (completeness direction of the test).

Audit of Balance

Substantive procedures are directed to obtaining evidence about the existence of film projects, completeness of the costs charged to them, valuation of the capitalized project costs, rights in copyright and ownership, and proper disclosure of amortization methods. The most important procedures are the same as the test of controls procedures; thus, when performed at the year-end date on the capitalized cost balances, they are dual-purpose audit procedures.

Either of the procedures described above as test of controls procedures should show evidence of projects that had never gone into production. (Auditors should be careful to obtain a list of actual projects before they begin the procedures.) Chances are good that the discovery of bad project codes with copying cost will reveal a pattern of Quickprint bills.

Knowing that controls over copying cost are weak, auditors could be tipped off to the possibility of a Welby-Quickprint connection. Efforts to locate Quickprint should be taken (telephone book, chamber of commerce, other directories). Inquiry with the state secretary of state for names of the Quickprint incorporators should reveal Welby's connection. The audit findings can then be turned over to a trained investigator to arrange an interview and confrontation with M. Welby.

Discovery Summary

In this case, internal auditors performed a review of project costs at the request of the manager of production, who was worried about profitability. They performed the procedures described above, noticed the dummy projects and the Quickprint bills, investigated the ownership of Quickprint, and discovered Welby's association. They had first tried to locate Quickprint's shop but could not find it in telephone, chamber of commerce, or other city directories. They were careful not to direct any mail to the post office box for fear of alerting the then-unknown parties involved. A sly internal auditor already had used a ruse at the post office and learned that Welby rented the box, but they did not know whether anyone else was involved. Alerted, the internal auditors gathered all the Quickprint bills and determined the total charged for nonexistent projects. Carefully, under the covert observation of a representative of the local district attorney's office, Welby was interviewed and readily confessed.

CASE 9.2
REAL CASH PAID TO PHONY DOCTORS

Problem

Cash disbursement fraud. Fictitious medical benefit claims were paid by the company, which self-insured up to $50,000 per employee. The expense account that included legitimate and false charges was "employee medical benefits."

Method

As manager of the claims payment department, Martha Lee was considered one of Beta Magnetic's best employees. She never missed a day of work in 10 years, and her department had one of the company's best efficiency ratings. Controls were considered good, including the verification by a claims processor that (1) the patient was a Beta employee, (2) medical treatments were covered in the plan, (3) the charges were within approved guidelines, (4) the cumulative claims for the employee did not exceed $50,000 (if over $50,000 a claim was submitted to an insurance company), and (5) the calculation for payment was correct. After verification processing, claims were sent to the claims payment department to pay the doctor directly. No payments ever went directly to employees. Martha Lee prepared false claims on real employees, forging the signature of various claims processors, adding her own review approval, naming bogus doctors who would be paid by the payment department. The payments were mailed to various post office box addresses and to her husband's business address.

Nobody ever verified claims information with the employee. The employees received no reports of medical benefits paid on their behalf. While the department had performance reports by claims processors, these reports did not show claim-by-claim details. No one verified the credentials of the doctors.

Paper Trail
The falsified claims forms were in Beta's files, containing all the fictitious data on employee names, processor signatures, doctors' bills, and phony doctors and addresses. The canceled checks were returned by the bank and were kept in Beta's files, containing "endorsements" by the doctors. Martha Lee and her husband were somewhat clever: They deposited the checks in various banks in accounts opened in the names and identification of the "doctors."

Martha Lee did not stumble on the paper trail. She drew the attention of an auditor who saw her take her 24 claims processing employees out to an annual staff appreciation luncheon in a fleet of stretch limousines.

Amount
Over the last seven years, Martha Lee and her husband stole $3.5 million, and, until the last, no one noticed anything unusual about the total amount of claims paid.

AUDIT APPROACH

Objective
Obtain evidence to determine whether employee medical benefits "existed" in the sense of being valid claims paid to valid doctors.

Control
The controls are good as far as they go. The claims processors used internal data in their work--employee files for identification, treatment descriptions submitted by doctors with comparisons to plan provisions, and mathematical calculations.

This work amounted to all the approval necessary for the claims payment department to prepare a check.

There were no controls that connected the claims data with outside sources, such as employee acknowledgment or doctor investigation.

Test of Controls
The processing and control work in the claims processing department can be audited for deviations from controls.
Procedure: Select a sample of paid claims and reperform the claims processing procedures to verify the employee status, coverage of treatment, proper guideline charges, cumulative amount less than $50,000, and accurate calculation. However, this procedure would not help answer the question: "Does Martha Lee steal the money to pay for the limousines?"

"Thinking like a crook" points out the holes in the controls. Nobody seeks to verify data with external sources. However, an auditor must be careful in an investigation not to cast aspersions on a manager by letting rumors start by interviewing employees to find out whether they actually had the medical claim paid on their behalf. If money is being taken, the company check must be intercepted in some manner.

Audit of Balance
The balance under audit is the sum of the charges in the employee medical benefits expense account, and the objective relates to the valid existence of the payments.
Procedure: The first procedure can be as follows: Obtain a list of doctors paid by the company and look them up in the state medical society directory. Look up their addresses and determine whether they are valid business addresses. You might try comparing claims processors' signatures on various forms, but this is hard to do and requires training. An extended procedure would be as follows: Compare the doctors' addresses to addresses known to be associated with Martha Lee and other claims processing employees.

Discovery Summary
The comparison of doctors to the medical society directory showed eight "doctors" who were not licensed in the current period. Five of these eight had post office box addresses, and discrete inquiries and surveillance showed them rented to Martha Lee. The other three had the same mailing address as her husband's business. Further investigation, involving the district attorney and police, was necessary to obtain personal financial records and reconstruct the thefts from prior years.

CASE 9.3
RECEIVING THE MISSING OIL

Problem
Fuel oil supplies inventory and fuel expense inflated because of short shipments.

Method
Johnson Chemical started a new contract with Madden Oil Distributors to supply fuel oil for the plant generators on a cost-plus contract. Madden delivered the oil weekly in a 5,000-gallon tank truck and pumped it into Johnson's storage tanks. Johnson's receiving employees were supposed to observe the pumping and record the quantity on a receiving report, which was then forwarded to the accounts payable department, where it was held pending arrival of Madden's invoice. The quantities received then were compared to the quantities billed by Madden before a voucher was approved for payment and a check prepared for signature by the controller. Since it was a cost-plus contract, Madden's billing price was not checked against any standard price.

The receiving employees were rather easily fooled by Madden's driver. He mixed sludge with the oil; the receiving employees did not take samples to check for quality. He called out the storage tank content falsely (e.g., 1,000 gallons on hand when 2,000 were actually in the tank); the receiving employees did not check the gauge themselves; and the tank truck was not weighed at entry and exit to determine the amount delivered. During the winter months, when fuel oil use was high, Madden ran in extra trucks more than once a week, but pumped nothing when the receiving employees were not looking. Quantities "received" and paid during the first year of the contract were (in gallons):

Jan.	31,000	May	18,000	Sep.	21,000
Feb.	28,000	June	14,000	Oct.	23,000
Mar.	23,000	July	15,000	Nov.	33,000
Apr.	19,000	Aug.	14,000	Dec.	36,000

Paper Trail
The Johnson receiving reports all agreed with the quantities billed by Madden. Each invoice had a receiving report attached in the Johnson voucher files. Even though Madden had many trucks, the same driver always came to the Johnson plant, as evidenced by his signature on the receiving report (along with the Johnson company receiving employees' initials). Madden charged $1.80 per gallon, making the charges for the 275,000 gallons a total of $495,000 for the year. Last year, Johnson paid a total of $360,000 for 225,000 gallons, but nobody made a complete comparison with last year's quantity and cost.

Amount
During the first year, Madden shorted Johnson on quantity by 40,000 gallons (loss = 40,000 x $1.80 = $72,000) and charged 20 cents per gallon more than competitors (loss = 235,000 gallons x $0.20 = $47,000) for a total overcharge of $119,000, not to mention the inferior sludge mix occasionally delivered.

AUDIT APPROACH

Objective
Obtain evidence to determine whether all fuel oil billed and paid was actually received in the quality expected at a fair price.

Control
Receiving employees should be provided the tools and techniques they need to do a good job. Scales at the plant entrance could be used to weigh the trucks in and out and determine the amount of fuel oil delivered. (The weight per gallon is a well-known measure.) They could observe the quality of the oil by taking samples for simple chemical analysis.

Instructions should be given to teach the receiving employees the importance of their job so they can be conscientious. They should have been instructed and supervised to read the storage tank gauges themselves instead of relying on Madden's driver.

Lacking these tools and instructions, they were easy marks for the wily driver.

Test of Controls
The control activity supposedly in place was the receiving report on the oil delivered. A procedure to (1) take a sample of Madden's bills, and (2a) compare quantities billed to quantities received, and (2b) compare the price billed to the contract would probably not have shown anything unusual (unless the auditor became suspicious of the same driver always delivering to Johnson).

The information from the "understanding the control system" phase would need to be much more detailed to alert the auditors to the poor receiving practices.
Procedure: Make inquiries with the receiving employees to learn about their practices and work habits.

Audit of Balance

The balances in question are the fuel oil supply inventory and the fuel expense.

The inventory is easily audited by reading the tank storage gauge for the quantity. The price is found in Madden's invoices. However, a lower-of-cost-or-market test requires knowledge of market prices of the oil. Since Johnson Chemical apparently has no documentation of competing prices, the auditor will need to make a few telephone calls to other oil distributors to get the prices. Presumably, the auditors would learn that the price is approximately $1.60 per gallon.

The expense balance can be audited like a cost of goods sold number. With knowledge of the beginning fuel inventory, the quantity "purchased," and the quantity in the ending inventory, the fuel oil expense quantity can be calculated. This expense quantity can be priced at Madden's price per gallon.

Analytical procedures applied to the expense should reveal the larger quantities used and the unusual pattern of deliveries, leading to suspicions of Madden and the driver.

Discovery Summary

Knowing the higher expense of the current year and the evidence of a lower market price, the auditors obtained the fuel oil delivery records from the prior year. They are shown below, and the numbers in parentheses are the additional gallons delivered in the current year.

Having found a consistent pattern of greater "use" in the current year, with no operational explanation, the auditors took to the field. With the cooperation of the receiving employees, the auditors read the storage tank measure before the Madden driver arrived. They hid in an adjoining building and watched (and filmed) the driver call out an incorrect reading, pump the oil, sign the receiving report, and depart. Then they took samples.

These observations were repeated for three weeks. They saw
short deliveries, tested inferior products, and built a case
against Madden and the driver.

Jan.	28,000 (3,000)	July	10,000	(5,000)
Feb.	24,000 (4,000)	Aug.	9,000	(5,000)
Mar.	20,000 (3,000)	Sep.	15,000	(6,000)
Apr.	17,000 (2,000)	Oct.	20,000	(3,000)
May	13,000 (5,000)	Nov.	28,000	(5,000)
June	11,000 (3,000)	Dec.	30,000	(6,000)

CASE 9.4
GO FOR THE GOLD

Problem
Fixed assets in the form of mining properties were overstated
through a series of "flip" transactions involving related parties.

Method
In 1989 Alta Gold Company was a public "shell" corporation
that was purchased for $1,000 by the Blues brothers.

Operating under the corporate names of Silver King and
Pacific Gold, the brothers purchased numerous mining claims
in auctions conducted by the U.S. Department of the Interior.
They invested a total of $40,000 in 300 claims. Silver King
sold limited partnership interests in its 175 Nevada silver
claims to local investors, raising $20 million to begin mining
production. Pacific Gold then traded its 125 Montana gold
mining claims for all the Silver King assets and partnership
interests, valuing the silver claims at $20 million. (Silver King
valued the gold claims received at $20 million as the fair value
in the exchange.) The brothers then put $3 million obtained
from dividends into Alta Gold, and, with the aid of a bank
loan, purchased half of the remainder of Silver King's assets

and all of Pacific Gold's mining claims by purchase. They paid off the limited partners. At the end of 1989, Alta Gold had cash of $16 million and mining assets valued at $58 million, with liabilities on bank loans of $53 million.

Paper Trail

Alta Gold had in its files the partnership offering documents, receipts, and other papers showing partners' investment of $20 million in the Silver King limited partnerships. The company also had Pacific Gold and Silver King contracts for the exchange of mining claims. The $20 million value of the exchange was justified in light of the limited partners' investments.

Appraisals in the files showed one appraiser's report that there was no basis for valuing the exchange of Silver King claims, other than the price limited partner investors had been willing to pay. The second appraiser reported a probable value of $20 million for the exchange based on proved production elsewhere, but no geological data on the actual claims had been obtained. The $18 million paid by Alta to Silver King also had similar appraisal reports.

Amount

The transactions occurred over a period of 10 months. The Blues brothers had $37 million cash in Silver King and Pacific Gold, as well as the $16 million in Alta (all of which was the gullible bank's money, but the bank had loaned to Alta with the mining claims and production as security). The mining claims that had cost $40,000 were now in Alta's balance sheet at $58 million, the $37 million was about to flee, and the bank was about to be left holding the bag containing 300 mining claim papers.

AUDIT APPROACH

Objective
Obtain evidence of the existence, valuation, and rights (ownership) in the mining claim assets.

Control
Alta Gold, Pacific Gold, and Silver King had no control system. All transactions were engineered by the Blues brothers, including the hiring of friendly appraisers. The only control that might have been effective was at the bank in the loan-granting process, but the bank failed.

Test of Controls
The only vestige of control could have been the engagement of competent, independent appraisers. Since the auditors will need to use (or try to use) the appraisers' reports, the procedures involve investigating the reputation, engagement terms, experience, and independence of the appraisers. The auditors can use local business references, local financial institutions who keep lists of approved appraisers, membership directories of the professional appraisal associations, and interviews with the appraisers themselves.

Audit of Balances
The procedures for auditing the asset values include analyses of each of the transactions through all their complications, including obtaining knowledge of the owners and managers of the several companies and the identities of the limited partner investors. If the Blues brothers have not disclosed their connection with the other companies (and perhaps with the limited partners), the auditors will need to inquire at the secretary of state's offices where Pacific Gold and Silver King are incorporated and try to discover the identities of the players in this flip game. Numerous complicated premerger transactions in small corporations and shells often signal manipulated valuations.

Loan applications and supporting papers should be examined to determine the representations made by Alta in connection with obtaining the bank loans. These papers may reveal some contradictory or exaggerated information. Ownership of the mining claims might be confirmed with the Department of Interior auctioneers or be found in the local county deed records (spread all over Nevada and Montana).

Discovery Summary
The inexperienced audit staff was unable to unravel the Byzantine exchanges, and they never questioned the relation of Alta to Silver King and Pacific Gold. They never discovered the Blues brothers' involvement in the other side of the exchange, purchase, and merger transactions. They accepted the appraisers' reports because they had never worked with appraisers before and thought all appraisers were competent and independent. The bank lost $37 million. The Blues brothers changed their names.

CASE 9.5
RETREAD TIRES

Problem
Inventory and income overstated by substitution of retread tires valued for inventory at new tire prices.

Method
Ritter Tire Wholesale Company had a high-volume truck and passenger car tire business in Austin, Texas (area population 750,000). J. Lock, the chief accountant, was a longtime trusted employee who had supervisory responsibility over the purchasing agents as well as general accounting duties. Lock had worked several years as a purchasing agent before moving into the accounting job. In the course of normal operations, Lock often prepared purchase orders; but the manufacturers were directed to deliver the tires to a warehouse in Marlin (a town of 15,000 population 100 miles northeast of Austin).

Ritter Tire received the manufacturers' invoices, which Lock approved for payment. Lock and an accomplice (brother-in-law) sold the tires from the Marlin warehouse and pocketed the money. At night, Lock moved cheaper retreaded tires into the Ritter warehouse so spaces would not seem to be empty. As chief accountant, Lock could override controls (e.g., approving invoices for payment without a receiving report), and T. Ritter (president) never knew the difference because the checks presented for signature were not accompanied by the supporting documents.

Paper Trail
Ritter Tire's files were well-organized. Each check copy had supporting documents attached (voucher, invoice, receiving report, purchase order), except the misdirected tire purchases had no receiving reports. These purchase orders were all signed by Lock, and the shipping destination on them directed delivery to the Marlin address. There were no purchase requisition documents because "requisitions" were in the form of verbal requests from salespersons.

There was no paper evidence of the retreaded tires because Lock simply bought them elsewhere and moved them in at night when nobody else was around.

Amount
Lock carried out the scheme for three years, diverting tires that cost Ritter $2.5 million, which Lock sold for $2.9 million. (Lock's cost of retread tires was approximately $500,000.)

AUDIT APPROACH

Objective
Obtain evidence of the existence and valuation of the inventory. (President Ritter engaged external auditors for the first time in the third year of Lock's scheme after experiencing a severe cash squeeze.)

Control

Competent personnel should perform the purchasing function. Lock and the other purchasing agents were competent and experienced. They prepared purchase orders authorizing the purchase of tires. (The manufacturers required them for shipments.)

A receiving department prepared a receiving report after counting and inspecting each shipment by filling in the "quantity column" on a copy of the purchase order. (A common form of receiving report is a "blind" purchase order that has all the purchase information except the quantity, which is left blank for the receiving department to fill in after an independent inspection and count.) Receiving personnel made notes if the tires showed blemishes or damage.

As chief accountant, Lock received the invoices from the manufacturers and approved them for payment after comparing the quantities with the receiving report and the prices with the purchase order. The checks for payment were produced automatically on the microcomputer accounting system when Lock entered the invoice payable in the system. The computer software did not void transactions for lack of a receiving report reference because many other expenses legitimately had no receiving reports.

The key weakness in the control system was the fact that no one else on the accounting staff had the opportunity to notice missing receiving reports in vouchers that should have had them, and Ritter never had the vouchers when checks were signed. Lock was a trusted employee.

Test of Controls

Because the control procedures for cross-checking the supporting documents were said to have been placed in operation, the external auditors can test the controls.

Procedure: Select a sample of purchases (manufacturers' invoices payable entered in the microcomputer), and (1) study the related purchase order for (i) valid manufacturer name and address; (ii) date; (iii) delivery address; (iv) unit price, with reference to catalogs or price lists; (v) correct arithmetic; and

(vi) approval signature. Then (2) compare purchase order information to the manufacturers' invoice; and (3) compare the purchase order and invoice to the receiving report for (i) date, (ii) quantity and condition, (iii) approval signature, and (iv) location.

Audit of Balance

Ritter Tire did not maintain perpetual inventory records, so the inventory was a "periodic system" whereby the financial statement inventory figure was derived from the annual physical inventory count and costing compilation. The basic audit procedure was to observe the count by taking a sample of locations on the warehouse floor, recounting the employees' count, controlling the count sheets, and inspecting the tires for quality and condition (related to proper valuation). The auditors kept their own copy of all the count sheets with their test count notes and notes identifying tires as "new" or "retread." (They took many test counts in the physical inventory sample as a result of the test of controls work, described below.)

Discovery Summary

Forty manufacturers' invoices were selected at random for the test of controls procedure. The auditors were good. They had reviewed the business operations, and Ritter had said nothing about having operations or a warehouse in Marlin, although a manufacturer might have been instructed to "drop ship" tires to a customer there. The auditors noticed three missing receiving reports, all of them with purchase orders signed by Lock and requesting delivery to the same Marlin address. They asked Lock about the missing receiving reports, and got this response: "It happens sometimes. I'll find them for you tomorrow." When Lock produced the receiving reports, the auditors noticed they were in a current numerical sequence (dated much earlier), filled out with the same pen, and signed with an illegible scrawl not matching any of the other receiving reports they had seen.

The auditors knew the difference between new and retread tires when they saw them, and confirmed their observations with employees taking the physical inventory count. When Lock priced the inventory, new tire prices were used, and the auditors knew the difference.

Ritter took the circumstantial evidence to a trained investigator who interviewed the manufacturers and obtained information about the Marlin location. The case against Lock led to criminal theft charges and conviction.

CASE 9.6
AMORTIZE *BANG THE DRUM* SLOWLY

Problem
Net asset values (unamortized costs of films) were overstated by taking too little amortization expense.

Method
Candid Production Company was a major producer of theatrical movies. The company usually had 15-20 films in release at theaters across the nation and in foreign countries. Movies also produced revenue from video licenses and product sales (T-shirts, toys, and the like).

Movie production costs are capitalized as assets, then amortized to expense as revenue is received from theater and video sales and from other sources of revenue. The amortization depends on the total revenue forecast and the current-year revenue amount. As the success or failure of a movie unfolds at the box office, revenue estimates are revised. (The accounting amortization is very similar to depletion of a mineral resource, which depends upon estimates of recoverable minerals and current production.)

Candid Production was not too candid. For example, its recent film of *Bang the Drum Slowly* was forecast to produce $50 million total revenue over six years, although the early box

office returns showed only $10 million in the first eight
months in the theaters. (Revenue will decline rapidly after
initial openings, and video and other revenue depend on the
box office success of a film.)

Accounting "control" with respect to film cost amortization
resides in the preparation and revision of revenue forecasts. In
this case, they were overly optimistic, slowing the expense
recognition and overstating assets and income.

Paper Trail
Revenue forecasts are based on many factors, including facts
and assumptions about number of theaters, ticket prices,
receipt sharing agreements, domestic and foreign reviews, and
moviegoer tastes. Several publications track the box office
records of movies. You can see them in newspaper
entertainment sections and in industry trade publications. Of
course, the production companies themselves are the major
source of the information. However, company records also
show the revenue realized from each movie.

Revenue forecasts can be checked against actual experience,
and the company's history of forecasting accuracy can be
determined by comparing actual to forecast over many films
and many years.

Amount
Over a four-year period, Candid Productions postponed
recognition of a $20 million amortization expense, thus
inflating assets and income.

AUDIT APPROACH

Objective
Obtain evidence to determine whether revenue forecasts
provide a sufficient basis for calculating film cost amortization
and net asset value of films.

Control
Revenue forecasts need to be prepared in a controlled process that documents the facts and underlying assumptions built into the forecast. Forecasts should break down the revenue estimate by years, and the accounting system should produce comparable actual revenue data so forecast accuracy can be assessed after the fact. Forecast revisions should be prepared in as much detail and documentation as original forecasts.

Test of Controls
The general procedures and methods used by personnel responsible for revenue forecasts should be studied (inquiries and review of documentation), including their sources of information both internal and external. Procedures for review of mechanical aspects (arithmetic) should be tested: Select a sample of finished forecasts and recalculate the final estimate.

Specific procedures for forecast revision also should be studied in the same manner. A review of the accuracy of forecasts on other movies with hindsight on actual revenues helps in a circumstantial way, but past accuracy on different film experiences may not directly influence the forecasts on a new, unique product.

Audit of Balance
The audit of amortization expense concentrates on the content of the forecast itself. The preparation of forecasts used in the amortization calculation should be studied to distinguish underlying reasonable expectations from "hypothetical assumptions." A hypothetical assumption is a statement of a condition that is not necessarily expected to occur, but nonetheless is used to prepare an estimate. For example, a hypothetical assumption is like an "if-then" statement: "If *Bang the Drum Slowly* sells 15 million tickets in the first 12 months
of release, then domestic revenue and product sales will be $40 million, and foreign revenue can eventually reach $10 million." Auditors need to assess the reasonableness of the

basic 15 million ticket assumption. It helps to have some early actual data from the film's release in hand before the financial statements need to be finished and distributed. For actual data, industry publications ought to be reviewed, with special attention to competing films and critics' reviews (yes, movie reviews!).

Discovery Summary
The auditors were not skeptical enough about optimistic revenue forecasts, and they did not weigh unfavorable actual/forecast history comparisons heavily enough. Apparently, they let themselves be convinced by exuberant company executives that the movies were comparable with *Gone with the Wind*! The audit of forecasts and estimates used in accounting determinations is very difficult, especially when company personnel have incentives to hype the numbers, seemingly with conviction about the artistic and commercial merit of their productions. The postponed amortization expense finally came to roost in big write-offs when the company management changed.

SUMMARY

The acquisition and expenditure cycle consists of purchase requisitioning, purchase ordering, receiving goods and services, recording vendors' invoices and accounting for accounts payable, and making disbursements of cash. Companies reduce control risk by having a suitable separation of authorization, custody, recording, and periodic reconciliation duties. Error-checking procedures of comparing purchase orders and receiving reports to vendor invoices are important for recording proper amounts of accounts payable liabilities. Supervisory control is provided by having a separation of duties between preparing cash disbursement checks and actually signing them. Otherwise, many things could go wrong, ranging from processing false or fictitious purchase orders to failing to record liabilities for goods and services received.

Two topics have special technical notes in the chapter. The *completeness assertion* is very important in the audit of liabilities because misleading financial statements often have contained unrecorded liabilities and expenses. The "search for unrecorded liabilities" is an important set of audit procedures. The *physical inventory observation* audit work gets a special section because actual contact with inventories (and fixed assets, for that matter) provides auditors with direct eyewitness evidence of important tangible assets.

Cash disbursement is a critical point for asset control. Many cases of embezzlement occur in this process. Illustrative cases in the chapter tell the stories of some of these schemes, mostly involving payment of fictitious charges to dummy companies set up by employees.

PRACTICAL CASE PROBLEMS
INSTRUCTIONS FOR CASES

These cases are designed like the ones in the chapter. They give the problem, the method, the paper trail, and the amount. Your assignment is to write the "audit approach" portion of the case, organized around these sections:

Objective: Express the objective in terms of the facts supposedly asserted in financial records, accounts, and statements.

Control: Write a brief explanation of desirable controls, missing controls, and especially the kinds of "deviations" that might arise from the situation described in the case.

Test of controls: Write some procedures for getting evidence about existing controls, especially procedures that could discover deviations from controls. If there are no controls to test, then there are no procedures to perform; go then to the next section. A "procedure" should instruct someone about the source(s) of evidence to tap and the work to do.

Audit of balance: Write some procedures for getting evidence about the existence, completeness, valuation, ownership, or disclosure assertions identified in your *objective* section above.

Discovery summary: Write a short statement about the discovery you expect to accomplish with your procedures.

CASE #9.1: THE PHANTOM OF THE INVENTORY--Overstated Inventory and Profits.

This case is a cross-reference to Case #6.5 in Chapter 6. Follow the instructions above. Write the "audit approach" section like the cases in the chapter, and also recalculate the income (loss) before taxes using the correct inventory figures. (Assume the correct beginning inventory two years ago was $5.5 million.)

CASE #9.2: PURCHASING STARS--Purchase Kickbacks.

In this case, let your initial objective be to select one vendor for investigation. Instead of a "test of controls" section, name the one vendor you would select from those in Case Exhibit # 9.2 and tell your reasons. In the "test of balances" section, tell how you would investigate the situation. In the "discovery summary" section, speculate about how your investigation might reveal the culprit.

Problem: Kickbacks taken on books or supplies inventory purchases caused inflated inventory, cost of goods sold, and expenses.

Method: Bailey Books, Inc., is a retail distributor of upscale books, periodicals, and magazines. Bailey has 431 retail stores throughout the southeastern states. Three full-time purchasing agents work at corporate headquarters. They are responsible for purchasing all the inventory at the best prices available from wholesales jobbers. They can purchase with or without obtaining competitive bids. The three purchasing agents are: R. McGuire in charge of purchasing books, M. Garza in charge of purchasing magazines and periodicals, and L. Collins (manager of purchasing) in charge of ordering miscellaneous items, such as paper products and store supplies.

One of the purchasing agents is suspected of taking kickbacks from vendors. In return, Bailey is thought to be paying inflated prices, which first go to inventory and then to cost of goods sold and other expense accounts as the assets are sold or used.

L. Collins is the manager in charge. Her duties do not include audit or inspection of the performance of the other two purchasing agents. No one audits or reviews Collins's performance.

Paper trail: The purchasing system is computerized, and detail records are retained. An extract from these records is in Case Exhibit #9.2.

Amount: This kickback scheme has been going on for two or three years. Several hundred thousand dollars may have been overpaid by Bailey Books.

CASE EXHIBIT #9.2 Summary of Purchasing Activity

BAILEY BOOKS, INCORPORATED
Selected Purchases 1993-1995

Vendor	Items Purchased	1993	1994	1995	Date of Last Bid	Percent of Purchases Bid (3-yr. Period)
Armour	Books	683,409	702,929	810,100	12/01/95	87%
Burdick	Sundries	62,443	70,949	76,722	----	----
Canon	Magazines	1,404,360	1,947,601	2,361,149	11/03/95	94
DeBois, Inc.	Paper	321,644	218,404	121,986	06/08/95	57
Elton Books	Books	874,893	781,602	649,188	07/21/95	91
Fergeson	Books	921,666	1,021,440	1,567,811	09/08/95	88
Guyford	Magazines	2,377,821	2,868,988	3,262,490	10/08/95	81
Hyman, Inc.	Supplies	31,640	40,022	46,911	10/22/95	----
Intertec	Books	821,904	898,683	949,604	11/18/95	86
Jerrico	Paper	186,401	111,923	93,499	10/04/95	72
Julian-Borg	Magazines	431,470	589,182	371,920	02/07/95	44
King Features	Magazines	436,820	492,687	504,360	11/18/95	89
Lycorp	Sundries	16,280	17,404	21,410	----	----
Medallian	Books	----	61,227	410,163	12/15/95	99
Northwood	Books	861,382	992,121	----	12/07/94	----
Orion Corp.	Paper	86,904	416,777	803,493	11/02/94	15
Peterson	Supplies	114,623	----	----	N/A	N/A
Quick	Supplies	----	96,732	110,441	11/03/95	86
Robertson	Books	2,361,912	3,040,319	3,516,811	12/01/95	96
Steele	Magazines	621,490	823,707	482,082	11/03/95	90
Telecom	Sundries	81,406	101,193	146,316	----	----
Union Bay	Books	4,322,639	4,971,682	5,368,114	12/03/95	97
Victory	Magazines	123,844	141,909	143,286	06/09/95	89
Williams	Sundries	31,629	35,111	42,686	----	----

CASE #9.3: LIKE A SON--Fictitious Vendors, Theft, and Embezzlement
Write the "audit approach" section like the cases in the chapter.

Problem: Fictitious purchases overstated inventory and inflated costs and expenses, causing misstated financial statements and operating losses.

Method: Simon Construction Company had two divisions. Simon, the president, managed the roofing division. Simon delegated authority and responsibility for management of the modular manufacturing division to John G. A widower, Simon had virtually adopted John when he ran away from an orphanage 20 years earlier, treating him like the son he never had, even building him a fine house on the outskirts of the city.

John and his secretary handled all the bids for manufacturing jobs, purchased all the material, controlled the physical inventory of materials, contracted for shipping by truck, supervised the construction activity, billed the customers when jobs were in progress and finished, approved all bid changes, and collected payments from the customers. With Simons' approval, John asked the company internal auditor not to interfere with his busy schedule. The secretary entered all the division's transactions into the computerized accounting system from a dedicated terminal in the manufacturing division office.

John did everything crooked, and the secretary was an accomplice. He rigged low bids and gave kickbacks to customers' purchasing agents, paid high prices to suppliers and took kickbacks, set up dummy companies to sell materials to Simon Construction at inflated prices, removed excess materials inventory and sold it and took the money, manipulated the inventory accounts to overstate the inventory and hide the thefts, and caused Simon Construction to pay trucking bills for a side business he owned. Simon exercised no control over John's operations.

Paper trail: Paper evidence was plentiful, if somebody looked for it. Bid records showed original low bids, later raised for basic construction (e.g., adding second floor, when the original request for bid included a second floor). Checks payable to "cash" were endorsed by people known to be customers' purchasing agents. Prices paid for materials and supplies were higher than the list prices shown in the competing suppliers' price books kept in the manufacturing division library. John's kickbacks were deposited in his own bank account. Dummy companies were incorporated in the same state, with John and the secretary listed as original incorporators. The physical inventory shown in the accounts simply did not exist. Trucking bills showed deliveries to locations where the manufacturing division had no jobs in progress.

Amount: John drained $1.2 million from Simon Construction over a nine-year period before he was caught. Auditors were engaged to analyze the situation when Simon finally noticed the reported losses in the manufacturing division and had a violent argument with John.

CASE #9.4: THE BULGING DESK DRAWERS--Liability Understatement. In this case, along with your "audit approach" solution, specify the discrepancies you notice by studying the excerpt from the accounts payable trial balance in Case Exhibit #9.4. Also, recalculate the income before taxes and write the adjusting journal entry you would propose. (*Hint*: The voucher numbers in the trial balance are assigned when the vendor invoices are recorded.)

Problem: Failure to record purchases of raw materials and expense items caused understated accounts payable, understated cost of goods sold, understated expenses, and overstated income.

Method: All Bright Company manufactured lamps. L. Mendoza, the company financial vice president, knew the company was under pressure to produce profits in order to maintain its loans at the bank. One of the surest ways accountants know to produce profits with a pencil is to fail to record purchases. This keeps expenses off the books and understates cost of goods sold figured on a periodic inventory basis. (Cost of goods sold = Beginning inventory + Purchases - Ending inventory.)

Mendoza opened the mail each day and removed the invoices from suppliers, putting them in the office desk drawer. Later, when the company could "afford it," some invoices were sent to the accounts payable department for recording. Mendoza did not always get them in sequence of arrival, but that didn't matter much to her. Anyway, the desk drawers were getting full.

The clerks in the accounts payable department knew about this manipulation. They would go through periods with very little to record, then a large stack of invoices would be delivered for recording. (Must have made a big sale, they gossiped.)

The clerks followed control procedures about matching invoices with receiving reports, and they always had a full file of "unmatched receiving reports" awaiting the arrival of invoices. Mendoza had the power to override controls that called for the timely recording of purchases, and the clerks could not record invoices they had not yet received.

Paper trail: The accounts payable clerks gave each invoice-receiving report-purchase order set a voucher number in numerical sequence. They dated the accounts payable and related debit recordings on the day they processed the vouchers. Their vouchers were always complete because they were under strict orders not to record any payables that were not supported by source documents.

The problem with the paper trail is that the recording did not get started until Mendoza delivered the invoices. However, there was a file of the unmatched receiving reports in the accounts payable department, forwarded from the receiving employees, and there was a trial balance of accounts payable produced for the auditors.

An excerpt from this trial balance is in Case Exhibit #9.4. The total accounts payable on the trial balance, not shown in Case Exhibit #9.4, was $1.8 million for the year ended December 31, 1995. (The signs of delayed recording of accounts payable are in the exhibit. Can you find them?)

Amount: Mendoza held back the recording of accounts payable for two years (the current year 1995, and one year ago 1994). One year ago, the accounts payable were understated by $500,000, of which $200,000 was unrecorded purchases for inventory and $300,000 was unrecorded operating expenses. In the current year (1995), the accounts payable were understated at December 31 by $750,000, of which $450,000 was for inventory purchases, and $300,000 was unrecorded operating expenses. The financial statements showed the following (dollars in 000s):

	Two Years Ago	One Year Ago	Current Year
Sales	$25,000	$29,000	$40,500
Cost of goods sold	(20,000)	(22,000)	(29,000)
Expenses	(5,000)	(8,000)	(9,000)
Income (loss) before taxes	0	$(1,000)	$2,500
Ending inventory	$6,000	$8,000	$10,200
Current assets	9,000	8,500	17,500
Total assets	21,000	21,600	34,300
Current liabilities	5,000	5,500	13,000
Long-term debt*	5,500	6,600	9,300
Stockholder equity	10,500	9,500	12,000

* Secured by inventory pledged to the bank.

CASE EXHIBIT #9.4   Excerpt from Accounts Payable Trial Balance: December 31, 1995

Voucher #	Vendor Name	Invoice #	Date Invoice	Date Due	Amount
26695	Industrial Uniforms	66681	01-Oct-95	01-Nov-95	112.11
26694	Industrial Uniforms	67127	08-Oct-95	08-Nov-95	112.11
27209	Industrial Uniforms	67582	15-Oct-95	15-Nov-95	112.11
27208	Industrial Uniforms	67981	22-Oct-95	22-Nov-95	112.11
27210	Industrial Uniforms	68462	29-Oct-95	29-Nov-95	112.11
27552	Industrial Uniforms	68972	05-Nov-95	05-Dec-95	112.11
27553	Industrial Uniforms	69463	12-Nov-95	12-Dec-95	112.11
27854	Industrial Uniforms	69851	19-Nov-95	19-Dec-95	112.11
29123	Industrial Uniforms	70851	03-Dec-95	03-Jan-96	112.11
28095	Industrial Uniforms	71353	10-Dec-95	10-Jan-96	112.11
29437	Industrial Uniforms	71831	17-Dec-95	17-Jan-96	112.11

Vendor total   1,233.21

27484	B&B Experimental Co	17490	04-Nov-95	04-Dec-95	2,354.50
27550	B&B Experimental Co	17492	04-Nov-95	04-Dec-95	371.25
27559	B&B Experimental Co	17495	08-Nov-95	08-Dec-95	148.50
27560	B&B Experimental Co	17493	08-Nov-95	08-Dec-95	396.00
27741	B&B Experimental Co	17502	09-Nov-95	09-Dec-95	560.25
27475	B&B Experimental Co	17508	12-Nov-95	12-Dec-95	145.11
29494	B&B Experimental Co	17512	16-Nov-95	16-Dec-95	1,284.25
27556	B&B Experimental Co	17474	18-Nov-95	18-Dec-95	265.50
27662	B&B Experimental Co	17514	22-Nov-95	22-Dec-95	519.75
28084	B&B Experimental Co	17523	26-Nov-95	26-Dec-95	938.34
28085	B&B Experimental Co	17546	30-Nov-95	30-Dec-95	893.62
28086	B&B Experimental Co	17549	06-Dec-95	06-Jan-96	1,607.72

Vendor total   9,484.79

29377	Cameo Corp	44298	06-Dec-95	28-Feb-96	1,429.02
29379	Cameo Corp	44300	06-Dec-95	28-Feb-96	1,747.93
29378	Cameo Corp	44413	07-Dec-95	28-Feb-96	259.33
29374	Cameo Corp	44412	07-Dec-95	28-Feb-96	808.33
29380	Cameo Corp	44415	07-Dec-95	28-Feb-96	844.71
29382	Cameo Corp	44414	07-Dec-95	07-Feb-96	1,553.19
29372	Cameo Corp	44596	09-Dec-95	28-Feb-96	3,781.01
29371	Cameo Corp	44682	10-Dec-95	28-Feb-96	1,262.59
29383	Cameo Corp	44684	10-Dec-95	10-Feb-96	4,094.82
29381	Cameo Corp	44681	10-Dec-95	28-Feb-96	926.51
29385	Cameo Corp	44685	10-Dec-95	28-Feb-96	3,750.44

CASE EXHIBIT #9.4 Excerpt from Accounts Payable Trial Balance: December 31, 1995

Voucher #	Vendor Name	Invoice #	Date Invoice	Date Due	Amount
29373	Cameo Corp	44680	10-Dec-95	28-Feb-96	1,124.78
29370	Cameo Corp	44983	10-Dec-95	28-Feb-96	3,973.39
Vendor total					25,556.05
27120	Central States Pension		15-Apr-95	15-Apr-95	10,558.23
27121	Central States Pension		15-May-95	15-May-95	10,558.23
27122	Central States Pension		15-Jun-95	15-Jun-95	10,558.23
27123	Central States Pension		15-Jul-95	15-Jul-95	10,558.23
27124	Central States Pension		15-Aug-95	15-Aug-95	10,558.23
27125	Central States Pension		15-Sep-95	15-Sep-95	10,558.23
27126	Central States Pension		15-Oct-95	15-Oct-95	10,558.23
Vendor total					73,907.61

CHAPTER 10
PAYROLL ACCOUNTING

The payroll accounting cycle covers numerous activities from hiring and firing to pay distribution. This chapter contains sections on (1) typical control activities in the cycle, (2) the audit evidence available in management reports and files, (3) control risk assessment (including detail test of controls procedures), and (4) case story-style explanations concerning discovery of errors, irregularities, and frauds.

PAYROLL CYCLE TYPICAL ACTIVITIES

Every company has a payroll. It may include manufacturing labor, research scientists, administrative personnel, or all of these. Subsidiary operations, partnerships, and joint ventures may call it "management fees" charged by a parent company or general partner. Payroll can take different forms. Personnel management and the payroll accounting cycle not only include transactions that affect the wage and salary accounts but also the transactions that affect pension benefits, deferred compensation contracts, compensatory stock option plans, employee benefits (such as health insurance), payroll taxes, and related liabilities for these costs.

Exhibit 10-1 shows a payroll cycle. It starts with hiring (and firing) people and determining their wage rates and deductions, then proceeds to attendance and work (timekeeping), and ends with payment followed by preparation of governmental (tax) and internal reports. One of these internal reports is a report of labor cost to the cost accounting department, thus linking the payroll cycle with cost accounting in the production cycle. Five functional responsibilities should be performed by separate people or departments. They are:

- Personnel and Labor Relations--hiring and firing.
- Supervision--approval of work time.
- Timekeeping and Cost Accounting--payroll preparation and cost accounting.
- Payroll Accounting--check preparation and related payroll reports.
- Payroll Distribution--actual custody of checks and distribution to employees.

EXHIBIT 10-1 Payroll Cycle

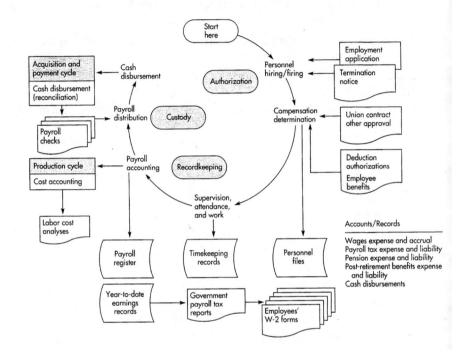

The elements that follow are part of the payroll control system.

AUTHORIZATION

A **personnel or labor relations department** that is independent of the other functions should have transaction initiation authority to add new employees to the payroll, to delete terminated employees, to obtain authorizations for deductions (such as insurance, saving bonds, withholding tax exemptions on federal form W-4), and to transmit authority for pay rate changes to the payroll department.

Authorization also takes place in the **supervision** function. All pay base data (hours, job number, absences, time off allowed for emergencies, and the like) should be approved by an employee's immediate supervisor.

Authorization is also a feature of the **timekeeping and cost accounting** function. Data on which pay is based (such as hours, piece-rate volume, incentives) should be accumulated independent of other functions.

APPROVAL OF FICTITIOUS OVERTIME

A supervisor at Austin Stoneworks discovered that she could approve overtime hours even though an employee had not worked 40 regular time hours. She made a deal with several employees to alter their work timecards and split the extra payments. Over a six-year period, the supervisor and her accomplices embezzled $107,000 in excess payments.

The employees' time cards were not reviewed after being approved by the supervisor. The company's payroll computer program did not have a valid data combination test that paid overtime only after 40 regular time hours were paid.

CUSTODY

The main feature of custody in the payroll cycle is the possession of the paychecks, cash, or electronic transfer codes used to pay people. (Electronic transfer codes refer to the practice by some organizations of transferring pay directly into employees' bank accounts.) A **payroll distribution** function should control the delivery of pay to employees so that unclaimed checks, cash, or incomplete electronic transfers are not returned to persons involved in any of the other functions.

Elements of custody of important documents are in the **supervision** function and in the **timekeeping** function. Supervisors usually have access to time cards or time sheets that provide the basis for payment to hourly workers. Likewise, the timekeeping devices (e.g., time clocks, supervisory approval of time cards or time sheets, electronic punch-in systems) have a type of custody of employees' time-base for payroll calculations.

RECORDKEEPING

The **payroll accounting** function should prepare individual paychecks, pay envelopes, or electronic transfers using rate and deduction information supplied by the personnel function and base data supplied by the timekeeping-supervision functions. Persons in charge of the authorization and custody functions should not also prepare the payroll. They might be tempted to pay fictitious employees.

Payroll accounting maintains individual year-to-date earnings records and prepares the state and federal tax reports (income tax and Social Security withholding, unemployment tax reports, and annual W-2 forms). The payroll tax returns (e.g., federal Form 941 that reports taxes withheld, state and federal unemployment tax returns) and the annual W-2 report to employees are useful records for audit recalculation and overall testing (analytical) procedures. They should correspond to company records. Most company employees responsible for these reports are reluctant to manipulate them.

PERIODIC RECONCILIATION

The payroll bank account can be reconciled like any other bank account. Otherwise, there is not much to count or observe in payroll to accomplish a traditional reconciliation--comparing "real payroll" to recorded wage cost and expense. However, one kind of reconciliation in the form of feedback to the **supervision** function can be placed in operation. Some companies send to each supervisor a copy of the payroll register, showing the employees paid under the supervisor's authority and responsibility. The supervisor gets a chance to reapprove the payroll after it is completed. This gives the opportunity to notice whether any persons not approved have been paid and charged to the supervisor's accountability.

The payroll report sent to cost accounting can be reconciled to the labor records used to charge labor cost to production. The cost accounting function should determine whether the labor paid is the same as the labor cost used in the cost accounting calculations.

NOT ENOUGH CONTROL, NO FEEDBACK, BYE-BYE MONEY

Homer had been in payroll accounting for a long time. He knew it was not uncommon to pay a terminated employee severance benefits and partial pay after termination. Homer received the termination notices and the data for the final paychecks. But Homer also knew how to keep the terminated employee on the payroll for another week, pay a full week's compensation, change the electronic transfer code, and take the money for himself. The only things he could not change were the personnel department's copy of the termination notices, the payroll register, and the individual employee pay records used for withholding tax and W-2 forms.

Fortunately, nobody reconciled the cost accounting labor charges to the payroll. The supervisors did not get a copy of the payroll register for post-payment approval, so they did not have any opportunity to notice the extra week. Nobody ever reviewed the payroll with reference to the termination notices. Former employees never complained about more pay and withholding reported on their W-2s than they actually received.

Homer and his wife Marge retired comfortably to a villa in Spain on a nest egg that had grown to $450,000. After his retirement, the company experienced an unexpected decrease in labor costs and higher profits.

EMPLOYEES ON FIXED SALARY

The functional duties and responsibilities described above relate primarily to nonsalaried (hourly) employees. For salaried employees, the system is simplified by not having to collect timekeeping data. In nonmanufacturing businesses, the cost accounting operations may be very simple or even nonexistent. The relative importance of each of these five areas should be determined for each engagement in light of the nature and organization of the company's operations.

AUDIT EVIDENCE IN MANAGEMENT REPORTS AND FILES

Payroll systems produce numerous reports. Some are internal reports and bookkeeping records. Others are government tax reports. Auditors should obtain and use these reports.

PERSONNEL FILES

The personnel and labor relations department keeps individual employee files. The contents usually include an employment application, a background investigation report, a notice of hiring, a job classification with pay rate authorization, and authorizations for deductions (e.g., health insurance, life insurance, retirement contribution, union dues, W-4 form for income tax exemptions). When employees retire, quit, or are otherwise terminated, appropriate notices of termination are filed. These files contain the raw data for important pension and post-retirement benefit accounting involving an employee's age, tenure with the company, wage record, and other information used in actuarial calculations.

A personnel file should establish the reality of a person's existence and employment. The background investigation report (prior employment, references, Social Security number validity check, credentials investigation, perhaps a private investigator's report) is important for employees in such sensitive areas as accounting, finance, and asset custody positions. One of the primary system controls is *capable personnel.* Experience is rich with errors, irregularities, and frauds perpetrated by people who falsify their credentials (identification, college degrees, prior experience, criminal records, and the like).

WHERE DID HE COME FROM?

The controller defrauded the company for several million dollars. As it turned out, he was no controller at all. He didn't know a debit from a credit. The fraudster had been fired from five previous jobs where money had turned up missing. He was discovered one evening when the president showed up unexpectedly at the company and found a stranger in the office with the controller. The stranger was doing all of the accounting for the bogus controller.

Source: Association of Certified Fraud Examiners, "Auditing for Fraud."

TIMEKEEPING RECORDS

Employees paid by the hour or on various incentive systems require records of time, production, piecework, or other measures of the basis for their pay. (Salaried employees do not require such detail records.) Timekeeping or similar records are collected in a variety of ways. The old-fashioned time clock is still used. It accepts an employee's time card and imprints the time when work started and ended. More sophisticated computer systems perform the same function without the paper time card. Production employees may clock in for various jobs or production processes in the system for assigning labor cost to various stages of production. These records are part of the cost accounting for production labor.

Timekeeping records should be approved by supervisors. This approval is a sign that employees actually worked the hours (or produced the output) reported to the payroll department. The payroll department should find a supervisor's signature or initials on the documents used as the basis for periodic pay. In computer systems, this approval may be automatic by virtue of the supervisory passwords used to input data into a computerized payroll system.

PAYROLL REGISTER

The payroll "register" is a special journal. It typically contains a row for each employee with columns for the gross regular pay, gross overtime pay, income tax withheld, Social Security tax withheld, other deductions, and net pay. The net pay amount usually is transferred from the general bank account to a special imprest payroll bank account. The journal entry for the transfer of net payroll, for example, is:

Payroll Bank Account	25,774	
General Bank Account		25,774

The payroll check amounts are accumulated to create the payroll posting to the general ledger, like this example:

Wages Clearing Account	40,265	
Employee Income Taxes Payable		7,982
Employee Social Security Payable		3,080
Health Insurance Premium Payable		2,100
Life Insurance Premium Payable		1,329
Payroll Bank Account		25,774

The payroll register is the primary original record for payroll accounting. It contains the implicit assertions that the employees are real company personnel (existence assertion), they worked the time or production for which they were paid (rights/ownership assertion), the amount of the pay is calculated properly (valuation assertion), and all the employees were paid (completeness assertion). The presentation and disclosure assertion depends on the labor cost analysis explained below.

Payroll department records also contain the canceled checks (or a similar electronic deposit record). The checks will contain the employees' endorsements on the back.

LOOK AT THE ENDORSEMENTS

An assistant accountant was instructed to "look at" the endorsements on the back of a sample of canceled payroll checks.

She noticed three occurrences of the payee's signature followed by a second signature. Although scrawled almost illegibly, the second signatures were identical and were later identified as the payroll accountant's handwriting. The payroll accountant had taken unclaimed checks and converted (stolen) them. When cashing these "third-party checks," banks and stores had required the payroll accountant to produce identification and endorse the checks that already had been "endorsed" by the employee payee.

The Lesson: Second endorsements are a red flag.

LABOR COST ANALYSIS

The cost accounting department can receive its information in more than one way. Some companies have systems that independently report time and production work data from the production floor directly to the cost accounting department. Other companies let their cost accounting department receive labor cost data from the payroll department. When the data is received independently, it can be reconciled in quantity (time) or amount (dollars) with a report from the payroll department. This is a type of reconciliation to make sure the cost accounting department is using actual payroll data and that the payroll department is paying only for work performed.

The cost accounting department (or a similar accounting function) is responsible for the "cost distribution." This is the most important part of the presentation and disclosure assertion with respect to payroll. The cost distribution is an assignment of payroll to the accounts where it belongs for internal and external reporting. Using its input data, the cost accounting department may make a distribution entry like this:

Production Job A	14,364	
Production Job B	3,999	
Production Process A	10,338	
Selling Expense	8,961	
General and Administrative Expense	2,603	
Wages Clearing Account		40,265

Payroll data flows from the hiring process, through the timekeeping function, into the payroll department, then to the cost accounting department, and finally to the accounting entries that record the payroll for inventory cost determination and financial statement presentation. The same data is used for various governmental and tax reports.

BEWARE THE "CLEARING ACCOUNT"

"Clearing accounts" are temporary storage places for transactions awaiting final accounting. Like the Wages Clearing Account illustrated in the entries above, all clearing accounts should have zero balances after the accounting is completed.

A balance in a clearing account means that some amounts have not been classified properly in the accounting records. If the Wages Clearing Account has a debit balance, some labor cost has not been properly classified in the expense accounts or cost accounting classifications. If the Wages Clearing Account has a credit balance, the cost accountant has assigned more labor cost to expense accounts and cost accounting classifications than the amount actually paid.

GOVERNMENTAL AND TAX REPORTS

Payroll systems have complications introduced by the federal income and Social Security tax laws. Several reports are produced. These can be used by auditors in tests of controls and substantive test of the balances produced by accumulating numerous payroll transactions.

Year-To-Date Earnings Records

The year-to-date (YTD) earnings records are the cumulative subsidiary records of each employee's gross pay, deductions, and net pay. Each time a periodic payroll is produced, the YTD earnings records are updated for the new information. The YTD earnings records are a subsidiary ledger of the wages and salaries cost and expense in the financial statements. Theoretically, like any subsidiary and control account relationship, their sum (e.g., the gross pay amounts) should be equal to the costs and expenses in the financial statements. The trouble with this reconciliation idea is that there are usually many payroll cost/expense accounts in a company's chart of accounts. The production wages may be scattered about in several different accounts, such as inventory (work in process and finished goods), selling, general, and administrative expenses. However, these YTD records provide the data for periodic governmental tax forms. They can be reconciled to the tax reports.

Government Payroll Tax Report

Federal Form 941 is the payroll tax report that summarizes a total amount paid to employees during each three-month period. It also summarizes the income tax withheld and provides a place to calculate the Social Security and Medicare taxes due (employee and employer shares). This is a quarterly report, although employer's deposits of withheld taxes into government accounts may be required more often according to IRS regulations. The YTD records provide the data for Form 941, but the form itself does not list individual employees and their amounts of earnings and taxes. If this report is filed electronically, the basic report data are available in magnetic form.

Federal Form 940 is the employer's annual federal unemployment (FUTA) tax return. It requires a report of the total amount (but not the detail by employee) of wages subject to the unemployment tax, calculation of the tax, and payment. State unemployment tax returns may differ from state to state. Some states require a schedule showing each employee's name, Social Security identification number, and amount of earnings. These details can be compared to the company's YTD earnings records.

Companies in financial difficulty have been known to try to postpone payment of employee taxes withheld. However, the consequences can be serious. IRS can and will padlock the business and seize the assets for nonpayment. After all, the withheld taxes belong to the employee's accounts with the government, and the employers are obligated to pay over the amounts withheld from employees along with a matching share for the Social Security and Medicare taxes.

Employee W-2 Reports
The W-2 is the annual report of gross salaries and wages and the income, Social Security, and Medicare taxes withheld. Copies are filed with the Social Security Administration and IRS, and copies are sent to employees for use in preparing their income tax returns. The W-2s contain the annual YTD accumulations for each employee. They also contain the employees' address and Social Security identifying number. Auditors can use the name, address, Social Security number, and dollar amounts in certain procedures (described later) to obtain evidence about the existence of the employees. The W-2s can be reconciled to the payroll tax reports.

CONTROL RISK ASSESSMENT

The major risks in the payroll cycle are:
- Paying fictitious "employees" (invalid transactions, employees do not exist)
- Overpaying for time or production (inaccurate transactions, improper valuation)
- Incorrect accounting for costs and expenses (incorrect classification, improper or inconsistent presentation and disclosure)

The assessment of payroll system control risk normally takes on added importance because most companies have fairly elaborate and well-controlled personnel and payroll functions. The transactions in this cycle are numerous during the year yet result in small amounts in balance sheet accounts at year-end. Therefore, in most audit engagements, the review of controls and test of controls audit of transaction details constitute the major portion of the evidence gathered for these accounts. On most audits, the substantive audit procedures devoted to auditing the payroll-related account balances are very limited.

GENERAL CONTROL CONSIDERATIONS

Control procedures for proper segregation of responsibilities should be in place and operating. By referring to Exhibit 10-1, you can see that proper segregation involves authorization (personnel department hiring and firing, pay rate and deduction authorizations) by persons who do not have payroll preparation, paycheck distribution, or reconciliation duties. Payroll distribution (custody) is in the hands of persons who do not authorize employees' pay rates or time, nor prepare the payroll checks. Recordkeeping is performed by payroll and cost accounting personnel who do not make authorizations or distribute pay. Combinations of two or more of the duties of authorization, payroll preparation and recordkeeping, and payroll distribution in one person, one office, or one computerized system may open the door for errors, irregularities, and frauds.

In addition, the control system should provide for detail control checking activities. For example: (1) periodic comparison of the payroll register to the personnel department files to check hiring authorizations and terminated employees not deleted, (2) periodic rechecking of wage rate and deduction authorizations, (3) reconciliation of time and production paid to cost accounting calculations, (4) quarterly reconciliation of YTD earnings records with tax returns, and (5) payroll bank account reconciliation.

Computer-based Payroll
Complex computer systems to gather payroll data, calculate payroll amounts, print checks, and transfer electronic deposits are found in many companies. Even though the technology is complex, the basic management and control

functions of ensuring a flow of data to the payroll department should be in place. Various paper records and approval signatures may not exist. They may all be imbedded in computerized payroll systems. Matters of auditing in a complex computer environment will need to be considered.

Internal Control Questionnaire
Information about the payroll cycle control structure often is gathered initially by completing an internal control questionnaire (ICQ). Auditors use extensive questionnaires on every audit.

DETAIL TEST OF CONTROLS AUDIT PROCEDURES

An organization should have detail control activities in place and operating to prevent, detect, and correct accounting errors. Exhibit 10-2 expresses the general control objectives with specific examples related to payroll.

EXHIBIT 10-2 Control Objectives (Personnel and payroll cycle)

General Objectives	Examples of Specific Objectives
1. Recorded payroll transactions are *valid* and documented.	Payroll accounting separated from personnel and timekeeping.
	Time cards indicate approval by supervisor's signature.
	Payroll files compared to personnel files periodically.
2. Valid payroll transactions are *recorded* and *none are omitted*.	Employees' complaints about paychecks investigated and resolved (written records maintained and reviewed by internal auditors).

EXHIBIT 10-2 Control Objectives (Personnel and payroll cycle) Continued

General Objectives	Examples of Specific Objectives
3. Payroll names, rates, hours, and deductions are *authorized*.	Names of new hires or terminations reported immediately in writing to payroll by the personnel department. Authorization for deductions kept on file. Rate authorized by union contract, agreement, or written policy and approved by personnel officer.
4. Payroll computations contain *accurate* gross pay, deductions, and net pay.	Payroll computations checked by person independent of preparation. Totals of payroll register reconciled to totals of payroll distribution by cost accounting.
5. Payroll transactions are *classified* correctly as direct or indirect labor or other expenses.	Employee classification reviewed periodically. Overall charges to indirect labor compared to direct labor and total product costs periodically.
6. Payroll transaction accounting and posting is complete.	Details of employee withholding reconciled periodically to liability control accounts and tax returns. Employee tax expense and liabilities prepared in conjunction with payroll.
7. Payroll costs and expenses are recorded in the *proper period*.	Month-end accruals reviewed by internal auditors. Payroll computed, paid, and booked in timely manner.

Auditors can perform detail test of controls audit procedures to determine whether controls that are said to be in place and operating actually are being performed properly by company personnel. A **detail test of control procedure** consists of (1) identification of the data population from which a sample of items will be selected for audit and (2) an expression of the action that will be taken to produce relevant evidence. In general, the *actions* in detail test of control audit procedures involve vouching, tracing, observing, scanning, and recalculating. If personnel in the organization are not performing their control activities very well, auditors will need to design additional procedures to try to detect whether control failures have produced payments to fictitious employees, overpayments for time or production, or incorrect accounting for costs and expenses.

Exhibit 10-3 contains a selection of detail test of controls audit procedures for auditing controls over payroll. Most of the illustrative procedures involve manual records, and B-5 refers to computerized systems. The samples are usually attribute samples, although payroll testing also can be designed in terms of variables sampling for substantive evidence of dollar errors and irregularities. On the right, Exhibit 10-3 shows the control objectives tested by the audit procedures.

EXHIBIT 10-3 Test of Controls Audit Procedures for Payroll

	Control Objective
A. Personnel Files and Compensation Documents	
1. Select a sample of personnel files:	
a. Review personnel files for complete information on employment date, authority to add to payroll, job classification, wage rate, and authorized deductions.	Authorization Classification Authorization
b. Trace pay rate to union contracts or other rate authorization. Trace salaries to directors' minutes for authorization.	Authorization
c. Trace pay rate and deduction information to payroll department files used in payroll preparation.	Completeness
2. Obtain copies of pension plans, stock options, profit sharing, and bonus plans. Review and extract relevant portions that relate to payroll deductions, fringe benefit expenses, accrued liabilities, and financial statement disclosure.	Validity Completeness Authorization Accuracy Acctg/posting

EXHIBIT 10-3 Test of Controls Audit Procedures for Payroll
　　　　　　Continued

	Control Objective
B. Payroll	
1. Select a sample of payroll register entries:	
a. Vouch employee identification, pay rate, and deductions to personnel files or other authorizations.	Authorization
b. Vouch hours worked to clock time cards and supervisor's approval.	Validity Authorization
c. Recalculate gross pay, deductions, net pay.	Accuracy
d. Recalculate a selection of periodic payrolls.	Accuracy
e. Vouch to canceled payroll check.	Accuracy
Examine employees' endorsement.	Validity
2. Select a sample of clock time cards. Note supervisor's approval and trace to periodic payroll registers.	Authorization Completeness
3. Vouch a sample of periodic payroll totals to payroll bank account transfer vouchers and vouch payroll bank account deposit slip for cash transfer.	Acctg/posting
4. Trace a sample of employees' payroll entries to individual payroll records maintained for tax reporting purposes. Reconcile total of employees' payroll records with payrolls paid for the year.	Completeness Accuracy
5. Review computer-printed error messages for evidence of the use of check digits, valid codes, limit tests, and other input, processing, and output application controls. Investigate correction and resolution of errors.	Accuracy Validity
6. Trace payroll information to management reports and to general ledger account postings.	Acctg/posting
7. Obtain control of a periodic payroll and conduct a surprise distribution of paychecks.	Validity

**EXHIBIT 10-3   Test of Controls Audit Procedures for Payroll
   Continued**

	Control Objective
C. Cost Distribution Reports	
1. Select a sample of cost accounting analyses of payroll:	
a. Reconcile periodic totals with payroll payments for the same periods.	Completeness
b. Vouch to time records.	Validity
2. Trace cost accounting labor cost distributions to management reports and postings in general ledger and subsidiary account(s).	Acctg/posting Classification
3. Select a sample of labor cost items in (a) ledger accounts and/or (b) management reports. Vouch to supporting cost accounting analyses.	Validity

DIRECTION OF THE TEST OF CONTROLS PROCEDURES

The test of controls procedures in Exhibit 10-3 are designed to test the payroll accounting in two directions. One is the *completeness direction*, in which the control performance of audit interest is the matching of personnel file content to payroll department files and the payroll register. Exhibit 10-4 shows that the sample for this direction is taken from the population of personnel files. The procedures trace the personnel department authorizations to the payroll department files (procedure A-1-c).

The other direction is the *validity direction* of the test. The control performance of interest is the preparation of the payroll register. Exhibit 10-4 shows that the sample for this test is from the completed payroll registers. The individual payroll calculations are vouched to the personnel files (procedure B-1-a).

EXHIBIT 10-4 Dual Direction Test of Payroll Controls

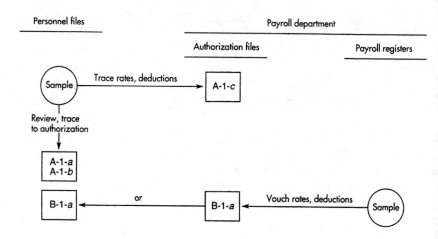

COVERT SURVEILLANCE

This sounds like spy work, and it indeed has certain elements of it.

Auditors can test controls over employees' clocking into work shifts by making personal observations of the process--observing whether anybody clocks in with two time cards or with two or more electronic entries, or leaves the premises after clocking in.

The auditors need to be careful not to make themselves obvious. Standing around in a manufacturing plant at 6 A.M. in the standard blue pinstripe suit uniform is as good as printing "Beware of Auditor" on your forehead. People then will be on their best behavior, and you will observe nothing unusual.

Find an unobtrusive observation post. Stay out of sight. Use a video camera. Get a knowledgeable office employee to accompany you to interpret various activities. Perform an observation that has a chance of producing evidence of improper behavior.

OVERT SURVEILLANCE
Surprise Payroll Distribution

Auditors may perform a surprise observation of a payroll distribution in connection with tests for overstatement. Such an observation involves taking control of paychecks and accompanying a company representative as the distribution takes place. The auditor is careful to see that each employee is identified and that only one check is given to each individual. Unclaimed checks are controlled, and in this manner the auditor hopes to detect any fictitious persons on the payroll. Auditors need to be extremely careful to notice any duplication of employee identification or instance of one person attempting to pick up two or more checks.

SUMMARY: CONTROL RISK ASSESSMENT

The audit manager or senior accountant in charge of the audit should evaluate the evidence obtained from an understanding of the internal control system and from the test of controls audit procedures. If the control risk is assessed very low, the substantive audit procedures on the account balances can be limited in cost-saving ways. As examples: a surprise payroll distribution may be considered unnecessary; the auditors may decide it is appropriate to place considerable reliance on management reports generated by the payroll system.

On the other hand, if tests of controls reveal weaknesses, improper segregation of duties, inaccurate cost reports, inaccurate tax returns, or lax personnel policies, then substantive procedures will need to be designed to lower the risk of failing to detect material error in the financial statements. The problem in payroll is that the irregularities of paying fictitious employees and overpaying for fraudulent time records do not normally misstate the financial statements as long as the improper payments are expensed. (The losses are expensed, as they should be!) The only misstatement is failing to distinguish and disclose "payroll fraud losses" from legitimate wages expense and cost of goods sold, but such losses are usually immaterial in a single year's financial statements, anyway. Nevertheless, auditors habitually perform procedures designed to find payroll fraud. It is more of a service to clients than a crucial part of the effort to detect material misstatements in financial statements.

AUDIT CASES: SUBSTANTIVE AUDIT PROCEDURES

The audit of account balances consists of procedural efforts to detect errors, irregularities, and frauds that might exist in the balances, thus making them misleading in financial statements. If such misstatements exist, they are characterized by the following features:

Method: A cause of the misstatement (accidental error, intentional irregularity or fraud attempt), which usually is made easier by some kind of failure of controls.

Paper trail: A set of telltale signs of erroneous accounting, missing or altered documents, or a "dangling debit" (the false or erroneous debit that results from an overstatement of assets).

Amount: The dollar amount of overstated assets and revenue, or understated liabilities and expenses.

Each audit program for the audit of an account balance or class of transactions like payroll contains an audit approach that may enable auditors to detect errors, irregularities, and frauds. Each application of procedures contains these elements:

Audit objective: A recognition of a financial statement *assertion* for which evidence needs to be obtained. The assertions are about existence of assets, liabilities, revenues, and expenses; their valuation; their complete inclusion in the account balances; the rights and obligations inherent in them, and; their proper presentation and disclosure in the financial statements.

Control: A recognition of the control activities that *should be* used in an organization to prevent and detect errors and irregularities.

Test of controls: Ordinary and extended procedures *designed to produce evidence about the effectiveness of the controls* that should be in operation.

Audit of balance: Ordinary and extended *substantive procedures designed to find signs* of errors, irregularities, and frauds in account balances and classes of transactions.

The next portion of this chapter consists of two cases that first set the stage with a story about an error, irregularity, or fraud--its method, paper trail (if any), and amount. This part of each case gives you the "inside story," which auditors seldom know before they perform the audit work. The second part of each case, under the heading of the "audit approach," tells a structured story about the audit objective, desirable controls, test of control procedures, audit of balance procedures, and discovery summary. The audit approach segment illustrates the manner in which audit procedures can be applied and the discoveries they may enable auditors to make. At the end of the chapter, some similar discussion cases are presented, and you can write the audit approach to test your ability to design audit procedures for the detection of errors, irregularities, and frauds.

CASE 10.1
TIME CARD FORGERIES

Problem
False claims for work time caused the overpayment of wages.

Method
A personnel leasing agency assigned Nurse Jane to work at County Hospital. She claimed payroll hours on agency time cards, which showed approval signatures of a hospital nursing shift supervisor. The shift supervisor had been terminated by the county several months prior to the periods covered by the time cards in question. Nurse Jane worked one or two days per week but submitted time cards for a full 40-hour workweek.

The leasing agency paid Nurse Jane, then billed County Hospital for the wages and benefits. Supporting documents were submitted with the leasing agency's bills.

Paper Trail
Each hospital work station keeps ward shift logs, which are sign-in sheets showing nurses on duty at all times. Nurses sign in and sign out when going on and going off duty.

County Hospital maintains personnel records showing, among other things, the period of employment of its own nurses, supervisors, and other employees.

Amount
Nurse Jane's wages and benefits were billed to the hospital at $22 per hour. False time cards overcharging about 24 extra hours per week cost the hospital $528 per week. Nurse Jane was assigned to County Hospital for 15 weeks during the year, so she caused overcharges of about $7,900. However, she told three of her crooked friends about the procedure, and they overcharged the hospital another $24,000.

AUDIT APPROACH

Audit Objective
Obtain evidence to determine whether wages were paid to valid employees for actual time worked at the authorized pay rate.

Control
Control activities should include a hiring authorization putting employees on the payroll. When leased employees are used, this authorization includes contracts for nursing time, conditions of employment, and terms including the contract reimbursement rate. Control records of attendance and work should be kept (ward shift log). Supervisors should approve time cards or other records used by the payroll department to prepare paychecks.

In this case, the contract with the leasing agency provided that approved time cards had to be submitted as supporting documentation for the agency billings.

Test of Controls
Although the procedures and documents for control were in place, the controls did not operate because nobody at the hospital ever compared the ward shift logs to time cards, and nobody examined the supervisory approval signatures for their validity. The scam was easy in the leasing agency situation because the nurses submitted their own time cards to the agency for payment. The same scam might be operated by the hospital's own employees if they, too, could write their time
cards and submit them to the payroll department.

Auditors should make inquiries (e.g., internal control questionnaire) about the error-checking activities performed by hospital accounting personnel. Test of control audit procedures are designed to determine whether control procedures are followed properly by the organization. Since the comparison and checking activities were not performed, there is nothing to test.

However, the substantive tests described below are identical to the procedures that could be called "tests of controls," but in this case they are performed to determine whether nurses were paid improperly (a substantive purpose).

Audit of Balances
Select a sample of leasing agency billings and their supporting documentation (time cards). Vouch rates billed by the agency to the contract for agreement to proper rate. Vouch time claimed to hospital work attendance records (ward shift logs). Obtain handwriting examples of supervisors' signatures and compare them to the approval signatures on time cards. Use personnel records to determine whether supervisors were actually employed by the hospital at the time they approved the time cards. Use available work attendance records to determine whether supervisors were actually on duty at the time they approved the time cards.

Discovery Summary
The auditors quickly found that Nurse Jane (and others) had not signed-in on ward shift logs for days they claimed to have worked. Further investigation showed that the supervisors who supposedly signed the time cards were not even employed by the hospital at the time their signatures were used for approvals. Handwriting comparison showed that the signatures were not written by the supervisors.

The leasing agency was informed and refunded the $31,900 overpayment proved by the auditors. The auditors continued to comb the records for more!

(Adapted from vignette published in *Internal Auditor*, April 1990.)

CASE 10.2
CLEVERLY HIDDEN PAYCHECKS

Problem
Embezzlement with fictitious people on the payroll.

Method
Betty Ruth processed personnel files for RD-Mart, a large
retail chain of clothing stores with about 6,400 employees in
233 store locations. She created fictitious files for fictitious
employees and notified the outside payroll processing service
of their names, addresses, social security numbers, salaries,
and deductions. The payroll service prepared the paychecks
and delivered them to Martha Lee in the accounting
department. Martha Lee placed the paychecks in overnight
express envelopes for delivery to the managers at RD-Mart's
46 stores in the Southeast Region. However, Martha Lee first
removed the fictitious paychecks. (Betty Ruth and Martha Lee
were long-time high school friends and conspirators in the
fraud.)

Martha Lee hired a print shop to print a private stock of
checks on the RD-Mart payroll bank account. These checks
looked exactly like the real payroll checks and were in the
payroll service's numerical sequence. After removing the
paychecks payable to the fictitious employees, Martha Lee and
Betty Ruth selected the checks with the same numbers from
their private stock. They then made the checks payable to
themselves in the proper net amount and deposited them in
their own bank accounts. For a signature, they bought a rubber
stamp that looked enough like the RD-Mart machine signature
to fool the bank.

Paper Trail
Payroll creates a large paper trail with individual earnings
records, W-2 tax forms, payroll deductions for taxes and
insurance, and Form 941 payroll tax reports. Betty Ruth's

fictitious employees were included in all these reports. Their
W-2 forms were mailed to a variety of addresses--some to post
office box numbers (rented by Martha Lee), and some to the
conspirators' own addresses. (The conspirators even prepared
federal income tax returns for the ghosts.)

RD-Mart's payroll bank account was truncated; that is, the
bank submitted a statement showing the check number and
amount of each paycheck but did not return the canceled
checks. The bank reconciler (a person in the treasurer's office)
was able to correspond the cleared check numbers and amounts
to the payroll service report of check numbers and amounts.
Nobody in the RD-Mart offices saw the canceled checks made
payable to Betty Ruth and Martha Lee.

Amount
The conspirators embezzled about $200,000 each year (one
$340 weekly gross paycheck alternating among 11-12 of the
Southeast Region stores all year). This was about two-tenths of
1 percent of the total RD-Mart payroll cost.

AUDIT APPROACH

Objective
Obtain evidence of the existence and validity of payroll
transactions.

Control
Different people should be responsible for hiring (preparing
personnel files), approving wages, preparing paychecks, and
distributing the checks. This segregation of duties was evident
in the RD-Mart offices. The company had prescribed activities
for authorizing personnel hires, personnel file preparation,
paycheck production, and check delivery. However, the store
managers did not receive any detail reports of employees paid,
so they had no post-payment opportunity to review their own
payrolls.

Test of Controls

Audit for transaction authorization and validity. A sample taken from the payroll service payroll registers can be vouched to personnel files. Since Betty Ruth had prepared authentic personnel files, this procedure will not show any exceptions. Likewise, a selection of personnel files traced to the payroll reports would show that all the people were paid.

Audit of Balance

The "balance" to audit is the accumulated total of payroll transactions. Analytical procedures will not show the total out of line with history because the fraud is small in relation to total payroll. The audit procedure to determine existence of the people is a surprise payroll distribution. A small selection of stores might not include one with a fictitious employee at the time of the observation. (Betty Ruth might be smart enough to "fire" the fictitious employees when the auditors are expected.)

If the intent is to search for fictitious employees, several computer-based screening methods can be employed: (1) run all the employee Social Security numbers through a program designed to find unissued numbers, (2) run a test to report all employees using the same address or telephone number, (3) run a report of employees who elect minimum insurance or pension deductions, (4) run a report of all employees using P.O. box addresses, (5) examine these reports to determine whether employees appear on one or more of them. If "suspects" appear, request the bank to send copies of the front and back of the canceled payroll checks.

Discovery Summary

The computer-generated search procedures turned up 300 suspect employees, of which 22 turned out to be the conspirators' ghosts. (They were ones with false Social Security numbers whose addresses were the same as Betty Ruth's and Martha Lee's homes.) The auditors requested these checks from the bank and quickly found the names on the checks not the same as the names in the payroll register. They identified the conspirators. Further investigation and covert observation of Martha Lee removing the paychecks established guilt. Further investigation by the district attorney obtained their bank accounts and revealed the deposits of the ill-gotten embezzlement gains.

SUMMARY

Payroll is a part of every business and an important part of every production cycle. Management and control of labor costs are important. The payroll cycle consists of hiring, rate authorization, attendance and work supervision, payroll processing, and paycheck distribution.

Payroll information systems produce many internal documents, reports, and files. A dozen or more of these sources of audit information are described in the chapter. This cycle is characterized by having mostly internal documentation as evidence and having relatively little external documentary evidence. The accounts in the payroll cycle are intangible. They cannot be observed, inspected, touched, or counted in any meaningful way. Most audit procedures for this cycle are analytical procedures and dual-purposes procedures that test both the company's control activities and the existence, valuation, and completeness assertions made by accumulating the results of numerous labor transactions.

Payroll accounting is a critical operation for expenditure control. Many cases of embezzlement occur in this process. Illustrative cases in the chapter tell the stories of some fictitious employee and false time embezzlements and thefts.

PRACTICAL CASE PROBLEM
INSTRUCTIONS FOR THE CASE

This case is designed like the ones in the chapter. It gives the problem, the method, the paper trail, and the amount. Your assignment is to write the "audit approach" portion of the case, organized around these sections:

Objective: Express the objective in terms of the facts supposedly asserted in financial records, accounts, and statements.

Control: Write a brief explanation of desirable controls, missing controls, and especially the kinds of "deviations" that might arise from the situation described in the case.

Test of controls: Write some procedures for getting evidence about existing controls, especially procedures that could discover deviations from controls. If there are no controls to test, then there are no procedures to perform; go then to the next section. A "procedure" should instruct someone about the source(s) of evidence to tap and the work to do.

Audit of balance: Write some procedures for getting evidence about the existence, completeness, valuation, ownership, or disclosure assertions identified in your *objective* section above.

Discovery summary: Write a short statement about the discovery you expect to accomplish with your procedures.

* * * * * * * * * *

CASE # 10.1: PAYROLL IN THE BLUE SKY--Inadequate Payroll Time Records. Write the "audit approach" section like the cases in the chapter.

Problem: SueCan Corporation deferred costs under the heading of defense contract claims for reimbursement and deferred tooling labor costs, thus overstating assets, understating cost of goods sold, and overstating income.

Method: SueCan manufactured electronic and other equipment for private customers and government defense contracts. Near the end of the year, the company used a journal entry to remove $110,000 from cost of goods sold and defer it as deferred tooling cost. This $110,000 purported to be labor cost associated with preparing tools and dies for long production runs.

The company opened a receivables account for "cost overrun reimbursement receivable" as a claim for reimbursement on defense contracts ($378,000).

Paper trail: The company altered the labor time records for the tooling costs in an effort to provide substantiating documentation. Company employees prepared new work orders numbered in the series used late in the fiscal year and attached labor time records dated much earlier in the year. The production orders originally charged with the labor cost were left completed but with no labor charges!

The claim for reimbursement on defense contracts did not have documentation specifically identifying the labor costs as being related to the contract. There were no work orders. (Auditors know that defense department auditors insist on documentation and justification before approving such a claim.)

Amount: SueCan reported net income of about $442,000 for the year, an overstatement of approximately 60 percent.

CHAPTER 11
COST ACCOUNTING

The production accounting cycle covers the activities related to internal cost accounting for manufacture of products. This chapter contains sections on (1) typical control activities in the cycle, (2) the audit evidence available in management reports and files, (3) control risk assessment (including detail test of controls procedures), and (4) case story-style explanations concerning discovery of errors, irregularities, and frauds.

PRODUCTION CYCLE TYPICAL ACTIVITIES

The basic production activities start with production planning, including inventory planning and management. Production planning can range from use of a sophisticated computerized long-range plan with just-in-time (JIT) inventory management to a simple ad hoc method ("Hey, Joe, we got an order today. Go make 10 units!") Exhibit 11-1 shows the activities and accounting involved in a production cycle. As you follow the exhibit, you can track the elements of a control system described in the sections below.

Most businesses try to estimate or forecast sales levels and seasonal timing, and they try to plan facilities and production schedules to meet customer demand. As shown in Exhibit 11-1, the production cycle interacts with the acquisition cycle (Chapter 9) and the payroll cycle (Chapter 10) for the acquisition of fixed assets, materials, supplies, overhead, and labor.

The physical output of a production cycle is inventory (starting with raw materials, proceeding to work in process, then to finished goods). Most matters of auditing inventory and physical inventory-taking are explained in Chapter 9. Exhibit 11-1 shows the connection of inventory to the revenue and collection cycle (Chapter 8) in terms of orders and deliveries.

EXHIBIT 11-1 Production Cycle

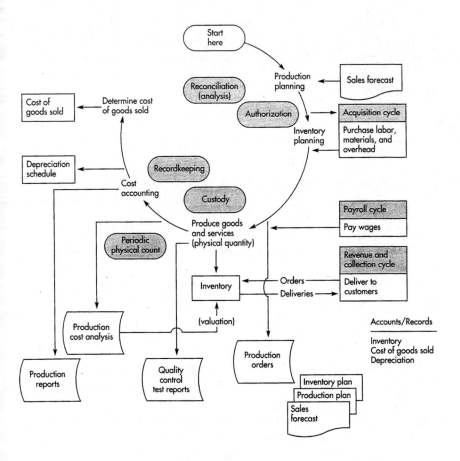

Most of the "transactions" in a production cycle are cost accounting allocations, unit cost determinations, and standard cost calculations. These are internal transactions produced entirely within the company's accounting system. Exhibit 11-1 shows the elements of depreciation cost calculation, cost of goods sold determination, and job cost analysis as examples of these transactions.

AUTHORIZATION

The overall production authorization starts with production planning, which usually is based on a **sales forecast**. Production planning interacts with inventory planning to produce **production orders**. These production orders specify the materials and labor required and the timing for the start and end of production. Managers in the sales/marketing department and production department usually sign off their approval on plans and production orders.

Authorization also can include plans and approvals for subcontracting work to other companies. The process of taking bids and executing contracts can be a part of the planning-authorization system.

The production order usually includes a **bill of materials** (a specification of the materials authorized for the production). This bill of materials is the source of authorization for the preparation of **materials requisitions**, and these requisitions are the authorization for the inventory custodian to release raw materials and supplies to the production personnel. These documents are the inventory recordkeepers' authorizations to update the raw materials inventory files to record the reductions of the raw materials inventory.

Later, when production is complete, the production reports, along with the physical units and the quality control test reports, are the authorizations for the finished goods inventory custodian to place the units in the finished goods inventory. These same documents are the inventory recordkeepers' authorization to update the inventory record files to record the additions to the finished goods inventory.

CUSTODY

Supervisors and workers, skilled and unskilled, have physical custody of materials, equipment, and labor while the production work is performed. They can requisition materials from the raw materials inventory, assign people to jobs, and control the pace of work. In a sense, they have custody of a "moving inventory." The work in process (an inventory category) is literally "moving" and changing form in the process of being transformed from raw materials into finished goods.

Control over this custody is more difficult than control over a closed warehouse full of raw materials or finished goods. Control can be exercised by holding supervisers and workers accountable for the use of materials specified in the production orders, for the timely completion of production, and for the quality of the finished goods. This accountability can be achieved with good cost accounting, cost analysis, and quality control testing.

RECORDKEEPING (COST ACCOUNTING)

When production is completed, production orders and the related records of material and labor used are sent forward to the cost accounting department. Since these accounting documents may come from the production workers, the effective separation of the recordkeeping function depends upon its receiving independent notices from other places, especially notifications of materials issued from the inventory custodian and the labor costs assigned by the payroll department.

The cost accounting department produces analyses of cost-per-unit, standard cost, and variances. Cost accounting also may determine the allocation of overhead to production in general, to production orders, and to finished units. Depending on the design of the company's cost accounting system, these costs are used in inventory valuation and ultimately in determination of the cost of goods sold. In many cases, the cost accounting department also is responsible for calculating the depreciation of fixed assets and the amortization of intangibles.

OVERHEAD ALLOCATION

The cost accounting department at Pointed Publications, Inc., routinely allocated overhead to book printing runs at the rate of 40 percent of materials and labor cost. The debit was initially to the finished books inventory, while the credit went to an "overhead allocated" account that was offset against other entries in the cost of goods sold calculation, which included all the actual overhead incurred. During the year, 10 million books were produced and $40 million of overhead was allocated to them. The auditors noticed that actual overhead expenditures were $32 million, and 3 million books remained in the ending inventory.

This finding resulted in the conclusion that the inventory was overstated by $2.4 million, the cost of goods sold was understated by $2.4 million, and the income before taxes was overstated by 8.2 percent.

	Company Accounting	Proper Accounting
Books produced	10 million	10 million
Labor and materials cost	$100 million	$100 million
Overhead allocated	$ 40 million	$ 32 million
Cost per book	$14.00	$13.20
	-------------	-------------
Cost of goods sold:		
Labor and materials cost	$100 million	$100 million
Overhead allocated		
to books	40 million	
Overhead incurred	32 million	32 million
Overhead credited to cost	(40 million)	
Ending inventory	(42 million)	(39.6 million)
	-------------	-------------
Total cost of goods sold	$90 million	$92.4 million

PERIODIC RECONCILIATION

The function of periodic reconciliation generally refers to comparison of actual assets and liabilities to the amounts recorded in the company accounts (e.g., comparing the physical count of inventory to the perpetual inventory records, comparing vendors' monthly statements to the recorded accounts payable). Exhibit 11-1 shows the periodic reconciliation of physical inventory to recorded amounts. The features and audit considerations of this reconciliation are covered in Chapter 9. The work-in-process inventory also can be observed, although the "count" of partially completed units is very judgmental. It can be costed at the labor, materials, and overhead assigned to its stage of completion. Most other periodic reconciliations in the production cycle take the form of analyses of internal information. These analyses include costing the production orders, comparing the cost to prior experience or to standard costs, and determining lower-of-cost-or-market (LCM) valuations. In a sense, the LCM calculations are a "reconciliation" of product cost to the external market price of product units.

AUDIT EVIDENCE IN MANAGEMENT REPORTS AND FILES

Most production accounting systems produce timely reports managers need to supervise and control production. These reports can be used by auditors as supporting evidence for assertions about work-in-process and finished goods inventories and about cost of goods sold. Auditors should obtain and use these reports.

SALES FORECAST

Management's sales forecast provides the basis for several aspects of business planning, notably the planning of production and inventory levels. If the auditors want to use the forecast for substantive audit decisions, some work to obtain assurance about its reasonableness needs to be performed. This work is not an examination or compilation of a forecast as contemplated by the attestation services standards. All the auditors need to accomplish is to learn about the assumptions built into the forecast for the purpose of ascertaining their reasonableness. In addition, some work on the mechanical accuracy of the forecast should be performed to avoid an embarrassing reliance on faulty calculations.

Forecasts can be used in connection with knowing management's plans for the year under audit, most of which will have already passed when the audit work begins. It will help the auditors understand the nature and volume of production orders and the level of materials inventory. Forecasts of the following year can be used in connection with valuing the inventory at lower-of-cost-or-market (e.g., slow-moving and potentially obsolete inventory), which influences the amount of cost of goods sold that is shown in the financial statements. Special care must be taken with using the forecast for the next year in connection with inventory valuation because an overly optimistic forecast can lead to a failure to write down inventory, accelerate the depreciation of fixed assets, and account for more cost of goods sold.

THE SALY FORECAST

The auditors were reviewing the inventory items that had not been issued for 30 days or more, considering the need to write some items down to market lower than cost. The production manager showed them the SALY forecast that indicated continuing need for the materials in products that are expected to have reasonable demand. The auditors agreed that the forecasts supported the prediction of future sales of products at prices that would cover the cost of the slow-moving material items.

Unfortunately, they neglected to ask the meaning of SALY in the designation of the forecast. They did not learn that it means "Same As Last Year." It is not a forecast at all. The products did not sell at the prices expected, and the company experienced losses the following year that should have been charged to cost of goods sold earlier.

PRODUCTION PLANS AND REPORTS

Based on the sales forecast, management should develop a plan for the amount and timing of production. The production plan provides general information to the auditors, but the production orders and inventory plan associated with the production plan are even more important. The production orders carry the information about requirements for raw materials, labor, and overhead, including the requisitions for purchase and use of materials and labor. These documents are the initial authorizations for control of the inventory and production.

Production reports record the completion of production quantities. When coupled with the related cost accounting reports, they are the company's record of the cost of goods placed into the finished goods inventory. In most cases, auditors will audit the cost reports in connection with determining the cost valuation of inventory and cost of goods sold.

DEPRECIATION SCHEDULE

The cost accounting department may be charged with the responsibility to prepare a schedule of the depreciation of fixed assets. In many companies, such a schedule is long and complicated, involving large dollar amounts of asset cost and calculated depreciation expense. It is not unusual to find the amount of depreciation expense exceeding a company's net income. (In the statement of cash flows, the depreciation added back to calculate the cash flow from operations can be larger than the net income carried forward from the income statement.) An abbreviated illustration of a fixed asset and depreciation schedule is in the table below.

FIXED ASSETS AND DEPRECIATION

| | Asset Cost (000s) | | | | Accumulated Depreciation (000s) | | | |
Description	Beginning Balance	Added	Sold	Ending Balance	Beginning Balance	Added	Sold	Ending Balance
Land	10,000			10,000	·			
Bldg 1	30,000			30,000	6,857	857		7,714
Bldg 2		42,000		42,000		800		800
Computer A	5,000		5,000	0	3,750	208	3,958	0
Computer B		3,500		3,500		583		583
Press	1,500			1,500	300	150		450
Auto 1	15		15	0	15		15	0
Auto 2		22		22		2		2
Total	46,515	45,522	5,015	87,022	10,922	2,600	3,973	9,549

The depreciation schedule is audited by recalculating the depreciation expense, using the company's methods, estimates of useful life, and estimates of residual value. The asset acquisition and disposition information in the schedule gives the auditors some points of departure for auditing the asset additions and disposals. When the schedule covers hundreds of assets and numerous additions and disposals, auditors can (a) use computer auditing methods to recalculate the depreciation expense and (b) use sampling to choose additions and disposals for test of controls and substantive audit procedures. The beginning balances of assets and accumulated depreciation should be traced to the prior year's audit working papers. This schedule can be made into an audit working paper and placed in the auditor's files for future reference.

GAAP AND REGULATORY DEPRECIATION

U.S. West took a $5.4 *billion* pretax charge against earnings, wiping out over one-third of the shareholders' equity. In stock trading, U.S. West's share price *increased* 4 percent. Wall Street sent two messages: (1) the company should be rewarded for honest bookkeeping, and (2) its bookkeeping has not been very honest in recent years.

U.S. West changed its depreciation accounting for telecommunications equipment from the long lives required by rate regulation agencies to the shorter useful lives appropriate under GAAP. U.S. West reportedly got tired of reporting phony net earnings required by regulators and decided to report GAAP depreciation in its public financial statements. (The company must still use the regulatory depreciation when reporting to the rate regulation agencies.)

Other telecommunications companies are waiting for the regulators to approve the more appropriate depreciation deductions. However, the capital markets clearly approve of U.S. West's new depreciation bookkeeping.

THE LESSON: Auditors should consider carefully the rational basis for useful lives clients incorporate in depreciation calculations.

Source: *Forbes*, July 4, 1994.

CONTROL RISK ASSESSMENT

Control risk assessment is important because it governs the nature, timing, and extent of substantive audit procedures that will be applied in the audit of account balances in the production cycle. These account balances include:

- Inventory:
    - Raw materials.
    - Work in process.
    - Finished goods.
- Cost of goods sold.
- Depreciation:
    - Depreciation expense.
    - Accumulated depreciation.

Several aspects of the audit of purchased inventories and physical quantities are covered in Chapter 9 (acquisition and expenditure cycle). With respect to inventory valuation, this chapter points out the cost accounting function and its role in determining the cost valuation of manufactured finished goods.

GENERAL CONTROL CONSIDERATIONS

Control procedures for proper segregation of responsibilities should be in place and operating. By referring to Exhibit 11-1, you can see that proper segregation involves authorization (production planning and inventory planning) by persons who do not have custody, recording, or cost accounting and reconciliation duties. Custody of inventories (raw materials, work in process, and finished goods) is in the hands of persons who do not authorize the amount or timing of production or the purchase of materials and labor, or perform the cost accounting recordkeeping, or prepare cost analyses (reconciliations). Cost accounting (a recording function) is performed by persons who do not authorize production or have custody of assets in the process of production. However, you usually will find that the cost accountants prepare various analyses and reconciliations directly related to production activities. Combinations of two or more of the duties of authorization, custody, cost accounting in one person, one office, or one computerized system may open the door for errors, irregularities, and frauds.

In addition, the control structure should provide for detail control checking activities. For example: (1) production orders should contain a list of materials and their quantities, and they should be approved by a production planner/scheduler; (2) materials requisitions should be compared in the cost accounting department with the list of materials on the production order, and the materials requisitions should be signed by the production operator and the materials inventory storeskeeper; (3) labor time records on jobs should be signed by production supervisors, and the cost accounting department should reconcile these cost amounts with the labor report from the payroll department; (4) production reports of finished units should be signed by the production supervisor and finished goods inventory custodian then forwarded to cost accounting. These control operations track the raw materials and labor from start to finish in the production process. With each internal transaction, the responsibility and accountability for assets are passed from one person or location to another.

Complex computer systems to manage production and materials flow may be found in many companies. Even though the technology is complex, the basic management and control functions of ensuring the flow of labor and materials to production and the control of waste should be in place. Manual signatures and paper production orders and requisitions may not exist. They may all be imbedded in computer-controlled manufacturing systems. Matters of auditing in a complex computer environment will need to be considered.

OVERCHARGING THE GOVERNMENT

Government contracting periodically gets in the news when companies charge unrelated costs to government contracts of various kinds (e.g., defense production, research contracts). Although the production plans and orders do not specify allowable costs for building the company baseball field or paying for the president's kennel fees while on business trips, costs like these have found their way into government contract reimbursement claims. Government contract auditors have found them, and companies have incurred penalties and requirements to reimburse the costs wrongly charged. Some companies summarily fire cost accountants who engage in cost manipulation on government contracts (McDonnell Douglas Company). Other organizations suffer in the glare of adverse publicity (Northrop Corporation, Massachusetts Institute of Technology, Stanford University).

Internal Control Questionnaire
Information about the production cycle control structure often is gathered initially by completing an internal control questionnaire. Auditors use extensive questionnaires on every audit.

DETAIL TEST OF CONTROLS AUDIT PROCEDURES

An organization should have detail control activities in place and operating to prevent, detect, and correct accounting errors. Exhibit 11-2 expresses the general control objectives in specific examples related to production.

EXHIBIT 11-2 Internal Control Objectives (Production cycle)

General Objectives	Examples of Specific Objectives
1. Recorded production transactions are *valid* and documented.	Cost accounting separated from production, payroll, and inventory control. Material usage reports compared to raw material stores issue slips. Labor usage reports compared to job time tickets.
2. Valid production transactions are *recorded* and *none omitted*.	All documents prenumbered and numerical sequence reviewed.
3. Production transactions are *authorized*.	Material usage and labor usage prepared by foreman and approved by production supervisor.
4. Production job cost transactions computations contain *accurate* figures.	Job cost sheet entries reviewed by person independent of preparation. Costs of inventory used and labor used reviewed periodically.
5. Labor and materials are *classified* correctly as direct or indirect.	Production foreman required to account for all material and labor used as direct or indirect.
6. Production *accounting and posting* is complete.	Open job cost sheets periodically reconciled to the work-in-process inventory accounts.
7. Production transactions are recorded in the *proper period*.	Production reports of material and labor used prepared weekly and transmitted to cost accounting. Job cost sheets posted weekly and summary journal entries of work in process and work completed prepared monthly.

Auditors can perform detail test of controls audit procedures to determine whether controls that are said to be in place and operating actually are being performed properly by company personnel. A **detail test of control procedure** consists of (1) identification of the data population from which a sample of items will be selected for audit and (2) an expression of the action that will be taken to produce relevant evidence. In general, the *actions* in detail test of control audit procedures involve vouching, tracing, observing, scanning, and recalculating. A specification of such procedures is part of an audit program for obtaining evidence useful in a final control risk assessment. If personnel in the organization are not performing their control activities very well, auditors will need to design substantive audit procedures to try to detect whether control failures have produced materially misleading account balances.

Exhibit 11-3 contains a selection of detail test of controls audit procedures for auditing controls over the accumulation of costs for work-in-process inventory. This is the stage of "inventory" while it is in the production process. Upon completion, the accumulated costs become the cost valuation of the finished goods inventory. The illustrative procedures presume the existence of production cost reports that are updated as production takes place, labor reports that assign labor cost to the job, materials-used and materials requisitions charging raw materials to the production order, and overhead allocation calculations. Some or all of these documents may be in the form of computer records. The samples are usually attribute samples. On the right, Exhibit 11-3 shows the control objectives tested by the audit procedures.

EXHIBIT 11-3 Test of Controls Audit Procedures for Work-in-Progress Inventory

	Control Objective
1. Reconcile the open production cost reports to the work-in-process inventory control account.	Completeness
2. Select a sample of open and closed production cost reports:	
a. Recalculate all costs entered.	Accuracy
b. Vouch labor costs to labor reports.	Validity
c. Compare labor reports to summary of payroll.	Acctg/posting
d. Vouch material costs to issue slips and materials-used reports.	Validity
e. Vouch overhead charges to overhead analysis schedules.	Accuracy

EXHIBIT 11-3 Test of Controls Audit Procedures for Work-in-Progress Inventory (Continued)

	Control Objective
f. Trace selected overhead amounts from analysis schedules to cost allocations and to invoices or accounts payable vouchers.	Validity
3. Select a sample of issue slips from the raw materials stores file:	
a. Determine if a matching requisition is available for every issue slip.	Completeness
b. Trace materials-used reports into production cost reports.	Completeness
4. Select a sample of clock timecards from the payroll file. Trace to job time tickets, labor reports, and into production cost reports.	Completeness
5. Select a sample of production orders:	
a. Determine whether production order was authorized.	Authorization
b. Match to bill of materials and manpower needs.	Completeness
c. Trace bill of materials to material requisitions, material issue slips, materials-used reports, and into production cost reports.	Completeness
d. Trace manpower needs to labor reports and into production cost reports.	Completeness

DIRECTION OF THE TEST OF CONTROLS PROCEDURES

The test of controls procedures in Exhibit 11-3 are designed to test the production accounting in two directions. One is the *completeness direction*, in which the control performance of audit interest is the recording of all the production that was ordered to be started. Exhibit 11-4 shows that the sample for this direction is taken from the population of production orders found in the production planning department. The procedures trace the cost department. The procedures keyed in the boxes (5-a, b, c, d) are cross-references to the procedures in Exhibit 11-3. A potential finding with these procedures is the cancellation of some production because of technical or quality problems, which should result in write-off or scrap of some partially completed production units.

**EXHIBIT 11-4 Test of Production Cost Controls: Completeness
    Direction**

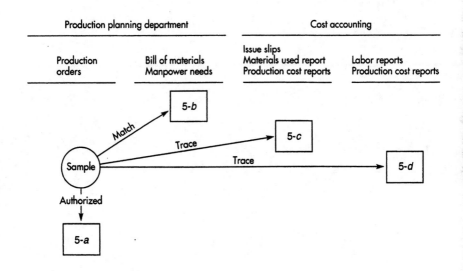

The other direction is the *validity direction* of the test. The control performance of interest is the proper recording of work in process and finished goods in the general ledger. Exhibit 11-5 shows that the sample for this test is from the production reports (quantity and cost) *recorded in the inventory accounts*. From these basic records the recorded costs can be recalculated, vouched to labor reports, compared to the payroll, and vouched to records of material used and overhead incurred. The procedures keyed in the boxes (2-a, b, c, d, e, f) are cross-references to the procedures in Exhibit 11-3. A potential finding with these procedures is improper valuation of the recorded inventory cost.

**EXHIBIT 11-5 Test of Production Cost Controls: Validity
              Direction**

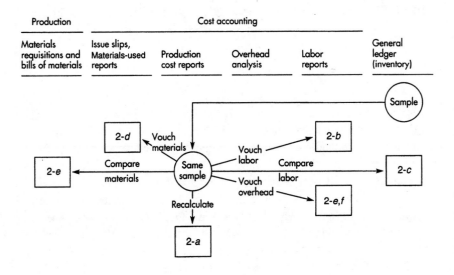

IMPROPER PRODUCTION LOSS DEFERRALS

According to the SEC, Litton Corporation incurred cost overruns on its shipbuilding contracts and postponed writing off a $128 million cost overrun by classifying it as an asset for financial reporting purposes. If it had been written off timely, the net income of $1 million for the year would have become a substantial loss. Litton wrote off the $128 million later.

* * * * * * * * * *

According to the SEC, International Systems & Controls Corporation (ISC) recorded and reported cost overruns on fixed price contracts, claims for price escalation, and kickback arrangements with suppliers as unbilled receivables. Additional uncollectible contract costs, which indicated losses on fixed price contracts, were buried in other unrelated contracts. ISC used the unbilled receivables account as a dumping ground for improper and questionable payments on the contracts. It tried to show them as legitimate reimbursable contract costs in order to avoid (a) writing them off as expense and (b) showing the true nature of the items. ISC used the unbilled receivables account to record cost overruns on fixed price contracts, misrepresenting them as an escalation payment due from the owner, but the contract did not provide for any such payment.

Source: I. Kellog, *How to Find Negligence and Misrepresentation in Financial Statements.*

SUMMARY: CONTROL RISK ASSESSMENT

The audit manager or senior accountant in charge of the audit should evaluate the evidence obtained from an understanding of the internal control system and from the test of controls audit procedures. If the control risk is assessed very low, the substantive audit procedures on the account balances can be limited in cost-saving ways. For example, the inventory valuation substantive tests can be limited in scope (i.e., smaller sample size), and overall analytical procedures can be used with more confidence in being able to detect material misstatements not otherwise evident in the accounting details.

   On the other hand, if tests of controls reveal weaknesses, depreciation calculation errors, and cost accumulation errors, the substantive procedures will need to be designed to lower the risk of failing to detect material error will need to be designed to lower the risk of failing to detect material error in the inventory and cost of goods sold account balances. For example, the depreciation cost may need to be completely recalculated and reviewed again by the auditors. A large number of inventoried production reports may need to be selected for valuation calculations. Cost overruns will need to be investigated with reference to contract terms to determine whether they should be carried as assets (e.g., inventory or unbilled receivables) or written off. Descriptions of major deficiencies, control weaknesses, and inefficiencies may be incorporated in a letter to the client describing "reportable conditions."

Computerized production cycle records are encountered frequently. Their complexity may range from simple batch systems, which automate the data processing, to transaction-driven integrated systems, which capture the production progress directly from automated devices on the production line. Computer audit techniques, such as test data, frequently are employed to audit controls in such systems, and generalized audit software may be employed to match data on different files.

AUDIT CASES: SUBSTANTIVE AUDIT PROCEDURES

The audit of account balances consists of procedural efforts to detect errors, irregularities, and frauds that might exist in the balances, thus making them misleading in financial statements. If such misstatements exist, they are characterized by the following features:

Method: A cause of the misstatement (accidental error, intentional irregularity, or fraud attempt), which is usually made easier by some kind of failure of controls.

Paper trail: A set of telltale signs of erroneous accounting, missing, or altered documents, or a "dangling debit" (the false or erroneous debit that results from an overstatement of assets).

Amount: The dollar amount of overstated assets and revenue, or understated liabilities and expenses.

Each audit program for the audit of an account balance contains an audit approach that may enable auditors to detect misstatements in account balances. Each application of procedures contains these elements:

Audit objective: A recognition of a financial statement *assertion* for which evidence needs to be obtained. The assertions are about existence of assets, liabilities, revenues, and expenses; their valuation; their complete inclusion in the account balances; the rights and obligations inherent in them; and their proper presentation and disclosure in the financial statements.

Control: A recognition of the control activities that *should be* used in an organization to prevent and detect errors and irregularities.

Test of controls: Ordinary and extended procedures *designed to produce evidence about the effectiveness of the controls* that should be in operation.

Audit of balance: Ordinary and extended *substantive procedures designed to find signs* of errors, irregularities, and frauds in account balances and classes of transactions.

The next portion of this chapter consists of two cases that first set the stage with a story about an error, irregularity, or fraud--its method, paper trail (if any), and amount. This part of each case gives you the "inside story," which auditors seldom know before they perform the audit work. The second part of each case, under the heading of the "audit approach," tells a structured story about the audit objective, desirable controls, test of control procedures, audit of balance procedures, and discovery summary. The audit approach segment illustrates the manner in which audit procedures can be applied and the discoveries they may enable auditors to make. At the end of the chapter, a similar discussion case is presented, and you can write the audit approach to test your ability to design audit procedures for the detection of errors, irregularities, and frauds.

CASE 11.1
UNBUNDLED BEFORE ITS TIME

Problem
Production "sold" as finished goods before actual unit completion caused understated inventory, overstated cost of goods sold, overstated revenue, and overstated income.

Method
Western Corporation assembled and sold computer systems. A system production order consisted of hardware and peripheral equipment specifications and software specifications with associated performance criteria. Customer contracts always required assembly to specifications, installation, hardware testing, software installation, and software testing, after which the customer could accept the finished installation and pay the agreed price for the entire package. Completion of an order usually took three to eight months.

For internal accounting purposes, Western "unbundled" the hardware and software components of the customer orders. Production orders were split between the two components. Standard production processing and cost accounting were performed as if the two components were independent orders. When the hardware was installed and tested (with or without customer acceptance), Western recorded part of the contract price as sales revenue and the related cost of goods sold. The amount "due from customers" was carried in an asset account entitled Unbilled Contract Revenue. No billing statement was sent to the customer at this time.

When the software component was completed, installed, tested, and accepted, the remainder of the contract price was recorded as revenue, and the cost of the software was recorded as cost of goods sold. A billing statement was sent to the customer. The Unbilled Contract Revenue, which now matched the customer's obligation, was moved to Accounts Receivable.

During the time either or both of the order components were in process (prior to installation at the customer's location), accumulated costs were carried in a work-in-process inventory account.

Paper Trail
Customer orders and contracts contained all the terms relating to technical specifications, acceptance testing, and the timing of the customer's obligation to pay. Copies of the technical specification sections of the contracts were attached to the separate hardware and software production orders prepared and authorized in the production planning department. During production, installation, and testing, each of these production orders served as the basis for the production cost accumulation and the subsidiary record of the work-in-process inventory. At the end, the production report along with the accumulated costs became the production cost report and the supporting documentation for the cost of goods sold entry.

Amount
Western Corporation routinely recorded the hardware component of contracts too early, recognizing revenue and cost of goods sold that should have been postponed until later when the customer accepted the entire system. In the last three years, the resulting income overstatement amounted to 12 percent, 15 percent, and 19 percent of the reported operating income before taxes.

AUDIT APPROACH

Objective
Obtain evidence of the actual occurrence of cost of goods sold transactions, thereby yielding evidence of the completeness of recorded inventory.

Control
The major control lies in the production planning department approval of orders that identify a total unit of production (in this case, the hardware and software components combined). Nothing is wrong with approving separate orders for efficiency of production, but they should be cross-referenced so both production personnel and the cost accounting department can see them as separate components of the same order unit.

Test of Controls
While the company conducted a large business, it had relatively few production orders (200-250 charged to cost of goods sold during each year). A sample of completed production orders should be taken and vouched to the underlying customer orders and contracts. The purpose of this procedure includes determining the validity of the production orders in relation to customer orders and determining whether the cost of goods sold was recorded in the proper period. (Procedures to audit the accuracy and completeness of the cost accumulation also are carried out on this sample.)

Even though the auditors can read the customer contracts, inquiries should be made about the company's standard procedures for the timing of revenue and cost of goods sold recognition.

Audit of Balances
The sample of completed production orders taken for the test of controls also can be used in a "dual purpose test" to audit the details of the cost of goods sold balance. In connection with the balance audit, the primary points of interest are the existence/occurrence and completeness of the dollar amounts accumulated as cost of the contracts and the proper cutoff for recording the cost.

The existence of the Unbilled Contract Revenue asset account in the general ledger should raise a red flag. Such an account always means that management has made an estimate of a revenue amount that has not been determined according to contract and has not yet been billed to the customer in accordance with contract terms. Even though the revenue is "unbilled," the related cost of goods sold still should be in the Cost of Goods Sold account. While accounting theory and practice permit recognizing unbilled revenue in certain cases (e.g., percentage of completion for construction contracts), the accounting has been known to harbor abuses in some cases.

Discovery Summary

When the company decided to issue stock to the public, a new audit firm was engaged. These auditors performed the dual purpose procedures outlined above, made the suggested inquiries, and investigated the Unbilled Contract Revenue account. They learned about management's unbundling policy and insisted that the policy be changed to recognize revenue only when all the terms of the contract were met. (The investigation yielded the information about prior years' overstatements of revenue, cost of goods sold, and income.) Part of the reason for insisting on the change of policy was the finding that Western did not have a very good record of quality control and customer acceptance of software installation. Customer acceptance was frequently delayed several months while systems engineers debugged software. On several occasions, Western solved the problems by purchasing complete software packages from other developers.

CASE 11.2
WHEN IN DOUBT, DEFER!

Problem
SaCom Corporation deferred costs under the heading of work in process, defense contract claims, and R&D test equipment, thus overstating assets, understating cost of goods sold, and overstating income. Disclosure of the auditor's fees was manipulated and understated.

Method
SaCom manufactured electronic and other equipment for private customers and government defense contracts. Near the end of the year, the company used a journal entry to remove $170,000 from cost of goods sold and to defer it as tooling, leasehold improvements,and contract award and acquisition costs.

The company capitalized certain expenditures as R&D test equipment ($140,000) and as claims for reimbursement on defense contracts ($378,000).

In connection with a public offering of securities, the auditors billed SaCom $125,000 for professional fees. The underwriters objected. The auditors agreed to forgive $70,000 of the fees, and SaCom agreed to pay higher fees for work the following year (150 percent of standard billing rates). SaCom disclosed audit fees in the registration statement in the amount of $55,000. This amount was paid from the proceeds of the offering.

Paper Trail
The $170,000 deferred costs consisted primarily of labor costs. The company altered the labor time records in an effort to provide substantiating documentation. The auditors knew about the alterations. The cost was removed from jobs that were left with too little labor cost in light of the work performed on them. The R&D test equipment cost already had been charged to cost of goods sold with no notice of deferral

when originally recorded. Deferral was accomplished with an adjusting journal entry. The company did not have documentation for the adjusting entry, except for an estimate of labor cost (44 percent of all labor cost in a subsidiary was capitalized during the period).

The claim for reimbursement on defense contracts did not have documentation specifically identifying the costs as being related to the contract. (Auditors know that defense department auditors insist on documentation and justification before approving such a claim.)

The audit fee arrangement was known to the audit firm, and it was recorded in an internal memorandum.

Amount
SaCom reported net income of about $542,000 for the year, an overstatement of approximately 50 percent.

AUDIT APPROACH

Objective
Obtain evidence of the validity of production costs deferred as tooling, leasehold improvements, contract award and acquisition costs, R&D test equipment, and claims for reimbursement on defense contracts.

Control
The major control lies in the requirement to document the validity of cost deferral journal entries.

Test of Controls
The test of controls procedure is to select a sample of journal entries, suspect ones in this case, and vouch them to supporting documentation. Experience has shown that nonstandard adjusting journal entries are the source of accounting errors and irregularities more often than standard repetitive accounting for systematic transactions. This phenomenon makes the population of adjusting journal entries a ripe field for control and substantive testing.

Audit of Balances

The account balances created by the deferral journal entries can be audited in a "dual purpose procedure" by auditing the supporting documentation. These balances were created entirely by the journal entries, and their "existence" as legitimate assets, deferrals, and reimbursement claims depends on the believability of the supporting explanations. In connection with the defense contract claim, auditors can review it with knowledge of the contract and the extent of documentation required by government contract auditors.

(As a separate matter, the auditors could "search for unrecorded liabilities," but they already know about the deferred accounting fees, anyway.)

Discovery Summary

By performing the procedures outlined above, the manager and senior and staff accountants on the engagement discovered all the questionable and improper accounting. However, the partners in the firm insisted on rendering unqualified opinions on the SaCom financial statements without adjustment. One partner owned 300 shares of the company's stock in the name of a relative (without the consent or knowledge of the relative). Another audit partner later arranged a bank loan to the company to get $125,000 to pay past-due audit fees. This partner and another, and both their wives, guaranteed the loan. (When the bank later disclosed the guarantee in a bank confirmation obtained in the course of a subsequent SaCom audit, the confirmation was removed from the audit working paper file and destroyed.)

The SEC investigated, and, among other things, barred the audit firm for a period (about six months) from accepting new audit clients who would file financial statements with the SEC. The SEC also barred the partners involved in supervising various portions of the audit work from involvement with new audit clients for various periods of time. (Adapted: ASR 196.)

SUMMARY

Production involves production planning, inventory planning, acquisition of labor, materials, and overhead (acquisition and payment cycle), custody of assets while work is in process and when finished products are stored in inventory, and cost accounting. Payroll is a part of every business and an important part of every production cycle (see Chapter 10). Management and control of production labor costs are important.

Production information systems produce many internal documents, reports, and files. Several of these sources of audit information are described in the chapter. This cycle is characterized by having mostly internal documentation as evidence and having relatively little external documentary evidence. Aside from the physical inventory in the production process, the accounts in the production cycle are intangible. They cannot be observed, inspected, touched, or counted in any meaningful way. Most audit procedures for this cycle are analytical procedures and dual-purposes procedures that test both the company's control procedures and the existence, valuation, and completeness assertions made by accumulating the results of numerous material, labor, and overhead transactions.

Companies reduce control risk by having a suitable separation of authorization, custody, recording, and periodic reconciliation duties. Error-checking procedures of analyzing production orders and finished production cost reports are important for proper determination of inventory values and proper valuation of cost of goods sold. Otherwise, many things could go wrong, ranging from overvaluing the inventory to understating costs of production by deferring costs that should be expensed.

Cost accounting is a central feature of the production cycle. Illustrative cases in the chapter tell the stories of financial reporting manipulations and the audit procedures that will detect them.

PRACTICAL CASE PROBLEM
INSTRUCTIONS FOR THE CASE

This case is designed like the ones in the chapter. It gives the problem, the method, the paper trail, and the amount. Your assignment is to write the "audit approach" portion of the case, organized around these sections:

Objective: Express the objective in terms of the facts supposedly asserted in financial records, accounts, and statements.

Control: Write a brief explanation of desirable controls, missing controls, and especially the kinds of "deviations" that might arise from the situation described in the case

Test of controls: Write some procedures for getting evidence about existing controls, especially procedures that could discover deviations from controls. If there are no controls to test, then there are no procedures to perform; go then to the next section. A "procedure" should instruct someone about the source(s) of evidence to tap and the work to do.

Audit of Balance: Wite some procedures for getting evidence about the existence, completeness, valuation, ownership, or disclosure assertions identified in your *objective* section above.

Discovery summary: Write a short statement about the discovery you expect to accomplish with your procedures.

CASE #11.1: TOYING AROUND WITH THE NUMBERS--Inventory and Deferred Cost Overstatement. Write the "audit approach" section like the cases in the chapter.

Problem: Mattel, Inc., a manufacturer of toys, failed to write off obsolete inventory, thereby overstating inventory, and improperly deferred tooling costs, both of which understated cost of goods sold and overstated income.

Method: "Excess" inventory was identified by comparing types of toys (wheels, general toys, dolls, games), parts, and raw materials with the forecasted sales or usage, Lower-of-cost-or-market (LCM) determinations then were made to calculate the obsolescence write-off. Obsolescence was expected, and the target for the year was $700,000. The first comparison computer run showed $21 million "excess" inventory! The company "adjusted" the forecast by increasing the quantities of expected sales for many toy lines. (Forty percent of items had forecasted sales greater than the recent actual sales experience.) Another "adjustment" was to forecast toy close-out sales not at reduced prices but at regular price. Also, certain parts were labeled "interchangeable" without the normal reference to a new toy product. These "adjustments" to the forecast reduced the "excess" inventory exposed to LCM valuation and write-off.

The cost of setting up machines, preparing dies, and other preparations for manufacture are "tooling costs." They benefit the lifetime run of the toy manufactured. The company capitalized them as prepaid expenses and amortized them in the ratio of current-year sales to expected product lifetime sales (much like a natural resource depletion calculation). To get the amortization cost lower, the company transferred unamortized tooling costs from toys with low forecasted sales to ones with high forecasted sales. This caused the year's amortization ratio to be smaller, the calculated cost write-off lower, and the cost of goods sold lower than it should have been.

Paper trail: The computer forecast runs of expected usage of interchangeable parts provided a space for a reference to the code number of the new toy where the part would be used. Some of these references contained the code number of the part itself, not a new toy. In other cases, the forecast of toy sales and parts usage contained the quantity on hand, not a forecast number.

In the tooling cost detail records, unamortized cost was classified by lines of toys (similar to classifying asset cost by asset name or description). Unamortized balances were carried forward to the next year. The company changed the classifications shown at the prior year-end to other toy lines that had no balances or different balances. In other words, the balances of unamortized cost at the end of the prior year did not match the beginning balances of the current year, except that the total prepaid expense amount was the same.

Amount: For lack of obsolescence write-offs, inventory was overstated $4 million. The company recorded a $700,000 obsolescence write-off. It should have been about $4.7 million, as later determined.

The tooling cost manipulations overstated the prepaid expense by $3.6 million.

The company reported net income (after taxes) of $12.1 million in the year before the manipulations took place. If pretax income were in the $20-$28 million range in the year of the misstatements, the obsolescence and tooling misstatements alone amounted to about 32 percent income overstatement.

CHAPTER 12
INVESTMENTS, LIABILITIES.
AND EQUITIES

The finance and investment accounting cycle covers several types of transactions that are typically large and infrequent. This chapter contains sections on (1) typical control activities related to the transactions, (2) control risk assessment (including detail test of controls procedures), and (3) case story-style explanations concerning discovery of errors, irregularities, and frauds for subtopics in (a) debt and stockholders equity capital, (b) long-term liabilities and related accounts, and (c) investments and intangibles. A closing section deals with additional aspects of clever accounting and fraud.

FINANCE AND INVESTMENT CYCLE:
TYPICAL ACTIVITIES

The finance and investment cycle contains a large number of accounts and records, ranging across tangible and intangible assets, liabilities, deferred credits, stockholders' equity, gains and losses, expenses, and income taxes. The major accounts and records are listed in Exhibit 12-1. These include some of the more complicated topics in accounting--equity method accounting for investments, consolidation accounting, goodwill, income taxes, and financial instruments, to name a few. It is not the purpose of this chapter to explain the accounting for these balances and transactions. The chapter concentrates on a few important aspects of auditing them.

Exhibit 12-1 shows a skeleton outline of the finance and investment cycle. Its major functions are financial planning and raising capital; interacting with the acquisition and expenditure, production and payroll, and revenue and collection cycles; and entering into mergers, acquisitions, and other investments.

EXHIBIT 12-1 Finance and Investment Cycle

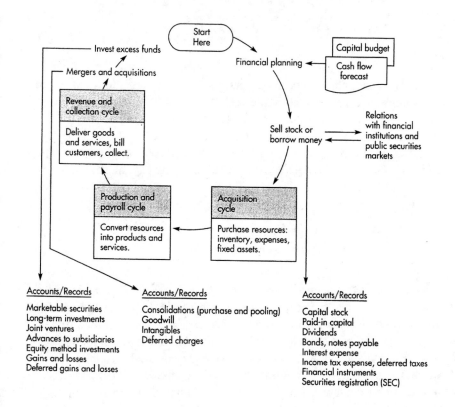

DEBT AND STOCKHOLDER EQUITY CAPITAL

Transactions in debt and stockholder equity capital are normally few in number but large in monetary amount. They are handled by the highest levels of management. The control-related duties and responsibilities reflect this high-level attention.

Authorization

Financial planning starts with the chief financial officer's (CFO's) **cash flow forecast**. This forecast informs the board of directors and management of the business plans, the prospects for cash inflows, and the needs for cash outflows. The cash flow forecast usually is integrated with the **capital budget**, which contains the plans for asset purchases and business acquisitions. A capital budget approved by the board of directors constitutes the authorization for major capital asset acquisitions (acquisition cycle) and investments.

Sales of capital stock and debt financing transactions usually are authorized by the board of directors. All the directors must sign registration documents for public securities offerings. However, authority normally is delegated to the CFO to complete such transactions as periodic renewals of notes payable and other ordinary types of financing transactions without specific board approval of each transaction. Auditors should expect to find the authorizing signatures of the chief executive officer (CEO), CFO, chair of the board of directors, and perhaps other high-ranking officers on financing documents.

Many financing transactions are "off the balance sheet." Companies can enter into obligations and commitments that are not required to be recorded in the accounts. Examples of such authorizations include: leases, endorsements on discounted notes or on other companies' obligations, letters of credit, guarantees, repurchase or remarketing agreements, commitments to purchase at fixed prices, commitments to sell at fixed prices, and certain kinds of stock options. These are among the business and financing options available to companies. They cause problems in financial reporting and disclosure.

THE FRAUD LOSSES HAPPENED LAST YEAR!

Retained earnings is usually not a very interesting capital account. It cannot be bought, sold, or stolen, but it can be the final resting place for some important accounting decisions.

AM International was the victim of a massive management fraud engineered by high-level executives and put over for awhile on the independent auditors and on everybody else. Reportedly, over $75 million in assets did not exist, even though they were reported in the audited financial statements.

After the corrupt management was terminated, the new management concluded that the losses resulting from the fraud should be a prior period adjustment to retained earnings and prior income statements in the amount of $250 million, counting the fictitious assets and the adverse impact of the events on the company's business. They wanted to start with a new, clean slate.

The argument was that the *accounting errors* occurred in earlier years, and all the related losses should be placed in the accounting for those years. Do you agree with this prior period adjustment accounting for this situation?

Custody

In large companies, custody of stock certificate books is not a significant management problem. Large companies employ banks and trust companies to serve as registrars and transfer agents. A **registrar** keeps the stockholder list and, from time to time, determines the shareholders eligible to receive dividends (stockholders of record on a dividend record date) and those entitled to vote at the annual meeting. A **transfer agent** handles the exchange of shares, cancelling the shares surrendered by sellers and issuing new certificates to buyers. The same bank or trust company usually provides both services.

Small companies often keep their own stockholder records. A stock certificate book looks like a checkbook. It has perforated stubs for recording the number of shares, the owner's name and other identification, and the date of issue. Actual unissued share certificates are attached to the stubs, like unused checks in a checkbook. The missing certificates are the ones outstanding in the possession of owners. Custody of the stock certificate book is important because the unissued certificates are like money or collateral. If improperly removed, they can be sold to buyers who think they are genuinely issued or can be used as collateral with unsuspecting lenders.

Lenders have custody of debt instruments (e.g., leases, bonds, and notes payable). A CFO may have copies, but they are merely convenience records. However, when a company repurchases its debt instruments, these come into the custody of trustees or company officials, usually the CFO. Until they are cancelled and destroyed, it is possible to misuse them by improperly reselling them to unsuspecting investors. (Refer to the box on "A New Meaning for 'Recylcing'.")

A NEW MEANING FOR "RECYCLING"

Something strange must have happened on the way to the dump. Hundreds of issues of long-term bonds were redeemed early and presented to Citicorp's Citibank in New York, acting as agent for the issues, according to the FBI. Many of the bonds still had not reached the maturity date marked on them. Citibank sent about $1 billion of cancelled U.S. corporate bonds to a landfill dump in New Jersey. But in the past year, some of those bonds have been turning up at banks in Europe and the United States. The banks have had a disturbing surprise: The bonds are worthless, though they still might look genuine to a layman or even to some bankers.

An FBI spokesman says a defunct company in New Jersey is being investigated. The company had a contract to destroy the bonds.

Note: Companies obtain a "destruction certificate" when bonds and stock certificates are canceled. The certificate obtained by Citibank apparently was fraudulent.

Source: *The Wall Street Journal*, March 3, 1992.

Recordkeeping

Records of notes and bonds payable are maintained by the accounting department and the CFO or controller. The recordkeeping procedures should be similar to those used to account for vendor accounts payable: payment notices from lenders are compared to the accounting records, due dates are monitored, interest payments are set up in vouchers for payment, and accruals for unpaid interest are made on financial reporting dates. If the company has only a few bonds and notes outstanding, no subsidiary records of notes are kept. All the information is in the general ledger accounts. (Companies with a large number of bonds and notes may keep control and subsidiary accounts, as is done for accounts receivable.) When all or part of the notes become due within the next year, the CFO and controller have the necessary information for properly classifying current and long-term amounts.

Another class of credit balances is treated here under the heading of "recordkeeping," for which the functions of authorization, custody, and reconciliation are not easy to describe. They are the "calculated liabilities and credits"--lease obligations, deferred income taxes, pension and post-retirement benefit liabilities, and foreign currency translation gains and losses, to name a few. These are accounting creations, calculated according to accounting rules and using basic data from company plans and operations. Management usually enjoys considerable discretion in structuring leases, tax strategies, pension plan and employee benefit terms, foreign holdings, and the like. These accounting calculations often involve significant accounting estimates made by management. Company accountants try to capture the economic reality of these calculated liabilities by following generally accepted accounting principles.

Periodic Reconciliation

A responsible person should periodically inspect the stock certificate book to determine whether the only missing certificates are the ones known to be outstanding in the possession of bona fide owners. If necessary, company officials can confirm the ownership of shares with the holders of record. Reports with similar information content can be obtained from registrars and transfer agents to verify that the company's record of the number of shares outstanding agrees with the registrars' number. (Without this reconciliation, counterfeit shares handled by the transfer agent and recorded by the registrar might go unnoticed.)

Ownership of bonds can be handled by a trustee having duties and responsibilities similar to those of registrars and transfer agents. Confirmations and reports from bond trustees can be used to reconcile the trustee's records to the company's records.

INVESTMENTS AND INTANGIBLES

A company can have many investments or only a few, and can have a large variety or a limited set of types of investments. Intangible assets may be in the form of purchased assets (e.g., patents, trademarks) or in the form of accounting allocations (e.g., goodwill, deferred charges). The sections below are phrased in the context of a manufacturing or service company for which investments and intangibles are fairly incidental in the business. Financial institutions (banks, thrifts), investment companies (mutual funds, small business investment companies--SBICs), insurance companies, and the like have more elaborate systems for managing their investments and intangibles.

THE LITTLE LEASE THAT COULD

The Park 'N Fly commuter airline was struggling. According to its existing debt covenants, it could not incur any more long-term liabilities. The company needed a new airplane to expand its services, so it "rented" one. The CFO pointed out that the deal for the $12 million airplane was a noncancellable operating lease because: (1) Park 'N Fly does not automatically own the plane at the end of the lease; (2) the purchase option of $1,500,000 is no bargain; (3) the lease term of 133 months is 74 percent, not 75 percent, of the estimated 15-year economic life; and (4) the present value of the lease payments of $154,330 per month, discounted at the company's latest borrowing rate of 14 percent, is $10.4 million, which is less than the 90 percent of fair value (0.90 X $12 million = $10.8 million) criterion in the FASB pronouncements.

The CFO did not record a long-term lease obligation (liability). Do you agree with this accounting conclusion?

Authorization

All investment policies should be approved by the board of directors or its investment committee. It is not unusual to find board or executive committee approval required for major individual investment transactions. However, auditors should expect to find a great deal of variation across companies about the nature and amount of transactions that must have specific high-level approval. The board of directors always is closely involved in major acquisitions, mergers, and stock buy-back plans.

AUTHORIZATION: HERE TODAY, GONE TOMORROW

The treasurer of Travum County had many responsibilities as a chief financial officer. She invested several million dollars of county funds with a California-based investment money manager. Soon thereafter, news stories of the money manager's expensive personal lifestyle and questionable handling of client's funds began to circulate, indicating that clients could lose much of their investments. At the same time, news stories about the treasurer's own credit-card spending habits were published locally, indicating that she had obtained a personal credit card by using the county's name.

Although no county funds were lost and no improper credit-card bills were paid, the county commissioners temporarily suspended the treasurer's authority to choose investment vehicles for county funds.

Custody

Custody of investments and intangibles depends on the nature of the assets. Some investments, such as stocks and bonds, are represented by negotiable certificates. The actual certificates may be kept in a brokerage account in a "house name" (the brokerage company), and, in this case, "custody" rests with the company official who is authorized to order the buy, sell, and delivery transactions. They also may be in the actual possession of the owner (client company). If they are kept by the company, they should be in a safe or a bank safe-deposit box. Only high-ranking officers (e.g., CFO, CEO, president, chair of board) should have combinations and keys.

Other kinds of investments do not have formal negotiable certificates, and "custody" may take the form of "management responsibility" instead of actual physical handling. Examples are joint ventures and partnerships in which the client company is a partner. Venture and partnership agreements are evidence of these investments, but they usually are merely filed with other important documents. Misuse of them is seldom a problem because they are not readily negotiable. Real custody rests with management's supervision and monitoring the venture or partnership operations.

Having "custody" of most intangibles is like trying to keep Jell-O in your pocket--good in theory but messy in practice. However, patents, trademarks, copyrights, and similar legal intangible rights may be evidenced in legal documents and contracts. These seldom are negotiable, and they usually are kept in ordinary company files. Accounting intangibles like goodwill and deferred charges (deferred tax credits and pension obligations on the liability side) are in the custody of the accountants who calculate them. Company managers may be assigned responsibility to protect exclusive rights granted by various intangibles.

DON'T USE OUR LOGO

The University of Texas at Austin has trademark rights over the "longhorn" symbol and a particular school color (burnt orange). The university actively prohibits businesses from using these symbols without permission. For example, a local cleaning business and a trash hauling business were informed that they must cease and desist using the longhorn-head logo on their buildings, signs, and trucks. The businesses complied by repainting and finding other ways to promote their business.

Recordkeeping

The procedures for purchase of stock and bond investments involve the voucher system described in the acquisition and expenditure cycle (Chapter 9). Authorization by the board of directors or other responsible officials is the approval for the accounting department to prepare the voucher and the check. The treasurer or CFO signs the check for the investment. If the company has few investments, no subsidiary records are maintained and all information is kept in the general ledger accounts. If the company has many investments, a control account and subsidiary ledger may be maintained.

The recordkeeping for many kinds of investments and intangibles can be complicated. The complications arise not so much from the original recording of transactions but from the maintenance of the accounts over time. This is the place where complex accounting standards for equity method accounting, consolidations, goodwill, intangibles amortization and valuation, deferred charges, deferred taxes, pension and post-retirement benefit liabilities, and various financial instruments enter the picture. High-level accountants who prepare financial statements get involved with the accounting rules and the management estimates required to account for such investments and intangibles. Management plans and estimates of future events and interpretations of the accounting standards often become elements of the accounting maintenance of these balances. These decisions are ripe areas for overstatement of assets, understatement of liabilities, and understatement of expenses.

Periodic Reconciliation

The most significant reconciliation opportunity in the investments and intangibles accounts is the inspection and count of negotiable securities certificates. This reconciliation is similar to a physical inventory in that it consists of an inspection of certificates on hand, along with comparison to the information recorded in the accounts. (When securities are held by a brokerage firm, the "inspection" is accomplished with a written confirmation.)

A securities count is not a mere handling of bits of paper. A securities count "inventory" should include a record of the name of the company represented by the certificate, the interest rate for bonds, the dividend rate for preferred stocks, the due date for bonds, the serial numbers on the certificates, the face value of bonds, the number or face amount of bonds and stock shares, and notes on the name of the owner shown on the face of the certificate or on the endorsements on the back (should be the client company). Companies should perform this reconciliation reasonably often and not wait for an annual visit by the independent auditors. A securities count in a financial institution that holds thousands of shares in multimillion-dollar asset accounts is a major undertaking.

When auditors perform the securities inspection and count, the same kind of information should be recorded in the audit working papers. Several elements of evidence are in this information: existence is established by inspecting the securities, ownership is established by viewing the client name as owner, valuation evidence is added by finding the cost and market value. If a security certificate is not available for inspection, it may be pledged as collateral for a loan and in the hands of a creditor. It can be confirmed or inspected, if the extended procedure of visiting the creditor is necessary. The pledge as collateral may be important for a disclosure note. A securities count and reconciliation is important for management and auditors because companies have been known to try to substitute others' securities for missing ones. If securities have been sold, then replaced without any accounting entries, the serial numbers will show that the certificates recorded in the accounts are not the same as the ones on hand.

CONTROL RISK ASSESSMENT

In the finance and investment cycle, auditors look for control activities, such as authorization, custody, recordkeeping, and periodic reconciliation. They especially look for information about the level of management involved in these functions. Tests of controls generally amount to inquiries and observations related to these features. Samples of transactions for detail tests of control performance are not normally a part of the control risk assessment work as they can be in the revenue and collection cycle, in the acquisition and expenditure cycle, in the payroll cycle, and in the production cycle. Because finance and investment transactions are usually individually material, each transaction usually is audited in detail. Reliance on control does not normally reduce the extent of substantive audit work on finance and investment cycle accounts. However, lack of control can lead to performance of significant extended procedures.

GENERAL CONTROL CONSIDERATIONS

Control procedures for suitable handling of responsibilities should be in place and operating. By referring to the discussion accompanying Exhibit 12-1, you can tell that these responsibilities are basically in the hands of senior management officials. You also can tell that different companies may have widely different policies and procedures.

It is hard to have a strict segregation of functional responsibilities when the principal officers of a company authorize, execute, and control finance and investment activities. It is not very realistic to maintain that a CEO can authorize investments but cannot have access to stockholder records, securities certificates, and the like. Real *segregation* of duties can be found in middle management and lower ranks, but it is hard to create and enforce in upper-level management.

In light of this problem of control, a company should have compensating control procedures. A **compensating control** is a control feature used when a standard control procedure (such as strict segregation of functional responsibilities) is not specified by the company. In the area of finance and investment, the compensating control feature is the involvement of two or more persons in each kind of important functional responsibility.

If involvement by multiple persons is not specified, then oversight or review can be substituted. For example, the board of directors can authorize purchase of securities or creation of a partnership. The CFO or CEO can carry out the transactions, have custody of certificates and agreements, manage the partnership or the portfolio of securities, oversee the recordkeeping, and make the decisions about valuations and accounting (authorizing the journal entries). These are normal management activities, and they combine several responsibilities. The compensating control can exist in the form of periodic reports to the board of directors, oversight by the investment committee of the board, and internal audit involvement in making a periodic reconciliation of securities certificates in a portfolio with the amounts and descriptions recorded in the accounts.

CONTROL OVER ACCOUNTING ESTIMATES

An **accounting estimate** is an approximation of a financial statement element, item, or account. Estimates often are included in basic financial statements because (1) the measurement of some amount of valuation is uncertain, perhaps depending upon the outcome of future events, or (2) relevant data cannot be accumulated on a timely, cost-effective basis (SAS 57, AU 342). Some examples of accounting estimates in the finance and investment cycle are shown in the box below.

A client's management is responsible for making estimates and should have a process and controls designed to reduce the likelihood of material misstatements in them. According to auditing standards (SAS 57, AU 342), specific relevant aspects of such controls include:

- Management communication of the need for proper accounting estimates.
- Accumulation of relevant, sufficient, and reliable data for estimates.
- Preparation of estimates by qualified personnel.
- Adequate review and approval by appropriate levels of authority.
- Comparison of prior estimates with subsequent results to assess the reliability of the estimation outcomes.
- Consideration by management of whether particular accounting estimates are consistent with the company's operational plans.

FINANCE AND INVESTMENT CYCLE ESTIMATES

Financial instruments: Valuation of securities, classification into trading versus investment portfolios, probability of a correlated hedge, sales of securities with puts and calls.

Accruals: Compensation in stock option plans, actuarial assumptions in pension costs.

Leases: Initial direct costs, executory costs, residual values, capitalization interest rate.

Rates: Imputed interest rates on receivables and payables.

Other: Losses and net realizable value on segment disposal and business restructuring, fair values in nonmonetary exchanges.

Auditors' test of controls over the production of estimates amounts to inquiries and observations related to the features listed immediately above. Such inquiries are: Who prepares estimates? When are they prepared? What data are used? Who reviews and approves the estimates? Have you compared prior estimates with subsequent actual events? Observations include: study of data documentation, study of comparisons of prior estimates with subsequent actual experience, study of intercompany correspondence concerning estimates and operational plans.

The audit of an estimate starts with the test of controls, much of which has a bearing on the substantive quality of the estimation process and of the estimate itself. Further substantive audit procedures include: recalculating the mathematical estimate, developing an auditor's own independent estimate based on alternative assumptions, and comparing the estimate to subsequent events to the extent they are known before the end of the field work.

AN ESTIMATED VALUATION BASED
ON FUTURE DEVELOPMENT

Gulf & Western Industries (G&W) sold 450,000 shares of Pan American stock from its investment portfolio to Resorts International (Resorts). Resorts paid $8 million plus 250,000 shares of its unregistered common stock. G&W recorded the sale proceeds as $14,167,500, valuing the unregistered Resorts stock at $6,167,500, which was approximately 67 percent of the market price of Resorts stock at the time ($36.82 per share). G&W reported a gain of $3,365,000 on the sale.

Four years later, Resorts stock fell to $2.63 per share. G&W sold its 250,000 shares back to Resorts in exchange for 1,100 acres of undeveloped land on Grand Bahamas Island. For its records, Resorts got a broker-dealer's opinion that its 250,000 shares were worth $460,000. For property tax assessment purposes, the Bahamian government valued the undeveloped land at $525,000.

G&W valued the land on its books at $6,167,500, which was the previous valuation of the Resorts stock. The justification was an appraisal of $6,300,000 based on the estimated value of the 1,100 acres when ultimately developed (i.e., built into an operating resort and residential community). However, G&W also reported a loss of $5,527,000 in its tax return (effectively valuing the land at $640,500).

> The SEC accused G&W of failing to report a loss of $5.7 million in its financial statements. Do you think the loss should have appeared in the G&W income statement?
>
> Source: I. Kellog, *How to Find Negligence and Misrepresentation in Financial Statements.*

CONTROL RISK ASSESSMENT FOR NOTES PAYABLE

From the preceding discussion, you can tell that test of controls audit procedures take a variety of forms--inquiries, observations, study of documentation, comparison with related data, and detail audit of some transactions. The detail audit of transactions, however, is a small part of the test of controls because of the nature of the finance and investment transactions, their number (few), and their amount (large). However, some companies have numerous debt financing transactions, and a more detailed approach to control risk assessment can be used, including the selection of a sample of transactions for control risk assessment evidence.

Auditors can select a sample of notes payable transactions for detail test of controls, provided that the population of notes is large enough to justify sample-based auditing. Exhibit 12-2 lists a selection of such procedures, with notation of the relevant control objectives shown on the right.

EXHIBIT 12-2 Test of Controls Audit Procedures for Notes Payable

	Control Objective
1. Read directors' and finance committee's minutes for authorization of financing transactions (such as short-term notes payable, bond offerings).	Authorization
2. Select a sample of paid notes:	
a. Recalculate interest expense for the period under audit.	Accuracy
b. Trace interest expense to the general ledger account.	Completeness
c. Vouch payment to canceled checks.	Validity

EXHIBIT 12-2 Test of Controls Audit Procedures for Notes Payable

	Control Objective
3. Select a sample of notes payable:	
a. Vouch to authorization by directors or finance committee.	Authorization
b. Vouch cash receipt to bank statement.	Validity

SUMMARY: CONTROL RISK ASSESSMENT

The audit manager or senior accountant in charge of the audit should evaluate the evidence obtained from an understanding of the internal control system and from test of controls audit procedures. These procedures can take many forms because management systems for finance and investment accounts can vary a great deal among clients. The involvement of senior officials in a relatively small number of high-dollar transactions makes control risk assessment a process tailored specifically to the company's situation. Some companies enter into complicated financing and investment transactions, while others keep to the simple transactions.

However, some control considerations can be generalized. Control over management's production of accounting estimates is characterized by some common features. In some cases, such as a company with numerous notes payable transactions, samples of transactions for detail testing can be used to produce evidence about compliance with controls.

In general, substantive audit procedures on finance and investment accounts are not limited in extent. It is very common for auditors to perform substantive audit procedures on 100 percent of these transactions and balances. The number of transactions is usually not large, and the audit cost is not high for complete coverage. Nevertheless, control deficiencies and unusual or complicated transactions can cause auditors to adjust the nature and timing of audit procedures. Complicated financial instruments, pension plans, exotic equity securities, related party transactions, and nonmonetary exchanges of investment assets call for procedures designed to find evidence of errors, irregularities, and frauds in the finance and investment accounts. The next section deals with some of the finance and investment cycle assertions, and it has some cases for your review.

ASSERTIONS, SUBSTANTIVE PROCEDURES, AND AUDIT CASES

This part of the chapter covers the audit of various account balances and gains and losses. It is presented in three sections--owners' equity, long-term liabilities and related accounts, and investments and intangibles. As in previous chapters, some cases illustrating errors, irregularities, and frauds are used to describe useful audit approaches. In addition, this chapter gives some assertions and procedures related to accounts in the cycle.

The cases begin with a description containing these elements:

Method: A cause of the misstatement (mistaken estimate or judgment, accidental error, intentional irregularity or fraud attempt), which usually is made easier by some kind of failure of controls.

Paper trail: A set of telltale signs of erroneous accounting, missing or altered documents, or a "dangling debit" (the false or erroneous debit that results from an overstatement of assets).

Amount: The dollar amount of overstated assets and revenue, or understated liabilities and expenses.

Each audit program for the audit of an account balance contains an audit approach that may enable auditors to detect misstatements in account balances. Each application of procedures contains these elements:

Audit objective: A recognition of a financial statement *assertion* for which evidence needs to be obtained. The assertions are about the existence of assets, liabilities, revenues, and expenses; their valuation; their complete inclusion in the account balances; the rights and obligations inherent in them; and their proper presentation and disclosure in the financial statements.

Control: A recognition of the control activities that *should be* used in an organization to prevent and detect errors and irregularities.

Test of controls: Ordinary and extended procedures *designed to produce evidence about the effectiveness of the controls* that should be in operation.

Audit of balance: Ordinary and extended *substantive procedures designed to find signs* of mistaken accounting estimates, errors, irregularities, and frauds in account balances and classes of transactions.

The cases first set the stage with a story about an accounting estimate, error, irregularity, or fraud--its method, paper trail (if any), and amount. This part of each case gives you the "inside story," which auditors seldom know before they perform the audit work. The second part of each case, under the heading of the "audit approach," tells a structured story about the audit objective, desirable controls, test of control procedures, audit of balance procedures, and discovery summary. The audit approach segment illustrates the manner in which audit procedures can be applied and the discoveries they may enable auditors to make. At the end of the chapter, some similar discussion cases are presented, and you can write the audit approach to test your ability to design audit procedures for the detection of mistaken accounting estimates, errors, irregularities, and frauds.

OWNERS' EQUITY

Management makes assertions about the existence, completeness, rights and obligations, valuation, and presentation and disclosure of owners' equity. Typical specific assertions include:
1. The number of shares shown as issued is in fact issued.
2. No other shares (including options, warrants, and the like) have been issued and not recorded or reflected in the accounts and disclosures.
3. The accounting is proper for options, warrants, and other stock issue plans, and related disclosures are adequate.
4. The valuation of shares issued for noncash consideration is proper, in conformity with accounting principles.
5. All owners' equity transactions have been authorized by the board of directors.

Documentation
Owners' equity transactions usually are well documented in minutes of the meetings of the board of directors, in proxy statements, and in securities offering registration statements. Transactions can be vouched to these documents, and the cash proceeds can be traced to the bank accounts.

Confirmation

Capital stock may be subject to confirmation when independent registrars and transfer agents are employed. Such agents are responsible for knowing the number of shares authorized and issued and for keeping lists of stockholders' names. The basic information about capital stock--such as number of shares, classes of stock, preferred dividend rates, conversion terms, dividend payments, shares held in the company name, expiration dates, and terms of warrants and stock dividends and splits--can be confirmed with the independent agents. Many of these items can be corroborated by the auditors' own inspection and reading of stock certificates, charter authorizations, directors' minutes, and registration statements. However, when the client company does not use independent agents, most audit evidence is gathered by vouching stock record documents (such as certificate book stubs). When circumstances call for extended procedures, information on outstanding stock in corporations having only a few stockholders may be confirmed directly with the holders.

CASE 12.1
UNREGISTERED SALE OF SECURITIES

Problem
A. T. Bliss & Company (Bliss) sold investment contracts in the form of limited partnership interests to the public. These "securities" sales should have been under a public registration filing with the SEC, but they were not.

Method
Bliss salesmen contacted potential investors and sold limited partnership interests. The setup deal called for these limited partnerships to purchase solar hot water heating systems for residential and commercial use from Bliss. All the partnerships entered into arrangements to lease the equipment to Nationwide Corporation, which then rented the equipment to end users. The limited partnerships were, in effect, financing conduits for obtaining investors' money to pay for Bliss's equipment. The investors depended on Nationwide's business success and ability to pay under the lease terms for their return of capital and profit.

Paper Trail

Bliss published false and misleading financial statements, which used a non-GAAP revenue recognition method and failed to disclose cost of goods sold. Bliss overstated Nationwide's record of equipment installation and failed to disclose that Nationwide had little cash flow from end users (resulting from rent-free periods and other inducements). Bliss knew--and failed to disclose to prospective investors--the fact that numerous previous investors had filed petitions with the U.S. tax court to contest the disallowance by the IRS of all their tax credits and benefits claimed in connection with their investments in Bliss's tax-sheltered equipment lease partnerships.

Amount

Not known, but all the money put up by the limited partnership investors was at risk largely not disclosed to the investors.

AUDIT APPROACH

Audit Objective

Obtain evidence to determine whether capital fund-raising methods comply with U.S. securities laws and whether financial statements and other disclosures are not misleading.

Control

Management should employ experts--attorneys, underwriters, and accountants--who can determine whether securities and investment contract sales do or do not require registration.

Test of Controls

Auditors should learn the business backgrounds and securities-industry expertise of the senior managers. Study the minutes of the board of directors for authorization of the fund-raising method. Obtain and study opinions rendered by attorneys and underwriters about the legality of the fund-raising methods. Inquire about management's interaction with the SEC in any presale clearance. (The SEC will give advice about the necessity for registration.)

Audit of Balances

Auditors should study the offering documents and literature used in the sale of securities to determine whether financial information is being used properly. In this case, the close relationship with Nationwide and the experience of earlier partnerships give reasons for extended procedures to obtain evidence about the representations concerning Nationwide's business success (in this case, lack of success).

Discovery Summary

The auditors gave unqualified reports on Bliss's materially misstated financial statements. They apparently did not question the legality of the sales of the limited partnership interests as a means of raising capital. They apparently did not perform procedures to verify representations made in offering literature respecting Bliss or Nationwide finances. Two partners in the audit firm were enjoined from violations of the securities laws. They resigned from practice before the SEC and were ordered not to perform any attest services for companies making filings with the SEC. (Source: SEC Litigation Release 10274, AAER 20, AAER 21.) They later were expelled from the AICPA for failure to cooperate with the Professional Ethics Division in its investigation of alleged professional ethics violations.

Source: *The CPA Letter*, January/February 1992.

CASE 12.2
TAX LOSS CARRYFORWARDS

Problem

Aetna Life & Casualty Insurance Company had losses in its taxable income operations in 1981 and 1982. Confident that future taxable income would absorb the loss, the company booked and reported a tax benefit for the tax loss carryforward. The SEC maintained that the company understated its tax expense and understated its liabilities (Aetna reported the tax benefit as a negative liability). Utilization of the loss carryforward was not "assured beyond a reasonable doubt," as then required by the accounting standards. (In 1992, FASB issued Statement No. 109 that changed the criterion to a "more likely than not" judgment.)

Method
Aetna forecasted several more years of taxable losses (aside from its nontaxable income from tax-exempt investments), then forecasted years of taxable income, eventually offsetting the losses and obtaining the benefit of the tax law allowing losses to be carried forward to offset against future taxable income. The company maintained there was no reasonable doubt that the forecasts would be achieved.

Paper Trail
The amounts of tax loss were clearly evident in the accounts. Aetna made no attempt to hide the facts. The size of the portfolio of taxable investments and all sources of taxable income and deductions were well known to the company accountants, management, and independent auditors.

Amount
At first, the carryforward tax benefit was $25 million, soon growing to over $200 million, then forecast to become an estimated $1 billion before it was forecast to reverse by being absorbed by future taxable income. In 1983, the first full year affected, Aetna's net income was 35 percent lower than 1981, instead of 6 percent lower with the carryforward benefit recognized.

AUDIT APPROACH

Audit Objective
Obtain evidence to determine whether realization of the benefits of the tax loss carryforward are "realizable beyond a reasonable doubt."

Control

The relevant control in this case concerns the assumptions and mathematics involved in preparing the forecasts used to justify the argument for recording the tax loss carryforward benefit. These forecasts are the basis for an accounting estimate of "realization beyond a reasonable doubt."

Test of Controls

Auditors should make inquiries and determine: Who prepared the forecasts? When were they prepared? What data were used? Who reviewed and approved the forecast? Is there any way to test the accuracy of the forecast with actual experience?

Audit of Balances

Aside from audit of the assumptions underlying the forecast and recalculations of the compilation, the test of balances amounted to careful consideration of whether the forecast, or any forecast, could meet the test required by accounting standards. The decision was a judgment of whether the test of "realization beyond a reasonable doubt" was met.

The auditors should obtain information about other situations in which recognition of tax loss carryforward benefits were allowed in financial statements. Other companies have booked and reported such benefits when gains from sales of property were realized before the financial statement were issued and when the loss was from discontinuing a business line, leaving other businesses with long profit histories and prospects in operation.

Discovery Summary

The SEC was tipped off to Aetna's accounting recognition of the tax loss carryforward benefit by a story in *Fortune* magazine, which described the accounting treatment. Aetna and its auditors argued on the basis of the forecasts. The SEC countered with the theory that forecasts were not sufficient to establish "realization beyond a reasonable doubt." The SEC won the argument. Aetna revised its previously issued quarterly financial statements, and the company abandoned the attempt to report the tax benefit

LONG-TERM LIABILITIES AND RELATED ACCOUNTS

The primary audit concern with the verification of long-term liabilities is that all liabilities are recorded and that the interest expense is properly paid or accrued. Therefore, the assertion of completeness is paramount. Alertness to the possibility of unrecorded liabilities during the performance of procedures in other areas frequently will uncover liabilities that have not been recorded. For example, when fixed assets are acquired during the year under audit, auditors should inquire about the source of funds for financing the new asset.

Management makes assertions about existence, completeness, rights and obligations, valuation, and presentation and disclosure. Typical specific assertions relating to long-term liabilities include:
1. All material long-term liabilities are recorded.
2. Liabilities are properly classified according to their current or long-term status. The current portion of long-term debt is properly valued and classified.
3. New long-term liabilities and debt extinguishments are properly authorized.
4. Terms, conditions, and restrictions relating to noncurrent debt are adequately disclosed.
5. Disclosures of maturities for the next five years and the capital and operating lease disclosures are accurate and adequate.
6. All important contingencies are either accrued in the accounts or disclosed in footnotes.

ENVIRONMENTAL LIABILITIES

The clock is ticking for corporations that missed the SEC's wakeup call to keep investors better informed about environmental liabilities. Companies may awaken to SEC enforcement actions, shareholder lawsuits, even criminal prosecution.

The focus on environmental disclosure is fairly recent--and it is gathering steam. Estimates of the nation's cost of hazardous waste cleanup range up to

> *$1 trillion*, but most shareholders have no idea the amounts specific companies must pay. Corporate annual reports tell very little.
>
> Companies must disclose any environmental trends or uncertainties they expect to have a material impact. The SEC is particularly interested in appropriate accounting and disclosure if a company is designated a "potentially responsible party" under the Superfund laws. (Auditors can identify such companies in a national "potentially responsible party" data base.)
>
> Source: *New York Times*, September 14, 1994.

Confirmation

When auditing long-term liabilities, auditors usually obtain independent written confirmations for notes and bonds payable. In the case of notes payable to banks, the standard bank confirmation may be used. The amount and terms of bonds payable, mortgages payable, and other formal debt instruments can be confirmed by requests to holders or a trustee. The confirmation request should include questions not only of amount, interest rate, and due date but also about collateral, restrictive covenants, and other items of agreement between lender and borrower. Confirmation requests should be sent to lenders with whom the company has done business in the recent past, even if no liability balance is shown at the confirmation date. Such extra coverage is a part of the search for unrecorded liabilities. (Refer to Chapter 9 for more on the "search for unrecorded liabilities.")

Off-Balance Sheet Financing

Confirmation and inquiry procedures may be used to obtain responses on a class of items loosely termed "off-balance sheet information." Within this category are: terms of loan agreements, leases, endorsements, guarantees, and insurance policies (whether issued by a client insurance company or owned by the client). Among these items is the difficult-to-define set of "commitments and contingencies" that often pose evidence-gathering problems. Some common types of commitments are shown in Exhibit 12-3.

Footnote disclosure should be considered for the types of commitments shown in Exhibit 12-3. Some of them can be estimated and valued and, thus, can be recorded in the accounts and shown in the financial statements themselves (such as losses on fixed-price purchase commitments and losses on fixed-price sales commitments).

EXHIBIT 12-3 Off-Balance Sheet Commitments

Type of Commitment	Typical Procedures and Sources of Evidence
1. Repurchase or remarketing agreements.	1. Vouching of contracts, confirmation by customer, inquiry of client management.
2. Commitments to purchase at fixed prices.	2. Vouching of open purchase orders, inquiry of purchasing personnel, confirmation by supplier.
3. Commitments to sell at fixed prices.	3. Vouching of sales contracts, inquiry of sales personnel, confirmation by customer.
4. Loan commitments (as in a savings and loan association).	4. Vouching of open commitment file, inquiry of loan officers.
5. Lease commitments.	5. Vouching of lease agreement, confirmation with lessor or lessee.

Analytical Relationships

Interest expense generally is related item by item to interest-bearing liabilities. Based on the evidence of long-term liability transactions (including those that have been retired during the year), the related interest expense amounts can be recalculated. The amount of debt, the interest rate, and the time period are used to determine whether the interest expense and accrued interest are properly recorded. By comparing the audit results to the recorded interest expense and accrued interest accounts, auditors may be able to detect: (1) greater expense than their calculations show, indicating some interest paid on debt unknown to them, possibly an unrecorded liability; (2) lesser expense than their calculations show, indicating misclassification, failure to accrue interest, or an interest payment default; or (3) interest expense equal to their calculations. The first two possibilities raise questions for further study, and the third shows a correct correlation between debt and debt-related expense.

Deferred Credits--Calculated Balances

Several types of deferred credits depend on calculations for their existence and valuation. Examples include: (1) deferred profit on installment sales involving the gross margin and the sale amount; (2) deferred income taxes and investment credits involving tax-book timing differences, tax rates, and amortization methods; and (3) deferred contract revenue involving contract provisions for prepayment, percentage-of-completion revenue recognition methods, or other terms unique to a contract. All of these features are incorporated in calculations that auditors can check for accuracy.

CASE 12.3
OFF-BALANCE SHEET INVENTORY FINANCING

Problem
Verity Distillery Company used the "product repurchase" ploy to convert its inventory to cash, failing to disclose the obligation to repurchase it later. Related party transactions were not disclosed.

Method
Verity's president incorporated the Veritas Corporation, making himself and two other Verity officers the sole stockholders. The president arranged to sell $40 million of Verity's inventory of whiskey in the aging process to Veritas, showing no gain or loss on the transaction. The officers negotiated a 36-month loan with a major bank to get the money Veritas used for the purchase, pledging the inventory as collateral. Verity pledged to repurchase the inventory for $54.4 million, which amounted to the original $40 million plus 12 percent interest for three years.

Paper Trail
The contract of sale was in the files, specifying the name of the purchasing company, the $40 million amount, and the cash consideration. Nothing mentioned the relation of Veritas to the officers. Nothing mentioned the repurchase obligation. However, the sale amount was unusually large.

Amount
The $40 million amount was 40 percent of the normal inventory. Verity's cash balance was increased 50 percent. While the current asset total was not changed, the inventory

ratios (e.g., inventory turnover, days' sales in inventory) were materially altered. Long-term liabilities were understated by not recording the liability. The ploy was actually a secured loan with inventory pledged as collateral, but this reality was neither recorded nor disclosed. The total effect would be to keep debt off the books, to avoid recording interest expense, and later to record inventory at a higher cost. Subsequent sale of the whiskey at market prices would not affect the ultimate income results, but the unrecorded interest expense would be buried in the cost of goods sold. The net income in the first year when the "sale" was made was not changed, but the normal relationship of gross margin to sales was distorted by the zero-profit transaction.

	Before Transaction	Recorded Transaction	Should Have Recorded
Assets	$530	$530	$570
Liabilities	390	390	430
Stockholder equity	140	140	140
Debt/equity ratio	2.79	2.79	3.07

AUDIT APPROACH

Audit Objective
Obtain evidence to determine whether all liabilities are recorded. Be alert to undisclosed related party transactions.

Control
The relevant control in this case would rest with the integrity and accounting knowledge of the senior officials who arranged the transaction. Authorization in the board minutes might detail the arrangements; but, if they wanted to hide it from the auditors, they also would suppress the telltale information in the board minutes.

Test of Controls

Inquiries should be made about large and unusual financing transactions. This might not elicit a response because the event is a sales transaction, according to Verity. Other audit work on controls in the revenue and collection cycle might turn up the large sale. Fortunately, this one sticks out as a large one.

Audit of Balances

Analytical procedures to compare monthly or seasonal sales probably will identify the sale as large and unusual. This identification should lead to an examination of the sales contract. Auditors should discuss the business purpose of the transaction with knowledgeable officials. If being this close to discovery does not bring out an admission of the loan and repurchase arrangement, the auditors nevertheless should investigate further. Even if the "customer" name were not a giveaway, a quick inquiry at the state secretary of state office for corporation records (online in some databases) will show the names of the officers, and the auditors will know the related party nature of the deal. A request for the financial statements of Veritas should be made.

Discovery Summary

The auditors found the related party relationship between the officers and Veritas. Confronted, the president admitted the attempt to make the cash position and the debt/equity ratio look better than they were. The financial statements were adjusted to reflect the "should have recorded" set of figures shown above.

INVESTMENTS AND INTANGIBLES

Companies can have a wide variety of investments and relationships with affiliates. Investments accounting may be on the market value method, cost method, equity method, or full consolidation, depending on the nature, size, and influence represented by the investment. Purchase-method consolidations usually create problems of accounting for the fair value of acquired assets and the related goodwill.

Specific assertions typical of a variety of investment and intangibles account balances are these:

1. Investment securities are on hand or are held in safekeeping by a trustee.
2. The accounting for investment cost and market value is appropriate.
3. Controlling investments are accounted for by the equity method.
4. Purchased goodwill is properly valued.
5. Capitalized intangible costs relate to intangibles acquired in exchange transactions.
6. Research and development costs are properly classified.
7. Amortization is properly calculated.
8. Investment income has been received and recorded.
9. Investments are adequately classified and described in the balance sheet, including disclosures of restrictions, pledges, or liens.

Unlike the current assets accounts, which are characterized by numerous small transactions, the noncurrent investment accounts usually consist of a few large entries. This difference has internal control and substantive audit procedure implications. The effect on the auditors' consideration of the control environment is concentration on the authorization of transactions, since each individual transaction is likely to be material in itself and the authorization will give significant information about the proper classification and accounting method. The controls usually are not reviewed, tested, and evaluated at an interim date but are considered along with the year-end procedures when the transactions and their authorizations are audited.

A few of the trouble spots in audits of investments and intangibles are in the box below.

TROUBLE SPOTS IN AUDITS OF INVESTMENTS AND INTANGIBLES

- Valuation of investments at cost, market, or value impairment that is other than temporary.
- Determination of significant influence relationship for equity method investments.
- Proper determination of goodwill in purchase-method consolidations. Reasonable amortization life for goodwill.
- Realistic distinction between purchase and pooling consolidations.

- Capitalization and continuing valuation of intangibles and deferred charges.
- Realistic distinctions of research, feasibility, and production milestones for capitalization of software development costs.
- Adequate disclosure of restrictions, pledges, or liens related to investment assets.

Confirmation

The practice of obtaining independent written confirmation from outside parties is fairly limited in the area of investments, intangibles, and related income and expense accounts. Securities held by trustees or brokers should be confirmed, and the confirmation request should seek the same descriptive information as that obtained in a physical inspection by the auditor (described earlier in this chapter).

Inquiries about Intangibles

Company counsel can be queried about knowledge of any lawsuits or defects relating to patents, copyrights, trademarks, or trade names. This confirmation can be sought by a specific request in the attorney's letter.

Income from Intangibles

Royalty income from patent licenses received from a single licensee may be confirmed. However, such income amounts usually are audited by vouching the licensee's reports and the related cash receipt.

Inspection

Investment property may be inspected in a manner similar to the physical inspection of fixed assets. The principal goal is to determine actual existence and condition of the property. Official documents of patents, copyrights, and trademark rights can be inspected to see that they are, in fact, in the name of the client.

Documentation Vouching

Investment costs should be vouched to brokers' reports, monthly statements, or other documentary evidence of cost. At the same time, the amounts of sales are traced to gain or loss accounts, and the amounts of sales prices and proceeds are vouched to the brokers' statements. Auditors should determine what method of cost-out assignment was used (i.e., FIFO, specific certificate, or average cost) and whether it is consistent with prior-years' transactions. The cost of real and personal property likewise can be vouched to invoices or other documents of purchase, and title documents (such as on land, buildings) may be inspected.

Market valuation of securities may be required in some cases. While a management may assert that an investment valuation is not impaired, subsequent sale at a loss before the end of audit field work will indicate otherwise. Auditors should review investment transactions subsequent to the balance sheet date for this kind of evidence about lower-of-cost-or-market valuation.

Vouching may be extensive in the areas of research and development (R&D) and deferred software development costs. The principal evidence problem is to determine whether costs are properly classified as assets or as R&D expense. Recorded amounts generally are selected on a sample basis, and the purchase orders, receiving reports, payroll records, authorization notices, and management reports are compared to them. Some R&D costs may resemble non-R&D cost (such as supplies, payroll costs), so auditors must be very careful in the vouching to be alert for costs that appear to relate to other operations.

External Documentation

By consulting quoted market values of securities, auditors can calculate market values and determine whether investments should be written down. If quoted market values are not available, financial statements related to investments must be obtained and analyzed for evidence of basic value. If such financial statements are unaudited, evidence indicated by them is considered to be extremely weak.

Income amounts can be verified by consulting published dividend records for quotations of dividends actually declared and paid during a period (e.g., Moody's and Standard & Poor's dividend records). Since auditors know the holding period of securities, dividend income can be calculated and compared to the amount in the account. Any difference could indicate a cutoff error, misclassification, defalcation, or failure to record a dividend receivable. In a similar manner, application of interest rates to bond or note investments produces a calculated interest income figure (making allowance for amortization of premium or discount if applicable).

Equity Method Investments

When equity method accounting is used for investments, auditors will need to obtain financial statements of the investee company. These should be audited statements. Inability to obtain financial statements from a closely held investee may indicate that the client investor does not have the significant controlling influence required by *APB Opinion* No. 18 (SAS 1, AU 332). When available, these statements are used as the basis for recalculating the amount of the client's share of income to recognize in the accounts. In addition, these statements may be used to audit the disclosure of investees' assets, liabilities, and income presented in footnotes (a disclosure recommended when investments accounted for by the equity method are material).

Amortization Recalculation

Amortization of goodwill and other intangibles should be recalculated. Like depreciation, amortization expense owes its existence to a calculation, and recalculation based on audited costs and rates is sufficient audit evidence.

Merger and acquisition transactions should be reviewed in terms of the appraisals, judgments, and allocations used to assign portions of the purchase price to tangible assets, intangible assets, liabilities, and goodwill. In the final analysis, nothing really substitutes for the inspection of transaction documentation, but verbal inquiries may help auditors to understand the circumstances of a merger.

Questions about lawsuits challenging patents, copyrights, or trade names may produce early knowledge of problem areas for further investigation. Likewise, discussions and questions about research and development successes and failures may alert the audit team to problems of valuation of intangible assets and related amortization expense. Responses to questions about licensing of patents can be used in the audit of related royalty revenue accounts.

Inquiries about Management Intentions

Inquiries should deal with the nature of investments and the reasons for holding them. Management's expressed intention that a marketable security investment be considered a long-term investment may be the only available evidence for classifying it as long term and not as a current asset. The classification will affect the accounting treatment of market values and the unrealized gains and losses on investments.

CASE 12.4
A CONSOLIDATION BY ANY OTHER NAME

Problem
Digilog, Inc., formed another company named DBS International (DBSI), controlled it, and did not consolidate its financial position and results of operations in the Digilog financial statements. Digilog income was overstated, and assets and liabilities were understated.

Method
Digilog, Inc., formed DBSI as a separate corporation to market Digilog's microcomputer equipment. DBSI was formed separately to avoid the adverse impact of reporting expected startup losses in Digilog's financial statements. Instead of owning stock in DBSI, Digilog financed the company with loans convertible at will into 90 percent of DBSI's stock. (Otherwise, the stock ownership was not in Digilog's name.) Since Digilog did not control DBSI (control defined as 50 percent or more ownership), DBSI was not consolidated, and the initial losses were not reported in Digilog's financial statements.

Paper Trail
Formation of DBSI was not a secret. It was authorized. Incorporation papers were available. Loan documents showing the terms of Digilog's loans to DBSI were in the files.

Amount
Several hundred thousand dollars of losses in the first two years of DBSI operations were not consolidated. Ultimately, the venture became profitable and was absorbed into Digilog.

AUDIT APPROACH

Audit Objective
Obtain evidence to determine whether proper accounting methods (cost, equity, consolidation) are used for investments.

Control
The relevant control in this case would rest with the integrity and accounting knowledge of the senior officials who arranged the transaction. Proper documentation of authorization and financing and operating transactions between the two corporations should be in the companies' files.

Test of Controls
Inquiries should be made about large and unusual financing transactions. Minutes of the board of directors' meetings should be studied to find related authorizations. These authorizations and supporting papers signal the accounting issues and the interpretations of generally accepted accounting principles required in the circumstances.

Audit of Balances
The central issue in this case was the interpretation of accounting standards regarding required consolidation. Existence, completeness, valuation, and ownership were not problematic audit issues. Accounting standards required consolidation of over-50 percent owned subsidiaries, and prohibited consolidation of subsidiaries owned less than 50 percent. Digilog's purpose in financing DBSI with loans instead of direct stock ownership was to skirt the 50 percent "ownership" criterion, thus keeping the DBSI losses out of the Digilog consolidated financial statements. The "test of the balance" (decision of whether to require consolidation) amounted to an interpretation of the substance versus form of "ownership" through convertible notes instead of direct stock holding.

Discovery Summary
Digilog, with concurrence of its independent audit firm, adopted the narrow interpretation of "ownership." Since Digilog did not "own" DBSI stock, DBSI was not "controlled," and its assets, liabilities, and results of operations were not

consolidated. The SEC disagreed and took action on the position that the convertible feature of the loans and the business purpose of the DBSI formation were enough to attribute control to Digilog. The company was enjoined from violating certain reporting and antifraud provisions of the Securities Exchange Act of 1934 and was required to amend its financial statements for the years in question (consolidating DBSI). The SEC also took action against the audit firm partner in charge of the Digilog audit. (Sources: SEC Litigation Release No. 10448 and Securities Act of 1933 Release No. 6542.) Later, the SEC amended its consolidation rules to make the over-50 percent consolidation criterion presumptive instead of determinative, along with language requiring consideration of substance over form in making consolidation accounting interpretations.

OTHER ASPECTS OF CLEVER ACCOUNTING AND FRAUD

The types of clever accounting and fraud that must be considered are those that affect the fair presentation of material equity accounts, investments, and intangibles. Improper accounting presentations are engineered more frequently by senior officials than by middle management or lower ranks. Top management personnel who deal with the transactions involved in investments, long-term debt, and stockholders' equity are not subject to the same kind of control as lower-level employees, and they generally are able to override detail procedural controls.

LONG-TERM LIABILITIES AND OWNERS' EQUITY

The kinds of clever accounting and fraud connected with liability and owners' equity accounts differ significantly from those associated with asset and revenue accounts. Few employees are tempted to steal a liability, although fictitious liabilities may be created as a means of misdirecting cash payments into the hands of an officer. Auditors should be alert for such fictions in the same sense that they are alert to the possibility of having fictitious accounts receivable.

Although employees have opportunities to commit fraud against the company, the area of liabilities and owners' equity also opens up possibilities for company fraud against outsiders. This class of fraud is most often accomplished through material misrepresentations or omissions in financial statements and related disclosures.

Officers and employees can use stock or bond instruments improperly. Unissued stock or bonds and Treasury stock or bonds might be used as collateral for personal loans. Even though the company may not be damaged or suffer loss by this action (unless the employee defaults and the securities are seized), the practice is unauthorized and is contrary to company interests. Similarly, employees might gain access to stockholder lists and unissued or Treasury bond coupons and cause improper payments of dividends and interest on securities that are not outstanding.

Proper custodial control of securities (either by physical means, such as limited-access vaults, or by control of an independent disbursing agent) prevents most such occurrences. An auditing procedure of reconciling authorized dividend and interest payments (calculated using declared dividend rates, coupon interest rates, and known quantities of outstanding securities) to actual payments detects unauthorized payments. If the company did not perform this checking procedure, auditors should include it among their own analytical recalculation procedures.

Many liability, equity, and off-balance sheet transactions are outside the reach of normal internal controls, which can operate effectively over ordinary transactions (such as purchases and sales) processed by clerks and machines. Auditors generally are justified in performing extensive substantive auditing of long-term liability, equity, and other high-level managed transactions and agreements since control depends in large part on the integrity and accounting knowledge of management.

Income tax evasion and fraud result from actions taken by managers. Evasion and fraud may be accomplished (1) by simple omission of income, (2) by unlawful deductions (such as contributions to political campaigns, depreciation on nonexistent assets, or depreciation in excess of cost), or (3) by contriving sham transactions for the sole purpose of avoiding taxation. Auditors should be able to detect errors of the first two categories if the actual income and expense data have been sufficiently audited in the financial statements. The last category--contrived sham transactions--is harder to detect because a dishonest management can skillfully disguise them. Some of the procedures outlined in Chapter 6 may be useful and effective.

Financial statements may be materially misstated by reason of omission or understatement of liabilities and by failure to disclose technical defaults on loan agreement restrictions. The procedures you have learned to discover unrecorded liabilities through a "search for unrecorded liabilities" may be used to discover such omissions and understatements (Chapter 9). If auditors discover that loan agreement terms have been violated, they should bring the information to the client's attention and insist on proper disclosure in notes to the financial statements. In both situations (liability understatement and loan default disclosure), management's actions, reactions, and willingness to adjust the financial figures and to make adverse disclosures are important insights for auditors' subjective evaluation of managerial integrity. An accumulation of inputs relevant to managerial integrity can have an important bearing on the auditors' perceptions of relative risk for the audit engagement taken as a whole.

A company, its individual managers, and the auditors can violate securities regulations if they are not careful. Auditors must know the provisions of the securities laws to the extent they can identify situations that constitute obvious fraud, and so they can identify transactions that might be subject to the law. Having once recognized or raised questions about a securities transaction, auditors should not act as their own attorney. The facts should be submitted to competent legal counsel for an opinion. Even though auditors are not expected to be legal experts, they have the duty to recognize obvious instances of impropriety and to pursue investigations with the aid of legal experts.

Similarly, auditors should assist clients in observing SEC rules and regulations on matters of timely disclosure. In general, the timely disclosure rules are phrased in terms of management's duties, and they do not require auditors to do any specific procedures or to make any specific disclosures. The regulations' purpose and spirit are to require management to disseminate to the public any material information, whether favorable or unfavorable, so investors can incorporate it in their decision making. Various rule provisions require announcements and disclosures very soon after information becomes known. Often, relevant situations arise during the year when the independent auditors are not present, so, of course, they cannot be held responsible or liable. However, in other situations, auditors may learn of the information inadvertently or the auditors' advice may be sought by the client. In such cases, auditors should advise their clients about the requirements of laws and regulations.

Presently, pressures are on the auditors to discover more information about off-balance sheet contingencies and commitments and to discover the facts of management involvement with other parties to transactions. Auditors' knowledge of contingencies and commitments that are not evidenced in accounting records depends in large part on information the management and its attorneys will reveal. Nevertheless, certain investigative procedures are available (Chapter 6). The current pressures on auditors to discover more information is a part of the public pressure on auditors to take more responsibility for fraud detection.

INVESTMENTS AND INTANGIBLES

Theft, diversion, or unauthorized use of investment securities can occur in several ways. If safekeeping controls are weak, securities simply may be stolen and the theft becomes a police problem, rather than an auditing problem. Somewhat more frequent, however, are diversions, such as using securities as collateral during the year, returning them for a count, then giving them back to the creditor without disclosure to the auditor. If safekeeping methods require entry signatures (as at a safe-deposit vault), auditors may be able to detect the in-and-out movement. The best chance of discovery is that the creditor will confirm the collateral arrangement. In a similar manner, securities may be removed by an officer and sold, then repurchased before the auditors' count. The auditors' record of the certificate numbers should reveal this change since the returned certificates (and their serial numbers) will not be the same as the ones removed.

Cash receipts from interest, royalties on patent licenses, dividends, and sales proceeds might be stolen. The accounting records may or may not be manipulated to cover the theft. In general, this kind of defalcation should be prevented by cash receipts control; but, since these receipts usually are irregular and infrequent, the cash control system may not be as effective as it is for regular receipts on trade accounts. If the income accounts are not manipulated to hide stolen receipts, auditors will find less income in the account than the amount indicated by their audit calculations based on other records, such as license agreements or published dividend records. If sales of securities are not recorded, auditors will notice that securities are missing when they try to inspect or confirm them. If the income accounts have been manipulated to hide stolen receipts, vouching of cash receipts will detect the theft, or vouching may reveal some offsetting debit buried in some other account.

Accounting values may be manipulated in a number of ways, involving purchase of assets at inflated prices, leases with affiliates, acquisitions of patents for stock given to an inventor or promoter, sales to affiliates, and fallacious decisions about amortization. Business history has recorded several cases of nonarm's-length transactions with promoters, officers, directors, and controlled companies (even "dummy" companies) designed to drain the company's resources and fool the auditors.

In one case, a company sold assets to a dummy purchaser set up by a director to bolster sagging income with a gain. The auditors did not know that the purchaser was a shell. All the documents of sale looked in order, and cash sales proceeds had been deposited. The auditors were not informed of a secret agreement by the seller to repurchase the assets at a later time. This situation illustrates a very devious manipulation. All transactions with persons closely associated with the company (related parties) should be audited carefully with reference to market values, particularly when a nonmonetary transaction is involved (such as stock exchanged for patent rights). Sales and lease-back and straight lease transactions with insiders likewise should be audited carefully.

SUMMARY

The finance and investment cycle contains a wide variety of accounts--capital stock, dividends, long-term debt, interest expense, income tax expense and deferred taxes, financial instruments, marketable securities, equity method investments, related gains and losses, consolidated subsidiaries, goodwill, and other intangibles. These accounts involve some of the most technically complex accounting standards. They create most of the difficult judgments for financial reporting.

Transactions in these accounts generally are controlled by senior officials. Therefore, internal control is centered on the integrity and accounting knowledge of these officials. The procedural controls over details of transactions are not very effective because the senior managers can override them and order their own desired accounting presentations. As a consequence, auditors' work on the assessment of control risk is directed toward the senior managers, the board of directors, and their authorizations and design of finance and investment deals.

PRACTICAL CASE PROBLEMS
INSTRUCTIONS FOR CASES

These cases are designed like the ones in the chapter. They give the problem, the method, the paper trail, and the amount. Your assignment is to write the "audit approach" portion of the case, organized around these sections:

Objectives: Express the objective in terms of the facts supposedly asserted in financial records, accounts, and statements.

Control: Write a brief explanation of control considerations, especially the kinds of manipulations that might arise from the situation described in the case.

Test of controls: Write some procedures for getting evidence about existing controls, especially procedures that could discover management manipulations. If there are no controls to test, then there are no procedures to perform; go then to the next section. A "procedure" should instruct someone about the source(s) of evidence to tap and the work to do.

Audit of balance: Write some procedures for getting evidence about the existence, completeness, valuation, ownership, or disclosure assertions identified in your *objective* section above.

Discovery summary: Write a short statement about the discovery you expect to accomplish with your procedures.

CASE #12.1: HIDE THE LOSS UNDER THE GOODWILL--Related Party Transaction "Goodwill." Write the "audit approach" section like the cases in the chapter.
Problem: A contrived amount of goodwill was used to overstate assets and disguise a loss on discontinued operations.

Method: Gulwest Industries, a public company, decided to discontinue its unprofitable line of business of manufacturing sporting ammunition. Gulwest had capitalized the startup cost of the business, and, with its discontinuance, the $7 million deferred cost should have been written off.

Instead, Gulwest formed a new corporation named Amron and transferred the sporting ammunition assets (including the $7 million deferred cost) to it in exchange for all the Amron stock. In the Gulwest accounts, the Amron investment was carried at $12.4 million, which was the book value of the assets transferred (including the $7 million deferred cost).

In an agreement with a different public company (Big Industrial), Gulwest and Big created another company (BigShot Ammunition). Gulwest transferred all the Amron assets to BigShot in exchange for (1) common and preferred stock of Big, valued at $2 million, and (2) a note from BigShot in the amount of $3.4 million. Big Industrial thus acquired 100 percent of the stock of BigShot. Gulwest management reasoned that it had "given" Amron stock valued at $12.4 million to receive stock and notes valued at $5.4 million, so the difference must be goodwill. Thus, the Gulwest accounts carried amounts for Big Industrial Stock ($2 million) BigShot Note Receivable ($3.4 million), and Goodwill ($7 million).

Paper trail: Gulwest directors included in the minutes an analysis of the sporting ammunition business's lack of profitability. The minutes showed approval of a plan to dispose of the business, but they did not use the words "discontinue the business." The minutes also showed approval of the creation of Amron, the deal with Big Industrial along with the formation of BigShot, and the acceptance of Big's stock and BigShot's note in connection with the final exchange and merger.

Amount: As explained above, Gulwest avoided reporting a write-off of $7 million by overstating the value of the assets given in exchange for the Big Industrial stock and the BigShot Ammunition note.

CASE #12.2: IN PLANE VIEW--Related Party Transaction Valuation.
Write the audit approach section like the cases in the chapter.

Problem: Whiz Corporation overstated the value of stock given in exchange for an airplane and, thereby, understated its loss on disposition of the stock. Income was overstated.

Method: Whiz owned 160,000 shares of Wing Company stock, carried on the books as an investment in the amount of $6,250,000. Whiz bought a used airplane from Wing, giving in exchange (1) $480,000 cash and (2) the 160,000 Wing shares. Even though the quoted market value of the Wing stock was $2,520,000, Whiz valued the airplane received at $3,750,000, indicating a stock valuation of $3,270,000. Thus, Whiz recognized a loss on disposition of the Wing stock in the amount of $2,980,000.

Whiz justified the airplane valuation with another transaction. On the same day it was purchased Whiz sold the airplane to the Mexican subsidiary of one of its subsidiary companies (two layers down; but Whiz owned 100 percent of the first subsidiary, which in turn owned 100 percent of the Mexican subsidiary). The Mexican subsidiary paid Whiz with US$25,000 cash and a promissory note for US$3,725,000 (market rate of interest).

Paper trail: The transaction was within the authority of the chief executive officer, and company policy did not require a separate approval by the board of directors. A contract of sale and correspondence with Wing detailing the terms of the transaction were in the files. Likewise, a contract of sale to the Mexican subsidiary, along with a copy of the deposit slip, and a memorandum of the promissory note was on file. The note itself was kept in the company vault. None of the Wing papers cited a specific price for the airplane.

Amount: Whiz overvalued the Wing stock and justified it with a related party transaction with its own subsidiary company. The loss on the disposition of the Wing stock was understated by $750,000.

CASE #12.3: SHARP HEDGE CLIPPERS--Loss Deferral on Hedged Investments. This case contains complexities that preclude writing the entire audit approach according to the instructions. Instead, respond to these requirements:

a.   What is the objective of the audit work on the investment account described in the Sharp Hedge Clippers case?

b.   What is your conclusion about the propriety of deferring the losses on the hedged investments sales and the futures contracts? About the proper carrying amount of the investment in the balance sheet?

c. Do you believe the successor auditors were independent? Competent? Discuss the practice of "shopping around" for an unqualified audit report.

Problem: Southeastern Savings & Loan Company (Southeastern) overstated its assets and income by improperly deferring losses on hedged investment transactions.

Method: In the course of its normal operations, Southeastern held investments in 15 percent and 16 percent GNMA certificates. Fearing an increase in interest rates and a consequent loss in the market value of these investments, Southeastern sought to hedge by selling futures contracts for U.S. Treasury bonds. If market interest rates increased, the losses in the GNMA investments would be offset by gains in the futures contracts.

However, interest rates declined, and Southeastern was caught in an odd market quirk. The value of the GNMAs increased with the lower interest rates, but not very much. (GNMAs are certificates in pools of government-backed mortgages, which pass through the interest and principle collections to the certificate holders.) As interest rates declined, the market perceived that the underlying mortgages would be paid off more quickly, that investors would receive all their proceeds earlier than previously expected, and that they would need to reinvest their money at the now-lower interest rates. Consequently, the 15 percent and 16 percent GNMAs held by Southeastern began trading as if the expected maturity were 4-5 years instead of the previously expected 8-12 years, which means that their prices did not rise as much as other interest-sensitive securities. On the other hand, the U.S. Treasury bonds with fixed maturity dates fell in price, and the futures hedge generated large losses.

Southeastern sold its 15 percent and 16 percent GNMAs and realized a $750,000 gain. Before and after these sales, the company purchased 8.0-12.5 percent GNMAs. The goal was to be invested in substantially different securities, ones that had a market return and the normal 8-12-year expected life payout. Later, Southeastern closed out its Treasury bond futures and realized a loss of $3.7 million. Still later, Southeastern sold GNMA futures contracts to hedge the investment in the 8.0-12.5 percent GNMA investments. The net loss of about $3 million was deferred in the balance sheet, instead of being recognized as a loss in the income statement.

Paper trail/accounting principles: The accounting for these transactions is complex and requires some significant judgments. In general, no gain or loss is recognized when the security sold is simultaneously replaced by the same or substantially the same security (a "wash" transaction), provided that any loss deferral does not result in carrying the investment at an amount greater than its market value. When a futures hedge is related to the securities sold, gains and losses on the futures contracts must be recognized when the hedged securities are sold, unless the sale of the hedged securities is part of a wash sale.

The significant accounting judgment is the identification of the disposition and new investment as a wash transaction. In turn, this requires a determination of whether the sale and reinvestment is "simultaneous" and involves "substantially the same security."

The "paper trail" is littered with information relevant to these judgments:

Criterion	Southeastern Transaction
Timing:	
Simultaneous sale/purchase or purchase/sale.	Some of the 15 percent and 16 percent GNMAs were sold six weeks after the 8.0-12.5 percent GNMAs were purchased.
Substantial similarity:	
Same issuer.	Both the securities sold and the securities purchased were GNMAs.
Similar market yield.	The yields on the two different GNMA series differed by about 3 percentage points.
Similar contractual maturity date.	The contractual maturity dates were the same.
Similar prospects for redemption.	The market priced the 15 percent and 16 percent GNMAs sold as though payback would occur in 4-5 years and the 8.0-12.5 percent GNMAs as though payback would occur in 8-12 years.
Carrying value:	
Asset carrying amount, including any deferred loss, shall not exceed securities' market value.	Asset value in financial statements exceeded the market value.

Paper trail/auditor involvement: Southeastern's independent auditors concluded that the losses should not be deferred. Southeastern fired the auditors and reported the disagreement in the 8-K reported filed with the SEC. After consulting several other auditors, who agreed with the former auditors, Southeastern finally found a CPA firm whose local partners would give an unqualified audit report on financial statements containing the deferral.

In February, the auditors who disagreed with the deferral were fired. The new auditors were hired on February 18 to audit the financial statements for the year ended the previous December 31. The unqualified audit report was dated March 28, 39 days after the new auditors were engaged by Southeastern's audit committee.

The new auditors were well aware of the accounting judgments required. They knew the former auditors and another CPA firm had concluded that the losses should not be deferred. They saw memoranda of the disagreement and the conclusion in the predecessor's working papers. They spoke with the predecessor partner on the engagement.

CHAPTER 13
FRAUD-DETECTION
AUDIT PROCEDURES

The AICPA generally accepted auditing standards (GAAS) contain two barriers for the performance of fraud-detection audit procedures. The first is the risk assessment prerequisite that can trigger a responsibility to perform them. The second is the concentration on management fraud almost to the exclusion of employee fraud. Fraud-detection procedures are usually regarded as costly. Many managements do not believe they are necessary and do not care to pay for them. However, independent auditors may find that some fraud-detection procedures are easy and may produce service benefits to clients.

TWO BARRIERS

Fraud-detection audit procedures are conditional. According to GAAS: "Considering the assessment of risk that fraud may cause the financial statements to contain a material misstatement, the auditor should plan the audit to include overall responses and specific procedures designed to determine whether fraud has occurred and whether the financial statements are materially misstated." The risk assessment comes first. It must show the auditors reasons to suspect errors and frauds in the accounts. This risk assessment demands the skills for noticing "red flags" and deciding that they are significant for planning subsequent procedures. Thus, performance of fraud-detection procedures is conditional upon (1) the existence of red flags, (2) the auditors' skill in noticing them, and (3) the auditors' willingness to follow them with fraud-detecting procedures. Performance of fraud-detecting procedures generally is not "normal" in most financial statement audits.

The auditing standards concentrate on management fraud--the production of materially false and misleading financial statements. This concentration of interest focuses on balance sheet accounts in terms of asset overstatement and liability understatement. It does not suggest high interest in the income statement. Many employee frauds are "expensed"; that is, they involve revenues that are never recorded or improper payments that are charged to expense accounts. When such frauds occur, the net income ("bottom line") is not wrong. After all, the fraud losses are in the income statement; they are just not separately identified and labeled. Granted, the income statement is not presented as it "should be" without the fraud, but independent auditors do not have a responsibility to give opinions on financial statements with relation to "no fraud" conditions. (Likewise, independent auditors do not give opinions on financial statements with relation to "what they could have been" had the organization obtained a new contract, produced better quality products, or achieved targeted expense reductions in the normal course of business.) Employee frauds may be large, but they are rarely large enough create material distortions of important income statement numbers and ratios and thus materially misstate an income statement.

CLIENT RELATIONS AND "NORMALITY"

Before SAS 82 was issued (effective December 15, 1997), independent auditors resisted any requirements to perform fraud-detecting procedures as a part of every audit. They tended to leap to the conclusion that a "fraud audit" is very costly and time-consuming. They regarded fraud-detecting procedures as "not normal." GAAS still somewhat supports this view by making such procedures conditional upon the risk assessment.

However, "normality" is in the eyes of the beholder. In the 1930s, confirmation of receivables and observation of inventories were not widely regarded as normal procedures. Under SEC pressure after the McKesson & Robbins affair, these two procedures were written into the auditing standards and made normal for all audits. Today, auditors regard confirmation and observation as standard procedures. Auditors perform them to try to detect errors and frauds, but they are not conditional. They are performed in all audits. Tomorrow, other procedures may become "normal" either through client demand or through external regulatory pressure.

Independent auditors also resist requirements that increase the effort and cost of audits. They are very sensitive to the audit fees clients are willing to pay. Fraud is an unpleasant topic, and many client managements need to be "sold" on the prospect that it may actually exist in their organizations. Independent auditors are generally not eager to undertake the task of persuading managements that they need fraud-detection work as part of the audit engagement.

Dealing with fraud can be troublesome. Some auditors do not relish being perceived as "snoops" out to catch the bad people. Managers and employees, especially the ones engaged in frauds, do not generally encourage auditors to find fraud. Independent auditors are very concerned about maintaining good relations with client managers. After all, they depend upon the managers for cooperation in the audit. The dynamics of client relations no doubt has helped shape auditing standards toward viewing fraud-detection procedures as aberrations in the normal audit. Independent auditors prefer to keep clients satisfied--at least not indignant--and present themselves as useful consultants rather than snoops.

Management consulting services are another matter. CPA firms have created forensic accounting and litigation support groups to provide a wide variety of services. Skills are available in CPA firms, but they apparently are confined mostly to the consulting business.

FRAUD-DETECTION AUDIT PROCEDURES

The remainder of this chapter presents a variety of audit procedures that can be used to detect fraud. The presentation is limited to procedures auditors generally do not include in standard audit programs. (Since space is limited, the fraud-detecting capability of "normal" audit procedures is not covered. Other fraud-detecting procedures are in the preceding chapters, especially Chapter 6.) The procedures are presented here do not address cost or feasibility. Auditors can decide whether to use them in consideration of all the circumstances in an engagement. Some of them can be performed with little cost. Others require considerable time and effort. Perhaps time will tell whether some of these procedures become "normal."

PROCEDURES FOR CASH RECEIPTS, SALES, ACCOUNTS RECEIVABLE

CASH RECEIPTS--LAPPING

> ● Select a sample of deposit slips, and compare listed checks by payee to subsidiary accounts receivable postings (remittance list or other bookkeeping document) for correspondence of name, date, and amount.

Lapping occurs when cash from a customer is misappropriated by an employee in the cash custody-bookkeeping loop. At a later date, the employee credits cash received from another customer to the first customer's account, and so on repeatedly. The audit procedure matches individual checks deposited by the client with the corresponding credits posted to customers' accounts. For example, if the deposit slip shows a check received from Customer B for $30 on February 14, but the daily posting shows no credit to Customer B but instead a credit for $30 to Customer A (not listed on the bank deposit), lapping is probable.

> ● When detail comparison of deposits to bookkeeping documents indicate lapping, obtain the customer's canceled check (or a front and back copy). Inspect the endorsement(s).

An employee engaged in lapping must convert the customers' payments to his or her own use. The endorsement on the customers' checks may lead to identification of the employee, the employee's bank account, or an accomplice. Endorsements to a bank for purchase of cashiers' checks and travelers' checks has been used to convert funds. (The receiving client ordinarily will not endorse customer payments to buy cashiers' checks or travelers' checks.)

CUSTOMER EXISTENCE

> ● Select a sample of customers, and verify their existence as bona fide businesses or persons, using (a) Better Business Bureau inquiry, (b) criss-cross and telephone directories, (c) Secretary of State incorporation records, (d) local partnership registration and assumed name records. Call

> the telephone number or visit the address. The sample should include customers with initials for company names and those with post office box addresses.

Fictitious sales may be charged to non-existent customers. An internal embezzlement can be perpetrated by selling to conspirators at discounted prices for a kickback.

Experience has shown instances of manipulators being unimaginative with names (using initials like "ABC Company") and being unwilling to go to the trouble to establish a false address other than a post office box. Auditors must exercise considerable care to notice clever use of private post box services. Fraudsters have used a real company name (e.g., General Motors) and a private box service to intercept mail that appears to be addressed to a legitimate company. Such addresses usually contain a street address as well as a "box number."

SALES RETURNS

> Investigate sales terms when large returns are recorded after year-end and quarter-end financial reporting dates.
>
> * Send accounts receivable confirmations to customers whose returns are recorded soon after year-end and quarter-end financial reporting dates.

Large amounts of sales returns after important financial reporting dates suggest that sales were recorded too early. If sales terms indicate liberal rights of return, sales and revenue recording may be not in conformity with generally accepted accounting principles. Questions and inquiries can also be used to try to learn of delays in recording returns.

Confirmations to such customers may reveal (a) customers' exceptions indicating no participation in the transactions (fictitious transactions without the knowledge of real customers), and (b) "return to sender" confirmation attempts indicating fictitious customers. Auditors need to be especially mindful of accounts receivable charged to customers who normally do not respond to confirmations (e.g., some governmental units and agencies and large multinational organizations).

> - Select a sample of recorded credit memos, and audit for timely recording with reference to dates in correspondence or other documentation.

Companies can inflate sales for the period and overstate accounts receivable by failing to record sales returns from customers. Delayed recording can be a red flag of this kind of activity.

> - Select a sample of recorded sales returns, and trace to inventory or similar records. If possible, inspect the physical property. Try to find original sales price record. Confirm returns with customers if feasible and necessary.

Employee return frauds have occurred by (a) employee theft of returned merchandise, (b) return of full price to a conspirator who paid a reduced sales price, (c) return of merchandise purchased at employee discount for full price refund. Documentation of "no return" original sales ticket or a discounted price ticket may be attached to credit memos.

UNAUTHORIZED SHIPMENTS

> - Select a sample of shipping records, and audit for authorization, shipment to a bona fide customer, shipment to a bona fide address, and complete recording as a cash or credit sale.

Employees have stolen inventory by falsifying shipping documents and directing shipments to themselves or conspirators. If the shipment is recorded as a sale, other audit procedures can be used to detect fictitious customers or destinations controlled by employees.

ACCOUNTS RECEIVABLE ACCURACY

- Verify the mathematical accuracy of the accounts receivable trial balance and its correspondence to the control account balance.

Companies have falsified the trial balance by omitting subsidiary accounts, adding false accounts, and miscalculating totals. Auditors should test the accuracy of the aging classifications to customer account details, particularly if the aged trial balance will be used to audit the allowance for doubtful accounts.

Employees have embezzled money by (a) taking cash or checks for themselves, (b) recording customer credit in a subsidiary customer account ledger, and (c) not recording customer credit in the control account. Out-of-balance conditions might signal this kind of embezzlement.

ACCOUNTS WRITTEN OFF

- Confirm amounts formerly due from customers but written off as uncollectible or inappropriately charged.

- When customers tell about previous payment, obtain the customer's canceled check (or a front and back copy). Inspect the endorsement(s).

- Verify customers to be bona fide businesses or persons using directories and state incorporation records.

Experience has shown cases in which high-level employees have personally collected charges and fees written off by the company. Sometimes, the charges may not have ever been recorded (e.g., bank loan fees forgiven). These confirmations and inquiries are delicate, and the typical positive accounts receivable confirmation forms are not well-suited. Appropriate strategies and methods will differ according to the company's and customers' circumstances.

Confirmation exceptions may tell of previous payment. An employee may have diverted the payment, even endorsing it for deposit to his or her own bank account or that of a dummy company or person.

- Analyze trends in writeoffs. Specifically, the activity classified by: (a) salesperson, (b) accounting period, (c) collection agency or collector.

- Determine who authorized writeoffs over a period of time. Identify any unusually amounts or trends by authorizer.

An unusually large amount of writeoffs attributable to a single salesperson could be a sign that the salesperson may be recording fictitious sales or may have a diversion scheme operating.

A large number of accounts written off at the same time could be the result of removing fictitious sales from the books (unless the company's standard policy is to review accounts at specified times during the year).

An increase in the number of written-off receivables assigned to a single collection agency should make an auditor consider the possibility of kickbacks, depending upon the engagement and review procedures imposed on the collection agency. Along the same lines, a decrease in the rate of collection by a collector or an agency could point to a collector or agency keeping funds rather than remitting the money to the company.

PROCEDURES FOR CASH DISBURSEMENTS, PURCHASING, ACCOUNTS PAYABLE

CASH DISBURSEMENTS

- Make inquiries to determine whether (a) checks are mailed immediately upon signing, and (b) blank checks (payee or amount blank) are signed in advance of delivery.

- Make inquiries and observe the physical security of blank check stock and the check-writing or electronic transfer system.

Checks held for delivery later are susceptible to alteration and diversion. If holding checks is suspected, perform additional procedures (below).

Checks signed in blank are susceptible to improper completion. Try to identify such checks, and examine them for correspondence to supporting documents and proper endorsements.

- Inspect a sample of paid vouchers for proper and complete cancellation (mutilation) of supporting documents.

- Hold supporting documents to the light and examine them for alterations or erasures. Be especially careful using photocopied documents in place of originals.

Documents that are not effectively canceled can be processed again for duplicate payments. If cancellation is faulty, identify vendors and try to find record (e.g., accounts payable subsidiary, if any) that will show repeated payments. Alphabetic sorting of computer records by vendor with an exception report based on frequent payments may identify duplicate payments. If any are identified, inspect canceled checks for endorsements--employee embezzlers may have diverted the payments to themselves.

- Examine bank statements to determine whether all canceled checks are filed with the statement. Obtain photocopies of missing checks from the bank.

Embezzlers often try to cover up by removing canceled checks made payable to, or endorsed by, themselves. Missing canceled checks are a signal. Bank reconcilers may not notice missing checks if the banks reconciliation is performed using only the numerical listing printed in the bank statement. Photocopies obtained from the bank can be examined for proper payees and endorsements.

Truncated bank statements (canceled checks routinely not returned to the payor) present a special problem. One ingenious embezzler (a) printed company checks in the company's numerical sequence, (b) intercepted legitimate checks and destroyed them, (c) substituted the same-numbered check from the private stock (payable to himself in the same amount as the legitimate check) and "signed" with a rubber stamp that looked like the company's check signature plate. The bank statement reconciler was able to correspond the bank statement check number and amount to the recorded cash disbursement, thus did not notice the trick. The company paid the legitimate vendor the "balance overdue" the next month. The embezzler was caught because he was too greedy--adverse cash flow alerted the business owner, and an investigation started. The investigator finally noticed the multiple payments recorded (scattered among numerous vendors), obtained the checks from the bank, and found the employee named as payee.

- Examine voided checks to determine (1) their existence on file and (2) the reason they were voided.

- If original voided checks cannot be located, look for them returned as canceled checks in bank statements.

PURCHASING

- Review the general ledger purchases account or similar records of purchases. Investigate for accuracy and validity (a) significant adjustments, (b) unusual entries, (c) unusual fluctuations in normal recurring activity. Large journal entries at the end of an accounting period are always suspect.

Significant adjustments may be errors in pricing, notable for later inventory pricing audit procedures. Unusual entries may charge costs to contracts improperly. Unusual fluctuations may indicate purchases for nonbusiness purposes (e.g., executive's home improvement).

- Obtain a listing of all vendors and their addresses. (If performed in prior years, the listing may be limited to new vendors and dormant vendors that become active.) Include purchase volume by vendor, if available.

- Select a sample of vendors, and verify their existence as bona fide businesses or persons, using (a) Better Business Bureau inquiry, (b) criss-cross and telephone directories, (c) Secretary of State incorporation records, (d) local partnership registration and assumed name records. Call the telephone number found or visit the address. The sample should include vendors with initials for company names ("ABD Company"),

> those with post office box addresses, and the vendors with the same address as other vendors. Cross-check vendor names, addresses, and telephone numbers with employees' names, addresses, and telephone numbers to detect possible employee connections to vendors.
>
> - If matches arise, examine related canceled checks for authorization, payee, and endorsements.

Purchasing frauds have utilized fictitious vendors. An internal embezzlement can be perpetrated by processing fictitious invoices from dummy vendors.

Experience has shown instances of fraudsters being unimaginative with names (using initials like "ABD Company") and being unwilling to go to the trouble to establish a false address other than a post office box, even using the same address or their own addresses and telephone numbers multiple times. They have incorporated dummy companies in their own names. They have been known to endorse checks with their own names.

> - Obtain reliable price lists from competing vendors and compare to the prices actually paid by the client.

Vendors and employees have been known to conspire to overcharge companies and split the proceeds with the employee accomplice.

> - Obtain authorizations of capital projects, especially construction projects (board of directors' minutes, accounting department) in as much detail as available. Examine delivery destinations on purchase orders for material and supplies for correspondence with construction sites.

Many executive homes and vacation houses have been built and improved with company funds. A university president built half an unauthorized research center with "cost overruns" on an authorized project before she was stopped.

> - Investigate purchase terms when large returns are recorded before year-end and quarter-end financial reporting dates.

> • Send accounts payable confirmations to vendors whose returns are recorded soon before year-end and quarter-end financial reporting dates.

Large amounts of purchase returns or discounts recorded before important financial reporting dates may be fictitious. The goods may not be returned at all but included in inventory, thereby understating cost of goods sold and accounts payable, and overstating income.

Confirmations to such vendors may reveal (a) vendors' exceptions indicating no participation in the transactions (fictitious transactions without the knowledge of real vendors), and (b) "return to sender" confirmation attempts indicating fictitious vendors.

> • Select a sample of recorded debit memos for purchase returns after year-end and quarter-end financial reporting dates, and audit for timely recording with reference to dates in correspondence or other documentation.

Companies can inflate inventory for the period and overstate accounts payable by recording fictitious (or early) purchases and inventory. While overstating accounts payable is not a typical ploy, a company may want to overstate inventory in connection with a loan agreement based on inventory levels.

ACCOUNTS PAYABLE

> • Verify the mathematical accuracy of the accounts payable trial balance and its correspondence to the control account balance.
>
> • Scan the detailed accounts payable listing for debit balances and old unpaid invoices. Send confirmations to these vendors.

Companies have falsified the trial balance by omitting subsidiary accounts, adding false accounts, and miscalculating totals. Auditors should test the accuracy of the aging classifications of overdue payables to vendor account details, particularly if the aged trial balance will be used to audit the going concern status of the company.

Embezzlers have used these manipulations to hide bogus vendors. Companies have used them to attempt to understate liabilities.

Confirmations may elicit independent evidence of disputed payables and unrecorded liabilities.

- Analyze statistics on returns, rebates, and allowances. Specifically, the activity classified by: (a) purchasing agent, (b) accounting period, (c) vendor.

An unusually large amount of returns and allowances attributable to a single purchasing agent could be a sign that the agent and one or more vendors have manipulated purchasing volume for the benefit of personal performance compensation or kickbacks.

A large number of purchase returns and allowances at the same time could be the result of removing fictitious payables from the books.

- Devise confirmations in a format that seeks qualitative as well as quantitative information.

- Investigate complaints from vendors and customers. Interview the client's employees and review correspondence files to learn of complaints.

The vendor may have information relating to late payments or abnormal purchasing patterns that may be useful in the fraud detection process.

Complaints could be a possible indication of fraud. Vendors may complain if payments are late (when the company records show timely payment). Customers may complain about product quality, which may lead to discovery of vendor substitution of low-quality material at high-quality prices.

- If credits have been written off (i.e., old payables, outstanding checks), consider potential liability under state escheat or unclaimed property laws.

Laws may vary by state. However, unclaimed property (e.g., old checks, securities) often reverts to the state. The company may not be entitled to reverse accounting entries and reclaim the property for itself.

PROCEDURES FOR INVENTORY

INVENTORY OBSERVATION

- When the client has no perpetual inventory records, photocopy all the count tags (or control other media) to create a physical inventory compilation. Select a sample of inventory and visit the warehouse or production area to test-count.

- Calculate the final priced inventory compilation and compare it to the physical count record, especially noting odd additions such as round numbers.

Without pre-existing perpetual records, auditors have been known to test-count and trace to the inventory compilation and overlook the need to audit in the other direction--from the compilation to the actual inventory. The actual inventory compilation may be produced later (too late), so the auditors need to create a "perpetual record substitute," then test it by selecting items and obtaining counts. The audited substitute record can be compared to the final priced inventory compilation.

Management personnel can add "overlooked" inventory after the counts are taken, sometimes in large round numbers. Auditors need to study the final compilation for such additions.

- Keep items selected for test counts secret from client personnel. Do not let client personnel identify "high-value" items for count without independent knowledge and verification.

- Keep audit records of client counting mistakes for an overall evaluation of counting accuracy.

Client personnel have accompanied auditors for the purpose of knowing which items are test-counted. They can then avoid these tested items when manipulations are made. One manager "helped" the auditors identify high-value items, then raised the counts on other items he knew the auditors did not test count and record.

Some auditors are very helpful to clients, assisting with correcting the counting errors as the inventory-taking proceeds, then reaching the conclusion that "no count errors were observed uncorrected." Of course, no errors remain in the items selected for test counts! The problem lies in the count accuracy in the items not test-counted. The auditors mislead themselves in this manner.

SHIPMENTS/INVENTORY HELD FOR CUSTOMERS

> • Audit sales documents and terms for inventory on hand but excluded from the inventory count with the explanation that the inventory is being held for the customer.

Fraudulent manipulation of "bill and hold" practices have created misleading financial statements. The terms of sales should unequivocally call for passage of risks of ownership to the customer. Send positive accounts receivable confirmations to these customers to give them a chance to respond if they have exceptions.

> • Investigate the locations indicated on shipping documents for correspondence with real customers' locations.

This is a difficult procedure designed to find inventory shipped to client-controlled locations yet recorded as sales to customers. Signals for identification of a sample include (1) locations in unlikely places, (2) nearby shipment destinations, (3) shipping terms naming the client as consignee, (4) shipments to locations on which the client pays rent or holds title. When auditors identify an address, they can search local real property records for ownership information. Questions and inquiries can follow. Send positive accounts receivable confirmations to "customers" identified as purchasers.

> • Obtain independent information about final sales to end-user customers. Compare to client sales/shipment information.

Several companies have engaged in "channel stuffing." This practice places excess products in wholesale/retail outlets long before actual sales to end-user customers. In some cases, channel stuffing has been construed as placing inventory on consignment (especially if payment terms depend on final sales and return privileges are granted). The understatement of inventory is a by-product of an overstatement of sales revenue. Send positive accounts receivable confirmations to identifiable shipment recipients to give customers a chance to express exceptions or tell about special arrangements with the client.

OBSOLESCENCE AND VALUATION

- Scan perpetual records for zero or small amount issuance entries.

- Design a scan for slow-moving inventory using criteria in addition to date of last issue.

Companies can process dummy issue entries of zero or small amounts simply to insert a recent issue date. If auditors rely only on the date of last issue to identify slow-moving inventory, they will be fooled.

PROCEDURES FOR PAYROLL

FICTITIOUS EMPLOYEES

- Search for fictitious employees
  1. Use a computer program or a lookup table to test all or a sample of social security numbers for legitimate issue.
  2. Sort employee social security numbers in numerical order and search (computer or manual) for duplicate numbers or numbers within a few digits of one another.
  3. List employee names in alphabetical order and check for duplicate names or similar names.
  4. Obtain a list of employee addresses and check for duplicates (addresses may include bank account numbers for direct deposit payroll).

5. Obtain a list of employees with abbreviations or initials for names or post office boxes for addresses.
6. Obtain a listing of all employees with few or no payroll deductions (e.g., insurance, savings bonds).
7. Obtain names of addressees on returned checks and undelivered W-2 and 1099 forms.
8. Obtain names of persons employed a short time.
9. Obtain names of persons terminated shortly before audit field work started.

Each of the signals in parts 1-8 of the procedure might identify questionable "people" on the payroll. However, finding a signal does not absolutely identify a "ghost." Each of the signals could be a mistake (duplicate social security number entered incorrectly) or a legitimate fact (near-duplicate social security numbers, same or similar names and addresses, initials for names, post office box addresses, same bank account as another employee, no insurance election, no forwarding address, short time employed). Each questionable "employee" can be investigated (quietly) through one or more of these information sources: personnel file, telephone book listing, criss-cross directory listing, job-site visit to look for name tag or to question supervisor as part of a plant tour, driver license information (state public records), and voter registration (public record). Auditors are advised to obtain information from two or more of these sources because a careful fraudster might provide for at least one of them.

Regarding part 9, a fraudster might try to be "smart" by getting ghosts off the payroll before the auditors arrive.

TERMINATED AND RETIRED EMPLOYEES

• Select all or a sample of final paychecks payable to terminated employees:
  1. Verify the date of termination to ensure that paychecks were not issued to cover periods after the employee had actually terminated.
  2. Compare the endorsements to the employees' signatures in personnel records.

- Select all or a sample of checks to retired employees:
  1. Evaluate company control procedures designed to determine death of retirees.
  2. Examine check endorsements for apparent change.
  3. Send confirmation-type inquiries to retirees.
  4. Determine whether retirees have made medical claims if the employer maintains post-retirement medical benefits.
  5. Search local death certificate records.
  6. Consider obtaining and using the Social Security Administration "death tape."

A supervisor or a payroll employee might keep a terminated employee the payroll for a short period after the employee has actually quit work.

Notification of the death of retirees is often uncertain and untimely. The U.S. Social Security Administration sends millions of dollars to dead people. Companies are in the same situation.

PAYROLL DEPARTMENT EMPLOYEES

- Search public records for assets of employees in the payroll chain of control (e.g., preparation, distribution) for signs of wealth not commensurate with salary income.

Employees who embezzle generally spend the money on themselves and members of their family, oftentimes acquiring traceable assets. Searches for assets may produce objective information about persons' lifestyles that are otherwise difficult to observe. Sources of information include public records of real property (large homes, vacation homes), personal property (auto and boat registrations), UCC filings of liens on property pledged for loans, registration of corporations or partnerships for other businesses, assumed name registrations, and newspaper and magazine articles. Searches should use the employees' names and names of known relatives and spouses. These public records are available in the offices of the local county clerk, the state secretary of state, and in several public computerized databases. Personal banking records can be obtained legally only with a proper subpoena based on cause, but fraudsters often deposit embezzled money in their own bank accounts.

CANCELED CHECKS AND CLEARANCE TIME LAG

- Audit cancelled payroll checks, looking for two endorsements, especially second endorsements by persons connected with company payroll functions. Look for deposit account numbers and locations and for bank codes.

- Determine whether all canceled check documents are retained in the payroll bank statement. (Compare checks to check numbers printed on the bank statement.)

- Determine whether too much time elapsed between payroll distribution and check deposit date.

Payroll embezzlers must convert a "ghost's" pay to his or her own use. Oftentimes, conversion is accomplished by cashing checks at a place the embezzling employee is known, including deposit in the employee's own bank account. The bank may require the fraudster to add a personal endorsement to the "ghost's" endorsement. Some banks stamp numbers indicating processing order or bank account numbers on the check. These bank imprints may reveal a suspicious pattern (e.g. several paychecks written over a month deposited at the same time at an unlikely bank far from the recipient's address).

Missing checks may be ones removed in an attempt to hide raised amounts or second endorsements. This procedure may identify a prospective fictitious employee.

If employees are required to sign for checks, compare signatures with the endorsement on the canceled check.

Most employees deposit or cash paychecks very quickly. A delay depositing a check may indicate that someone needs extra time to procure the check and falsely cash it. Examine endorsements on such checks carefully.

VACATION HOURS AND SICK DAYS

- Scan company records of vacation and sick days earned and used.

A fraudster may pay himself or herself for more time than allowed.

TAXES WITHHELD

- Select all or a sample of individual earnings records and compare to W-2 forms. Recalculate the withheld amounts. Include payroll preparation employees in the sample.

In one ingenious fraud, a payroll preparation employee credited herself for small amounts of many other employees' income tax withheld. The other employees did not notice differences in their W-2's, and the employee received a large tax refund based on a large amount withheld. (In this case, the payroll employee stole from the other employees.)

OUTSIDE PAYROLL SERVICES AND
TEMPORARY EMPLOYMENT AGENCIES

- Reconcile information shown in the payroll processing service reports of payroll to the client company payroll information. Audit special orders given to the payroll service to correct prior payroll errors.

- Investigate ownership of the payroll service company.

- Audit temporary employment service billings for agreement with contracts.

- Investigate ownership of the temporary employment agency.

Outside payroll processing service arrangements differ. However, the service is merely a substitute for internal processing. A service must use information supplied by the client, and this information can be subject to the same audit procedures. Errors are inevitable--wrong hours, wrong rate, wrong deductions, and the like. Company personnel must submit information to correct errors, and these submissions may be subject to manipulation. Auditors should not be lulled into thinking that an outside payroll preparation service insulates payroll from fraud. State incorporation records can be consulted to try to determine whether any client insiders incorporated the payroll service.

Temporary employment agencies are substitutes for in-house personnel services. The time and rate billings need to be audited in a manner similar to internal data. State incorporation records can be consulted to try to determine whether any client insiders incorporated the employment agency.

DIRECT DEPOSIT (WIRE TRANSFER)

- Obtain proper clearance from company officials to make bank inquiries about the names of persons who own bank accounts to which paychecks are deposited directly. Compare to names on payroll.

A payroll embezzler could manage to alter or input his or her own account to receive the paycheck prepared for a ghost or terminated employee.

PAYROLL TAX DEPOSITS

- Audit cancelled checks credited for payroll tax deposits, looking for company check, endorsement (if any), date of deposit.

Payroll tax deposit timing and frequency are governed by IRS rules. Fraudsters have been known to (1) divert the payroll tax payment for a few days to earn interest, then make the deposit late with a non-company check, and (2) steal the tax deposit.

PAY RAISES, OVERTIME, AND BONUSES

- Obtain a schedule of unusually large or frequent pay raises Find and audit authorization documents.

- Obtain names of persons consistently paid for significant overtime. Audit time records. Carefully question supervisors or other employees.

- Audit the calculation of bonuses in comparison to policy or formula. Find appropriate authorization (e.g., union contract, employment contract, directors' minutes).

Someone with power to change the payroll system could enter false salary raises, overpaying some employees, and sharing the proceeds.

Falsified time records may account for improper payment for overtime. However, supervisors may be in collusion to approve time and split the overpayments. Auditors are well advised to try to use independent work records (e.g., job cost sheets, production schedules, production reports) before attempting to make on-site observations or ask fraud questions.

Periodic bonuses might be miscalculated or manipulated in favor of an employee, with division of proceeds with payroll employees. Frauds have occurred with payment of bonuses to executives without proper approval by the board of directors.

PROCEDURES FOR EMPLOYEE EXPENSE ACCOUNTS

UNUSUAL AMOUNTS

- Compare expense account payments with employees' history of payments and with similar employees (e.g., sales representatives).

- Compare expense account payments with budget amounts. Investigate unusual increases and decreases.

Unexplained variances may indicate that false expense reports were submitted. Unexplained decreases may mean that former false expense reporting has stopped.

DATES AND NUMBER SEQUENCE

- Compare expense report receipt dates submitted by employees to a calendar showing the dates each employee was out of town.

- Audit a sample of employees with attention to numerical sequence on various types of restaurant, hotel, and club receipts. Expenses on different dates should not be in close numerical order.

If the dates do not coincide, employees may have submitted false reports. Numerical sequence has been the clue to employees' ploy of picking up a pad of blank receipts to submit expenses. (Receipts with consecutive numbers have been submitted to support expenses on widely separate travel dates.)

PROCEDURES FOR PROPERTY, PLANT, AND EQUIPMENT

ASSET EXISTENCE AND OWNERSHIP

- Select a sample of recorded assets and determine that title (ownership record) is in the name of the client organization.

Controlling owners (e.g., principal shareholders, partners) often "contribute" assets to the entity but neglect to formalize the legal ownership in the entity. Controlling owners have been known to "move" assets around among a group of related companies.

- Select a sample of assets acquired in prior years and inspect them.

- Select a sample of small, easily-movable assets and inspect (inventory) them.

Beware of the temptation to consider prior years' audited property assets as items that need no inspection in the current year. Unrecorded dispositions (e.g., dispositions, authorized removals by owners, unauthorized removal by employees) cause account balances to be overstated. A common employee fraud is theft or embezzlement of supplies and equipment. Notebook computers, modern telephones, and similar electronics are small but expensive.

- Identify any new product lines or business divisions started in the current audit period. Determine whether related research and development costs and start-up costs were expensed or properly capitalized.

Companies often are very shrewd about manipulating classification of R&D, development costs, and start-up or pre-opening costs. Generally, they prefer to capitalize as much as possible to make income appear better than warranted.

ASSET VALUATION

- Determine whether any vendors sell both property assets and inventory items to the client. Audit the prices charged for property assets:
  1. Obtain independent price quotes.
  2. Compare prior period prices for the same assets from the same or from a different vendor.

Companies and vendors might agree (collude) to "allocate" higher prices to property and equipment and lower prices to inventoried items. The result is overstatement of property assets and income, with understatement of inventory and cost of goods sold. (The misstatements may be in the other direction if the motive is to understate assets and income.)

- Obtain appraiser's reports for purchases of real estate and investigate the reputation, engagement terms, and independence of the appraisers. Use: (a) local business references, (b) local financial institutions that keep lists of approved appraisers, (c) membership directories of professional appraiser associations. Consider interviewing the appraisers or their personnel.

Land and building "flips" were a problematic accounting issue for financial institutions in the 1980s. Old schemes never die. In a flip transaction, land or building properties were sold multiple times among colluding parties, with each party raising the price for each successive transaction. The end result was highly inflated asset prices which sometimes passed standard audit scrutiny. Appraisers were often in on the action.

- Obtain documents relating to the purchase of land and buildings.
    1. Determine the identities of the owners and managers of corporate parties to the transaction.
    2. Determine the identities of limited partner parties to the transaction.
    3. Examine loan applications and supporting papers for management representations concerning the property.
    4. For like-kind exchanges and noncash exchanges, audit the valuation determination.

This procedure is related to flip transactions and other transactions that do not involve flips. It is designed to produce information about related parties. One signal of fraudulent valuation manipulations is the use of numerous shell corporations and complicated transactions. Transactions that are more convoluted than necessary should be suspect. Determining the identities of the people and organizations involved in transactions might reveal related party transactions and conflicts of interest which increase the probability of fraud. Loan documents may reveal representations of the asset's price which contradict other recorded values.

Like-kind exchanges and noncash exchanges (e.g., debt, stock, dissimilar property) are often characterized by related party relations among the buyers and sellers. Valuations of noncash considerations are subject to manipulation and faulty judgment.

ACCOUNTING POLICIES

- Examine the client's insurance claims and attempt to perform a physical inspection of the damaged/lost assets. Interview plant personnel about damages and losses.

This procedure is designed to determine whether damaged or lost assets are in fact still in use. Company employees can commit fraud by filing false loss claims with an insurance carrier.

- Learn the client's policy for expensing small asset purchases. Select a sample of these expenses and determine whether multiple small purchases represent a larger purchase that has been broken down in order to avoid capitalization.

Most companies do not attempt to overstate expenses. However, some see the expense route as a tax-advantaged treatment. Expensing might be used to persuade minority shareholders to sell in light of low reported profits. The normal audit of the repairs and maintenance account can be designed to discover this type of expensing maneuver.

DISCLOSURE

- Search UCC filings for evidence of property pledged as collateral for loans.

Failure to disclose pledges of assets is fraudulent. Desperate managements have been known to pledge the same assets many times. They usually do not tell the auditors voluntarily, but the lenders will likely file UCC liens. These filings are available on computer data bases.

- Audit lease documents for operating leases and sale-and-leaseback transactions.

Operating leases and sale-leasebacks are popular methods of "off-balance sheet financing." Sometimes these transactions are carefully structured in form to avoid the substance of asset purchases and debt obligations. In borderline cases, disclosure may be the available means of reporting them.

PROCEDURES FOR INCOME TAXES

TRANSFER PRICING

- Review all pertinent issues of transfer pricing between company segments in different countries.

- Review tax records, confirming that a realistic position has been taken in the pricing of transferred goods.

Transfer pricing is possibly the most pervasive issue in international trade. The opportunity for fraud exists when the tax rate in one country is lower than that of another country. When companies price the goods transferred among independent segments of one company, the strategy is to lower the net income of the segment in the country with the higher tax rate and raise the income of the segment in another country with a lower tax rate. I.R.C. § 482 authorizes the IRS to allocate gross income, deductions, and credits between related taxpayers to the extent necessary to prevent evasion of taxes or to clearly reflect the income of related taxpayers.

EXCESSIVE SALARIES

- Identify excessive salaries and loans made to shareholders, officers, employees and other related parties at any favorable terms.

- Examine the documentation and determine whether loans are term or demand and determine whether the loan should be recast as constructive dividends, or whether interest should be imputed.

- Determine whether salaries are reasonable compared to industry standards.

A corporation may attempt to disguise income paid to related parties, thereby shifting the taxable income and the deduction of the item. For example, a corporation may increase an officer's compensation by loaning the officer money at a below-market interest rate. The officer receives the benefit of the low interest loan but pays no taxes on this phantom income. Related party loans at below market rates can be recast by the IRS to more clearly reflect the substance of the transaction (I.R.C. § 482), transferring the phantom income to the person receiving the true benefit of the transaction. Excessive salaries can be construed as dividends.

TAX EXEMPT INCOME

- Review the validity of tax exempt income.

- Verify the existence and propriety of the paying entity.

A traditional aspect of the U.S. tax structure is the immunity of governmental units from taxation by other units. Auditors should confirm that income recorded as tax exempt is valid by reviewing the bond indenture and confirming tax exempt status.

ASSET DEPRECIATION

- Confirm asset acquisition and disposition dates for application of tax depreciation conventions.

- Interview operations or other personnel to confirm date property was placed in or taken out of service.

Entities typically use the half-year convention to calculate tax depreciation expense for assets acquired. This allows the businesses to allocate one half-year of depreciation to each asset, regardless of when the assets were acquired. However, I.R.C. § 168(d) dictates that if the aggregate basis of property placed in service during the last three months of the tax year exceed 40% of the aggregate basis of property placed in service the entire year, the mid-quarter convention must be used; that is, the assets placed in service in the last quarter must be depreciated for only the last quarter. This convention was created to deny the benefits of the half year convention to entities waiting until the end of the year to acquire major assets. The area that still may provide room for manipulation is the date the property was placed in or taken out of service. Since many assets are purchased in stages, auditors need to determine the date these assets were actually placed in service. Auditors can interview plant personnel who have this information.

WASH SALES OF SECURITIES

> • Review sales of stocks, options, or securities sold at a loss for sale dates. Audit for the possibility of wash sales.

Because unrealized losses may not be deducted from taxable income, taxpayers may be tempted to sell securities to recognize losses for tax purposes. If the taxpayer believes the investment is sound, the identical security can be repurchased soon thereafter, thus restoring the investment position. To prevent this type of manipulation, I.R.C. § 1091 disallows loss recognition if the taxpayer acquires similar securities within 30 days before or after the sale generating the loss. (The acquisition of the same securities for the purpose of restoring an investment position upon a sale at a loss is a "wash sale" transaction. The transaction is not illegal, but tax recognition of the loss is not allowed.)

DIVIDEND INCOME EXCLUSION

> • Verify dividends received deduction for exclusions related to period of ownership and debt financing.
>
> • Confirm dividends paid with issuing organization or by reference to published dividend records.

I.R.C. § 243 allows corporations a deduction for dividends received equal to a percentage of the dividends, according to the percentage of voting power and value owned by the recipient. For domestic corporations: when less than 20% is owned, 70% of dividends received may be excluded from the recipient's income; when 20% to 79% is owned, 80% may be excluded; when 80% or more is owned, 100% may be excluded. The dividends received deduction is disallowed for dividends received on stock owned for 45 days or less and for stock that is financed with debt.

ACKNOWLEDGEMENTS

The procedures in this chapter were initially adapted and developed in student assignments for the graduate Fraud Examination course conducted at The University of Texas at Austin. These students deserve credit: Kevin Boardman, Darrell Brimberry, Scott Davidson, Carmelo Felix, Leena Kelhu, Karen Krock, Amanda Kuhler, Joe Lanza, Julie McHugh, David Reese, Jamie Rickey, Liisa Rudduck, Sara Scribner, Melinda Steffey, and James Vaughn. The students were assisted with comments and observations from: Jack Robertson (Professor, The University of Texas), Joseph Wells (Chairman, The Association of Certified Fraud Examiners), Charlotte Bell (Association of Certified Fraud Examiners), Steve Hendrix (Association of Certified Fraud Examiners), Peter McLaughlin (Lindquist, Avey, Macdonald & Baskerville), Mike Vandervoort (University of Texas Internal Audit Department), and John Fisher Weber (Builders' Square Loss Prevention Department).

CHAPTER 14
AUDITORS' AND INVESTIGATORS' RESPONSIBILITIES

This chapter summarizes the responsibilities specified in professional literature for external auditors, internal auditors, government auditors, and fraud examiners. The term **external auditors** refers to independent CPAs who audit financial statements for the purpose of rendering an opinion. **Internal auditors** and **Certified Internal Auditors** are persons who can be both independent and CPAs but are employed within organizations. **Government auditors** are auditors whose work is governed by the GAO audit standards, whether they be audit employees of governments or of public accounting firms engaged to perform government audits. **Fraud examiners** are people engaged specifically for fraud investigation work, particularly persons qualified as **Certified Fraud Examiners**.

EXTERNAL AUDITORS' RESPONSIBILITIES

The official AICPA auditing standards are rigorous. Relevant standards concern errors and frauds (SAS 82, AU 316), illegal acts by clients (SAS 54, AU 317), auditing accounting estimates (SAS 57, AU 342), and communication with audit committees (SAS 61, AU 380).

CONSIDERATION OF FRAUD IN A FINANCIAL STATEMENT AUDIT (SAS 82)

SAS 82 was issued early in 1997 with a December 15, 1997 effective date. It uses the "fraud" word that was so conspicuously omitted from earlier statements on auditing standards, which spoke of "errors and irregularities." SAS 82 is reasonably explicit with guidance on fraud risk factors. It contains numerous requirements for obtaining reasonable assurance of material fraud detection, overall audit responses, specific procedural responses, documentation, and reports to management and the board of directors.

Excerpts of the explicit SAS 82 requirements (but not the more general discussion of guidance, which is more thoroughly covered in other chapters in this book anyway) are below. The ones marked with the symbol ● are specifications that are new in SAS 82. The others are essentially the same as the requirements in SAS 53, which was superseded by SAS 82.

1. Assess the risk of material misstatement of financial statements due to fraud by fraudulent financial reporting (management fraud) and by misappropriation of assets (employee fraud).
2. Consider this risk assessment at the beginning and throughout the audit in designing audit procedures to be performed.
3. ● Inquire of management its understanding regarding risk of fraud in the company and (a) whether any frauds are known to have occurred, and (b) whether any fraud risk factors have been identified.
4. ● Document the fraud risk assessment in the audit working papers, including (a) risk factors identified, and (b) the auditors' overall and/or specific responses.
5. ● Pay attention to well-known fraud risk factors.
6. ● Pay attention to information that indicates financial stress of employees or adverse relations between the company and its employees (but no requirement to plan the audit to discover such information).
7. ● Determine whether the company has specific controls that mitigate identified fraud risks or whether specific control deficiencies exacerbate these risks.
8. ● Consider the effectiveness of clients' programs that include steps to prevent, detect, and deter fraud. Ask persons overseeing such programs whether they have identified any fraud risk factors.

CLIENTS' PROGRAMS

SAS 82 makes no reference to the corporate sentencing guidelines, but they include a provision for mitigating a penalty if a company has "an effective program to prevent and detect violations of law." Such programs show companies' *due diligence* in seeking to prevent and detect criminal conduct by its employees. The seven elements of due diligence are in this book in Chapter 1, page 37.

---

9. ● Decide whether the fraud risk assessment calls for (A) an overall response, and/or (B) a response specific to a particular account balance or class of transactions:

(A) Overall Response
- (i)   Exercise professional skepticism.
- (ii)   Assign personnel with appropriate knowledge, skill, and ability.
- (iii)   Study more carefully management's selection and application of accounting principles.
- (iv) ●   Be sensitive to management's ability to override controls related to fraud risk factors.
- (v) ●   Alter audit procedures with regard to nature (obtain more reliable or additional corroborative information), timing (closer to year-end), and extent (larger sample sizes or more extensive analytical procedures).

(B) Specific Procedural Response
- (i) ●   Perform procedures on a surprise or unannounced basis (e.g., visits, inventory observation).
- (ii) ●   Observe inventory-taking close to year-end.
- (iii) ●   Add oral contacts to the written confirmation procedure.
- (iv)   Review and investigate in detail the client's quarter- and year-end adjusting entries.
- (v) ●   Investigate unusual transactions near year-end for the possibility of related parties and sources of financial resources that support such transactions.
- (vi) ●   Perform substantive analytical procedures at a detailed level.
- (vii) ●   Conduct interviews with people in fraud risk areas.
- (viii) ●   Coordinate audit work with other independent auditors, if any.
- (ix) ●   Perform additional work on specialists' assumptions, methods, and findings.
- (x) ●   Confirm sales contract terms with customers.
- (xi) ●   Conduct inventory observations carefully (e.g., surprise basis, multiple locations on same date, open boxes, assay quality of substances).

10. Consider whether discovered misstatements indicate fraud and evaluate implications even of immaterial misstatements (● but no requirement to determine an *intent* element of fraud).
11. When the possibility of material fraud exists, review the audit plan, discuss further investigation with a higher level of management, and attempt to obtain additional evidence.
12. ● When fraud is detected, consider the implications for the integrity of managers and employees and the possible effect on the audit. [SAS 47 amendment prompted by SAS 82]
13. Withdraw from the engagement if fraud risk is significant and management cooperation is unsatisfactory, and communicate the reasons for withdrawal to the audit committee of the board of directors.
14. When evidence of fraud exists, tell management (appropriate higher level) even about inconsequential matters, and tell the audit committee about fraud involving senior managers.
15. Disclose possible fraud in limited circumstances by:
    ○ Complying with legal and regulatory requirements (including reporting a change of auditors on SEC Form 8-K, reporting control matters and disagreements according to Item 304 of SEC Regulation S-K).
    ○ Responding to a successor auditor's inquiries (SAS 7).
    ○ Responding to a subpoena.
    ○ Communicating with a funding or other agency when required in audits of entities that receive governmental financial assistance.

External auditors are *not* responsible for:

● Determining the element of *intent* in a possible fraud situation.
○ Authenticating documents (lack of training).
○ Finding intentional misstatements concealed by collusion and falsified documents when using procedures designed to find unintentional misstatements. (**Collusion** is the circumstance in which two or more people conspire to conduct fraudulent activity in violation of an organization's internal controls.) [SAS 1, AU 230 amendment prompted by SAS 82]
● Obtaining *absolute* assurance that material misstatements in financial statements will be detected.
○ Insuring or guaranteeing that all material misstatements will be discovered. [SAS 1, AU 230 amendment prompted by SAS 82]

o General reporting of frauds to outside agencies or parties.
● Planning the audit to discover information that indicates particular employees' financial stress or adverse relationships between the company and its employees.

ILLEGAL ACTS BY CLIENTS (SAS 54)

SAS 54 deals with two kinds of "illegal acts:" (1) **Direct-effect illegal acts** produce direct and material effects on financial statement amounts (e.g., violations of tax laws and government contracting regulations for cost and revenue recognition), and they come under the same responsibilities as errors and frauds (SAS 82); and (2) **Illegal acts** is the term used to refer to violations of laws and regulations that are *far removed* from financial statement effects (e.g., violations relating to insider securities trading, occupational health and safety, food and drug administration, environmental protection, and equal employment opportunity). The far- removed illegal acts come under a responsibility for general awareness, particularly in matters of contingent liability disclosure, but not routine responsibility for detection and reporting. Excerpts from SAS 54 are below.

1. Be aware of the types of illegal acts that might occur in the organization under audit and the "signals" of them.
2. Perform audit procedures when specified information indicates that possible illegal acts may have a material indirect effect on financial statements.
3. Make inquiries about management's policies and procedures for compliance with laws and regulations.
4. Obtain written management representations concerning the absence of violations of laws and regulations.
5. Consider both the quantitative and qualitative materiality of known and suspected illegal acts.
6. Consider the implications of illegal acts for other aspects of the audit, specifically the reliability of management representations.
7. Assure that the company's audit committee is informed about illegal acts known to the auditor, except those that are clearly inconsequential. (When senior management is involved, auditors should communicate directly with the audit committee.)

8.   Evaluate the adequacy of financial statement disclosure regarding illegal acts.
9.   Withdraw from the engagement if management will not accept a qualified, adverse, or disclaimed opinion regarding statement presentation problems, and communicate the reasons in writing to the board of directors.
10.   Withdraw from the engagement if management does not take remedial action the auditor considers necessary.
11.   Disclose illegal acts to outside agencies in limited circumstances by:

- Reporting a change of auditors on SEC Form 8-K.
- Responding to a successor auditor's inquiries.
- Responding to a subpoena.
- Communicating with a funding or other agency when required in audits of entities that receive governmental financial assistance.

External auditors are *not* responsible for:

- Final determination that a particular act is illegal (lack of legal, judicial expertise.)
- Assuring that illegal acts will be detected or that related contingent liabilities will be disclosed.
- Designing audit procedures to detect illegal acts in the absence of specific information brought to the auditors' attention.
- General reporting of illegal acts to outside agencies or parties.

AUDITING ACCOUNTING ESTIMATES (SAS 57)

SAS 57 is related to fraudulent financial reporting because numerous fraud cases have involved manipulation of estimates. This area is difficult because an **accounting estimate** is an *approximation* of a financial statement element, item, or account made by an organization's management. (Examples include: allowance for loan losses, net realizable value of inventory, percentage-of-completion revenue, and fair value in nonmonetary exchanges.)

According to SAS 57, management is responsible for making the accounting estimates, and auditors are responsible for evaluating their reasonableness in the context of the financial statements taken as a whole.

Auditors are supposed to keep track of the differences between: (1) management's estimates and (2) the closest reasonable estimates supported by the audit evidence. And they are supposed to evaluate: (1) the differences taken altogether for indications of a systematic bias and (2) the combination of differences with other likely errors in the financial statements found by other audit procedures.

COMMUNICATION WITH AUDIT COMMITTEES (SAS 61)

SAS 61 sets forth requirements intended to assure that audit committees are informed about the scope and results of the independent audit. The auditing standards place great faith in audit committees and boards of directors. All companies with securities traded on the exchanges (e.g., New York, American, NASDAQ) are required to have audit committees. External auditors are required to make oral or written communications on numerous topics, some of which are listed below.

1. Internal control structure.
2. Material misstatements in financial statements.
3. Selection or changes in significant accounting policies.
4. Accounting for significant unusual transactions.
5. Effect of controversial accounting policies.
6. Accounting estimates.
7. Significant audit adjustments.
8. Disagreements with management on significant accounting and auditing matters.
9. Management's consultation with other accountants (possible "opinion shopping").
10. Serious difficulties dealing with management (e.g., delays, evidence availability) when conducting the audit.

INTERNAL AUDITORS' RESPONSIBILITIES

Internal auditors' attitudes about fraud responsibilities cannot be generalized. Some internal auditors hesitate to get involved because they believe a watchdog role will damage their image and effectiveness as internal consultants. Others have flocked to the fraud investigation education programs run by the Association of Certified Fraud Examiners because they want to add the fraud expertise dimension to their skills.

The scope of work sections of the internal audit standards give the basic charge to internal auditors for fraud awareness auditing: Internal auditors review the reliability and integrity of financial and operating information (IIA section 310); review the systems established to ensure compliance with policies, plans, procedures, laws, and regulations (IIA section 320); and review the means of safeguarding assets and verify the existence of assets (IIA section 330). This charge was expanded in *Statement on Internal Auditing Standards No. 3*, entitled "Deterrence, Detection, Investigation, and Reporting of Fraud." An abbreviated list of some points of guidance from SIAS 3 is below.

The internal auditing standards appear to be carefully written to impose no positive obligation for fraud detection and investigation work in the ordinary course of assignments. However, internal auditors are encouraged to be aware of the various types of frauds, their signs (red flags), and the need to follow up the notice of signs and control weaknesses to determine whether a suspicion is justified; then, alert management to call in the experts. SIAS 3 cautions that internal auditors are *not* expected to guarantee that fraud will be detected in the normal course of most internal audit assignments.

1. Exercise due professional care and be alert to signs of wrongdoing, errors and omissions, inefficiency, waste, ineffectiveness, and conflicts of interest.
2. Consider the possibility of noncompliance with policies, procedures, laws, and regulations.
3. Inform management of suspected wrongdoing.
4. Review the systems used to safeguard assets from various types of losses, including those resulting from theft and improper or illegal activities.
5. Be aware of signs and indicators of fraud.
6. If significant control weaknesses are detected, conduct additional tests directed toward identification of other indicators of fraud.
7. Assist fraud investigations conducted by lawyers, investigators, security personnel, and other specialists.
8. Report fraud findings to management, the board of directors, or the audit committee of the board, being careful not to report to persons who might be involved in a fraud scheme.

GOVERNMENT AUDITORS' RESPONSIBILITIES

The Generally Accepted Government Auditing Standards (GAGAS) are applicable for audits conducted by government employees and by public accounting firms engaged to perform audits on governmental organizations, programs, activities, and functions. Consequently, the government standards control a significant portion of audits by public accountants. The basic governmental audit requirements are to know the applicable laws and regulations, design the audit to detect abuse and illegal acts, and report to the proper level of authority. A few more details about these requirements are below.

Auditors are supposed to prepare a written report on their tests of compliance with applicable laws and regulations, including all material instances of noncompliance and all instances or indications of illegal acts that could result in criminal prosecution. Reports should be directed to the top official of an organization and, in some cases, to an appropriate oversight body, including other government agencies and audit committees. Persons receiving the audit reports are responsible for reporting to law enforcement agencies.

Compliance auditing in governmental audits is a matter of considerable concern, and the AICPA has issued SAS 74 (AU 801) entitled "Compliance Auditing Applicable to Governmental Entities and Recipients of Governmental Financial Assistance." SAS 74 tailors the discussion of responsibilities regarding errors and fraud (SAS 82), and illegal acts (SAS 54), GAO standards, and certain government bulletins to the special requirements of governmental entities and other recipients of government financial assistance.

GAO FIELD WORK STANDARDS FOR FINANCIAL AUDITS:

Auditors should design audits to accomplish the following:
1. Provide reasonable assurance of detecting irregularities material to the financial statements.
2. Provide reasonable assurance of detecting material misstatements resulting from direct-effect illegal acts.
3. Be aware of the possibility of indirect-effect illegal acts. If information comes to attention, apply specific audit procedures to ascertain whether an illegal act has occurred.

4.   Provide reasonable assurance of detecting material misstatements resulting from noncompliance with provisions of contracts or grants. If information comes to attention, apply specific audit procedures to ascertain whether the noncompliance has occurred.

GAO THIRD FIELD WORK STANDARD FOR PERFORMANCE AUDITS:

Auditors should design audits to accomplish the following:
5.   Provide reasonable assurance about compliance with laws, regulations, and other compliance requirements.
6.   Be alert to indications of illegal acts or abuse.

Other aspects of responsibility under these Generally Accepted Government Auditing Standards for detecting and reporting errors, irregularities, and illegal acts include the following:

7.   Be aware of characteristics and types of potential material irregularities.
8.   Understand the relevant laws and regulations, perhaps consulting with attorneys.
9.   Exercise due care in pursuing indications of irregularities and illegal acts so as not to interfere with future investigations or legal proceedings.
10.   Under required circumstances, report indications of irregularities to law enforcement or regulatory authorities.
11.   Be aware of characteristics and types of potential noncompliance with contracts and grants.
12.   Be alert to situations or transactions that could indicate illegal acts or abuse (although "abuse" is so subjective that auditors are not expected to provide reasonable assurance of detecting it).

FRAUD EXAMINERS RESPONSIBILITIES

If you try to make an informal ranking of the strength of commitment in official audit standards to fraud matters, it appears that the government auditors (General Accounting Office GAGAS) have the highest commitment to fraud matters, followed by the external auditors (AICPA standards), then the internal auditors (SIAS 3). Of course, fraud examiners have the strongest spirit of fraud detection and investigation. They differ significantly from external, internal, and government auditors. When they take an assignment, fraud is already known or strongly suspected. They do not fish around for fraud while performing "normal" work. In fact, the Association of Certified Fraud Examiners teaches that assignments are not started without **predication**, which means a reason to believe fraud may have occurred. The Professional Standards and Practices for Certified Fraud Examiners are reproduced below.

PROFESSIONAL STANDARDS AND PRACTICES FOR CERTIFIED FRAUD EXAMINERS (JULY 1, 1991)

I.   GENERAL STANDARDS

A. **Independence and Objectivity**
CFEs are responsible for maintaining independence in attitude and appearance, approaching and conducting fraud examinations in an objective and unbiased manner, and assuring that examining organizations they direct are free from impairments to independence.

B. **Qualifications**
CFEs must possess skills, knowledge, abilities, and appearance needed to perform examinations proficiently and effectively. CFEs responsible for directing fraud examinations must assure they are performed by personnel who collectively possess the skills and knowledge necessary to complete examinations in accordance with these Standards. CFEs must maintain their qualifications by

fulfilling continuing education requirements and adhering to the Code of Ethics of the Association of Certified Fraud Examiners.

C. **Fraud Examinations**

CFEs must conduct fraud examinations using due professional care, with adequate planning and supervision to provide assurance that objectives are achieved within the framework of these Standards. Evidence is to be obtained in an efficient, thorough, and legal manner; and reports of the results of fraud examinations must be accurate, objective, and thorough.

D. **Confidentiality**

CFEs are responsible for assuring they and the examining organizations they direct exercise due care to prevent improper disclosure of confidential or privileged information.

II. SPECIFIC STANDARDS

A. **Independence and Objectivity**

1. *Attitude and Appearance*

Independence of attitude requires impartiality and fairness in conducting examinations and in reaching resulting conclusions and judgments. CFEs must also be sensitive to the appearance of independence so that conclusions and judgments will be accepted as impartial by knowledgeable third parties. CFEs who become aware of a situation or relationship that could be perceived to impair independence, whether or not actual impairment exists, should inform management immediately and take steps to eliminate the perceived impairment, including withdrawing from the examination, if necessary.

2. *Objectivity*

To assure objectivity in performing examinations, CFEs must maintain an independent mental attitude, reach judgments on examination matters without undue influence from others, and avoid being placed in positions where they would be unable to work in an objective professional manner.

3. *Organizational Relationship*
The CFE's reporting relationship should be such that the attitude and appearance of independence and objectivity are not jeopardized. Organizational independence is achieved when the CFE's function has a mandate to conduct independent examinations throughout the organization, or by a reporting relationship high enough in the organization to assure independence of action.

B. Qualifications

1. *Skills, Knowledge, Abilities, and Experience*
CFEs cannot be expected to have an expert level of skill and knowledge for every circumstance that might be encountered in a fraud examination. Nevertheless, CFEs must have sufficient skill and knowledge to recognize when additional training or expert guidance is required. It is the responsibility of a CFE to assure that necessary skills, knowledge, ability, and experience are acquired or available before going forward with a fraud examination.

CFEs must be skilled in obtaining information from records, documents, and people; in analyzing and evaluating information and drawing sound conclusions; in communicating the results of fraud examinations, both orally and in writing; and in serving as an expert witness when appropriate.

CFEs must be knowledgeable in investigative techniques, applicable laws and rules of evidence, fraud auditing, criminology, and ethics.

2. *Continuing Education*
CFEs are required to fulfill continuing education requirements established by the Association of Certified Fraud Examiners. Additionally, CFEs are responsible for securing other education necessary for specific fraud examinations and related fields in which they are individually involved.

3. *Code of Ethics*
CFEs are to adhere to the Code of Professional Ethics of the Association of Certified Fraud Examiners.

C. Fraud Examinations

1. *Due Professional Care*

   Due professional care is defined as exercising the care and skill expected of a prudent professional in similar circumstances. CFEs are responsible for assuring that there is sufficient predication for beginning a fraud examination; that said examinations are conducted with diligence and thoroughness; that all applicable laws and regulations are observed; that appropriate methods and techniques are used; and that said examinations are conducted in accordance with these Standards.

2. *Planning and Supervision*

   CFEs must plan and supervise fraud examinations to assure that objectives are achieved within the framework of these Standards.

3. *Evidence*

   CFEs must collect evidence, whether exculpatory or incriminating, that supports fraud examination results and will be admissible in subsequent proceedings, by obtaining and documenting evidence in a manner to ensure that all necessary evidence is obtained and the chain of custody is preserved.

4. *Reporting*

   CFE reports of the results of fraud examinations, whether written or verbal, must address all relevant aspects of the examination, and be accurate, objective, and understandable.

   In rendering reports to management, clients, or others, CFEs shall not express judgments on the guilt or innocence of any person or party, regardless of the CFE's opinion of the preponderance of evidence. CFEs must exercise due professional care when expressing other opinions related to an examination, such as the likelihood that a fraud has or has not occurred, and whether or not internal controls are adequate.

D. Confidentiality

CFEs, during fraud examinations, are often privy to highly sensitive and confidential information about organizations and individuals. CFEs must exercise due care so as not to purposefully or inadvertently disclose such information except as necessary to conduct the examination or as required by law.

* *

REPORTING ERRORS, FRAUDS, AND ILLEGAL ACTS

Auditors must report their findings about frauds. Some official standards are available for guidance.

INDEPENDENT AUDITORS (AICPA)

Standards for independent external auditors contain materiality thresholds related to reporting auditors' knowledge of errors, frauds , and illegal acts. Immaterial errors are supposed to be reported to management at least one level above the people involved (SAS 82, AU 316). The idea is that small matters can be kept in the management family. However, errors material to the financial statements must be adjusted and handled by management persons responsible for the financial statements to the satisfaction of auditors, or else the audit report will be qualified.

Frauds get slightly different treatment, but a materiality standard is still in effect. The auditors should inform the audit committee of the board of directors of all frauds except ones that are clearly inconsequential. Frauds involving senior management are never inconsequential. In the AICPA audit standards, room is always left for auditors' discretion to determine whether something is minor enough not to matter and not to report. However, management and directors must deal with frauds to the satisfaction of the auditors. If uncertainties persist about possible frauds and management's actions, the audit report should be qualified, explaining all the unsavory reasons, or the auditors may withdraw from the engagement.

Clients' illegal acts also come under the "clearly inconsequential" materiality standard. Ones that are consequential should be reported to the organization's audit committee, and the financial statements should contain adequate disclosures about the organization's illegal acts (SAS 54, AU 317). Independent external auditors always have the option to withdraw from the engagement if management and directors do not take action satisfactory in the circumstances.

Under the AICPA audit standards, disclosures of frauds and clients' illegal acts to outside agencies are limited (SAS 82 and SAS 54). If the auditors get fired, the firm can cite these matters in the letter attached to SEC Form 8-K, which requires explanation of an organization's change of auditors. A fired auditor can tell the successor auditor about them when the successor makes the inquiries required by audit standards (SAS 7, AU 315). Auditors must respond when answering a subpoena issued by a court or other agency with authority, which will happen in a lawsuit or prosecution. When performing work under GAO audit standards, auditors are required to report irregularities and illegal acts to the client agency under the audit contract, which may be an agency or office different from the organization audited.

INTERNAL AUDITORS (IIA)

Statement on Internal Audit Standards No. 3 requires internal auditors to inform management of suspected wrongdoing. They are expected to report fraud findings to management, the board of directors, or the audit committee of the board, being careful not to report to persons who might be involved in a fraud scheme. The Institute of Internal Auditors' standards are silent about any responsibility to report matters to outside parties.

SUMMARY

Various auditing standards for independent auditors, internal auditors, government auditors, and fraud examiners hold a wide array of conceptual and technical responsibilities for detecting and reporting errors, irregularities, illegal acts, and frauds. In general, the government auditing standards (GAGAS) are the most demanding, followed by the AICPA standards for independent auditors and the IIA standards for internal auditors. Fraud examiners are different from these auditors because examiners are expected to have an adversarial role in finding the persons involved in a suspected fraud. Most of the professional standards for reporting fraud-related matters involve communications within an organization. Public reporting may emerge in connection with accounting requirements for full disclosure in financial statements. Aside from this difficult area, public and quasi-public reporting may arise in cases of government regulation requirements and judicial prosecutions.

SELECTED BIBLIOGRAPHY
OF FRAUD-RELATED PUBLICATIONS

Akst, Daniel. *Wonderboy Barry Minkow: The Kid Who Swindled Wall Street*. Scribner's, New York, 1990.

Albrecht, W.S., G.W. Wernz, and T.L. Williams, *Fraud: Bringing Light to the Dark Side of Business*. Irwin Professional Publishing, Burr Ridge, IL, 1995.

Albrecht, W. Steve, Marshall B. Romney, David J. Cherryington, I. Reed Payne, and Allen J. Roe, *How to Detect and Prevent Business Fraud*. Prentice-Hall, Inc., 1982.

Albrecht, W. Steve, Ph.D., CFE, CPA, CIA, Keith R. Howe, DBA, CIA, Marshall B. Romney, Ph.D., CPA. *Deterring Fraud: The Internal Auditor's Perspective*. The Institute of Internal Auditors Research Foundation, Altamonte Springs, FL, 1984.

American Institute of Certified Public Accountants
- "Consideration of Fraud in a Financial Statement Audit." SAS No. 82.
- "Illegal Acts by Clients." SAS No. 54.
- "Auditing Accounting Estimates." SAS No. 57.
- "Communication with Audit Committees." SAS No. 61.
- "Compliance Auditing Considerations in Audits of Governmental Entities and Other Recipients of Governmental Financial Assistance." SAS No. 74.

Androphy, Joel M. *White Collar Crime*. Shepard's/McGraw-Hill, Inc., Chicago, IL, 1992.

Arkins, Stanley S.; Barry A. Bohrer; Donald L. Cuneo; John F. Donohue; Jeffrey M. Kaplin; Robert Kasanof; Andrew J. Levander; and Sanford Sherizen. *Prevention and Prosecution of Computer and High Technology Crime*. Matthew Bender, 1988.

Barefoot, J. Kirk, CPP. *Employee Theft Investigation*. Butterworth Publishers, Stoneham, MA, 1979.

Blankenship, Michael B, ed., *Current Issues in Criminal Justice*. Vol. 3, Understanding Corporate Criminality. Garland Publishing, Inc., 1993.

BloomBecker, Buck. *Spectacular Computer Crimes: What They Are and How They Cost American Business Half a Billion Dollars a Year!* Dow Jones-Irwin, Homewood, IL, 1990.

Bologna, Jack. *Corporate Fraud: The Basics of Prevention and Detection*. Butterworth Publishers, Boston, MA, 1984.

Bologna, G. Jack, and Robert J. Lindquist. *Fraud Auditing and Forensic Accounting: New Tools and Techniques*. John Wiley & Sons, New York, 1987.

Bologna, Jack. *Handbook on Corporate Fraud*. Butterworth-Heinemann, Boston, MA, 1993.

Bologna, J., R.J. Lindquist, and J.T. Wells, *The Accountant's Handbook of Fraud and Commercial Crime*. John Wiley & Sons, NY, 1993.

Bologna, J., and Paul Shaw, *Forensic Accounting Handbook*. Assets Protection Publishing, Madison, WI, 1993).

Brian, Brad D. and Barry F. McNeil, eds. *Internal Corporate Investigations: Conducting Them, Protecting Them*. American Bar Association, Chicago, IL, 1992.

Buckwalter, Art. *Investigative Methods*. Butterworth Publishers, Woburn, MA, 1984.

Carr, James G. 1988 *Criminal Procedure Handbook*. Clark Boardman Company, Ltd., New York, 1988.

Cissell, James C. *Federal Criminal Trials*. The Michie Company, Charlottesville, VA, 1983.

Clinard, Marshall B., and Peter C. Yeager. *Corporate Crime*. Macmillan Publishing Co., Inc., New York, NY, 1980.

Coleman, James William. *The Criminal Elite: The Sociology of White Collar Crime*. Second Edition, St. Martin's Press, Inc., New York, NY, 1989.

Computers at Risk: Safe Computing in the Information Age. National Research Council, Academy Press, 1991.

Cressey, Donald R. *Other People's Money: A Study in the Social Psychology of Embezzlement*. The Free Press, Glencoe, Ilinois, 1953.

Davia, H.R., Coggins, P.C., Wideman, J.C., and Kastantin, J.T., *Management Accountant's Guide to Fraud Discovery and Control*. John Wiley & Sons, Inc., New York, 1992

Dortch, Richard, I*ntegrity: How I Lost It and My Journey Back*. [PTL Ministry] New Leaf Press, Green Forest, AK, 1991).

Domanick, Joe. *Faking It In America: Barry Minkow and the Great ZZZZ BEST Scam*. Contemporary Books, Chicago, IL, 1989.

Drake, John D. *The Effective Interviewer: A Guide for Managers*. AMACOM, New York, NY, 1989 ed.

Ekman, Paul. *Telling Lies*. The Berkley Publishing Group, New York, NY, 1986.

Epstein, M.J., and A.D. Spalding, *The Accountant's Guide to Legal Liability and Ethics*. R.D. Irwin, Homewood, IL, 1993..

Elliott, Robert K., and John J. Willingham. *Management Fraud: Detection and Deterrence*. Petrocelli Books, Inc., NY, 1980.
False Identification: The Problem and Technological Options. Paladin Press, Boulder, CO, 1988.

Federal Bureau of Investigation. *Money Laundering: A Guide for Insurance Companies*. Washington, D.C.: U.S. Department of Justice, 1993.

Federal Rules of Criminal Procedure. West Publishing Company, St. Paul, MN, 1988 ed.

Frank, P.B., M.J. Wagner, and R.L. Weil, *Litigation Services Handbook: The Role of the Accountant as Expert Witness.* John Wiley & Sons, NY, 1990.

Government Accounting Office. *Guide for Incorporating Internal Control Evaluations Into GAO Work.* March 1987.

Government Accounting Office. *Standards and Policies for Evaluating and Reporting on Controls for Computer-Based Systems.*

Grau, Joseph J., Ph.D., ed., and Ben Jacobson, Investigative Consultant. *Criminal and Civil Investigation Handbook.* McGraw-Hill Book Company, New York, 1981.

Hafner, Katie, and John Markoff. *Cyberpunk: Outlaws and Hackers on the Computer Frontier.* Simon & Schuster, New York, NY, 1991.

Hayes, Read, CPP. *Retail Security and Loss Prevention.* Butterworth-Heinemann, Stoneham, MA, 1991.

Henderson, M. Allen. *Flim Flam Man: How Con Games Work.* Paladin Press, Boulder, CO, 1985.

Houghton, C.W., and J.A. Fogarty, "Inherent Risk," *Auditing: A Journal of Practice and Theory.* (Spring, 1991) pp. 1-21.

Inbau, Fred E., John E. Reid, Joseph P. Buckley. *Criminal Interrogation and Confessions.* Williams & Wilkins, Baltimore, MD, 1986.

Inciardi, James A. *Criminal Justice.* 3rd ed., Harcourt Brace Jovanovich, Publisher, San Diego, CA, 1990.

Internal Revenue Service Criminal Investigation Division, *Financial Investigations: A Financial Approach to Detecting and Resolving Crimes,* Department of the Treasury--IRS, U.S. Government Printing

Office, Superintendent of Documents, Mail Stop SSOP, Washington, D.C. 20402-9328. ISBN 0-16-041830-5.

Institute of Internal Auditors. *Standards for the Professional Practices of Internal Auditing, SIAS No. 3.*. Alta Monte Springs, FL.

Kellogg, Irving. *How to Find Negligence and Misrepresentations in Financial Statements*. Shepard's/McGraw-Hill, Colorado Springs, CO, 1983.

Kochan, N., M. Potts, R. Whittington, *Dirty Money*. National Press Books, NY, 1992.

Kramer, W. Michael. *Investigative Techniques in Complex Financial Crimes. National Institute on Economic Crime*. Washington, D.C, 1988.

Loebbecke, J.K., M.M. Eining, and J.J. Willingham, "Auditors' Experience with Material Irregularities: Frequency, Nature, and Detectability," *Auditing: A Journal of Practice and Theory*. (Fall, 1989), pp. 1-28.

MacInaugh, Edmond A. *Disguise Techniques: Fool All of the People Some of the Time*. Paladin Press, Boulder, CO, 1984.

Maggin, Donald L. *Bankers, Builders, Knaves, and Thieves: The $300 Million Scam at ESM*. Contemporary Books, Chicago, IL, 1989.

Mautz, R.K., and Hussein A. Sharaf. *The Philosophy of Auditing*. American Accounting Association monograph no. 6, Sarasota. American Accounting Association, 1961.

Mayer, Martin, *The Greatest-Ever Bank Robbery: The Collapse of the Savings and Loan Industry*. Charles Scribner's Sons, NY, 1990).

McClintick, David, *Indecent Exposure*. Dell Publishing Co., Inc., NY, 1982.

Minkow, Barry, *Clean Sweep*. Thomas Nelson Publishers, Nashville, TN, 1995.

Murphy, T. Gregory. *Asset Forfeiture: Uncovering Assets Laundered Through a Business*. Washington, D.C.: U.S. Department of Justice, Bureau of Justice Assistance, 1992.

Naftalis, Gary P., ed. *White-Collar Crimes*. American Law Institute-American Bar Association, Philadelphia, PA, 1980.

National Commission on Fraudulent Financial Reporting. *Report of the National Commission on Fraudulent Financial Reporting*. New York: American Institute of Certified Public Accountants, October, 1987.

Nossen, R.A., and J.W. Norvelle, *Detection, Investigation, and Prosecution of Financial Crimes*. Thoth Books, 1993.

Pankau, Edmond J., *Check It Out*. Contemporary Books, Chicago, IL. 1992.

Pilzer, P.Z. *Other People's Money: The Inside Story of the S&L Mess*. Simon and Schuster, NY, 1989.

Pizzo, Stephen, Mary Fricker, and Paul Muolo, *Inside Job: The Looting of America's Savings and Loans*. McGraw-Hill, NY, 1989.

Powis, Robert E. *The Money Launderers: Lessons From the Drug Wars (How Billions of Illegal Dollars are Washed Through Banks and Businesses)*. Probus Publishing Company, Chicago, IL, 1992.

Robertson Jack C., Ph.D., CPA, CFE. *Auditing*. Eighth Edition. IRWIN, Homewood, IL, 1996.

Securities Exchange Commission.
- *Matter of USF&G Corp. and James M. Raley, Jr.*, Accounting and Auditing Enforcement Rel. No. 182, Exchange Act Rel. No. 25403 (February 29, 1988).
- *SEC v. Time Energy Systems, Inc., et al.*, Civil Action No. 86-1370 (D.D.C.), Litigation Rel. No. 11106, Accounting and Auditing Enforcement Rel. No. 99 (May 10, 1986).
- *Electro-Catheter Corp., Robert I. Bernstein and John J. Teryilan*, Civil Action No. 87-0267 [NHJ] (D.D.C.), Litigation Rel. No.

11803, Accounting and Auditing Enforcement Rel. No. 196 (July 15, 1988).

- *SEC v. Automatix Inc.*, Civil Action No. 86-1596 (D.D.C.); *SEC v. John Dias*, Civil Action No. 86-1597 (D.D.C.), Litigation Rel. No. 11121, Accounting and Auditing Enforcement Rel. No. 100 (June 10, 1986).

- *SEC v. Storage Technology Corporation*, Civil Action No 87-0175, Litigation Rel. No. 11340, Accounting and Auditing Enforcement Rel. No. 125 (January 27, 1987).

- *SEC v. Endotronics, Inc.*, Civil Action No. 3-88-277 (D. Minn.), Litigation Rel. No. 11729, Accounting and Auditing Enforcement Rel. No. 189 (May 9, 1988).

- *SEC v. Edgar Bolton*, No. 85 Civ. 4787 (JES) (S.D.N.Y.), Litigation Rel. No. 11699, Accounting and Auditing Enforcement Rel. No. 185 (April 12, 1988).

- *SEC v. Michael Clinger, Walter G. Solomon and Avi Oren*, Accounting and Auditing Enforcement Rel. No 142 (July 27, 1987).

- *SEC v. George Risk Industries, Inc.*, Civil Action No. 88-2553 (D.D.C.), Litigation Rel. No. 11864, Accounting and Auditing Enforcement Rel. No. 199 (September 13, 1988).

- *In the Matter of Petrofab International, Inc.*, Securities Act Rel. No. 6769, Accounting and Auditing Enforcement Rel. No. 186 (April 20, 1988).

- *SEC v. Ronald R. Walker, et al.*, Civil Action No. 86-523 (W.D. Mo.), Litigation Rel. No. 11071, Accounting and Auditing Enforcement Rel. No. 96 (April 22, 1986). Litigation Rel. No. 11267 (October 20, 1986).

- *Avanti Associates First Mortgage Fund 84 Limited Partnership, et al.*, Civil Action No. 88-2124-PHX-PGR (D. Az.) (filed December 28, 1988); Litigation Rel. No. 11961, Accounting and Auditing Enforcement Rel. No. 214 (January 11, 1989).

- *American Biomaterials Corporation*, Civil Action No. 88-1063 (D.D.C.), Litigation Rel. No. 11710, Accounting and Auditing Enforcement Rel. No. 187 (April 19, 1988).

- *United States v. Larry B. Groover.* United States District Court for the District Court of Utah, Case No. 89-CR-02318. Accounting and Auditing Enforcement Rel. No. 285, Litigation Rel. No. 12724 (December 4, 1990).

- *Matter of American Savings and Loan Association of Florida*, FHLBB Enforcement Review Committee Resolution No. ERC 88-24 (March 31, 1988); Exchange Act Rel. No. 34-25788, Accounting and Auditing Enforcement Rel. No. 194 (June 8, 1988).
- *Rocky Mount Undergarment Co., Inc., et al.*, Civil Action No. 89-014-5 (E.D.N.C.), Litigation Rel. No. 11960 Accounting and Auditing Enforcement Rel. No. 212 (January 9, 1989).
- *SEC v. Arthur Rogovin and Albert DeBiccari*, Civil Action No. 86-1740 (S.D.N.Y.), Litigation Rel. No. 11018 (March 6, 1986).
- *In the Matter of Michael P. Richer, Melvyn J. Goodman and Robert S. Hardy*, Exchange Act Rel. No. 25528, Accounting and Auditing Enforcement Rel. No. 184 (March 29, 1988).
- *In the Matter of John E. Harrington and Gregory B. Arnott*, Exchange Act Rel. No. 22686, Accounting and Auditing Enforcement Rel. No. 81 (December 5, 1985).
- *In the Matter of Michael S. Hope, et al.*, Exchange Act Rel., No. 23513, Securities Act Rel. No. 6655, Accounting and Auditing Enforcement Rel. No. 109 (August 6, 1986).
- *In the Matter of Marsh & Mclennan Companies, Inc.*, Exchange Act Rel. No. 24023, Accounting and Auditing Enforcement Rel. No. 124 (January 22, 1987).
- *SEC v. Cardillo Travel Systems, Inc. et al.*, Accounting and auditing Enforcement Rel. No. 143 (August 4, 1987); Litigation Rel. No. 11675 (March 1, 1988).
- *DeLaurentis Entertainment Group, Inc.*, Exchange Act Rel. No. 24786, Accounting and Auditing Enforcement Rel. No. 144 (August 10, 1987).
- *SEC v. Oak Industries, Inc.*, Civil Action No. Enforcement Rel. No. 63 (June 25, 1985).
- *SEC v. The Charter Co.*, Civil Action No. 86-713-CIV-J-12 (M.D. FL.), Litigation Rel. No. 11135, Accounting and Auditing Enforcement Rel. No. 104 (June 24, 1986).
- *In the Matter of Continental Illinois Corporation*, Exchange Act Rel. No. 24142, Accounting and Auditing Enforcement Rel. No. 128 (February 27, 1987).
- *Matter of E.F. Hutton Group, Inc.*, Exchange Act Rel. No. 25524; Accounting and Auditing Enforcement Rel. No. 183 (March 29, 1988).

- *SEC v. Levin International Corporation*, Accounting and Auditing Enforcement Rel. No. 217 (February 23, 1989).
- *In the Matter of Fluid Corporation*, Order Instituting Proceedings Pursuant to Section 12(j) of the Securities Exchange Act of 1934 and Section 54(c) of the Investment company Act of 1940, Findings, and Order of the Commission, Accounting and Auditing Enforcement Rel. No. 276, Investment Company Act Rel. No. IC-17756, Admin. Proc. File No. 307394.
- *SEC v. Trailer*, Accounting and Auditing Enforcement Rel. No. 278, Litigation Rel. No. 12645 (September 28, 1990).
- *SEC v. Allegheny International, Inc.*, Civil Action No. 87-2472, Litigation Rel. No. 11533, Accounting and Auditing Enforcement Rel. No. 151 (D.D.C. September 9, 1987).
- *Matter of the Registration Statement of Alta Gold Co.*, Securities Act Rel. No.6801, Accounting and Auditing Enforcement Rel. No. 203 (September 30, 1988)
- *Savin Corporation*, Civil Action No. 85-3605 (D.D.C.), Litigation Rel. No. 10928, Accounting And Auditing Enforcement Rel. No. 80 (November 12, 1985).

Seidler, L., F. Andrews, and M.J. Epstein, *The Equity Funding Papers: The Anatomy of a Fraud*. McGraw-Hill, NY, 1977.

Siegel, Larry J. *Criminology*. 4th ed., West Publishing Co., St. Paul, MN, 1992.

Snyder, Neil H.; O. Whitfield Broome, Jr.; William J. Kehoe; James T. McIntyre, Jr.; and Karen E. Blair. *Reducing Employee theft: A Guide to Financial and Organization Controls*. Quorum Books, New York, NY, 1991.

Somers, Leigh Edward. *Economic Crimes: Investigative Principles and Techniques*. Clark Boardman Company, Ltd., New York, NY, 1984.

Sterngold, James,*Burning the House Down: How Greed, Deceit, and Bitter Revenge Destroyed E.F. Hutton*. Summit Books, NY.

Stewart, James B., *Den of Thieves* (S&Ls). Simon & Schuster, NY, 1992).

The Annals of the American Academy of Political and Social Science. *White-Collar Crime*. Vol. 525, Sage Periodicals Press, Newbury Park, CA, January 1993.

Thornhill, William T., *Forensic Accounting: How to Investigate Financial Fraud*. R.D. Irwin, Burr Ridge, IL, 1995).

Tidwell, Gary. *Anatomy of a Fraud*. John Wiley & Sons, Inc., NY, 1993.

U.S. General Accounting Office. *Government Auditing Standards*. rev. ed. Washington, D.C., U.S. Government Printing Office, July, 1994.

Vaughan, Diane. *Controlling Unlawful Organizational Behavior: Social Structure and Corporate Misconduct*. The University of Chicago Press, Chicago, IL, 1983.

Villa, John K. *Banking Crimes: Fraud, Money Laundering, and Embezzlement*. Clark, Boardman, Callaghan, Deerfield, IL, 1991.

Walsh, Timothy J., CPP, and Richard J. Healy, CPP. *Protection of Assets Manual*. The Merrit Company, Santa Monica, CA, 1984.

Wells, Joseph T. CFE, CPA; W. Steve Albrecht, Ph.D., CFE, CPA; Jack Bologna, JD, CFE; Gilbert Geis, Ph.D.; W. Michael Kramer, JD, CFE; and Jack Robertson, Ph.D., CPA, CFE. Fra*ud Examiners Manual*. 2nd Edition. Austin, TX: National Association of Certified Fraud Examiners, 1993.

Wells, Joseph T., CFE, CPA. *Fraud Examination: Investigative and Audit Procedures*. Quorum Books, New York, 1992.

Wells, Joseph T., "Six Common Myths About Fraud," *Journal of Accountancy*. (February, 1990), pp. 82-88.

Wells, Joseph T., CFE, CPA; Tedd A. Avey, BComm, CA; G. Jack Bologna, JD, CFE, BBA; and Robert J. Lindquist, CFE, FCA. The *Accountant's Handbook of Fraud and Commercial Crime*. Published in Canada by the Canadian Institute of Chartered Accountants, Toronto, Ontario, 1992.

Wold, Geoffrey H. and Robert F. Shriver. *Computer Crime: Techniques for Preventing and Detecting Crime in Financial Institutions*. Bankers Publishing Company, Rolling Meadows, IL, 1989.

Zulawtski, David E., and Douglas E. Wicklander, *Practical Aspects of Interview and Interrogation*. CRC Press, Boca Raton, FL, 1993.